BIOSPHERE
POLITICS

Also by Jeremy Rifkin

BIOSPHERE POLITICS

A New Consciousness for a New Century

JEREMY RIFKIN

Crown Publishers, Inc.
New York

Published by Crown Publishers, Inc., 201 East 50th Street, New York, New York 10022. Member of the Crown Publishing Group.

CROWN is a trademark of Crown Publishers, Inc.

Manufactured in the United States of America

Library of Congress Cataloging-in-Publication Data

Rifkin, Jeremy.
    Biosphere politics: a new consciousness for a new
century / Jeremy Rifkin.—1st ed.
        p.   cm.
    1. Human ecology—Philosophy.   2. Civilization—Philosophy.
3. Nonrenewable natural resources.   4. Environmental policy.
5. Twenty-first century—Forecasts.   I. Title.
GF21.R52   1991
304.2—dc20   90-22052
                                                                         CIP

ISBN 0-517-57746-1

10 9 8 7 6 5 4 3 2 1

First Edition

Carol
for the love, joy, and companionship of a lifetime

ACKNOWLEDGMENTS

I would like to give special thanks to Donald E. Davis. Don worked closely with me in the researching of *Biosphere Politics*. His depth of knowledge in the fields of social ecology and Western cultural history has been invaluable in helping to select the range of material included in the book. Don has assisted me in the past, serving as research coordinator for *Time Wars* and as a contributor to *The Green Lifestyle Handbook*.

I greatly appreciate Don's considerable contribution to *Biosphere Politics*. I have learned much from him and have been inspired by his scholarship as well as his activist commitment to a new biosphere consciousness. Above all, I value his friendship.

So many hours have been spent over the years with Andy Kimbrell discussing the ideas that have found their way into *Biosphere Politics* that it's difficult to know how much of the thinking in this book is attributable to either of us alone. To a great extent the book represents a collaborative intellectual journey and, while I assume ultimate responsibility for the text, I greatly appreciate Andy's many insightful contributions which appear throughout the work.

Andy's editing of the manuscript helped transform a working draft into a finished work. Andy is one of those rare individuals who combines intellectual brilliance with a craftsman's eye for editing. I greatly value his personal support and close friendship.

ACKNOWLEDGMENTS

I would like to thank the following people for their help, support and encouragement while preparing the book: Anna Awimbo, Clara Elizabeth Mack, Helen E. Mathis, Carolyn C. Bennett, Beulah W. Bethea, Regina Thompson, and Cassandra Spears.

I would also like to thank my agents, Jim Stein and Michael Carlisle, who have given so much of themselves, both professionally and personally. I would like to extend a special note of gratitude to my editor at Crown Publishers, Jim Wade, for shepherding *Biosphere Politics* through its various stages. It's a pleasure to work with an editor with whom I share so many intellectual and personal sensibilities. I greatly appreciate Mr. Wade's enthusiasm for *Biosphere Politics* and his many thoughtful suggestions which have been incorporated into the book.

Mr. Wade is the kind of editor authors dream of working with and only occasionally have the opportunity of doing so. Jim believes that ideas have consequences and cares deeply about the need to stimulate critical thinking. He is one of the few people I have met in the publishing world who still asks us to take time to reflect.

I would like to thank my wife, Carol Grunewald Rifkin, for her editorial critique of the final manuscript. Her editorial suggestions have been incorporated into virtually every page of the book. I am grateful for the many constructive changes she made and deeply appreciate both her love of the English language and her extraordinary word-smithing skills, which have helped transform this work. Most of all, I'd like to thank Carol for helping me to understand better and empathize with the other species we live with. Her deep personal commitment to the animal kingdom has inspired me to think in new ways. I hope that many of the values we share have been adequately expressed in *Biosphere Politics*.

CONTENTS

Part Two: Geopolitics and the Death of Nature

Part Three: The Culture of Privacy

Part Four: Securing the Body Politic

INTRODUCTION

IN EVERY CULTURE, concepts of security are inextricably intertwined with human beings' relationships to the natural world. Securing sustenance, securing the state, and securing peace of mind are always bound up, in one way or another, with securing the environment. Strangely enough, in much of contemporary scholarship, concepts of security and concepts of nature have been treated as separate realms. Questions of security are generally relegated to the fields of political science, economics, and military history. Questions involving the environment and nature are most often the preserve of the biologists, chemists, and physicists, and secondarily the philosophers and poets.

Today the public is becoming increasingly aware of the connections that link politics, economics, war making, and the environment. Still, national governments have yet to integrate environmental principles and concerns into their foreign policies, and business leaders still prefer to think of the environment merely as a "resource" or "externality."

Now, however, a new series of environmental problems have emerged that are global in impact and threaten the continued existence of planetary ecosystems and the future of civilization. Global warming, ozone depletion, acid rain, deforestation, desertification, and species extinction are forcing our species to turn its attention, for the first time in our history, to the question of global environmental security. Questions of personal and national security, economic and military security, which have dominated the affairs of modern man and woman, have suddenly become dwarfed by the magnitude of environmental changes that threaten to alter the very biochemistry of our planet.

A younger generation is beginning to understand that preserving global environmental security is essential to guaranteeing the political and economic security of each human being and every community and nation. Despite the new ecological awareness, society has repeatedly shied away from a frank and open discussion of the roots of the contemporary environmental crisis.

The environmental threats facing the planet are not simply the result of scientific miscalculation. Nor are they merely the consequence of ill-conceived management decisions. Ironically, it is the notion of security upon which our entire modern worldview is based that has led us to the verge of ecocide. A thorough understanding of the current ecological crisis will require a vigorous examination of the social forces and philosophical currents that underlie our contemporary views of economic, political, and military security. More important still, saving the earth will require a fundamental change in our thinking about security and a new worldview that is more compatible with our species' awakening ecological consciousness.

The past several centuries have been dominated by the mechanistic thinking of the Enlightenment, with its emphasis on the privatization and commodification of nature and man; detachment and isolation from the natural world; and a near pathological obsession with creating a secure, autonomous existence, independent of the forces of nature. The nation-state and its appendages, the modern business corporation and the professional military establishment, have emerged as the primary institutional vehicles for implementing the modern notions of individual and collective security. Geopolitics, in turn, has evolved as the primary expression of nation-state ideals and objectives.

In less than a century, the practice of geopolitics has pushed the world to the brink of both nuclear Armaggedon and environmental catastrophe, forcing us to reconsider the basic assumptions of security that animate the modern worldview.

Introduction

Fortunately, the elements of "a new way of thinking" about security have been in the making for nearly a quarter of a century and are now steadily edging forward from the margin to the center of human consciousness, providing the context for a wholesale challenge to the existing world order. A new political vision is beginning to take shape and form, offering both hope and inspiration for the first generation of the twenty-first century.

Biosphere politics is the culmination of a twenty-five-year odyssey of intellectual discovery and political activity that has begun to change the thinking and redirect the sociality of a generation of human beings around the planet. The term "biosphere" was coined at the beginning of the twentieth century and refers to the thin chemical envelope, extending from the ocean depths to the stratosphere, that sustains all the various forms of life on the planet. The new politics envisions the earth as a living organism, and the human species as a partner and participant, dependent on the proper functioning of the biosphere and at the same time responsible for its well-being.

Biosphere politics unites the thinking of three great social currents of the post–World War II era into a unified philosophical vision: first, the movements for participatory democracy and economic justice, including the anticolonial struggles of the third world, the civil rights, student, and women's movements in the first world, and the newly emerging human rights and pro-democracy movements in the Soviet Union and Eastern Europe; second, the various movements to preserve and sustain the environment, including the animal rights and sustainable agriculture movements, and the new environmentally oriented peace movements; and third, the movements centering around therapeutic consciousness and transformational politics, including the many new forms of personal therapy, the human potential movement, holistic health, and the new spiritual reawakening taking place both inside the Judeo-Christian communities and outside, in Eastern and nontraditional religious and spiritual practices.

Each of these three social currents has been inspired by a deep human yearning to reestablish a sense of participation in community life: the political community and institutional life of the body politic; the community of nature and the outward life of

3

the environment; and the spiritual community and the inner life of the soul.

The struggle for direct and intimate participation in the communities of life has been accompanied by the beginnings of a fundamental shift in human consciousness—first among the generation of the 1960s and now among their sons and daughters coming of age in the 1990s. The new consciousness eschews the strictly utilitarian thinking of previous generations that turned human beings into mere factors of production and consumption and that reduced nature to resources and commodities to be exploited in the marketplace. Champions of the new consciousness believe that human beings and the other creatures with whom we share the earth embody an intrinsic sacred value, not just utilitarian value, and deserve both our respect and stewardship.

The twin ideals of intimate reparticipation in the communities of life and resacralization of nature form the cornerstone of a new vision of security. When combined with the idea of the earth as a living organism, the three concepts form a powerful trinity and serve as a foundation for a new overarching worldview for the twenty-first century.

The new biosphere politics offers a strong antidote and alternative vision to the politics of the modern era. Unlike geopolitics, which views nature exclusively as strategic resources, biosphere politics views the environment as the irreducible context that sustains all of life and sets the conditions and limits for all other human thought and activity. In the biospheric era, the exploitation of nature gives way to a sense of reverence for the natural world and a sustainable relationship with the environment.

The conventional geopolitical notion of spheres of influence becomes an arcane concept in a biospheric framework and ultimately an obstacle in the way of achieving any kind of lasting peace. The idea of securing an autonomous existence, independent of the forces of nature, is incongruous in a world defined as a living organism.

For that reason, the transition into a biospheric culture will likely mark the end of the nation-state as the dominant political institution and the multinational corporation as the primary economic institution.

The biospheric era will spawn new political and economic arrangements more in keeping with our new ecological understanding of the earth as a living organism. New forms of governance will be grounded in the local biome and regional ecosystems. At the global level, the biosphere itself will become the governing region for the human species.

In the first four parts of *Biosphere Politics* we will examine the origin and development of our modern concepts of security and describe the impact they have had on the environment and the economic, political, and cultural life of Western civilization.

In Part One, "Enclosing the Global Commons," we will contrast the medieval notion of security with our modern ideas on the subject. We will trace the developments that led to a fixation with moneyed relationships, technological prowess, and the commodification and exploitation of the natural world. In the process we will explore a little-known but decisive political phenomenon in the history of Western culture: the five-hundred-year journey to "enclose" the vast reaches of the global commons—the landmasses, oceans, atmosphere, electromagnetic spectrum, and gene pool. This section will explore the relationship between the worldwide enclosure movements and humanity's futile quest for security in the modern world. The section ends with a description of the tragic environmental and economic toll wrought by modern man in his relentless drive to free himself from the forces of nature and secure an autonomous existence.

Part Two, "Geopolitics and the Death of Nature," is given over to an examination of the unique role played by the nation-state, the business corporation, and the professional military establishment in the struggle to enclose and commercially exploit the global commons. We will also review the "science" of geopolitics that has emerged in the past century to advance the security interests of nation-states and multinational corporations.

Geopolitical thinking is largely responsible for the ruin of much of the earth's environment, the oppression of millions of human beings forced to live in constant fear of military reprisal and, worse still, the specter of a nuclear holocaust. The retrospective of geopolitics in this section clears the way for the introduction of a new theory of international affairs that is more likely to advance the personal and collective security interests of human-kind.

In Part Three, "The Culture of Privacy," we will deepen the discussion of political security to include the politics of culture. Conventional politics has dwelled almost exclusively on the narrow questions of institutional arrangements and power relationships. In this section we will go below the surface and examine the changes in living patterns and life-styles over the past half millennium with an eye toward understanding the many ways our modern notions of security have been imprinted on the intimate details of daily life.

The fourth part of the book, "Securing the Body Politic," penetrates even deeper into the realm of human physicality and consciousness in an effort to better understand the basic human drives that have given shape and form to our modern notions of security. We will examine modern man and woman's desperate flight from nature, including their own animal natures and even their own bodily senses.

In the final section, "The Coming of the Biospheric Age," we will challenge the geopolitical orthodoxy with a call for a new biosphere politics centered on reestablishing community, resacralizing relationships, and restoring the health of the earth. We will look at the new temporal and spatial concepts that govern biospheric consciousness and examine the new challenges that lie in wait along the way to an ecologically sustainable future.

For too long, discussion of the mounting environmental problems facing the planet and civilization has been separated from the main currents of intellectual thought. This book attempts to infuse biospheric thinking and the new ecological awareness into the social sciences and humanities. Reorienting the various intellectual disciplines toward a biospheric perspective is an essential intellectual task if we are to create an ecological worldview to guide future generations.

It is my firm belief that a new ecological sensibility is emerging among the younger generation. A new commitment to the environment and the welfare of future generations needs to be accompanied by a well-reasoned critique of both the existing world order and the conventional geopolitical thinking that has accompanied it. At the same time, human civilization is in need of a bold new biospheric political vision that is strong enough to unite present and future generations in the formidable task of healing the earth◻I have written *Biosphere Politics* in the hope of contributing to that process.

PART ONE

ENCLOSING THE GLOBAL COMMONS

1

SECURING THE WORLD

ONE BY ONE, the old shibboleths are falling by the wayside. Pieces of the Berlin Wall were sold in Western department stores in 1989. Free elections have been held in the Soviet Union and the Eastern bloc countries. Soviet troops are leaving Eastern Europe. U.S. troops are pulling out of Western Europe. The Cold War has ended. Talk of American imperialism and Evil Empires has been shunted off the world stage to make room for discussion of the global shopping center.

The young are no longer eager to give their bodies over to the defense of the empire, the free world, or the proletarian struggle. They no longer banter with each other over the merits of the free market, or how best to control the means of production. Nor are their thoughts directed to what manner of utopia lies at the end of history. Their dreams are no longer filled with visions of capitalist cornucopias or classless societies. Modern science has become suspect, its stature and authority diminished by too high expectations, staggering costs, and far too many disappointments. Technology still dazzles, but no longer inspires awe. Once an idol, it is now treated as commonplace by most.

The ideological foundations that inspired the thinking and ignited the passions of the modern era are cracking under the weight of new realities. Thomas Paine, the great American revolutionary, once said, "Every generation must be free to remake the

11

world anew." Never before have the opportunities been so great to redirect both the consciousness and the affairs of civilization. Yet, where there should be festive celebration of a new world in the making, there exists instead a deep angst about our future and the world our children's generation will inherit.

Ironically, in a society that is obsessed with the notion of personal and national security, we feel less secure than at any other time in our existence. Our fears have been fueled, of late, by a new genre of threats that all but overwhelm our sensibilities.

Today, upward of three million Americans are homeless, living on the streets of our major cities, and their numbers are growing steadily each year.[1] Nearly six million additional individuals are one paycheck away from falling through the economic "safety net" and becoming another homeless victim in the growing legion of urban poor.[2]

Drug abuse is an increasing problem among every class and within every region of the country. One out of every twenty-four Americans reports that he or she has used cocaine in the last twelve months,[3] and one out of every seven now admits using illicit drugs.[4] Despite billions of dollars spent in prevention and enforcement programs, local and state officials are not sanguine about winning the war against drugs.

Crime is also on the rise. The prisons are overflowing with repeat offenders, and court dockets are woefully backed up, straining the capacity of the judicial system to administer justice effectively. The statistics are grim. One out of every 160 Americans is the victim of a violent crime—murder, armed robbery, rape—every twelve months. One out of every twenty Americans is the victim of property crimes each year.[5] The public fear has reached staggering proportions. There are over 200 million firearms of various kinds presently in circulation in the United States, enough to arm virtually every man, woman, and child.[6]

Fears and anxieties about the future are compounded by the escalating government debt, which now exceeds $3 trillion. The debt has tripled in the past ten years and is expected to increase by 50 percent by the middle of the decade unless draconian measures are taken to curb the government's profligate spending practices.[7]

Perhaps most important of all, the earth itself is now endangered by an escalating number of environmental threats. The planet—its soil, its flora and fauna, its protective arch of atmospheric gases—is graying under the relentless assault of modern science and technology, industrial production, market forces, and unrestrained consumption. These environmental crises threaten to extinguish much of the life of the planet in the years ahead.

Already, the ecological devastation wrought by the industrial age and global market economy has contributed to the impoverishment of nearly 20 percent of our species.[8] Political tensions continue to mount as millions of environmental refugees find themselves homeless and increasingly desperate.[9]

The physical impoverishment of the second and third world has been matched by a deepening spiritual impoverishment among the rich and the well-to-do of the first world. As the breath of life has been sucked from the planet, the meaning of life has become a matter of increasing doubt. Not surprising, for as we have focused our attention more and more on the "how" of things, we have become far less able to reflect on the "why" of our existence. Today, a growing number of our species find themselves dispossessed in both body and soul.

The future lies very much in doubt as civilization careens toward the twenty-first century. With the old ideological moorings losing their hold over the body politic, and new political realities emerging faster than at any time in human memory, questions of security begin to loom ever larger in the public consciousness.

References to security abound in contemporary culture. The term flashes by us a thousand times a day, in a thousand different guises. Yet we seldom pause to ask what we really mean by economic and environmental security, political and military security, spiritual and emotional security. We assume that security has always meant the same thing to human beings in every culture, and that those before us went about securing their existence in much the same way, although with less technological prowess and intellectual sophistication. Nothing could be further from the truth. Our contemporary ideas about security would have seemed quite strange to our ancestors just a few hundred years ago.

Notions of security differ significantly between cultures and between periods of history. Understanding those differences can

13

shed some much needed light on the grave problems facing contemporary society as it attempts to secure itself and the planet in
the years ahead.

Those of us living in the industrial world are accustomed to
thinking of personal security almost exclusively in monetary
terms. Our bank accounts and nonliquid assets serve as the ground
of our being. While we have come to define ourselves and others
largely in financial terms, even to the point of judging our intrinsic
worth by the way of dollars accrued, this approach to security is
quite novel in the history of human affairs. In fact, it wasn't so
long ago that our ancestors defined their economic security in very
different terms. For the people of medieval Europe, security was
tightly bound up with the land on which they lived and from
which they derived their primary means of survival.

We live in a highly mobile society, where individuals and families often change residence every few years. For us, it is difficult
even to comprehend the overriding importance that place used to
have in the lives of human beings. Yet, at the dawn of the urban
industrial revolution, most of our ancestors in Europe were still
living in remote village hamlets, walking along the same well-worn
paths, tending the same plots of soil their families had stewarded
for over six hundred years. Sustenance ruled over acquisition, and
the economic survival of each individual and family rested with
the fortunes of the larger community and the benevolence of the
changing seasons. Novelties and innovations were entertained, on
occasion, but only with the proviso that they be thoroughly integrated into the existing order, without damaging time-honored
covenants and traditions.[10]

Economic security in medieval Europe was a communal affair.
In the medieval village men and women valued their relationships
and obligations. They valued the cooperation of their neighbors
and found pleasure in performing time-honored tasks. Values
were wrapped up in the intangibles: the loyalty of a friend, the
physical strength of a fellow worker, the sage advice of a village
elder. To be sure, the dark side of human life could be found as
well. In every village there were petty jealousies, a modicum of
greed, a fair share of idle gossip, and a fear and loathing of
outsiders. Life in medieval Europe could be menacing, disruptive,

and harsh. In most respects, life was a stark affair, and very often needlessly brutal. However, the issue at hand is not how secure medieval man and woman were by our modern standards, but, rather, the very different way they perceived the notion of security in their lives and times.

While medieval man and woman looked to the land for their economic security, they looked to the heavens for their emotional security. They were bonded in a highly organized vertical structure that swept upward like the great vaulted columns of the medieval cathedral. St. Thomas Aquinas, the great schoolman of the medieval Church, defined nature as a great ladder or chain of being, a vertical world stretching from the lowest of God's creations up to the gates of heaven. Every species had a rung assigned to it on the great ladder, and all the rungs were filled. Aquinas's world was tightly knit with a careful gradation of ranks accompanied by a detailed catechism of instructions governing mutual responsibilities and obligations.[11] Security in this world depended on human beings faithfully playing out the parts that Providence assigned to them in this grand hierarchy. The social imperative included Christian cooperation with one's neighbors in the commune and fealty to God's representatives, which in descending order included the pope, the monarch, and the lord of the manor. By faithfully exercising their obligations and duties in this world, medieval man and woman could rest assured that everlasting security would be their final reward in the next world.

Even the mundane tasks of daily life in the commune took on a celestial purpose. Medieval man and woman were stewards of God's creation. They tilled God's garden and by doing so they bore witness to His heavenly kingdom and helped ensure their own individual salvation. The Protestant reformer Martin Luther was once asked what he would do tomorrow if Christ were to suddenly reappear on earth, to which he replied, "I would plant a tree."

The medieval concept of security was challenged, and eventually shattered, by two major developments, both of which helped lay the groundwork for our modern views about security. First, a money economy began to dominate the life of European culture. The substitution of moneyed relationships for communal obligations and sacred trusts profoundly altered the consciousness of

15

Western man and woman and changed the course of Western history. Security in the modern age rested increasingly in fiduciary rather than organic relationships, and it is this fundamental severance of natural bonds that helped set the context for man's near total alienation from the natural world.

Second, the new preoccupation with money and commercial relationships was accompanied by a new fascination with the power of technology. A Promethean spirit swept across the Holy Roman Empire. Everywhere, it seemed, men were suddenly constructing machines of every kind and character to help expropriate and convert the resources of nature into the assets of civilization. Machines became the new icons of a materialist culture.

Increasingly surrounded by commercial and mechanical relationships, Western man and woman fell victim to a new illusion: a belief in their own invulnerability to the forces of nature. Not surprisingly, autonomy became the new unchallenged symbol of security in the modern world as Western society found innovative ways to detach and isolate itself from the environment at large.

The obsession with money, machines, and autonomy spawned "a new way of thinking" about man and nature, one more in keeping with the utilitarian concerns of a commercial culture. The new worldview that emerged was immersed in worldly rather than otherworldly security. In place of communion with Christ and external salvation, the man and woman of the modern age were inspired and beguiled by visions of technological progress and the prospects of material cornucopias.

In contemporary discussions, little, if any, serious attention is given to the intellectual roots of our modern ideas about security. Yet, it is the unique way of thinking about security that emerged in the early modern age that has helped condition so much of the actions of modern man and woman. A thorough understanding of the modern worldview, with its emphasis on money, machines, and autonomy, is a necessary first step toward understanding the current plight of humanity and the planet. Only by critically examining the intellectual assumptions that underlie the modern notions of human security will it be possible to begin redirecting the future course of civilization in a more ecologically sustainable fashion.

2

WHAT DOTH IT PROFIT A MAN . . . ?

HISTORIAN ELLIOT SMITH provides an interesting insight into the origins of money in ancient Egypt. A cowrie shell found in the Red Sea was believed to contain life-giving powers, and it became coveted as an amulet to ward off danger and death. Its supernatural powers even extended to the dead, whose souls it protected. Egyptians identified this immortality symbol with the divine cow goddess, Hathor, the great mother and nurturer of all creation. At some point in Egyptian history the people began to make models of the magical shell in clay and stone, in the belief that the power could be transferred from one to the other. Eventually they settled on using a yellow metal found in the Nubian desert as their model. The gold amulets became more popular than the original shells and the gold became imbued with the life-giving powers of the goddess Hathor.[1]

In India, according to Arthur Hocart, gold became identified with the fire god Agni and was often substituted for the sun in religious rituals. Hocart steers us to a line from the *Satapatha Brahamana:*

> For this gold plate is the same as truth. Yonder sun is the same as truth. It is made of gold, for gold is life and he [the sun] is life. Gold is immortality, and he is immortality. It is round, for he is round. Indeed, this gold plate is the sun.[2]

Coins and gods have enjoyed an intimate relationship through-out recorded history. Gold and silver have long been valued as symbols, or representatives, of the sun and moon gods. In fact, as Hocart and other economic historians point out, gold coins were a "supernatural utility" long before they became an "economic utility." The value attached to money, says Hocart, was quite different from today. "A little of it was given away in exchange for quantities of stuff because a few ounces of divinity was worth pounds of gross matter."[3]

The great temples of the ancient empires along the Nile and Euphrates served as the first banks. Inside the sanctuaries the priests assumed the role of exchequer, exchanging divine security, in the form of gold, for grain and other foodstuffs. Gold, the first permanent form of money, was endowed with sacred powers. Those who possessed it remained safe and secure in body and soul.[4]

Virtually everywhere money has emerged it has been associated, in one form or another, with security. The very word *money* is derived from the Latin word *moneo,* which means "to warn."[5] According to Roman mythology, Juno Regina, the wife of Jupiter, was the queen of the heavens and the goddess of security and protection who warned the Roman rulers of dangers ahead. Her temple was used as the first mint, and she served as the guardian of finance.[6]

Money has always represented power, and as Ernest Becker observed, "All power is in essence power to deny mortality."[7] Up until the modern era money symbolized divine power. All sacred coins were divinely inspired promissory notes, guaranteeing the holder a measure of bodily security in this world, and the pros-pect of eternal security in the next. In the modern age money metamorphosed into a new species. The sacred power of money was replaced with a new secular power. Money now represents a lien on other people's time and toil. The nineteenth-century so-cial reformer John Ruskin lays bare the truth about modern money:

> [Money] signifies the accumulation in the hands of individuals of legal and moral claim upon, or power over, the labor of

18

others. What is really desired under the name of riches is essentially the power over other men.[8]

The battle in the late medieval era between the ecclesiastical authorities and the bourgeoisie over the use of money marks one of the decisive turning points in Western history. At stake were two different notions of security, one sacred and centered on eternal salvation, the other profane and directed toward a material cornucopia. The Church prohibited usury. In Matthew 6:24 it is written: "No man can serve two masters. For either he will hate the one and love the other, or else he will stand by the one and despise the other. We cannot serve God and Mammon."

Usury was a rare event in the early Middle Ages as most of Europe was still a subsistence-based economy relying on barter as the dominant form of trade and exchange. As population, cities, and trade began to expand in the twelfth century, money became more important in regulating economic transactions and exchanges. A new class of merchants and bankers began to lend money at interest, reaping tremendous profits in the process.

The Church argued that usury was a mortal sin punishable by eternal damnation. In support of this contention, they cited chapter and verse from both testaments. In Exodus 22:25, God warns His chosen people: "If you lend money to one of your poor neighbors among my people, you shall not act like an executioner to him by demanding interest from him."

Of all the unworthy professions—and the Church's list was a long one, including bathkeepers, innkeepers, butchers, fullers, dyers, cooks, and barbers—usurers were considered the most culpable because of their avarice. Only prostitutes and acrobats shared the same Church ire, being condemned by their very nature.

As usury became more widespread, the Church fought back with new additions to canon law, condemning the practice. St. Anselm likened usury to theft, which was expressly forbidden by the fourth commandment: "Thou shall not steal." By the thirteenth century Church authorities were worried that the widespread use of usury by landlords was depriving peasants of their cattle and tools, threatening agriculture, and raising the possibility of famine.[9]

The Church made it clear that it was not opposed to the "just" price or "fair market" price but considered usury an improper gain and, therefore, theft. According to St. Thomas Aquinas:

> Money was invented chiefly for exchange to be made. So the prime and proper use of money is its use in disbursement in the way of ordinary transactions. It follows that it is, in principle, wrong to charge for money lent, which is what usury consists of.[10]

At the heart of the controversy over usury, or profit, was the question of use of time. The merchants argued that "Time is money."[11] For the merchants time was critical. Their success depended on their ability to use time to their advantage: knowing when the best time was to buy cheap and sell dear and how long inventory should be allowed to stay on hand; determining the time it would take for goods to arrive, or how long it would take to ship them to their destination; anticipating changes in exchange rates, the rise and fall of prices, changes in labor availability over time, and the time necessary to make a product. The merchant who garnered the most knowledge of how to predict, use, and manipulate these various time frames commanded the best prices and made the most profit.

The Church argued that time belonged exclusively to God, who dispenses it freely in his temporal kingdom. Time is a gift God grants so that human beings may use it to prepare for their future salvation. By usurping time, the merchants, bankers, landlords, and entrepreneurs were usurping God's authority. Summing up the official position of the Vatican, Thomas Chobham argued that in charging interest, "the usurer sells nothing to the borrower that belongs to him. He sells only time which belongs to God. He can therefore not make a profit from selling someone else's property."[12] If time belonged exclusively to God, then to assure personal duration in this world, and salvation in the next, one must choose to surrender freely to Him. Earthly security was only obtained by bathing in time freely dispensed by the Lord.

If, however, time was reducible to a commodity that could be bought and sold, then the more profit one could amass, the more time one could buy for oneself. By charging greater interest and reaping greater profits one could buy other people's time as well, thus adding to the amount of time available.

How, then, did human beings ensure their perpetuation and survival? By faith in God or by the accumulation of money? Medieval historian Jacques Le Goff sums up the significance of the great battle to define humanity's future. "The conflict, then, between the Church's time and the merchant's time takes its place as one of the major events in the mental history of these centuries."[13]

The protracted debate between the Church and the merchants over profit and usury extended far beyond the question of "just" price. At the core of the dispute was the troubling question of how best to define economic relationships and to achieve personal security. The Church expressed the traditional wisdom. Economics was, first and foremost, a social act based on reciprocity. The goal was to strengthen the bonds of community and to steward God's creation in anticipation of the coming of the kingdom.

To place this epochal struggle in its proper perspective, we need to appreciate fully the different way economics was regarded in the pre-modern era. Bronislaw Malinowski reminds us that economics began as an exercise in "gift giving" and was steeped in indebtedness and appreciation.[14] From the temples of Sumer, to the alms plate at the Cathedral of Chartres, the act of exchange in Western history served a common goal. The economics of gift giving allowed the community periodically to cleanse its collective soul of the heaviness of expropriation that weighed so forcefully on it. Even in contemporary culture, we retain a facade of the ancient practice of economics at Christmastime, when the entire society engages in an elaborate orgy of gift giving and receiving.

Cultural historian Elias Canetti once remarked that "Each of us is a King in a field of corpses."[15] If we were to stop for a moment and reflect on the number of creatures and Earth's resources, and materials we have expropriated and consumed in our lifetime to perpetuate our existence, we would be appalled at the carnage and depletion that has been required to secure our existence. The sense of guilt and indebtedness runs deep in the human psyche and stretches over the expanse of human experience. Giving gifts to the gods, the priests, and other members of the community

21

was a sacrificial act, a humbling of the soul, borne of the awareness that one's good fortune and security depended not on personal wiliness alone, but rather on the benevolence of larger forces
in the world.

Even on a secular plane, ancient economics was practiced in a
different dimension. For example, it was not unusual, Malinowski
reminds us, in the ritual of gift giving for two parties to exchange
the exact thing back and forth. One person might give a pig to a
second person only to have the same pig given back a short time
later. To our modern sensibilities, such activity seems odd and
hardly deserving of the term economics. We need to remember
that the function of exchange served different ends in the past.[16]

Exchange of goods was, for most of history, a social act, a way
of forging bonds and deepening relationships. Ancient economics,
both sacred and secular, was based in reciprocity, not in seeking
advantage. Exchanges between people were meant to be equivalent in value. Like their ancestors, medieval man and woman
perceived their economic security in terms of indebtedness to God,
nature, and the larger community. By the late medieval era,
however, the merchants had already begun to express the vague
outlines of a new form of security based on personal financial
autonomy, achieved by the exercise of raw power in the marketplace.[17]

Today, we are raised with the notion that to be secure is to be
financially autonomous. Amassing wealth is viewed as the primary
rite of passage to a secure, autonomous existence. In the modern
world "possession" has been substituted for gift giving, and *caveat
emptor*, let the buyer beware, has become the faint whisper underlying every transaction.

Personal financial autonomy is an idea completely unique to the
present moment and nowhere to be found in the historical record
of past civilizations. Indeed, it may well be one of the most
significant innovations of the past five hundred years, as it has
shaped the contours of contemporary life as no other single force.

The modern concept of economic security did not take hold
overnight. The Church proved to be a formidable adversary, for a
time blocking the aspirations of the merchant class. The threat of
eternal damnation tempered the avarice of many. Lewis Mumford

reminds us that in a world where everyone believes literally in an afterlife, "even kings trembled" before the Church.[18] Ecclesiastical authority might have prevailed over the merchants, forestalling the modern age altogether, had the Church not compromised at a critical point in the great struggle.

During the first millennium of the Church's reign, the afterlife was divided into two regions, heaven and hell. For the Christian who led an exemplary or near exemplary life, eternal salvation in heaven was the ultimate reward. For those who allowed themselves to fall prey to the devil, eternal damnation in hell was to be their final judgment. Then, in the thirteenth century, the Church introduced an innovation into its practice and doctrine that was to provide the opening for the final triumph of the merchant class.[19]

The Vatican created a new region in the afterlife, purgatory, which was to be reserved for all those who had sincerely repented their mortal sins before death, even if they had not made an overt act of penance. While the repentant sinner would face punishment in purgatory, comparable to hell, the sentence would be limited, after which he or she would be lifted up into heaven for all of eternity. The length of stay in purgatory depended both on the weight and number of sins committed over a lifetime, and the intervention of friends and loved ones on the sinner's behalf after death. By prayer, offerings, and intercessions, family and friends could shorten the punishment and the sentence. Here was the great escape hatch that eventually helped undermine the authority of the Church and embolden the capitalist class to make a successful bid for world dominance.[20]

Before the introduction of contrition in the confessional, and purgatory in the afterlife, a Christian had only one choice open to him if he were to avoid eternal damnation. He must confess his mortal sins and make penance in the form of restitution. The Church's position was unwavering. Stephen of Bourbon wrote: "If the userer wishes to avoid damnation he must *cough up* [the Latin term is a very strong one, *evomet* or *evomat*, which means to vomit it up] in restitution the dishonestly acquired money and confess his fault. Otherwise he will *cough them up* during his punishment in Hell."[21] When the Church did finally yield on the question of restitution, the consequences were devastating and far-reaching.

Beginning in the thirteenth century, the userer could gain entrance to heaven through a short detour through purgatory by merely expressing his contrition. It was no longer necessary to make retribution to those victims who suffered at his hands. Jacques Le Goff notes the importance of these changes in Church doctrine for the future course of Western culture:

> For the usurer who was ready for final contrition, Purgatory was the hope and soon the quasi-certainty of being saved, of being able to have both his money here below, and his eternal life beyond the grave. . . . The hope of escaping hell, thanks to Purgatory, permitted the userer to propel the economy and society of the thirteenth century ahead, toward capitalism."[22]

It was Jesus who said, "What doth it profit a man if he should gain the world and lose his soul." Modifications in Church law after the thirteenth century ensured the profiteer that he could have the best of both worlds.

Human beings' changing relationship to money in Western history is a chronicle of the increasing loss of faith in God and increasing attachment to secular power over men and nature. Shakespeare, whose work often juxtaposed the conflicting sensibilities of the medieval and modern world, foresaw the great changes in thinking that were taking place when he said that money is the new "visible God." The victory of the merchants over the Church, then, represents a historic substitution of allegiance. Man's indebtedness to God was replaced with indebtedness to the merchant, banker, and factory owner. In contemporary society credit has substituted for faith and has come to fill the vacuum left in the wake of divine dethronement.

In a modern market economy, the bonds between people are reduced to a fiduciary relationship centered on raw power. Human relationships are no longer largely structured around religious traditions, sacred trusts, family and communal obligations, or fraternal love, but rather on a form of commercial indenture. Money allows people to use or borrow other people's time and labor. In a market economy, every person has his price, as money becomes "the sole measure of a man."[23]

Today we are all so thoroughly indoctrinated in the modern money economy that its cold and inhuman demeanor goes largely unnoticed. Oftentimes its utilitarian nature is even the source of adulation. Champions of the "free" market are fond of singing the praises of the Scottish economist Adam Smith, whose economic philosophy provided a convenient rationale for a society in which each human being competes with others in pursuit of his or her own self-interest.

In the money economy, Thomas Hobbes observed: "A man's labor also is a commodity, exchangeable for benefits as well as any other thing."[24] Hobbes's vision has dominated the modern mind. In contemporary society, even our most personal relationships are increasingly structured around monetary payment. We pay psychiatrists to listen to our woes. We pay domestic help to clean our homes and look after our children. We pay restaurants to cook our meals. All of these relationships, which we take for granted, are bought. We pay for nurture, care and consideration, advice and counsel, understanding and loyalty. Our connection to others is more and more determined by the monetary power we are able to exercise over their time and labor. Our relationships remain secure only as long as our bank accounts remain full.

At no other time and place in history have social and economic relationships been played out in such an abstract, detached, superficial, and forced context. Sociologist Max Weber summed up the salient features of the new money economy earlier in this century:

> The market community, as such, is the most impersonal relationship of practical life into which human beings can enter with one another. Where the market is allowed to follow its own tendencies, its participants do not look toward the person of each other, but only toward the commodity. There are no obligations of brotherliness or reverence, and none of those spontaneous human relations that are sustained by personal unions. They all would just obstruct the free development of the bare market relationship. Such absolute de-

personalization is contrary to all elementary forms of human relations.[25]

Money serves a variety of functions, then, in the modern world. It is the primary means by which human beings secure their existence. Money is both a medium to facilitate exchange of goods and services between people and a convenient tool for measuring the worth of each individual. Money is the glue that cements an increasing number of relationships between people. Money confers status and power. Stored money, in the form of capital, allows some human beings to exert control over the lives of others. Most important of all, modern man and woman have become obsessed with the illusion that money buys autonomy, and that autonomy and security are one and the same thing.

3

THE HARLOT AND THE MACHINE

THE COMMODIFICATION OF human relationships and economic activity set in motion a great transfer of power in Western civilization. Divine power, which had ruled over nature and the affairs of society through most of human history, was circumvented and eventually usurped altogether. A new breed of commercial adventurers effectively wrested the mantle of sovereignty away from the heavens and appropriated it for themselves. At the same time, the medieval preoccupation with doing good works became subsumed by the new compulsion to make things work. Man's interest in profit and power became intricately bound up with his increasing interest in technological prowess.

Of course, human beings have always been interested in toolmaking as a means of extending their personal power over the world. The musket is an extension of our throwing arm. The printed book is an extension of our memory. The steam locomotive extends our legs and feet. Technologies are appendages of our physical and mental processes, providing us with greater power to affect, control, and overcome the limitations of time and space. We look to technology, then, to secure the world around us so that we may, in turn, feel secure.

Although tools have always played a significant role in human affairs, it is only in the industrial age that we have come to rely almost exclusively on science and technology to secure our existence in the world. Whereas medieval man felt secure as long as God's grace shined down upon him, modern man feels secure as long as he is able to invent new tools to extend his dominion over nature and his fellow human beings. In times of crisis, we look to the saving grace of science and new technological innovations to secure our existence against a hostile or threatening reality.

The "desacralization of nature" began in the seventeenth century as European intellectuals began to tear down the cosmological order that had given meaning and purpose to medieval Christian life. Francis Bacon, the father of modern science, led the assault on the medieval citadel of thought. Bacon surveyed the history of Western science and concluded that it had utterly failed to secure human existence. The Socratic tradition, with its emphasis on the why of things, was to Bacon's way of thinking singularly unsuccessful at enhancing the well-being of humanity. The Greeks, he complained, "assuredly have that which is characteristic of boys: they are prompt to prattle, but cannot generate; for their wisdom abounds in words but is barren of work."[1] Bacon was far more interested in practical benefits and argued that the Greeks, for all their musings, had not "adduced a single experiment which tends to relieve and benefit the condition of man."[2]

Bacon developed a radical new methodological approach to science that emphasized "how" over "why" and power over revelation. Using what he called the "scientific method," Bacon said that it would be possible to separate oneself from nature and, acting as a neutral observer, amass "objective knowledge" about the world. The goal, Bacon declared, was to "enlarge the bounds of human empire to the affecting of all things possible."[3]

For Bacon, knowledge was power. He provided a much needed scientific impetus for harnessing the riches of nature. By relying on the scientific method, nature could be "forced out of her natural state and squeezed and molded."[4] Bacon's conception of science was immersed in power. Over and over again in his writings, he emphasized coercion and control. With the scientific method at our disposal, Bacon boasted, we have "the power to conquer and subdue" nature and "to shake her to her foundations."[5]

Bacon introduced, for the first time in history, the idea of perpetual warfare against nature. The goal of the new science was to "establish and extend the power of dominion of the human race itself over the universe."[6] The environment was viewed as a menacing subterranean reality surrounding the small islands of order that man had created for himself. It was no longer enough, Bacon contended, to simply keep "her" at bay. Bacon argued for an all-out mobilization against what he referred to as this "common harlot."[7] Bacon called on his contemporaries to put their intellectual skills and resources on a wartime footing to subdue, overwhelm, conquer, and enslave the forces of nature. He warned that nature itself was relentless, and that even a slight lapse in vigilance could result in the world falling back "into the old Chaos." It was Bacon, then, far more than Machiavelli, who provided the methodology for exercising power in the modern world.[8]

It is not surprising that today, nearly four hundred years after Bacon's call to arms, more than one third of all the scientists in the world work on military-related research and development. Most of the rest are employed directly or indirectly by multinational corporations looking for new ways to exploit and commodify nature.

Even though we still think of the scientific method as a metaphysical tool, it has served a much more expedient function in the modern age. Bacon provided future generations with a radical new blueprint for exercising technological power over nature and it is in that context that his methodology must ultimately be judged.

Traditionally, power was exercised directly, whether it be over people or nature. Power was intimate, physical, of the body. Bacon introduced a new concept of power based on separation, detachment, and withdrawal. The new power was rational and analytical. The passion of direct engagement was replaced with cold technological coercion from a distance. Above all, Bacon's scientist was an autonomous force. He created a safe haven for himself in the form of the objective observer. He erected a new barrier of defense, separating himself from the things of the world by means of the "neutrality" of science. Armed with the scientific method, man could act on the world without having to participate in and be vulnerable to it.

Bacon inverted and secularized St. Thomas Aquinas's great dictum. The schoolman of the Church had counseled the faithful to be in this world but not of it. Bacon's disciples also chose to be in this world but not of it. Their gaze, however, was not on the otherworldly domain of eternal salvation but, rather, a future material cornucopia over which they could rule.

While Bacon helped construct the scientific methodology for the modern age, it was a mathematician, René Descartes, who provided the all-encompassing worldview. In place of St. Thomas Aquinas's great chain of being, Descartes reconceptualized the universe to resemble a giant clockwork mechanism.

The introduction of the steam engine and other forms of automated machinery unleashed a great new source of previously untapped energy and power. In the presence of the steam-driven loom and other machines, with their gigantic pistons, valves, pulleys, and cylinders, and their relentless belching, hissing, and stamping, even God's majesty began to wane. The slow, plodding movements of the ox pulling a plow in the fields, the quiet evening breeze turning a rural windmill were sublime images, unbefitting man's new Promethean drive for sovereignty over nature.

René Descartes captured the new intellectual fascination with machines by constructing a bold new cosmology.[9] He envisioned all of nature as a giant machine, run by well-ordered mechanical principles. God, the benevolent and caring shepherd of Christendom, was replaced with God the remote and cold technician, who created and set in motion a self-regulating machinelike universe that was orderly, predictable, and self-perpetuating.

Descartes's vision became a recurrent theme and finally an obsession for generations of scholars. Here was a view of nature and the universe that was conveniently compatible with the new technological revolution sweeping the European continent. Everywhere European men and women looked, machines of all kinds were being assembled and hurried into place to extract ores from the earth, to convert wool into textiles, to drive engines on rails, to print words on paper. Surrounded by the new technological wizardry, the great thinkers of the day projected the attributes of the machines far beyond the village commons, recasting all of nature to conform with the tools they were using to expropriate it. In the new scheme of things, nature was deadened and turned into passive machine parts that could be set into motion only by the introduction of energy from an outside source, much the same way that a clock requires winding up and a machine requires steam or fuel to operate.

Sir Isaac Newton provided the science for the new cosmology in his three laws of matter and motion, which among other things states that a body at rest remains at rest unless acted upon by an outside force. In the new mechanistic view, God became the outside force, a detached clockmaker who assembles the cosmic machine and then sets it in perpetual motion by winding it up. On earth, the entrepreneur, merchant, industrialist, and scientist became God's counterparts, the skilled technicians who used the same mechanical laws and principles that operated in the universe to assemble the stuff of nature and set in motion the industrial production of the modern age. They mined and extracted the ores, burned the trees to create the charcoal, stoked the furnaces, primed the pumps, converted the material, transported the goods, and exchanged the products. They were, in fact, the prime movers, the outside source of power that transformed "worthless" matter into valuable wealth.

In the new mechanistic universe, even the longstanding conception of animals was recast in machine terms. Descartes likened animals to "soulless automata" whose movements were little different from those of the automated puppetry that danced upon the Strasbourg clock. When an animal whimpers or screams, Descartes declared, it is not showing feeling or pain, but only emitting sounds and noises from its internal gears and mechanisms. "It seems reasonable," Descartes suggested, that "since art copies nature, and men can make various automata which move without thought, that nature should produce its own automata, much more splendid than artificial ones. Those natural automata are the animals."[10] Karl Marx observed that Descartes and the other intellectuals of the modern age were seeing with the eyes of the manufacturing period.

Descartes transformed the machine from tool to idol, refashioning all of nature in its image. The landlords, merchants, industrialists, and scientists could rest assured that their mechanical manipulation and expropriation of man and nature was appropriate because it conformed "to the natural order of things."

According to Descartes's own account, the universe, in all of its majesty, was revealed to him in a series of dreams on the night of November 10, 1619. Descartes believed that the universe, nature, and all of existence operates by mechanistic principles, and underlying the machinelike universe are the laws of mathematics.

> As I considered the matter carefully, it gradually came to light that all those matters only are referred to mathematics in which order and measurement are investigated, and that it makes no difference whether it be in numbers, figures, stars, sounds, or any other object that the question of measurement arises. I saw, consequently, that there must be some general science to explain that element as a whole, which gives rise to problems about order and measurement. This, I perceived, was called universal mathematics. Such a science should contain the primary rudiments of human reason, and its province ought to extend to the eliciting of true results in every subject.[11]

Descartes's revelation was matched by his sense of excitement over the possibilities that lay ahead with the new mathematical conception of nature. "To speak freely, I am convinced that it [mathematics] is a more powerful instrument of knowledge than any other that has been bequeathed to us by human agency, as being the source of all things."[12]

Descartes's vision stripped nature of its aliveness, its spontaneity. He reduced the world and everything in it from quality to quantity, leaving modern man and woman with only a rational and calculable domain. Descartes believed that just as we could use mathematical reasoning to unlock the workings of machines, we could use the same laws to unlock nature's secrets, making it a hostage to human manipulation. With mathematics as both tool and weapon, Descartes declared that we could "make ourselves masters and possessors of nature."[13]

Descartes's mathematical vision fit quite comfortably into a world where people and nature were already being redefined by their market value and reduced to a numerical status. In the industrial world, everything had a number attached to it—the price of a man's labor, the value of a piece of land, the time taken to ship goods to market, credits and debits, assets and liabilities, stocks and inventories, bushels and pecks, gross tonnage of cargo, net yields, volumes. The new moneyed economy flattened all phenomena and relationships to a strictly quantitative basis. In the industrial age, only those things that could be measured, counted, or assigned a commercial value were real.

The philosopher Bertrand Russell once said that mathematics has "a beauty cold and austere." In Descartes's mathematical universe, there was no room for joy, passion, exuberance, empathy, faith, sorrow. None of these qualities can be reduced to quantities. They can't be assigned a market value. They can't be coerced, or purchased. They are qualities that must be given freely. They are the intangibles that animate human existence. Descartes's reality was, in the words of the scientist-philosopher Alfred North Whitehead, "a dull affair, soundless, scentless, colorless; merely the bumping of material endlessly, meaninglessly."[14]

Descartes constructed his universe during a period of great upheaval. Food shortages, plagues, wars, the opening of commercial markets, new machine technologies, the colonization of new territories, the consolidation of city-states into monarchies and nation-states made the times both uncertain and tumultuous. The Church seemed powerless to explain or even comprehend the nature, scope, or direction of the social and economic changes that were taking place in Europe. The carefully constructed Christian worldview was far too otherworldly and labyrinthine to withstand the secular forces that were battering down the walls of the medieval world.

Descartes, like many of his contemporaries, sought a new form of security that could make sense out of the mounting chaos and restore a sense of order to a world adrift. He found his security in the domain of numbers and in the mechanical realm of pendulums and pistons. In a world where old certainties were fast crumbling, mathematics and mechanics appeared a welcome reprieve, if not a godsend. These tools offered predictability, rationality, order, and above all, control over the forces of nature and the follies of human beings.

Mathematics and mechanics can be used to manage people, events, and forces from a safe distance and can be controlled by a select few: the scientists who understand the arcane nature of the world of numbers and the industrialists who possess the capital to make and run the machines. Mathematics and mechanics also conjure up the notion of autonomy. Mathematics is by nature autonomous. Its internal logic is not subject to outside coercion. The rules of the game are set in advance. Its laws cannot be tampered with or undermined. In all dimensions it represents the purest conception of autonomy.

The industrial machine also seemed an appropriate symbol of the new quest for autonomy. Automated machinery is the embodiment of power. Compared to human and animal power it seems far more predictable and self-sufficient. Machinery almost runs on its own. It is tireless, it does not easily wear out, and is not subject to whims and caprices. It is a force that can be controlled even while it exercises control. Once set in motion it is virtually autonomous, needing only an occasional infusion of energy and periodic maintenance. It is understandable, then, that the great thinkers of the early modern era might have concluded that by using mathematics and mechanics to secure the world, they were in fact helping to secure an autonomous human existence in the process.[15]

It wasn't long before Enlightenment thinkers extended Descartes's mechanistic worldview to the economy, providing a convenient philosophical rationale for the commercial exploitation of man himself. Borrowing from the Cartesian metaphor, Adam Smith argued that an invisible hand ruled over the marketplace, assuring the proper functioning of economic life. This invisible hand was likened to the mechanical pendulum of a clock, meticulously regulating supply and demand, labor, energy, and capital, automatically assuring the proper balance between production and consumption of the earth's resources. If left unencumbered by outside interference or regulation, the invisible hand of capitalism would run like a perpetual motion machine, securing each individual's autonomy within an autonomous, self-regulating economy. Even today, economists continue to view the economic process in Cartesian terms when they speak of the "market mechanism."

In the new scheme of things, then, the invisible hand becomes the overseer and the marketplace the battleground in man's war against nature and his fellow human beings. Detached, impartial, automatic, and autonomous, the new god governing the marketplace understands only the language of numbers. In its domain all phenomena are reduced to commodity values: cost per unit, price per pound, dollar per hour, wages per week, rents per month, profits per quarter, and interest compounded semi-annually. The floors of the stock exchanges on Wall Street, in London, Tokyo, and Hong Kong provide the forums for a highly ritualized life-and-death struggle. With each shout, hand motion, and gesture, each change of number on the big board, the lives of people around the world are secured or threatened, the earth's resources exhumed and consumed. This is the veneer of economic security upon which most of the world community is precariously perched.

Perhaps no figure in the early modern era was more influential in establishing the political framework for the new mechanistic worldview than John Locke. His ideas on the utilitarian value of nature provided a rationale for the commercial exploitation of the environment that is still regarded as gospel by many in both the government and private sectors. Locke argued that "Land that is left wholly to nature, is called as indeed it is waste."[16] The great political philosopher believed that the living creatures and inanimate materials that make up the earth have no intrinsic value, only utilitarian value. In a state of nature everything is worthless, as it is not serving human needs. Earthly phenomena become valuable only after human labor and machine technology transform them into useful material, products, goods, and services.

Locke, like Bacon, Descartes, and many of the seminal thinkers of the sixteenth and seventeenth centuries, divided the planet into two separate realms—nature, which was made up of spare parts or raw resources, and society, which was made up of autonomous individuals looking to maximize their self-interest by the constant expropriation of nature's resources and their fellow human beings.

Locke believed that as long as human beings remain vulnerable to the forces of nature, their security could never be assured. He argued that true security could only be achieved if "man effectively emancipated [himself] from the bounds of nature."[17] The key to human liberation was the accumulation of wealth and greater consumption. The more planetary resources each person could effectively garner and consume, the more autonomous he would become and the more secure his existence. For Locke, security and consumption became virtually synonymous. As a person can never be too secure, Locke argued that every person has a right to "heap up as much as these durable things [gold, silver, and so on] as he pleases, the exceeding of the bounds of his just property not lying in the largeness of his possession, but the perishing of anything uselessly given."[18]

Like other architects of the pre-Enlightenment, Locke was convinced that technological progress would spur the increased expropriation and consumption of the earth's resources and ensure a more autonomous and secure existence for humankind. Locke provided the new warrior of modernity with his final marching orders: "The negation of nature is the way to happiness."[19]

Today we are so indoctrinated in the modern worldview that we seldom, if ever, pause to ponder the impact it has had on our personal and institutional relationships and our attitudes toward nature. Of course, that is the power of a worldview. When certain ideas become so thoroughly integrated into the thinking of a culture that they become second nature, they assume the same status as the air people breathe. Analytical and rational modes of thinking, mechanistic views of nature, reducing phenomena to purely quantifiable standards of measurement, the neutrality of science, knowledge as power, self-interest as the motivating force in history, the invisible hand of the marketplace, and utilitarianism are among the critical intellectual assumptions that, together, provide a unified intellectual schema for the modern notion of an autonomous, secure existence.

Modern man and woman's actions in the world flow inextricably from these Enlightenment ideas about nature and human security. These powerful intellectual constructs make up the rules of engagement in the contemporary war against nature. This being the case, it is naïve to believe it possible to extricate ourselves from the global environmental and economic crises facing the planet lest we are prepared to confront the set of ideas about security that gave rise to our current predicament.

From the very beginning of the modern era, the new set of assumptions about the nature of security has had a profound effect on shaping a wholesale change in human beings' economic and social relationships. Nowhere was the impact of the new thinking more poignant and directed than in the European enclosure movement, a little known social upheaval that had far-reaching consequences, changing the very basis of human beings' relationship to the environment and society.

While the Enlightenment worldview provided the philosophical justification for the separation from nature, it was the enclosure movement that began the actual process of physically separating man and woman from the land and their ancestral ground. The enclosure movement substituted money relationships and technological mastery for communal obligations and divine authority, forcing a fundamental change in the quest for security in daily life. In both its earliest incarnations and modern guises the enclosure movement has played a central role in restructuring economic, social, and environmental relationships. An examination of the history and anthropology of the worldwide enclosure movement is crucial to understanding the crisis engendered by our modern notions of security.

4

A PRIVATE NATURE

THE PROCESS OF separating people from each
other and their ancestral ground began with the dismantling of the
European commons half a millennium ago. Much of the economic
life of medieval Europe centered around the village commons.
Although feudal landlords owned the commons, they leased it to
peasant farmers under various tenancy arrangements. Freeholders
enjoyed perpetual tenancy, from generation to generation, and
could not be arbitrarily removed from their land by the landlord.
Leaseholders enjoyed a limited tenancy agreement, generally extending through three lifetimes, at which point the landlords could
renew or change the conditions of the lease or withhold the lease
altogether. Customary tenants, on the other hand, were without
legal rights and their tenancy depended solely on the goodwill of
the landlord.

In return for their right to cultivate the land, tenant farmers had
to turn over a percentage of their harvest to their landlord or
devote a comparable amount of time working the landlord's fields.
With the introduction of a moneyed economy in the late medieval
era, peasant farmers were increasingly required to pay rent or
taxes in return for the right to farm the land.

Medieval European agriculture was communally organized.
Peasants pooled their individual holdings into open fields that
were jointly cultivated. Common pastures were used to graze their

animals. Village commons peppered the European landscape. For the most part, they were self-sufficient and proved to be highly resilient to climate and other environmental and political assaults. They remained so as long as they continued to be organized communally for subsistence purposes.

The most remarkable feature of the village commons, and unfortunately the least known, is their democratic form of governance. Peasant councils administered the commons. Decisions on crop rotation, the time to plant and harvest, the number of animals that could graze on the commons, the introduction of new crops, the cutting of forests, the allocation of water, and the use of farm animals and plows were all made jointly and democratically by the members of the commune.

The village commons prospered for over six hundred years along the base of the feudal pyramid, under the watchful but often nominal presence of the landlords, monarch, and pope. Then, beginning in the 1500s, new and powerful political and economic forces were unleashed, first in Tudor England, and later on the continent, which undermined and ultimately destroyed the communitarianism of the village commons and the economic security that had bound humans to one another and the land for centuries.

Enclosing means "surrounding a piece of land with hedges, ditches, or other barriers to the free passage of men and animals."[1] Enclosure placed the land under private control, severing any right the community formerly had to use it. The enclosure movement was carried out by several means, including acts of Parliament, the common agreement of all the members of the village commune, and license by the king.

Some historians have called the enclosure movement "the revolution of the rich against the poor."[2] Between the sixteenth and nineteenth centuries, a series of political and legal acts were initiated in countries throughout Europe that enclosed publicly held land. These acts fundamentally altered the economic relationship between people, and between people and the natural environment, paving the way for the emergence of the industrial and urban revolutions. In the process, millions of peasants were dislodged from their ancestral homes and forced to migrate into the new industrial cities where, if they were fortunate, they might secure subsistence employment in the new industrial factories, which were eager to take advantage of their desperate plight.

The European enclosure movement marked the beginning of a worldwide process of privatization and commodification of the land, ocean, and atmosphere of the earth that is still being carried out today in every unattended or unclaimed ecological niche. Yet, few among us are more than vaguely aware of either the political history or environmental consequences of this radical reorientation in human beings' relationship to nature. The English enclosure movement predates that of the rest of Europe and provides a representative picture of the impact that privatizing of commonly held land had on the life of the individual, the community, and the course of events in Western civilization.

England experienced two major waves of enclosure, the first in the 1500s under the Tudor monarchy, the second in the late 1700s and early 1800s during King George III's reign.[3] In the earlier period, increased urban demand for food triggered an inflationary spiral which, in turn, increased the cost to landlords whose land rents had been fixed at pre-inflationary rates. At the same time, an expanding textile industry was clamoring for more wool, making sheep grazing an increasingly attractive and lucrative prospect. Those two forces conspired, creating an irresistible lure to enclose the land.

With the financial help of a new and wealthy bourgeois class of merchants and bankers, landlords began to buy up the common lands, turning them to pastureland for sheep. The enclosure of the commons swept through England as large areas of once common land were brought under private control, forcing peasants off the land and into the cities. Seemingly overnight, sheep took over the English countryside.

The landlords defended their actions, pointing out that a single shepherd tending sheep on enclosed land could bring in far greater returns at far less expense than could be expected from the paltry fixed rents paid by dozens of tenant farmers on the commons. The cost of farm labor had risen dramatically in the 1500s in the wake of the mass deaths of rural populations during the plague of the preceding century. Many landlords complained bitterly of the scarcity of farmhands and reasoned that conversion of arable land to pasture would greatly reduce their labor bill, as indeed it did.

Fenced off the land, the peasants reacted. Protests and open rebellion ensued. Sir Thomas More captured the bitter spirit of the times in his *Utopia*, a scathing attack on the avarice and greed of the landlord class.

> Your sheep, that were wont to be so meek and tame and so small eaters, now, and I hear say, become so great devourers and so wild, that they eat up and swallow down the very men themselves. They consume, destroy, and devour whole fields, houses and cities.[4]

"Sheep eat men," declared More, echoing the sentiments of hundreds of thousands of farm families, who watched helplessly as sheep grazed on grassland that just a few years earlier had been tilled for oats and rye to feed their own children. Everywhere people were reduced to starvation while sheep were fattened and fleeced to rush wool to the new textile factories popping up all over England and on the continent. British Board of Agriculture statistics tell the story. An acre of arable land on the commons could produce 670 pounds of bread. That same acre, when enclosed, could only support a handful of sheep producing less than 176 pounds of mutton.[5] By maintaining production high up on the food chain to increase the wealth of a few, valuable calories were lost—calories that could have been used to feed a hungry population. This story would be repeated over and over again in the modern age as the enclosure movement, in various guises, was used to radically redefine the use of the land. In each instance the land, long regarded as home, became transformed into a mere resource, changing the basis of economic security for large numbers of human beings.

In the first wave of enclosures in medieval England, many peasants became resigned to a new status as landless people, a fate previously experienced only by the wandering Jew in the long sweep of European history. Without a home, the newly disenfranchised peasants became the first refugees of the modern age. Their existence marginalized, they were no longer treated as a

41

community but, rather, as a class, their worth henceforth determined in dollars and measured strictly by their labor value per hour worked, rather than by their long-standing ancestral rights.

While some peasants accepted their new condition, others fought back, determined to regain their former economic status. Throughout England the banner cry went up: "Enclosures make fat beasts and lean poor people." The peasants found a partial ally in the crown. The Tudor monarchs, and later the Stuart kings, were quite interested in commercial development of agriculture. They were opposed, however, to rapid and extensive enclosures that resulted in the wholesale depopulation of the English countryside. Concerned that massive dislodgement of the rural population might ignite peasant insurrection and rebellion, and that abandoned countryside might even make much of England vulnerable to military attack by foreign powers, the monarchy supported weak anti-enclosure legislation.

The crown had ample reason to be worried. The economic foundations of English life were being torn asunder with unfathomable consequences.[6] The entire country was being privatized. The land was being transformed into a marketable resource; agriculture was being reduced to a commodity status; and from Newcastle to Cornwall there were abandoned homes, deserted villages, and boarded-up churches.

This was a new and unprecedented form of warfare—economic warfare—whose consequences bore a striking resemblance to the ravages of military action. The scenes in the English countryside were to become familiar ones in the modern age as a new class of entrepreneurs and capitalists swept into ecological niches and traditional communities around the world, forcing people off the land, which they transformed into a "resource" for short-term market exploitation.

Caught between the greed of the wealthy landlord class with whom they closely identified, and the fury of the newly landless peasant class, the monarchy tried to maintain a delicate balancing act designed to enrich its own coffers while dampening the public rage. Legislation was passed in 1533 to limit the spread and impact of enclosures, but it was not strictly enforced and did little to stem the movement to privatize English soil. By the middle of the eighteenth century nearly half of the agricultural land had been transferred to private possession.

The second and decisive wave of enclosures began around 1760 and extended into the 1840s, roughly corresponding to the reign of King George III.[7] England and the continent were beginning to industrialize. Trade routes were expanding and new markets were opening up overseas. A growing urban population required more food, and an emerging bourgeoisie was demanding a greater variety of foodstuffs as well. Wealthy landlords were anxious to meet the new consumer demands. They made their final drive to enclose the remaining English countryside, transforming the last vestiges of a subsistence-based rural economy into a new, market-oriented agriculture.

The enclosure movement brought with it a change in temporal as well as spatial conception. In fact, the history of this period is as much about the enclosure of time as space. The time orientation of the commune adhered strictly to the temporal requirements of nature. Agricultural activity was shaped by the changing seasons and the rhythms of the larger environment. In the incipient market economy, the whims and caprices of consumer preferences began to exercise a greater influence over how the land was to be used. Private landlords were willing and able to change their practices and policies to innovate and adjust to the ever-changing demands of the market.

The changing time orientation dictated by the forces of the marketplace was to have far-reaching consequences in the ensuing centuries. The signs were already apparent. Private landlords anxious to keep pace with new consumer demands pushed ahead with agricultural innovations to increase the productivity of their land. Age-old practices of soil conservation were often compromised or abandoned altogether to accelerate production. Agricultural land, which had remained fertile for hundreds of years under the stewardship of the village communes, was exhausted as the time demands of the market edged out the time requisites of the ecosystem.

In every region of the world where land has been enclosed and converted from subsistence agriculture to a marketplace orientation over the past several hundred years, the "time demands" exerted by a growing urban market have strained the carrying capacity of the soil, threatening erosion and long-term desertification. Today American farmers, buffeted by high costs and lower prices, are overusing the land, exhausting the soil base, and threatening the food supply for future generations. Over one third of the prime topsoil of North America has eroded away in this century, much of it in the last several decades as farmers have attempted to meet the ever accelerating production pace set by domestic and foreign markets.

It is often argued that the enclosure acts freed the individual from the iron grip of the collective will. In actuality, privatization of land allowed a few individuals to pursue their own naked self-interests without having to be accountable to the larger community. Privatization severed the bonds of intimate community, leaving each member to fend for himself against his neighbor.

Interestingly, this new form of individual rights, the right to freely exploit nature and people, was purchased at the expense of another even more basic individual right that had been protected by law for hundreds of years. Under English law, enclosure of a common often required the unanimous consent of the freeholders of the commune. Even if one member opposed enclosure it was generally sufficient to block the conversion.

We moderns are so thoroughly indoctrinated by the idea that individual rights are a creature of capitalism and the Industrial Revolution that we find it difficult to entertain the notion that long before our own Bill of Rights was signed into law, peasant freeholders living within the village commons in medieval England enjoyed an even more basic right: the right to maintain their ancestral land even against the will of the majority; the right to turn over the same ground, to drink from the same well, to gaze on the same landscape and vistas that had provided context, home, and existence for one's family for as far back as any could remember: in short, the right to pass along to one's children a largesse of common experiences, shared settings, and tasks—the right to join past, present, and future into a unified experience. This is what the freeholder protected when he exercised his right under law not to be moved. That right was highly coveted and fiercely championed.

One documented voice from those years long ago conveyed the sentiments of many at the time:

> The freeholder's right of commons is his several right as much as his tenancy of his home. I defy you to enclose one square yard; I defy you severally; I defy you jointly; you may meet in your court, you may pass what resolutions you please; I shall condemn them; for I have a right to put my beast on this land and every part of it; the law gives me this right and the King protects it.[8]

Increasing commercial pressure to enclose the remaining commons finally resulted in the passage of special acts of Parliament stripping members of the commons of their rights to hold out against the privatization of the land. In most instances these acts sanctioned enclosure if three fourths or four fifths of the members of the commons agreed. Votes, however, were weighed by the amount or value of the land owned, ensuring that the wealthy landlords and rich farmers would prevail.

Enclosure fundamentally restructured the way people perceived themselves, each other, and the soil. English historian Gilbert Slater asks us to imagine "what a village cataclysm took place" when an act of Parliament was passed to enclose a village commons.[9] Commissioners descended on the village with account books in hand. They went door to door, plot to plot, assigning a monetary value on every property. The commissioners then rearranged the entire commons, cutting up the arable land and pastures into neat, orderly rectangles, each with a separate owner. All past relationships and mutual obligations were severed. Suddenly and arbitrarily, the customs and traditions of lifetimes were declared null and void. Neighbors were no longer expected to help plough each other's fields, or mend village fences together, or share in the grazing of draft animals on the common pasture.

Enclosure introduced a new concept of relationships into European civilization that changed the basis of economic security and the perception of social life. Henceforth, land and people were no longer treated as ends but rather as means. The ground people walked on was no longer valued solely or even primarily in terms of shared experiences. It was no longer something people belonged to, but rather a commodity people possessed. Land was reduced to a quantitative status and measured by what it could be exchanged for. So, too, with people. Relationships were reorganized. Neighbors became employees or contractors. Reciprocity was replaced with hourly wages. People sold their time and labor where they used to share their toil. With enclosure, a myriad of relationships had to be restructured overnight. People began to view each other and everything around them in financial terms. Virtually everyone and everything became negotiable and could be purchased at an appropriate price.

Philosophers—like Thomas Hobbes—welcomed the change. Hobbes attacked the roots of communalism that nourished the village commons and anchored the feudal order. Hobbes viewed human life as a "short, nasty, and brutish affair" and argued that man is constantly engaged in a war of all against all. Since perpetual warfare and competition for scarce resources is inherent to human nature, the village commons could never be an effective arrangement for organizing economic life. Hobbes ridiculed the notion of communal obligations and relationships, arguing that they were based on an illusion rather than reality. "For he that should be modest and tractable and perform all he promises . . . should then make himself a prey to others and procure his own certain ruin."[10]

Hobbes was the first to articulate the idea "of the tragedy of the commons," the notion that each person will inevitably compete with others for the limited land and resources available to all. Hobbes championed the idea of commercial enclosure, arguing that it more accurately reflected the true nature of human motivation. Hobbes skirted the historical fact, however, that the village commons successfully maintained itself and sustained the lives of its members for over six hundred years in Europe. The emerging bourgeois class chose to ignore history altogether, casting their lot with a philosophy that justified both their new relationship to the land and people and their newly acquired fortunes.

Max Weber called this great restructuring of relationships the "disenchantment of the world"—life, land, existence, reduced to abstract quantifiable standards of measurement. The European enclosure movement set the stage for the modern age. The privatization of the land and the commodification of human and environmental relationships marked the triumph of the rational and analytical over the sacred. As Karl Marx later observed, the enclosure movement also provided an army of surplus labor for the new industrial factories in England and on the continent. Landless peasants became the first generation of alienated workers.

The European enclosure movement helped create the necessary conditions for the emergence of integrated national economies. The passing of agricultural land into private hands was accompanied by technological innovations in transportation, providing more reliable and efficient means of connecting town and country. Improvement in river navigation, the dredging of canals, the enlarging of paths into paved toll roads, and the laying down of rails brought villages, towns, and cities into an interconnected framework for the first time. Ironically, the increasing atomization and isolation of European peasants and laborers provided a rather striking contrast to the increasing complexification and integration of economic life. The communal self-sufficiency that characterized medieval life on the manor estate and the village common gave way to a diversified market economy on the European continent. Expanding markets, improved transportation, and overseas trade required new forms of regulation, coordination, and control. Regional integration of all these activities helped spawn the modern nation-state.

In a little more than three hundred years the enclosure movement had succeeded in fundamentally restructuring people's concept of security. Medieval man and woman lost far more than their ancestral land during the waves of enclosure. The privatization of the commons shattered the entire structure of medieval life and, with it, the spiritual as well as economic security that for hundreds of years had provided a sense of place and purpose. Exposed and directionless, European peasants became easy prey to a new phalanx of sovereigns, first in the form of wealthy landlords, later capitalist merchants and factory owners, and finally the bureaucrats and autocrats of the nation-state.

At the same time, the new bourgeois class turned its gaze from

47

the heavens to the farthest points on the horizon, where new markets lay in wait. The Western World constructed a new base for security, which was firmly entrenched along a horizontal plane. Security was to be found in walls and fences, guns, and great masted sailing ships, mechanisms, and machines. Security came to be measured more in technological prowess and earthly possessions, and less in faith and good works. In return for the great loss—the loss of intimate communion with the body and blood of Christ—the new man and woman were offered a form of security that was secular in nature, tangible, and accumulative. Henceforth, money and machines were to be the new guarantors.

5

COWS DEVOUR PEOPLE

TODAY, THE WORLDWIDE enclosure movement shows little sign of abatement, as nation-states and multinational corporations continue to commodify every last vestige of the earth's endowment as well as an increasing number of human relationships, all in the name of profit, autonomy, and security. Nowhere is the modern enclosure movement more in evidence than in Central and South America, where companies like Volkswagen, Nestlé, Mitsubishi, and Swift Armour are enclosing millions of acres of tropical rain forests to establish ranching operations for the increasingly lucrative export trade in meat.

From the jungles of Rondônia, deep inside the Amazon, to the ancient forest ranges of El Salvador and Honduras, millions of peasant farmers, rubber tappers, and native Indians are being forced off their ancestral land to make room for cattle. The rich tropical forests, which contain the remaining genetic diversity of the planet, are being systematically razed and burned to open up pastureland for grazing.

In Brazil, Chico Mendez, the head of the rubber tappers' union, was murdered in 1987 by cattle ranchers anxious to move the peasants off the land from which their families had eked out a sustainable living for generations. His martyrdom has been repeated countless times and in many different forms as native populations have been forced by bayonets and banks to abandon their land to wealthy corporate landlords who have amassed fortunes in the conversion of the commons to private ranching fiefdoms.

"Cows devour people" can be heard from the river edge of the Rio Grande to the rolling plains of the Argentine pampas—an entire continent turned into a giant grazing land to feed the cows that will, in turn, feed the stomachs of well-off American, European, and Japanese families, who prefer to eat high up on the planetary food chain. The statistics are grim and eerily reminiscent of the toll in human suffering that acompanied the early enclosure movement in Europe, when "sheep ate men."

In Brazil, 44 percent of the domestic food crop is now used to feed livestock (in Mexico the figure is 32 percent).[1] The poor literally go hungry in order to fatten cattle for beef exports. Black beans, a staple of the Brazilian peasant diet, are now out of reach for many families, as corporate cattle ranchers have switched to growing soybeans to feed livestock. In many other Latin American countries, land that might have been cleared to raise corn for human consumption two decades ago is now being converted exclusively into pastureland for cattle. Where the same acre could produce over twelve hundred pounds of corn per year, it now can sustain barely fifty pounds of beef.[2] Most of the meat produced is shipped to U.S. and European markets. In Mexico alone, a major cattle-producing country, one third of the peasants go through their entire lives never tasting beef.[3] In Central America up to one half of the beef produced each year is shipped abroad, mostly to the U.S., where it is made into frankfurters, hamburgers, frozen dinners, baby food, luncheon meat, and dog food.[4] In Costa Rica in one recent year cattle ranchers exported over sixty million pounds of beef while the consumption of beef within the country dropped to thirty-three pounds per capita.[5] Food economist Frances Moore Lappé notes that half that country's children are malnourished while the land is being used to provide cheap meat for millions of U.S. families.[6]

Many U.S. multinational corporations are rushing to enclose Latin American land to save on the high cost of raising cattle domestically. American grain companies, which own many of the largest cattle-raising and meat-packing operations, also benefit from the enclosure of Central and South American land and the conversion to cattle ranching. An increasing amount of grain grown in the American farm belt is being exported to Central and South America as feed grain for the growing number of cattle.[7]

In the frenzied scramble to secure windfall profits, the multinational corporations are stripping Latin America of the rich biological endowment upon which future generations will depend for their survival. Over twenty thousand square kilometers of tropical forest are razed and burned each year to make room for cattle grazing.[8] In Central America, over half the forests have been cleared since 1960, and if the present rate of destruction continues, the entire region will be stripped bare before the turn of the century.[9]

Lappé provides a graphic account of the destruction inflicted when Western technology is turned against one of the oldest living ecosystems of the world:

> Already, legions of Caterpillar tractors, gargantuan 35-ton D-9s mounted with angle plows weighing 2500 pounds each, are bulldozing the forests at 2700 yards an hour, uprooting everything in sight. In some areas their job calls for two D-9s with a heavy chain between them, rolling a huge hollow steel ball 8 feet in diameter and weighing 6000 pounds. As the tractors move forward, the chains jerk out the trees, destroying the extensive matted root system and exposing the tropical soil.[10]

Astronauts in outer space report the twinkling of thousands of fires burning along millions of acres of the Amazon on their fly-bys, as the forest is cleared and burned to make room for pasture. The tragic irony is that the land being cleared and enclosed is poorly suited for grazing. The soil base in tropical ecosystems is extremely thin and contains very little nutrients. These ancient ecosystems exist in a climax state, quickly recycling energy back from roots to canopy with very little allowed to remain on the forest floor. After just a few short years of grazing—generally three to five years—the soil is depleted, forcing the cattle ranchers to clear more virgin lands.

Like the earlier European enclosure movement, the conversion of land away from subsistence toward export has resulted in the amassing of great wealth by capitalist entrepreneurs and the creation of a new landless peasant class. In Guatemala, for example, 2.2 percent of the population owns 70 percent of the agricultural land, most of it used for cattle ranching.[11] In Costa Rica fewer than two thousand cattle ranchers own over half of the agricultural land in the country.[12] Throughout Central America over half of the rural families—35 million people—are landless or own too little land to support themselves.[13] In Brazil, one percent of the farms cover 43 percent of the nation's farmland.[14] Some of the cattle ranches owned by multinational companies are as large as 3.7 million acres, or half the size of the Netherlands.[15] Meanwhile seven million farm families own no farmland at all.[16]

Today, millions of peasants, forced off their land throughout Central and South America, remain in the countryside barely able to eke out their survival. Others migrate to urban areas where there is little or no prospect of employment. Thousands of landless refugees enter places like Mexico City each week, taxing basic services beyond their capacity. The enclosure of the Central and South American commons has precipitated widespread political unrest and turmoil as a newly disenfranchised class of landless peasants, turned proletariat, rally to the cry for economic and social justice and the restoration of ancestral rights to their homeland.

Meanwhile, in the United States, Americans are exposed to a nightly ritual of news coverage showing the burning of the Amazon forests and the spilling of blood in the streets of El Salvador, Nicaragua, and other Latin American countries. We see the bloated bellies of the babies and the despair written on the faces of the *campesinos*. It is a heavy price to pay to trim a nickel off the price of every American hamburger. Each year American consumers save $500 million by importing cheap beef from Latin America.[17]

6

GATHERING UP
THE WAVES

THE GLOBAL ENCLOSURE and commodification of the land commons was made possible by the conquest of the oceans. The Greek city-states of the premodern era were the first to articulate a comprehensive theory of sea power in the Western world. Athens's economic domination over the Mediterranean was, to a large part, due to the superiority of its naval fleets, both merchant and military. Thucydides, whose writings were rediscovered and extolled by the British in the modern era, warned: "There is no city that does not need to export or import; and these things it will not be able to do unless it accepts the bidding of the power that rules the sea."[1]

Before the sixteenth century, European maritime activity was limited to the narrow seas that enveloped the European landmass. The Baltic, Mediterranean, and North Sea had long been used to ferry raw resources and finished goods between regional trading centers. These narrow seas were highly contested, as city-states continually attempted to assert military dominance and ensure favored treatment for their own merchant and fishing fleets. As regional markets and trade began to expand in the late medieval era, city-states and monarchies began to claim sovereign control over entire seas.

The Venetian city-state, the dominant commercial power in the Mediterranean, was the first to attempt to enclose the oceanic commons, declaring its sovereignty over the entire Adriatic Sea in A.D. 1279.[2] Shortly thereafter, Genoa announced the enclosure of the Ligurian Sea. In Northern Europe, Sweden attempted to enclose the Gulf of Bothnia. Denmark made similar claims on the straits leading to the Baltic Sea and attempted to collect tributes from vessels seeking passage through the sea corridor. In 1273, Norway followed the lead of its Scandinavian neighbors, announcing its annexation of the northern seas "bounded by Norway, the Shetland and Faroe Islands, Iceland, Greenland, and Spitsbergen."[3] The British usurped sovereign jurisdiction over the seas extending from the British Isles to the North Sea as well as parts of the Atlantic Ocean.

The first serious attempt to enclose the great oceanic commons of the planet came in the late 1400s as Portugal and Spain, the first global naval powers, wrestled for control over vast stretches of the Atlantic, Indian, and Pacific oceans. In the Treaty of Tordesillas, signed in 1494, the two nations divided the oceans of the world along a line "between the north and south poles, that ran 370 degrees west of the Cape Verde Islands." The treaty gave Spain exclusive jurisdiction over the oceans west of the demarcation line, including the Gulf of Mexico and Pacific Ocean, while Portugal gained control of the oceans to the east, including the South Atlantic and Indian oceans.[4]

By the early seventeenth century, all of the emerging European powers were vying with one another for dominance over the oceanic commons. The English explorer and adventurer Sir Walter Raleigh declared, "Whosoever commands the sea commands the trade: whosoever commands the trade of the world, commands the riches of the world, and consequently the world itself."[5]

These early attempts to enclose the oceans proved ineffective. The ocean expanse was simply too vast to patrol and secure. Beginning in the early seventeenth century, European powers shifted their attention from the oceans to coastal waters. King James I enclosed the fisheries off the British and Irish coasts in 1609. All vessels flying foreign flags were required to purchase licenses to operate in "British waters."[6] Other nations scrambled to enclose their coastal waters as well. The question of how far coastal waters extend out to the sea has divided nations ever since. The Italians argued for a one-hundred-mile zone, the distance that could be sailed in two days. Most of the treaties of the period were far more moderate. It became accepted practice to mark the outer limits of coastal waters as the visual horizon, or "line of sight." Of course, even that calculation was open to varying interpretations, as some nations preferred to rely on the telescope, as opposed to the naked eye, thus extending the "line of sight from three miles to fifty miles."[7] In the eighteenth century, a new measurement for enclosing coastal waters gained currency. The Dutch jurist Cornelius Van Bynkershoek suggested the cannon shot, arguing that sovereignty ought not extend beyond the distance that could be defended by land-based artillery. Even here, disputes arose. When Van Bynkershoek made his suggestion, the range of artillery barely exceeded a mile. By the time Napoleon assumed power a century later, the artillery range had increased to three miles. The three-mile limit remained the international standard up to the eve of the Second World War.[8]

A far more aggressive drive to enclose the oceanic commons began after World War II with an announcement by President Truman that the United States would extend its coastal waters to include "jurisdiction and control" of the gas and oil deposits and minerals along the seabed of the continental shelf. Truman's proclamation touched off a frenzy of counterclaims by other nations, each seeking to enclose "their" continental shelves and offshore fisheries. By the early 1970s, seventeen nations had claimed sovereignty over coastal waters, extending two hundred miles out to sea.[9]

A law-of-the-seas convention was finally drafted in 1982 under the auspices of the United Nations, guaranteeing signature nations sovereignty twelve miles out to sea and exclusive economic rights two hundred miles out on open oceans. These exclusive economic zones gave each nation "sovereign rights for the purpose of exploring and exploiting, conserving and managing the living and nonliving resources of the oceans, seabeds, and subsoil."[10] The great ocean grab effectively enclosed 36 percent of the world's ocean areas, containing 90 percent of the commercially exploitable fish and 87 percent of the projected offshore oil reserves along continental shelves. Although many nations have yet to ratify the convention, it has established the new parameters of state sovereignty, bringing much of the oceanic commons under the grip of enclosure.[11]

Today, the commercially exploitable resources of the ocean are being rapidly exhausted just like those of the enclosed land masses of the earth. Fish provide 20 percent of the animal protein in the human diet and 5 percent of the protein fed to animals.[12] The major commercial fishing powers—Japan, the United States, the Soviet Union, China, Norway, and Chile—who together account for 37 percent of the world catch, are overtaxing the carrying capacity and depleting the stock in the world's major oceans, including the North and South Atlantic, the Mediterranean, the southern oceans, and North Pacific.[13]

It was only a hundred years ago that T. H. Huxley wrote that the great oceanic storehouses of cod, herring, and mackerel "were inexhaustible because the multitude of those fishes are so inconceivably great that the number we catch is relatively insignificant."[14] Huxley, for all his vision, was unable to anticipate the technological breakthroughs in fishing methods of the twentieth century, which allowed the maritime nations to deplete and exhaust vast regions of the oceanic commons in a matter of decades. After the Second World War, fishing armadas—made up of hundreds of ships, or floating factories, each performing a specialized function—became commonplace in the great oceans and coastal waters. Today, gutting, filleting, canning, and freezing equipment on board the factory ships allow them to remain at sea for long periods of time. The result has been a dramatic rise in the worldwide catch of fish, from twenty million tons in 1950 to seventy million tons in 1970.[15] With worldwide demand for fish expected to rise to between 113 and 125 million tons per year by the year 2000, the great oceans of the world are likely to be largely "fished out" in the coming decades.[16] Again, over 90 percent of the world catch takes place inside the newly enclosed two-hundred-mile exclusive economic zones established by the U.N. Convention on the Sea.[17]

As with the land, wherever enclosure and commodification of the earth's oceanic commons has occurred, resource optimization, profit maximization, and other market forces have combined, leaving the environment stripped bare. The exhaustion of the marine fisheries in the ocean is analogous to the widespread desertification of the land.

Even with the enclosure of 36 percent of the high seas, disputes have arisen over commercial use of the remaining oceanic commons. The industrial nations are interested in commercial exploitation of the seabed, especially the rich deposits of magnesium, cobalt, and copper found in nodule form along the floor of the great oceans. The seabed also contains boron, aluminum, lithium, fluorine, and uranium, as well as deposits of oil and gas, sulfur, coal, tin, and potash. As mining and extracting technology becomes more efficient, the high-technology nations have become increasingly interested in the commercial potential.[18] Over one hundred nations, primarily in the third world, have joined together to urge that the high seas be kept open as a shared commons to be used collectively and equitably by all nations.[19] Many of the first world nations, which now enjoy the technological know-how to exploit this bonanza of resources, are resisting the initiative, hoping to reap commercial advantage from the unrestrained exploitation of this heretofore hidden source of mineral wealth.

The struggle between rich and poor nations and the multinational corporations over the minerals in the vast oceanic seabed is likely to be heated in the years to come, especially as land-based mineral reserves are depleted. Attempts to enclose even more of the ocean area of the globe are likely in the future.

7

RIDING ON THIN AIR

T HE ENCLOSURE OF the terrestrial and oceanic commons established a historic precedent for the enclosure of the remaining ecological realms of the planet. At the beginning of the twentieth century, mercantilists turned to the heavens with an eye toward enclosure.

The sky, which from time immemorial has been the home of the gods, was suddenly a region of intense political and commercial interest. This grand sacred domain was transformed in the wake of the Wright brothers' historic twenty-second flight over Kitty Hawk, North Carolina, in 1903. The pantheon of gods was pushed off the heavenly commons to make room for the German zeppelin, the French Spad plane, and the American Curtiss hydroplane. With human beings now populating the sky, nation-states and corporations scurried to divide up and convert the atmosphere of the planet into a commercial realm that could be exploited for financial and political gain.

Sir Joseph Banks, president of the Royal Society of London, anticipated the wrangling that would accompany the commercial enclosure of the sky in 1783. He wrote to his friend Benjamin Franklin, who had informed him of his great excitement upon witnessing man's first air flight aboard a hot-air balloon over Paris.

The present day, which has opened a road into the air, is an epoch . . . and the more immediate effect it will have upon the concerns of mankind, greater than anything since the invention of shipping, which opened our way upon the face of the water from land to land.[1]

Franklin's enthusiasm soon became tempered by the sobering thought of the military implications of air travel. Writing in 1784, Franklin sounded a prophetic jeremiad.

Where is the prince that can afford so to cover his country with troops for its defense, as that ten thousand men descending from the clouds might not in many places do an infinite deal of mischief before a force could be brought together to repel them.[2]

The commercial and military exploitation of the atmospheric commons have gone hand in hand in the twentieth century, although on occasion the objectives of one conflicted with the goals of the other. The potential military significance of air travel became apparent in 1909, when Louis Blériot, a French pilot, made a thirty-seven-minute solo flight across the English Channel, landing on English soil.[3] The Channel, which had always protected the island from military conquest from the continent, was suddenly less formidable. Almost effortlessly, a tiny aircraft had accomplished a feat that had eluded great naval forces from the Spanish Armada to French warships. The question of control over the atmospheric commons became paramount as nations wrestled over the issue of protecting their security.

In 1913, the British Parliament passed the world's first aerial navigation act. The legislation regulated the entry of foreign aircraft into England and established zones that were off limits to planes from other countries. Virtually the entire English Channel was included in the prohibited area to ensure military security. The act, which was amended and strengthened in 1913, was the first to claim national sovereignty of the airspace over territorial boundaries. France and Germany quickly followed suit, establishing air corridors in their respective countries, claiming the right of

total sovereignty over the airspace within their political boundaries.[4]

While military security issues dominated the discussion over the
enclosure of the atmospheric commons, the increasing commercial
prospects of air travel began to pose new problems. Effective
commerce in the air depended on open access to the skies.
Transporting passengers and cargo effectively between nations
"would be clearly best secured if aircraft above a certain altitude
were allowed to fly freely in any direction without let or hindrance
imposed upon them by the municipal legislation of the state over
whose territories they might pass."[5] The British favored charting a
middle course, striking a compromise between military security
needs and commercial interests. It was proposed that state
sovereignty over the atmosphere extend only up to an agreed-upon
altitude, above which all carriers were extended free right of
passage. Some jurists used international maritime laws as an analogy: while nations exercised sovereign control over territorial
waters, beyond a prescribed outer limit all maritime commerce
enjoyed free and open access to the ocean. Britain was particularly
keen on keeping part of the atmospheric commons open to protect
commercial ties with its own colonies, which were scattered
around the world. If England were forced to pay tribute, and had
to adhere to an array of travel restrictions crossing the European
continent to reach its eastern empire in India and Asia, it would
lose commercial advantage and risk dissolution of its colonial
possessions.

The commercial arguments were compelling and enjoyed strong
support before the First World War. By 1917, however, after
several years of firsthand experience with the military potential of
air power, the nations of the world were virtually unanimous in
their support of total sovereignty of the airspace over their national boundaries.

On October 13, 1919, the nations of the world drafted the
"Convention Relating to the Regulation of Aerial Navigation."
The first article of the convention stated unequivocally that "Every
power has complete and exclusive sovereignty over the airspace
above its territory."[6] From that time on, the atmosphere was
divided up by the nations of the world, severing the aerial com-

mons for the first time in human history. (At a subsequent convention, held in 1944 in Chicago, the allied nations formally agreed to allow open access to the airspace over the oceans of the world, free of influence by any nation.)

The decision to enclose the atmospheric commons greatly benefited the nations with expansive and continuous landmasses. The Soviet Union, with one sixth of the land surface of the planet, suddenly acquired over one sixth of all of the airspace over the global landmass, without firing a shot.

Today, all nations enjoy exclusive sovereignty over their airspace. International regulatory agencies have been established and multilateral agreements have been signed governing rates nations can charge air carriers operating in and through domestic airspace. Air corridors have also been established in every nation to regulate the flow of commercial traffic. Local, regional, and national governments have even established air-rights laws and zoning within their countries governing how much of the sky a corporate or private landlord can own or claim exclusive use to above his property. Landlords can and often do sell their air rights to others at appropriate market rates. In highly dense urban areas where space is at a premium, air rights and ownership have become extremely important economic factors and coveted assets.

The skies are now filled around the world with commercial and military traffic. Passengers, cargo, soldiers, and missiles are being ferried through the heavens daily, making the atmosphere an intricate and essential part of the global market economy. In less than one hundred years the great atmospheric commons has been divided up, nationalized, partially privatized, and reduced to a commodity negotiable in the open marketplace.

8

THE ELECTRONIC PULSE
OF THE PLANET

IN THE PRESENT CENTURY the enclosure movement has been extended into virtually every conceivable earthly region. Today governments and commercial interests are even dividing up and commodifying spheres within spheres, reducing the entire planet to a market complex made up of exploitable resources. For example, the transition into a global information economy has increased the commercial value of the electromagnetic spectrum. Hertzian waves crisscross the atmospheric commons providing the bands for sending information and broadcasting entertainment around the world. The electromagnetic commons, an invisible environment running through the atmospheric environment, is becoming a source of heated political debate as nations and multinational corporations vie for access to a limited number of bands and channels. The planet's electrical commons is used by hundreds of geo-stationary satellites in the collecting and transferring of information around the globe.

The enclosure of the electromagnetic commons has proceeded apace with the invention and widespread commercial use of electronic communications and information technology. The enclosed bands are regulated by the International Telecommunications Union, which was established in 1865.[1] Questions over the commercial use of the electromagnetic bands are proliferating as high-technology nations and global corporations push ahead to create a new global information society. Anthony Smith, author of *The Geopolitics of Information,* argues, "As the information debate has progressed, the issue of spectrum allocation has become intensely politicized, and arguments concerning a particular use of the short wave, or a particular band within the gigahertz range, have taken on the same kind of ideological coloration as arguments over oil resources or frontiers or coffee prices."[2]

The debate over the use of the electromagnetic spectrum often pits the northern industrial countries against the developing nations of the Southern Hemisphere. In the 1970s, third world nations joined together demanding access rights to frequencies used for broadcast satellites, despite the fact that they had no satellites of their own.[3] They won the battle in 1979 and were awarded their own national frequencies on the gigahertz range, ensuring them access if and when they joined the satellite club.[4]

A far more serious squabble has erupted in recent years over the use of the high frequency (HF) or shortwave bands. The northern industrial nations have already enclosed most of the HF bands over the century, locking out third world countries that desperately need access to the spectrum to develop their own domestic communications networks. The HF band is already overutilized, and now multinational companies are pushing to monopolize as much of the spectrum as possible to serve a growing middle-class market for cellular telephones, beepers, and other luxury items. On the other hand, poor nations, especially in Africa, rely on shortwave radio to communicate and disseminate information to remote regions, to coordinate basic social services and a range of military and civilian programs. They contend that their security needs should outweigh what they consider to be frivolous and tangential needs of wealthy consumers in the rich nations.[5]

There is also the question of using the electromagnetic band to violate the sovereign rights of countries. At the beginning of the 1980s over four thousand satellites were orbiting the earth, monitoring, collecting, and disseminating vital information on everything from climate conditions to the location of mineral reserves.[6] The LANDSAT satellite program, initiated by the United States and used in cooperation with programs in some fifty-five nations, monitors a variety of activities and processes, including "crop yield forecasts, forest management, water resource management, geological surveys and mineral exploration, marine resource management, coastal engineering, and identification of potential areas of natural hazards."[7] Some argue that the collection and dissemination of this information violates national sovereignty and often provides the monitoring nations with information that can be used to exact a commercial advantage in the global market.

Anthony Smith points out that U.S. companies can use the Freedom of Information Act to secure LANDSAT data on the discovery of mineral deposits before officials in the host country are even aware of the find. Multinational mining companies can then take advantage of the advance information by buying up tracts of land before the government is aware of its potential value. Some nations have demanded an international agreement which would, among other things, require nations or corporations operating satellites to secure approval from a country before surveillance, ensure that the information gained be made available to nations being surveyed, and obtain permission before transferring information about the surveyed nation to a third party.[8]

Smith is not sanguine about the prospects of tailoring the awesome power of the new electronic media to the needs of geographically bound nation-states.

> . . . the passing of laws may not in itself help matters, since a great deal of data cannot really be said to be "stored" in any one place. It flits about the globe from computer to computer. It is not the case that all data has a final resting place like files on a shelf. It defies territoriality, however hard national governments may seek to pin it down. . . . The whole history of the nation as a political unit of mankind has been predicated on territoriality . . . it is physically impossible to impose upon data the same kinds of controls that are imposed upon goods. . . .[9]

9

A PRICE TAG
ON GENES

In the 1970s, molecular biologists began splicing genes. The development of this powerful process established the conditions for the final enclosure of the planet. The vast interior commons that makes up the insides of nature, the cells, is now being enclosed and converted to commercial property that can be manipulated and exchanged in the world market.

The high-technology nations are just beginning to make a long-term transition out of fossil fuel–based technologies into biologically based technologies. The transition from the industrial age to the biotechnical age is creating new interest in the commercial exploitability of DNA.

Human beings share a biological commons with all other living creatures. DNA is the shared chemical substance that makes up each creature and binds together every life form, from microbes to man, in a common heritage. Up until the early 1970s, human beings could manipulate living creatures through traditional breeding techniques but could not manipulate the DNA code itself. Now with gene-splicing technologies scientists can, for the first time, recombine genetic material within and between species. For example, scientists have inserted human growth hormone genes into the permanent genetic code of pigs, sheep, and mice. The human genes expressed themselves in the animals and continue to be passed along to each succeeding generation of offspring.

Similarly, researchers have inserted the gene that emits light in a firefly into the genetic code of tobacco plants. The plant's leaves glow twenty-four hours a day. Gene-splicing techniques allow scientists to bypass species boundaries altogether, defying the limits imposed by natural evolutionary development.[1]

Multinational corporations throughout the world are retooling plants and building new laboratories and production facilities to harness the gene to commercial advantage. Corporate prospectuses are already overflowing with superlatives, touting the market potential of genetically engineered production in fields ranging from medicine to agriculture.

In the years ahead, the planet's shrinking gene pool is going to become a source of increasing monetary value as multinational corporations scour the earth for valuable genetic traits that have commercial potential. A battle of enormous proportions has already emerged between the high-technology nations of the north and the poor developing nations of the south over the enclosure of the planet's gene pool.

The contest for control of genetic resources has dominated the political agenda at the United Nations Food and Agricultural Organization's biannual meetings for over a decade. Some third world leaders argue that multinational corporations and Northern Hemisphere nations are attempting to enclose the biological commons, most of which is found in the rich tropical regions of the Southern Hemisphere. The Southern Hemisphere nations contend that genetic resources are part of their national heritage, just like oil is for the Middle East, and they should be compensated for their use. The multinational corporations and Northern Hemisphere nations maintain that the genes increase in market value only when manipulated and recombined by advanced gene-splicing techniques, and therefore they have no obligation to compensate countries from which the genes are taken.

Two examples, one from agriculture, the other from the pharmaceutical field, illustrate the vast potential as well as the bitter struggle that surrounds the enclosure of the genetic commons.

Years ago, scientists discovered a rare perennial strain of maize growing in a mountain forest of south central Mexico. Only a few thousand stalks of the perennial existed, in three tiny patches, and these were about to be bulldozed by farmers and loggers. The newly discovered strain was found to be resistant to leaf fungus, which had devastated the U.S. corn crop in 1970, costing farmers over two billion dollars. The commercial value of the strain "could total several millions of dollars a year," according to geneticists and seed company experts.[2]

The rosy periwinkle, found in the tropical rain forest of Madagascar, offers the other graphic example of the potential profits that lie in store with the enclosure of the genetic commons. A few years ago, researchers discovered that the rare periwinkle plant contained a unique genetic trait that could be used as a pharmaceutical to cure childhood leukemia. The pharmaceutical companies that have developed the drug are making windfall profits, while Madagascar has not received so much as a penny of compensation for the expropriation of one of its natural resources.

Governments around the world have already set up gene storage facilities to preserve rare strains of plants whose genetic traits may prove commercially useful in the future. The U.S. National Seed Storage Laboratory at Fort Collins, Colorado, contains over 400,000 accessions—seeds—from all over the world. Many nations are also beginning to establish additional gene banks to store rare microorganisms and frozen animal embryos. In the years ahead, the commercial value of many of these rare strains of plants and breeds of animals will increase dramatically as the world market relies on genetic technologies to produce materials and products.[3]

In the age of biotechnology, the economic and political forces that control the genetic resources of the planet will exercise tremendous power over the world ecomomy, just as in the industrial age access to and control over fossil fuels and rare minerals helped determine control over world markets. It is no wonder, then, that governments and multinational corporations are scouting continents in search of the new green gold, hoping to locate microbes, plants, and animals with rare genetic traits that might have future market potential.

Recent developments in tissue culture technology underscore the significance of the genetic enclosure movement. Vanilla is a good case in point. Over 98 percent of the world's vanilla crop is produced by three small island nations—Madagascar, Comoros, and Réunion. The vanilla plant is also grown in Indonesia. Madagascar alone produces over 70 percent of the world's harvest each year. Some seventy thousand native farmers on this one island rely on the vanilla crop for their livelihood.[4] Now biotechnology companies in the United States and Europe are producing vanilla extract in laboratory vats, using new tissue culture techniques. The new process eliminates the seed, the plant, the bean, the planting, the cultivation, and the harvest. In a few years, when the process becomes commercially available, it will eliminate the thousands of peasant farmers whose survival depends on the vanilla plant.[5]

With cell tissue technology, the genetic composition of the tissue culture becomes the valuable asset. Once the researchers find the most market-efficient, commercially exploitable genetic strain, it can be reproduced endlessly without having to compensate the host country. Pat Mooney and Cary Fowler, who have written extensively on the potential impact that the new biotechnologies will likely have on third world economies, explain how the tissue cell process works:

> The basic technique used to produce vanilla flavor by means of tissue culture technology involves the selection of high-yielding cell tissue from the vanilla plant. The cell tissues are then propagated in suspended cultures. Careful regulation of culture conditions, nutrient mediums, and metabolic regulators are then used to induce the production of the desired chemical flavored compound—vanilla.[6]

Recently, researchers at Texas Tech University successfully grew cotton fiber from tissue cells chemically treated in a vat of nutrients. Other scientists have successfully grown orange and lemon vesicles from tissue culture. In Japan, one company is already selling tobacco grown exclusively from cells cultured in giant indoor vats.[7] As scientists learn more about turning on and off, recombining, and transferring genes, they will be able, with far greater precision, to engineer specific qualities directly into the laboratory production of food, fiber, and pharmaceutical products, ensuring a competitive and expanding market.

The genetics revolution is precipitating a new kind of enclosure movement. Where earlier enclosure movements forced the peasants off the land, this latest enclosure movement will eventually force the commercial crops off the land, leaving the peasant with land that no longer has market value. In the years to come, an increasing number of agricultural activities are going to be taken indoors and enclosed in vats and caldrons, sealed off from the outside world.

With these new processes the multinational corporations will be able to exert far greater economic control over world markets, with far less risk to themselves. Controlling genes in a laboratory in New Jersey is far less troublesome than controlling climate, land, and workers on an island off the eastern coast of Africa. By distancing themselves, the multinational corporations can exercise economic power without having to be dependent on the forces of nature or be accountable to people in communities on whom they previously relied in the production process. *Food Technology* magazine summed up the economic and political advantages of the new genetic imperialism:

> Many of our flavors and other products come from remote parts of the world, where the political instability of governments or the vagaries of weather yield inconsistent supply, cost, and product quality from season to season. In a plant tissue culture process, all parameters . . . can be controlled.[8]

The U.S. Government has spearheaded the commercial drive to exploit the genetic commons. Beginning in the 1930s, Congress passed special legislation to allow the patenting of selective plant varieties. In 1980, in a highly controversial Supreme Court decision, the justices ruled, by a five-to-four margin, that a microorganism genetically engineered by the General Electric Company to eat up oil spills could be patented. Justice William Brennan, speaking for the minority opinion, argued persuasively and passionately that the patent laws never had been meant to include animals, even microorganisms. Chief Justice Warren Burger, speaking for the majority, argued that living creatures that were manipulated and engineered in novel ways not found either in nature or in traditional breeding techniques qualify as manufactured products and are fully protected under the existing patent laws.

Seven years later, the U.S. Patent Office extended the Supreme Court ruling to the entire living kingdom, arguing that any genetically engineered animal may be patented. For example, under the agency ruling, if a human gene is inserted into the genetic code of a pig, both the process and the animal are patentable, the only test of patentability being novel intervention. In one regulatory stroke, the U.S. Patent Office moved to enclose the entire genetic pool, from mice to primates. The Patent Office decision came down with only one disclaimer, excluding genetically engineered human beings from the patent laws because the Thirteenth Amendment to the Constitution forbids human slavery.

The U.S. Patent Office has already granted a patent to Harvard University for a genetically engineered mouse and the process used to create it. Dozens of other patent applications for genetically engineered fish and animals are currently winding their way through the review process.[9]

Although human beings have kept animals as property since the early neolithic era, the granting of patent privileges over animals genetically engineered in a laboratory represents a radical new departure for civilization. By extending patent protection to genetically engineered microbes, plants, and animals, the United States becomes the first nation in the world to eliminate formally any last teleological distinction that might exist between life and inanimate objects. If the current patent policy is allowed to stand, our children will grow up in a world where the line between animate and inanimate will have been virtually eliminated for the first time in history, with all of nature finally debased to a commodity status.

The granting of patent privileges over genetically engineered microorganisms, plants, and animals represents the culmination of a five-hundred-year movement to enclose the planetary commons that began inauspiciously on the village green in small rural hamlets scattered throughout England and the European continent. Now even the building blocks of life itself have been enclosed, privatized, and reduced to marketable products.

10

ENVIRONMENTAL SHRAPNEL

THE ENCLOSURE OF the global commons has fundamentally changed humanity's relationship to the earth. Nature, once an independent force, both revered and feared, has been reduced to an assortment of exploitable resources, all negotiable in the open marketplace. The privatization and commodification of the earth has elevated humanity from servant to sovereign, and made nature an object of pure commercial exchange. The great landmasses, the vast oceans, the atmosphere and electromagnetic spectrums, and now the gene pool have all been desacralized and increasingly rationalized, their worth measured almost exclusively in monetary terms.

The seizure and commercial exploitation of Earth's ecosystems have left the planet environmentally devastated and much of human civilization impoverished. The rich bounty of coal, oil, and natural gas, which for millennia remained hidden in the seams of the planet, has been exhumed, pumped, and extracted to run the engines of the machine age. Luxurious tropical plants—maize, sugar, cocoa, coffee, and tobacco—have been snatched away and transported to the temperate landmasses, where they have been marshaled into straight rows and put to work. Today, their descendants are grown on the great agricultural plains, providing food, drink, and fiber primarily for the wealthy classes of the first and second worlds. The wilds have been trampled and paved, their creatures trapped, shot, and clubbed to death to provide luxurious furs and exotica, from ivory tusks used as adornments to the pulverized powder of the rhino horn, a much coveted aphrodisiac that fetches a high price in Asian markets. The great oceans of the world have been sectioned off into hunting corridors. Thousands and thousands of miles of dragnets are hoisted over the sides of fishing schooners and trollers each day, siphoning off what remains of the oldest living community on the planet.

The man and woman of the industrial era are surrounded by the spoils of war. The booty of the planetary commons has been placed at our feet. We turn up our thermostat and consume the oil from the underbelly of the Arabian deserts. We turn on our TVs and radios, stereos and video-cassette recorders, and all of the materials with which they were constructed, even the packages they were shipped in, come from someplace on the vast earth commons where they once existed in a vegetative, animal, or mineral state. The newspaper on our front porch came from the giant fir trees of the Alaska forest. The mahogany for the furniture in our living rooms was cut down in the dense jungle of Rondônia along the Amazon River basin. The beef patties in our freezer came from cows that once grazed on the pasturelands of Central America.

In our homes and neighborhoods, our offices and factories, we have engaged in an orgy of consumption unknown in previous times. The rich nations of the industrial north have literally expropriated and consumed the planetary commons to grease the wheels of commerce and satiate an ever more profligate life-style.

While the North enjoys what's left of the plunder, the people of the southern clime have been left to sift through the environmental rubble, hoping to scratch out a meager existence. The devastation wrought by the great war against nature far exceeds the toll of any military venture in history. Today, 800 million people go to bed hungry, mostly across the southern tier. Hundreds of millions of people have no running water to drink or bathe in. One hundred million people have no homes to live in and must spend their lives on the streets and pavements, their children never knowing the security of a roof.

The forest cover that anchors the soil and whose canopy provides habitat for most of the animal species of the planet is being systematically razed. Two thousand years ago, the tropical rain forest alone extended over five billion acres, covering 12 percent of the earth's land surface.[1] In less than one hundred years over half of the forest has now been cut and burned, leaving whole areas of the earth bare and unprotected, rendering entire regions lifeless. Over fifty million acres of tropical rain forest are destroyed every year—enough trees to fill all of England and Scotland combined.[2] The U.N.'s Food and Agricultural Organization estimates that if the rate of destruction continues, by the turn of the century over one fifth of the rain forests will be eliminated. Some of these forests, like the ones in Southeast Asia, have existed in a continuous sustainable state for over seventy million years.[3]

In the United States, schoolchildren on the Eastern seaboard no longer grow up hearing the melodious tones of the North American songbirds when springtime comes. The wood thrush, the Wilson warbler, the yellow-billed cuckoo, the Baltimore oriole—their numbers are fast dwindling as their winter homes in the forests along the neck of Central America have been bulldozed to make room for cattle ranches operated by multinational corporations.[4] The birds' loss, though significant, is just another statistic buried amid the carnage of the great war against nature. According to recent biological surveys, the planet is now losing a species of plant or animal life to extinction every sixty minutes. The loss of entire species in the tropics exceeds the natural rate of extinction by as much as ten thousand times. Within the next decade, we may lose nearly 20 percent of all the remaining species of life on earth. Most of these species exist in remote areas and have not yet been seen by human eyes.[5]

Everywhere the soldiers of modern commerce have tread, they have left degraded earth behind them. The topsoil of the planet is eroding faster than international agencies can chronicle the losses. It is estimated that in the United States alone, over one third of the valuable topsoil used to grow the grains that feed much of the world has blown or washed away.[6]

Desertification is spreading on all the continents of the world. Desertification is caused by overgrazing cattle and other domestic animals and by overcultivation, salinization, and deforestation.

According to the U.N. Environmental Program, over 35 percent of the land surface of the earth is now threatened by desertification.[7]

As nation after nation has moved to enclose the land commons, traditional pastureland and subsistence agricultural practices have given way to the raising of commercial livestock as cash crops for export markets. The commodification of lands and resources and the rush for profits has destabilized traditional rural communities and overtaxed the carrying capacity of the soil.

Multinational corporations, wealthy land owners, and politicians have joined forces in a worldwide land grab, seizing the best land and leaving tens of millions of peasants to fend for themselves on marginal land. Today, over 850 million people, or 20 percent of the world's human population, live on land ruined by desertification.[8] Both the prime land and the marginal land is being exhausted in a desperate attempt to maintain market position and feed mouths. In Africa alone, desertification has spread to twenty-two nations.[9] African land is literally blowing away, scattering dust around the world. "Dust fallout across the Atlantic from the African continent measured at Barbados in the West Indies increased from 8 micrograms per cubic meter in 1967 and 1968, to 15 micrograms in 1972, and 24 micrograms in 1973."[10] In the drought years of 1968–73, and again from 1982–84, nearly 250 million people died of starvation south of the Sahel, all victims of man's war against nature.[11]

Millions of people still remain trapped in rural areas surrounded by the spreading desert sheet. Some farm families now have to walk for days to find enough firewood to cook their meals. Others have begun to rely on dried cow dung as a source of fuel. Continued deforestation and loss of vital animal fertilizer weakens and erodes the already impoverished soil. As the soil erodes and blows away, the land loses its capacity to retain water; overgrazing of cattle consumes what little water is left. The process of land degradation and land loss has become self-perpetuating and irreversible in many parts of the world.

Lacking the bare essentials of survival, millions of human beings have taken to the road, migrating hundreds, even thousands, of miles to urban slums, where all that awaits them are meager government relief packages. Some families, especially the children, take to scavenging refuse dumps on the margins of cities hoping to find edible leftovers cast off by the wealthy professional and commercial classes, who live far removed from the shanty towns in well-protected, fashionable suburbs.

These people are the new war refugees, victims of man's war against nature. In Burkina Faso, Chad, Niger, Senegal, Mali, and Mauritania millions of families are abandoning the land and streaming into urban areas that more closely resemble resettlement camps than functioning communities. By the year 2000, the collective urban population of these six African countries will have increased by 224 percent.[12]

This urban influx is being repeated around the world in the cities of the sub-Sahara in Africa, in the Punjab, on the streets of Mexico City, and in the barrios of Los Angeles. This new class of environmental refugee is the human cost of the war against nature. They are a constant reminder of the price we pay for cheap pet food, inexpensive paper products, and ample gasoline to run our automobiles.

Today, over 1.3 billion people in the developing world live in abject poverty; their average life expectancy is only fifty-seven years.[13] Three out of every ten children born die before the age of five. Many of the deaths occur because there isn't enough clean water to provide basic hygiene and sanitation.[14] In Port-au-Prince, Haiti, four families share a common latrine and eight to ten families share a common shower.[15] Over 500 million people lack the minimum calories required to survive.[16] Nearly fifteen million children die each year of malnutrition and starvation.[17] In Calcutta, half of the families live in cramped one-room households. In Mexico City, one third of the families share the same fate.[18]

The enclosure of the global commons and the conversion of land from crops for local subsistence to cash crops for export has created a new form of exploitation. The environmental and human toll never shows up on the electronic boards of the international commodities exchanges, or in the neatly stacked rows of numbers printed out on the computer screens in Wall Street investment houses. Occasionally, the human environmental toll is factored in by economists who use the term "externalities" to refer to the unanticipated secondary cost of doing business. Even the term "externality" conjures up the idea of marginality.

The United States and the nations of Europe and the Far East consume the earth from a distance. The process is carried out in a technologically mediated, mathematically planned way. The international market economy is the most detached form of warfare ever devised.

The United States makes up less than 5 percent of the total population on earth. Yet, we currently consume over 30 percent of all the resources.[19] The statistics fail to convey the greed and ruthlessness that underlie the modern war against man and nature. The numbers can't be felt; the grim reality they mask can't be experienced directly. The humiliation and pain, the human sorrow, the desperation and despair, the environmental pillage seem so far removed from the clean, brightly lit rows of the supermarket, so far away from the warm, cheerful living rooms of suburban homes, so unconnected to the efficient whir of activity in our offices and factories.

Sequestered from the pitch of battle, we continue to think of the environmental and economic crisis as something that happens "out there." On occasion, however, even our safe havens are breeched by an incident or event that tears through the complex structure that has been constructed to secure the earth's riches and our own autonomy.

The Exxon oil spill in Prince William Sound off the coast of Alaska was greeted first with outrage and later by some soul searching. The leak of millions of gallons of oil into one of the most pristine wildlife areas of the world shocked the sensibilities of millions of Americans. The public was exposed to a constant barrage of nightly television coverage of the devastation: the oil-soaked coastline, sea otters encased in sludge gasping for breath, angry fishermen lashing out at Exxon officials. Anger gave way to sober thought by some about our own culpability. The Exxon gasoline was, after all, destined for our filling stations and our own automobiles. The Exxon credit card lined many American billfolds. Suddenly, the vague distances that separated us from the ongoing war against nature vanished in an instant. A connection, regardless how tenuous, was made between the self-serve islands at the local gas station and an environmental war zone five thousand miles away in a remote part of Alaska.

A few years ago, the American public found itself amused, if not slightly embarrassed, by the furtive journey of a Long Island garbage barge that had been turned away at foreign ports of call when it attempted to dump its cargo. The incident underscored rather graphically the often exploitive environmental and economic relationship that lies hidden away and unnoticed between industrial nations and developing countries. Many third world nations, desperate for earnings of any kind, have shown a willingness to accept garbage from the industrialized nations, making them victims of environmental abuse at both ends. Their people, land, and resources are often exploited at the front end to provide raw materials and finished goods for export. Consequently, their environments become degraded, and depleted, in the process. Faced with a devalued natural environment and mounting international debt, these countries often have no other choice but to take back industrial waste products for burial, increasing the environmental damage at the back end as well.

The garbage barge odyssey forced Americans to think about where our waste goes after we discard it in the trash. The United States and other industrialized nations have been consuming the planet so fast that we have run out of places to bury our own refuse. In 1987, we discarded more than 200 million tons of municipal solid waste. This included more than 18 million tons of metals, 16 million tons of glass, 80 million tons of paper, and 4 million tons of rubber.[20] In recent years, the average American used 10 tons of mineral resources, including 1,340 pounds of metal and 18,900 pounds of nonmetallic minerals. In a lifetime, each American uses, on average, approximately 700 tons of mineral resources, including nearly 50 tons of metals. If we add fossil fuels and wood, the per capita use more then doubles, to 1,400 tons.[21] Some of these resources come from the United States, while vast amounts come from other countries.

America's consumption of the earth's resources has now outstripped the nation's ability to dispose of the waste within its borders. By the early 1990s over one half of U.S. landfills will be used up, forcing a garbage crisis upon the country.[22] With less

space available, the cost of burying a ton of garbage has skyrock-
eted from $5 a ton to $30 a ton in Minneapolis in less than six
years and from $20 to $40 a ton in Philadelphia.[23] Over 3.7
million tons of waste from the U.S. and European nations is
shipped to other countries each year, primarily poor nations,
where the disposal costs are cheaper and the environmental safe-
guards less stringent.[24]

Seeing our own garbage hauled halfway around the world in
search of a resting place helped drive home the nature of the
economic and environmental relationships that bind the world
into a single international market. Three hundred years after the
architects of the modern age set us on a course to secure our
autonomy from nature, we find ourselves unable to secure our
own garbage.

Many other incidents over the past several years have had a
similar jarring effect on American consciousness. The mounting
environmental crisis has forced a recognition of the deep and
complex relationships that exist between our production and consumption practices and the fate of people and the sustainability of
land and resources around the world. In 1989, the U.S. Department of Agriculture prohibited the shipment of grapes from Chile
into U.S. supermarkets, fearing pesticide contamination. Cesar
Chavez and the Farmworkers Union asked American consumers
to boycott grapes grown in California because the pesticide being
sprayed on the crops is causing illness among American
farmworkers. In Bhopal, a 1984 chemical accident at the Union
Carbide plant killed 2,500 people and injured over 100,000 others. Tens of thousands of the victims continue to suffer from
"blurred vision, disabling lung diseases, intestinal bleeding, and
neurological and psychological disorders."[25] Stockholders in the
Union Carbide corporation found themselves caught in a crisis
thousands of miles away. Some stockholders began to question
publicly the lax management practices that allowed the Bhopal
accident to occur. Serious questions were raised in the wake of the
Bhopal tragedy regarding the responsibility of U.S. corporations to
provide environmental safety standards abroad comparable to
those required in the United States.

The steady barrage of environmental assaults pierce our consciousness like so much schrapnel. The incidents generally happen without warning and appear arbitrary and capricious. Often the media treats them as if they were natural calamities, violent acts inflicting great damage over which we have little or no control: an oil spill on the high seas, the discovery of a toxic waste dump near a schoolyard, infectious wastes washed up on the shore forcing the closing of summer beaches, a smog alert warning senior citizens not to venture outdoors for twenty-four hours. With each passing year, the American public becomes increasingly aware of and concerned over these mounting incidents. Still, each event is treated in isolation, compartmentalized, duly recorded and analyzed, and then generally left to fade into history. If blame is affixed, it generally falls on a negligent worker, less frequently on faulty equipment or machine failure, and only on rare occasions on insensitive or callous management. Our lives are threatened for the moment, our security and autonomy temporarily suspended. But in the aftermath of each incident, life seems to return to normal, without any of us having to question seriously the underlying motives or overriding assumptions that make up the belief system of the modern world.

By maintaining the illusion that much of the environmental damage being inflicted is the result of human error, freak accident, or even the unsavory activity of unscrupulous business executives, the whole set of philosophical, scientific, technological, and economic relationships that have been constructed during the industrial age to manipulate and mold the natural world are left unaddressed in public debate.

Now, however, a new genre of environmental threats has emerged over the past decade that is so enormous and far-reaching that it cannot simply be acknowledged, cleaned up, and then forgotten. The greenhouse effect and ozone depletion represent the first truly global environmental crises in recorded history. Although societies have experienced traumatic, sometimes devastating environmental events in the past, the damage has always been limited in time and space. Great civilizations, from Sumer to Rome, have fallen victim both to human-induced and natural calamities. Still, the environmental impact, in all of these instances, spread through only a particular region, affecting a particular people, and then generally for only a few generations or centuries.

Global warming and the depletion of the ozone shield around the planet are phenomena of a very different type. For the first time in our species' history, human activity has affected the biochemistry of the entire planet. If we were to measure human accomplishment to date in terms of sheer impact, these two unfolding crises would have to be regarded as the most significant events in our short history.

Deforestation, soil erosion, toxic waste, pesticide buildup, and many of the other environmental threats exist on a limited horizontal plane. The greenhouse effect and ozone depletion are overarching; they envelop the planetary sphere. They meet us regardless of which way we turn. They cannot be pushed aside, any more than we can step outside of them or enclose ourselves inside and away from them. Omnipresent, their existence already casts a powerful shadow over our world. In the years to come, these two great environmental problems will become more pervasive, their effects descending and spreading until the entire earth is "shaken to its foundation."

11

ICARUS AND
THE GREAT CATACLYSM

GLOBAL WARMING REPRESENTS the final conflict in the war against nature. It is the entropic bill, come due, for the machine age. For nearly a decade, scientists and government officials have been holding meetings, commissioning studies, publishing reports, and rendering policy statements on the issue of global warming. Left unacknowledged and unstated in all of the formal discussions and declarations is the central meaning of the greenhouse effect. The war against nature, which began just a few hundred years ago with such confidence and enthusiasm, with such bravado, has been lost.

Modern man and woman have attempted to secure the global commons by privatizing, commodifying, and consuming the earth's endowment. Now, in a final twist of historical irony, we find ourselves enveloped by the spent energy of the industrial era, trapped under a thick layer of industrial gases that were emitted to run the machines, extract the minerals, grow the crops, graze the livestock, store the produce, and ship the goods of the modern age. The greenhouse gases—carbon dioxide, chlorofluorocarbons (CFCs), nitrous oxide, and methane—that now bloat the atmosphere are the chemical record of the age of growth and consumption. The spent molecules chronicle a five-hundred-year war against nature. Now, after a long and protracted battle to capture, enclose, and consume the global commons, we are, in turn, being enclosed by the discarded waste of our own consumption.

Some scientists, business leaders, and public officials continue to characterize the greenhouse crisis as a "scientific experiment" gone awry. In fact, global warming is the inevitable outcome of the modern way of thinking about nature and security first espoused by Francis Bacon, René Descartes, Isaac Newton, John Locke, Adam Smith, and the other architects of the modern age. The global warming phenomenon of the past several centuries offers an inverse history of the modern period. A careful examination of its emergence, development, and ultimate impact sheds light on the dark side of the age of progress.

A thin blanket of greenhouse gases has existed in the earth's atmosphere for as long as there has been life. Carbon dioxide and other atmospheric gases allow solar radiation to enter the earth's atmosphere. The earth's surface absorbs much of the solar energy, converting it to infrared energy or heat. The heat then rises from the earth's surface and bombards the carbon dioxide and other gaseous molecules in the atmosphere, forcing the molecules to vibrate. The gas molecules act as reflectors, sending some of the heat back toward the surface of the earth, creating a warming effect. The greenhouse phenomenon is an essential feature of the earth's atmosphere, providing a warm temperature band conducive to the emergence and sustenance of life on the planet. The natural greenhouse cover has remained relatively constant over the long period of evolutionary history.

In the industrial age, massive amounts of coal, oil, and natural gas have been burned to propel the machine culture. The carbon dioxide released into the atmosphere has increased dramatically over previous periods of history, blocking the release of heat from the planet. In 1750, the earth's atmosphere contained approximately 288 ppm (parts per million) of CO_2. Today, the atmosphere contains 346 ppm.[1] From the outset of the American Civil War until today, the industrial nations have released more than 185 billion tons of carbon into the atmosphere from burning fossil fuels.[2] According to current projections, the CO_2 content in the atmosphere will likely double by the year 2030, with world temperatures rising to unprecedented levels.[3]

The burning of fossil fuels accounts for nearly 50 percent of the increase in the greenhouse gases.[4] Each of the billions of CO_2 molecules vibrating in the heavens represents a trace of the great war against nature and modern man's drive to consume the global commons. Approximately 16 percent of the spent CO_2 comes from heating and lighting our homes and running our electrical appliances. The average American home uses up 1,253 gallons of oil per year and contributes ten tons of CO_2 to the atmosphere every twelve months. In total, our homes in the United States are responsible for 770 million tons of CO_2 emissions annually.[5]

The average American automobile gets twenty-five miles to a gallon of gasoline and spews an additional five tons of CO_2 into the atmosphere every twelve months. Today, there are 127 million automobiles on the roads in the United States, emitting 635 million tons of CO_2 into the skies each year. The trucks, trains, and airplanes that move cargo and passengers contribute additional carbon into the atmospheric commons. Overall, transportation is responsible for 38 percent of all carbon emissions in the United States.

Much of the spent CO_2 in the atmosphere comes from our highly mechanized agriculture, which uses up 12 percent of the energy consumed in the United States.[6] Some of the energy is used to run the tractors, milking machines, reapers, and other machines. Additional energy is consumed in the use of massive amounts of petrochemical fertilizers and pesticides. Still more energy is used in marketing the produce. Modern mechanized agriculture uses more energy inputs per unit of output than any other agricultural system in history. To produce "just one can of corn containing 270 calories," the agricultural sector uses up 2,790 calories of energy.[7]

The transition from subsistence to market-based agriculture has been accompanied by a dramatic increase in energy use. Today, only 20 percent of the energy used in agriculture goes into growing the food. The remaining 80 percent is burned in processing, packaging, and distributing the produce to market.[8] The food-processing industry is now the fourth largest industrial user of energy in the United States. Some sources estimate that food processing consumes nearly 6 percent of the country's total energy budget. Every container and package of food on the shelves and in the freezers of the local supermarket is represented by millions of CO_2 molecules in the atmosphere.[9]

The military is the largest institutional consumer of energy in the United States. Over 80 percent of the federal energy budget goes to maintaining military equipment, weapons, and ordnance.[10] When defense contracting firms are added to the mix, the military uses 6 percent of all the energy consumed in the United States.[11] Every rifle, tank, airplane, and missile requires energy to build, maintain, and operate. Every soldier requires additional energy to clothe, feed, and transport. All the energy consumed by the giant military-industrial complex is represented by spent CO_2 molecules in the atmosphere.

Virtually the entire industrial culture is built with and operated by the burning of fossil fuels. Our factories and offices, our communications systems and transportation networks, our plastic packaging and synthetic clothes are all either fossil fuel–based or –dependent. Every day, part of the vast industrial production process of the planet migrates into the atmosphere in the form of CO_2, blocking more and more heat from escaping the planet.

While CO_2 is the major greenhouse gas, CFCs, nitrous oxide, and methane also contribute to global warming. CFCs are man-made chemicals used in a variety of industrial processes and consumer products. CFCs are more powerful blocking agents than CO_2 and are accumulating at an alarming rate in the atmosphere. CFCs are also responsible for destroying the delicate ozone layer in the upper atmosphere that protects Earth's inhabitants from deadly ultraviolet radiation. The average refrigerator contains 2.5 pounds of CFC. Home and automobile air conditioners contain a comparable amount of the chemical. When the CFCs are drained during the servicing of refrigerators and air conditioners, or when they leak out after the machines are abandoned in landfills, they migrate into the atmosphere, adding to the ever-growing blanket of greenhouse gases hovering over the planet.

Similarly, millions of fast-food containers are made up of CFC molecules, which eventually find their way up into the sky. Some kinds of insulation used in homes and offices contain CFCs. Every day CFCs blow out chimneys of electronic plants in Silicon Valley and into the atmosphere, after being used to clean computer chips that go into stereos, clocks, automated teller machines, and thousands of other products.

Nitrous oxide is another potent greenhouse gas, emitted from petrochemical fertilizer used in modern agriculture around the world. In 1950, only 14 tons of petrochemical fertilizer were being used per year. By 1988, over 135 million tons were being applied to the land in a futile attempt to maintain production on depleted and eroded soils.[12] Most of today's worldwide agricultural output is grown on an oil base, which means that every blade of wheat and stalk of corn that is harvested is represented by nitrous oxide molecules in the atmosphere.

Methane completes the list of major greenhouse gases. Bacteria release methane gas in the process of breaking down organic matter. While methane is emitted from peat bogs, rice paddies, and landfalls, termites and cattle and other livestock account for much of the increase in methane emission over the past several decades.

Methane levels in the atmosphere remained relatively constant until the industrial era. In the past 350 years, however, methane concentration in the atmosphere has nearly doubled.[13] Over 140 million tons of methane are now being released into the atmosphere each year.[14]

Scientists first became alarmed over the dramatic increase in methane concentration when they compared current levels with ancient air samples taken from ice deposits in Greenland. The geological records showed less than half the methane concentration in the atmosphere three thousand years ago as we have today. Scientists at NASA's Langley research center have concluded that the methane concentration in the atmosphere may have increased 40 percent in the past thirty-five years.[15] Methane is still found in much smaller concentrations than CO_2 in the atmosphere, but because it is twenty times as strong in its ability to block heat, it has become a major greenhouse gas. Some scientists predict that by the year 2030 methane emissions could increase global warming by 20 to 40 percent.[16]

Much of the increase in methane is indirectly attributable to massive worldwide deforestation. Live trees produce substances, including alkaloids and terpenes, that help check the growth of the termite population. When the trees are cleared, termites are able to feed off the dead wood chips without being killed by the chemical secretions. The termite population often increases by a factor of ten in cleared forests. With the queens laying up to eighty thousand eggs per day, some entomologists now estimate that there are three fourths of a ton of termites for every human being on the planet. The ever-expanding termite population is suspected of being a major culprit in the rising levels of methane emission.[17]

Cattle account for the greatest rise in methane concentration in the atmosphere. Today, over 1.2 billion cows are being grazed in countries around the world.[18] Each cow emits an average of four hundred liters of methane into the atmosphere every twenty-four hours.[19] Collectively, the one billion plus cows on earth release approximately 54.3 million metric tons of methane annually.[20]

As mentioned earlier, cattle production is increasing as a cash crop around the world to feed the demands of wealthy consumers in the United States, Europe, and now Japan who prefer to eat high up on the world's food chain. By the early 1980s, Americans were consuming an average of 77 pounds of red meat per year and spending nearly 3.5 percent of their disposable income on the purchase of beef.[21] Again, as with the other greenhouse gases, every hamburger, steak, and roast consumed by American families is recorded somewhere in the atmosphere by methane molecules emitted from the cow that eventually found its way to the dining room table.

The thickening greenhouse blanket in the atmosphere is a continuing reminder that the rich industrial nations of the north are living far beyond the earth's means. We are consuming and discarding planetary resources faster than the earth can absorb and recycle the spent energy and replenish the stock. The United States alone is responsible for 27 percent of all CO_2 emissions.[22]

Since the late 1970s, scientists have been studying the greenhouse phenomenon with increasing concern. After years of monitoring, computer simulation studies, published reports, and conferences, a consensus has begun to emerge. While the data are still sketchy, many scientists now predict a 4- to 9-degree Fahrenheit rise in temperature on the planet between now and the latter part of the twenty-first century.[23] A temperature change of this magnitude is likely to plunge the world's ecosystems and human civilization into the throes of a cataclysm unlike anything ever experienced during the short span of human history.

To grasp the enormity of the crisis, it is necessary to understand the self-regulating nature of Earth's temperature range. Just as every species lives within a narrow temperature band, so does the planet. Earth's mean temperature has not varied more than 3.6 degrees Farenheit since the last ice age, eighteen thousand years ago. A rise of 4 to 9 degrees Fahrenheit will mean that the earth could experience the passage of an entire geological epoch in less than one human lifetime, forcing ecosystems and social systems to make radical adjustments in an evolutionary moment. The potential for wreaking havoc on the delicate web of economic and environmental relationships that have emerged since the dawn of recorded history is almost unfathomable.

By the year 2030, northern American cities like New York and Boston may have the tropical climate of Miami. The Midwest farm belt could well be experiencing droughts, and in some regions complete desertification, threatening both the domestic food supply and the export of foodstuffs to the hundreds of millions of people abroad who rely on the American breadbasket to sustain them. Great rivers like the Mississippi may well turn into giant mud flats during the summer months, preventing commercial navigation for the first time. A new generation of super hurricanes, with 50 percent greater intensity, are likely to battle coastal regions each year, devastating port cities like Galveston, Norfolk, and Baltimore.

The worldwide consequences of global warming are likely to be equally severe. Scientists predict a three- to five-foot rise in seawater level by the year 2050 as a result of thermal heat expansion of the oceans. If the polar icecaps melt, the rise in water level could be even higher. Salt water will inundate coastal regions, infiltrating fresh water rivers and lakes, contaminating the already scarce drinking water for millions of people. The rising wall of water will likely destroy many low-lying island nations. The Maldives off India, the Marshall Islands in the Pacific, and the Caribbean islands may well be submerged under the great oceans. Like the mythical Atlantis, they may well cease to exist, except in the collective memory of the human race. The submerging of land-masses will create a new kind of refugee. Millions of people will be without a homeland, because for the first time in recorded history, whole countries will disappear from the face of the earth.

Low-lying nations will have to spend billions of dollars building dikes and shoring up coastal areas if they are to stave off the onslaught. Even then, scientists predict that Egypt could lose 15 percent of its arable land along the Nile delta, displacing one seventh of its population. A loss of this magnitude is expected to lower the GNP of Egypt by as much as 14 percent or more.[24] The Environmental Protection Agency (EPA) predicts that a five-foot rise in sea level will destroy up to 90 percent of America's remaining wetlands.[25] Countries like the Netherlands are likely to exhaust much of their capital building massive dikes to hold off the rising water levels.

Global warming will also fundamentally alter rainfall patterns around the planet. As rainfall shifts location and changes in concentration, existing lakes, rivers, and streams will begin to evaporate and in some cases dry up altogether. The upper Colorado river basin is predicted to lose 40 percent of its water.[26] Some climatologists predict a similar decline of 40 percent in the rainfall in the American Midwest.[27] The worldwide shift in rainfall is going to force a wholesale rebuilding of dams and irrigation systems. It is estimated that the cost of retooling U.S. dams and irrigation systems could range between $7 billion and $23 billion.[28] Worldwide over 18 percent of all the agricultural land is currently irrigated. The cost of massive restructuring could exceed $200 billion.[29]

The dramatic rise in planetary temperature will have its biggest impact on the earth's ecosystems. According to the Bellagio Report, a study undertaken by some of the world's leading climatologists in 1987, the greenhouse effect is likely to result in massive forest die back before the end of the first decade of the twenty-first century. Forests will not be able to migrate fast enough to keep up with the shift in their temperature range. Writing in the journal *Science*, Richard Akerr points out that "Each 1 degree centigrade of warming pushes climatic zones 100 to 150 km [60–95 miles] northward."[30] Consider the impact on one ecosystem alone. Within sixty years, the climate that nurtures Yellowstone National Park will have shifted well into Canada.[31] Trees are not capable of migrating at the speed set by the greenhouse phenomenon. In every region of the globe, entire ecosystems—trees, insects, microbes, animals—will be trapped by these rapid shifts in climate and left behind to die.

Economic systems, because they are highly dependent on ecosystems, are going to find it difficult, if not impossible, to adjust to the rapid shift in climate and the wild fluctuations in rainfall patterns and other environmental variables. The subsequent disruptions in the world's market economy are likely to be unprecedented and incalculable.

Virtually every nation in the world is currently making economic decisions and future development plans based on the false assumption that the climatic environment their ancestors have experienced for thousands of years will continue to exist fifty years from now. At the conclusion of the World Climate Program in 1985, scientists from twenty-five industrialized and developing nations warned that:

> Many economic and social decisions are being made today on long-term projects such as irrigation and hydro power, drought relief, agriculture, land use, structural designs, coastal engineering projects, and energy planning based on the assumption that past climatic data are a reliable guide to the future. This is no longer a good assumption since the increasing concentration of greenhouse gases are expected to cause a significant warming of the global climate in the next century."[32]

Even the most mundane economic activities, which we generally take for granted, are likely to be disrupted. For example, consider the design process. Present-day buildings, bridges, dams, roads, sewer systems, canals, and machinery of all kinds are designed for climatic stress tolerances that will no longer be applicable fifty to one hundred years from now. Jesse Ansubel, of the National Academy of Engineering, expresses the feelings of deep anxiety emerging within the development community when he asks, "What do you do when the past is no longer a guide to the future?"[33]

While the greenhouse effect threatens the survival of the earth's ecosystems and economic systems, a second global environmental crisis has emerged whose consequences are likely to be every bit as devastating. In 1985 scientists discovered a gaping hole in the ozone layer over the Antarctic. Ozone in the upper atmosphere provides a protective shield preventing excessive amounts of deadly ultraviolet rays from penetrating the earth. It was discovered that CFCs, a potent greenhouse gas, are also destroying the ozone. The CFCs migrate to the upper atmosphere, where they are broken down by the sun's rays, releasing atoms of chlorine which, in turn, destroy ozone.

In 1985 scientists recorded a 50 percent loss of ozone over the Antarctic. By 1987 the loss of ozone had increased to 60 percent.[34] More troubling, recently scientists discovered still another tear in the ozone over the mid-Northern Hemisphere.[35] NASA predicts a 10 percent depletion in the worldwide ozone layer by the year 2050. The EPA predicts that a reduction of that magnitude will result in an additional two million skin cancer cases annually.[36]

The increase in ultraviolet radiation damages the immune system, making people vulnerable to a range of traditional infectious diseases, as well as new diseases. "It is no exaggeration to say that the health and safety of millions of people around the world are at stake," says Donald Douglas of the National Resources Defense Council.[37]

The increased ultraviolet radiation is also going to have an effect on plant and animal life. At the University of Maryland, botanist Alan Teramura found that ultraviolet radiation results in tissue and cell damage in two thirds of the two hundred species tested.[38] According to Richard Adams of Oregon University, a 15 percent reduction in atmospheric ozone by the year 2050 could cause crop losses in excess of $2.5 billion a year in the United States alone.[39]

Studies suggest that the most serious potential effect of increased ultraviolet radiation is likely to be on the photosynthesis and metabolism of plankton, the microscopic marine organisms that are the base of the ocean food chain. A recent study in the Antarctic has reported serious ultraviolet radiation damage to plankton, raising questions about the survival of aquatic life around the world.[40]

Global warming and ozone depletion are among a handful of events in human history that are of such an extraordinary nature that they assume almost mythical proportions. Indeed, modern man's journey invites comparison to the ancient story of Icarus, the young man who invented wax wings to fly up into the heavens. Icarus desired to be like the gods, but in his arrogance he overreached, flying too close to the sun. His wings of wax melted and he plummeted to his doom.

Modern man has donned his own wings, the mechanical appendages of the industrial age, and set off on a journey into the secular heaven of material salvation. Along the way, he consumed the raw energy of the earth's commons to propel him ever upward and outward. He put his faith in science and technology, hoping against hope that he could eclipse time and space altogether and experience the autonomous existence of a god. But like Icarus, he too overreached. His spent energy blocked the sun's heat from escaping the planet. His manmade chemicals tore open a hole in the earth's atmosphere, exposing him to the sun's deadly ultraviolet radiation.

Global warming and ozone depletion tell the story of the fall of Homo faber. Modern man's elevation has proved illusory and short-lived. The global environmental crisis has dashed the hopes and dampened the spirit of the industrial age. The godlike autonomy we sought has now metamorphosed into a cruel joke as we find ourselves more vulnerable and less secure than at any time in our history.

PART TWO

GEOPOLITICS AND THE DEATH
OF NATURE

12

THE CORPORATE STATE

THE GRAVE ENVIRONMENTAL threats facing the planet and human civilization have been the subject of increasing public concern in recent years. Yet, government officials and business leaders around the world have shown little enthusiasm for mobilizing public opinion and marshaling public resources to address what may well be the greatest threat to human security in recorded history. The reluctance to assume a leadership role lies less in the personal shortcomings of world leaders than in the nature of the institutional setting they represent.

The nation-state and the business corporation are, by their very nature, designed to enclose ecosystems, commodify and privatize nature, optimize the expropriation of scarce resources, expand production and consumption, and advance utilitarian self-interest. The present environmental and economic crises have been brought on, in large part, by these self-same institutions. They are the vehicles that are chiefly responsible for implementing the ideas of the Enlightenment. For that reason it is essential to understand the unique role they have played in humanity's attempt to control the forces of nature and secure an autonomous existence.

The nation-state is a curious social construction quite unlike any of its predecessors. Village communities, dating all the way back to the neolithic era, had always claimed a form of organic legitimacy, their authority rooted in the sacred geometry of place.

The nation-state is an altogether different creation. It is a pure intellectual abstraction, bound together neither organically nor spiritually. While in the past it often claimed divine origin, in its present form it is a highly sophisticated secular institution that has been carefully sculptured over the centuries to perform a specific task: the commodification, transformation, exchange, and consumption of the earth's endowment. The nation-state is the first governing body in history that owes its existence almost exclusively to economic considerations.

As discussed in Chapter 4, "A Private Nature," the transition from a subsistence to a market economy, the expansion of trade, and the improvement in forms of communication and transportation required a new form of institutional control that could keep pace with commercial developments which were cutting across communities, continents, and oceans. The feudal principalities, and later the free city-states, were too parochial in teleology and too limited in geographic range to serve the needs of an incipient world economy.

The medieval form of governance was often an unreliable, hit-or-miss arrangement reflecting the idiosyncracies of the local rulers. Government was personalized to such an extent that it could be portable, set up wherever the royal family established residence. It was not uncommon for feudal lords to make periodic rounds of their domain traveling from estate to estate with their entire government entourage. Personal representatives would be dispatched from the lord's estate to collect rents and taxes from the villagers of the district, thus ensuring a high degree of personal supervision over the subjects. By the fourteenth century this unpredictable form of governance began to give way as increased population, urbanization, and expanded trade exerted increasing pressure on the rather flimsy, makeshift apparatus of rule that had prevailed for centuries.[1]

In its place, a more permanent form of governance began to take shape, one better suited to accompany the transition to a commercial economy. By the sixteenth century, trade between communities, both near and far, became increasingly intertwined, complex, and contentious, requiring political regulation on a more expansive geographical plane. Overland and overseas expansion of markets for both raw materials and consumer products required more sophisticated and expensive forms of transportation and communication which only a very large political unit could hope to finance, build, and manage. Taxes had to be raised and finance capital had to be secured to dredge canals, pave roads, and construct ships. Feudal principalities and free cities were forced, by economic necessity, to federate and finally be absorbed into monarchies and then national states.[2]

The nation-state brought with it the modern bureaucracy and a new type of relationship between ruler and ruled. In medieval Europe, political rule had been based on local tradition, custom, and, often, oral agreements. The nation-state bureaucracies eliminated the human bonds, preferring to codify all relationships between government and subjects in abstract legal documents and accounts stored in permanent archives or written court records. The new form of governance was detached, abstract, analytical, and, above all, centralized. The body politic, like nature and the marketplace, was draped in the Cartesian vision and administered with the cool rational objectivity of Baconian science.

The boundaries of the emerging nation-state were fixed neither by tradition nor revelation. Rather, they were artificial constructs, continually growing to meet the needs of an expanding market. Where past political leaders ruled over subjects and claimed authority as God's emissaries, the new secular politicians increasingly ruled over territorial resources and markets and, by the twentieth century, preferred to rest their claims to leadership on managerial expertise.

The transition to the nation-state took place over five hundred years, the path of development paralleling the worldwide enclosure of the global commons. Since the end of World War II, the number of nation-states has increased from fifty to nearly two hundred.[3] Although never officially noted, one of the great anthropological milestones in human history was passed in the present century when the last remaining square foot of soil on the planet—short of the Arctic and Antarctic—was formally enclosed by nation-states and every human being was confined within a political boundary.

Much of the success of the nation-state is attributable to the rise of the business corporation, which helped the fledgling powers subdue overseas territories, enclose the earth's resources, and secure expanded trading markets. The modern business firm was nurtured on Italian soil during the early Renaissance. Amalfi, Venice, Genoa, and other Italian city-states introduced the *societas maori,* or maritime firms, which were a partnership arrangement generally involving a financial backer for a trading excursion and the captain of a merchant ship. These early prototypes of the business firm were short-lived arrangements, usually extending to only the length of a particular voyage. At about the same time, the *compagnia* came into existence. These were joint liability firms in which all the members were liable for debts incurred by the company. Many of the great corporate enterprises of Italy and France grew out of powerful family businesses of the Renaissance.[4]

As markets expanded and business opportunities opened up, a new economic arrangement, the limited liability firm, became popular. The first record of such an enterprise is dated May 8, 1532, in Florence.[5] Eager to draw on outside capital, merchants and manufacturers devised an institution guaranteeing limited liability to those who contributed funds. Unlike the family-based joint liability firms, where every member was liable for debts incurred by the business, under the new arrangement shareholders were only liable to the extent of their investment. A French ordinance, one of the first of its kind, passed in 1673, stated "the parties to a limited partnership will be liable only to the equivalent of their shareholding."[6]

The final metamorphosis to the modern business corporation came with the introduction of the joint stock company. The first recorded English joint stock venture, the Muscovy Company, was chartered in 1553. The joint stock company was ideally suited to meet the needs of an expanding economy, as capital could be raised from a much larger pool of investors. Equally important, investors were no longer strictly limited to a particular geographic region or social milieu. While the joint stock company was a legal creation of the state, its stockholders might come from other cities or even countries.[7]

In the early years of the capitalist era, the state and the business corporation enjoyed a close working relationship. Each profited from the success of the other. The state provided the corporation with legal protection at home and military protection abroad. In return, the new capitalist enterprises quickened the pace of commerce and manufacturing and increased the tax revenue for the state.

The symbiotic relationship between the forces of capitalism and the new national powers reached a peak with the state chartering of the great European merchant companies in the seventeenth and eighteenth centuries. These early predecessors of today's giant multinational corporations owe their existence largely to Vasco da Gama's legendary voyage to India in 1498. Gama reached India by way of the Cape of Good Hope. He returned to Portugal triumphant, with riches from the East worth sixty times the cost of his voyage. His booty included silks and ivory as well as pepper and precious spices—cloves, cinnamon, nutmeg, and ginger. The news of his success traveled fast and far to countries throughout Europe. The Portuguese, then the Dutch and English, launched a furious competition for the lucrative Eastern trading markets.[8]

The Dutch were the first to exploit the idea of establishing an overseas merchant company to secure the Indian market. The Dutch East India Company of the Netherlands was incorporated in 1602 with 500,000 pounds of capital. The Dutch charter granted the company an exclusive monopoly over trade in the East. The corporate charter even empowered the company to negotiate treaties, make wars, build forts, and subdue overseas territories. Like the other great trading companies that were to follow, the Dutch East India Company was set up as "a great instrument of war and conquest."[9]

All the great European trading companies—the Virginia and Plymouth companies, the Russia Company, the British East India Company—were granted exclusive trading monopolies in the colonies in return for enclosing territory and securing foreign markets and revenue for the home country. These corporate enterprises often rivaled the power of sovereign states and served as political surrogates in far-flung regions of the world.

The British East India Company offers the best example of how the enormous power was exercised by the first global corporations. Chartered on December 31, 1600, the company was given an exclusive monopoly over Indian trade. In the ensuing decades, the company often reaped yearly profits of 100 percent or more.[10] As its economic fortunes waxed, its charter was amended, giving it more and more autonomy in the conduct of its affairs abroad. In 1661, the British crown revised the East India Company charter to include "the privileges accorded by previous grants, and gave additional rights of jurisdiction over all Englishmen in the East, and power to maintain fortifications and to raise troops for their defense."[11] In its heyday, the East India Company ruled over virtually all of India and its 250 million inhabitants, boasted the largest professional army in the world, and deployed forty-three warships.[12]

The worldwide enclosure movement was made possible, in large part, by the commercial and colonial practices of these giant commercial enterprises. These appendages of the nation-state brought the modern war against nature to every corner of the globe. Nature was enclosed and commodified and native people were subdued and colonized. The great merchant trading companies also brought the Enlightenment worldview with them wherever they established a beachhead and regime. Around the planet, whole cultures were reoriented to the exacting standards of the clock and schedule, the assumptions of mechanistic thinking, and the objective detachment of modern scientific inquiry. By the turn of the nineteenth century, much of the human population of Earth had adopted bits and pieces of the Western frame of mind. Efficiency and material progress became the secular watchwords of the age, as the corporation and nation-state beat a path across the global commons.

13

GUNPOWDER
AND GLOBAL REACH

THE INDUSTRIAL JOURNEY has been blazed with incendiaries. The enclosure and commodification of the global commons has been secured, at every step of the way, with firepower. From French artillery pointing menacingly at the walls of the ancient Florentine city-state to powerful intercontinental missiles swooping up from the ocean depths en route to a rendezvous with distant military targets, fiery explosions have echoed across five centuries, providing the refrain for man's mercurial quest for security in the modern age.

The nation-state and the giant merchant trading companies were able to extend their reach over the global commons with the establishment of a professional military regime in each country. The state, the corporation, and the professional military together make up the trinity that to this day exercises near complete dominion over the earth, its resources, and its inhabitants.

The professional military owes its existence to gunpowder. The repercussions of this single technological revolution have been enormous, conditioning the way we have come to view ourselves, our civilization, and our world. Before gunpowder, military security was for the most part bound up in defensive actions. Walled cities provided security for communities for thousands of years. The first walled settlement at Jericho dates back to 7000 B.C. In medieval Europe every castle was protected by thick walls, and usually surrounded by a moat.[1] The free cities were also fortified with walled defenses. While these barriers did not assure absolute protection from warring bands or armies of conquest, they were adequate to fend off most attacks. Machiavelli observed that the "cities of Germany . . . are fortified in such a manner that to reduce them would be tedious and difficult, for they all have the necessary moats and bastions and always keep in the public store-houses food and drink and fuel for one year."[2]

Up until the advent of gunpowder, defensive military action often prevailed, limiting the possibility of widespread wars of conquest. After the gunpowder revolution, holding the high ground became far more problematic. The first indication of the far-reaching potential of gunpowder came in 1494, when Charles VIII of France invaded Italy. Using infantry and the new technology of artillery, the French ruler decimated the once seemingly inpenetrable walls of the Italian city-states.[3] Like the dropping of the atomic bombs on Hiroshima and Nagasaki almost five centuries later, the use of incendiary weapons changed the basic notion of security and unleashed forces that would eventually undermine the medieval way of life.

Gunpowder technology provided the means literally to break down the old order. Political historian John Herz notes that as the gunpowder revolution spread, "a feeling of insecurity swept all of Europe."[4] One can imagine the sheer terror these first modern machines must have engendered among the people. The introduction of the cannon, and later the musket, signaled the death knell for the medieval knight and the ritualized form of combat that characterized the Middle Ages. More important, gunpowder provided the aristocracy and the merchant class with a new form of offensive warfare that could be used to extend their power over large tracts of land, allowing them to take control over an expanded trading territory.

With the introduction of firearms, security moved from a vertical to a horizontal plane, and from a defensive to an offensive posture. One by one, the fortified castles and walled-in cities of medieval Europe were overrun and rendered defenseless. A new spirit of conquest, of lust for territorial advantage, began to take hold. The new aggressive military temperament matched the new spirit of commercial conquest that was beginning to characterize the age. Together, these two forces created the foundation of the modern territorial state and the industrial age.

With gunpowder, the merchant class and aristocracy were able to secure the gains of enclosure on the sea as well as on the land. In fact, it was on the high seas that the gunpowder revolution had, perhaps, its biggest impact. A new generation of small, light-weight, and powerful bronze cannons replaced the older wrought-iron models. The Portuguese were the first to exploit the naval potential of these new armaments by mounting them on warships. The Spanish, then the British and French, quickly followed suit. Mounted artillery ended the long tradition of boarding ships to engage in hand-to-hand combat. On sea, as on land, the gunpowder revolution introduced a new form of warfare, fought from a distance. Historian Paul Kennedy points out that armed sailing ships "heralded a fundamental advance in Europe's place in the world. With these vessels, the naval powers of the West were in a position to control the oceanic trade routes and to overcome all societies vulnerable to the workings of sea power."[5]

With armed galleons at their disposal, the emerging nation-states of Europe were able to extend their trading markets into the Americas in the West and Cathay in the Far East. Countries fought with each other to secure and enclose the great oceanic commons. Armed ships bombarded ancient ports and raised their flags over small islands and whole continents. Populations were routed, subdued, and domesticated. European nations traded in Chinese silk and looted Peruvian silver. Tobacco, sugar, indigo, and rice were planted and harvested in the new colonial territories and shipped backed to the home markets. The Newfoundland fisheries were opened up for commercial exploitation, providing European cities with a new, seemingly inexhaustible source of cheap protein. Whaling on the high seas became commercially lucrative. It has been said that the modern nation-state was built, in part, off the back of the great Atlantic whales. The whale provided oil for lighting, lubrication, and hundreds of other items that became indispensable to urbanized existence and industrial production.

The volume of oceanic trade increased dramatically in the wake of the gunpowder revolution and the securing of overseas territories. Transatlantic trade increased "eightfold between 1510 and 1550, and threefold again between 1550 and 1610."[6]

Lewis Mumford once remarked that "all the great national states, and the empires formed around a national core, are at bottom war-states; their politics are war politics; and the all-absorbing preoccupation of their governing classes lies in collective preparation for armed assault."[7] Coercion and force are indispensable elements in the drive to commercially exploit the earth's riches. While Adam Smith served up paeans of praise to an invisible hand, it was the loaded cannon and armed infantrymen that often had to clear the way for commerce when more subtle market forces were inadequate to the task.

The military cost of securing vast tracts of the earth for commercial exploitation proved to be exorbitant. Medieval Europe had been primarily organized around defense. Securing walled cities and castles had been relatively inexpensive. Financing knights and temporary armies for occasional forays had been more expensive, but even during the Crusades, the cost was generally manageable. The new offensive form of warfare, in contrast, required the expenditure of vast sums of money. Outfitting and maintaining professional standing armies, financing the manufacturing of artillery and muskets, constructing warships, transporting men and machines, munitions and matériel over expanded terrain changed the cost as well as the form of warfare. Only a pooling of vast financial and terrestrial resources could provide the necessary means to wage modern warfare. The nation-state brought together a powerful alliance of merchants, bankers, industrialists, and aristocrats around a common goal: the financing of a military-industrial complex that could secure the global commons.

Financing large armies and navies and wars of conquest became a primary concern of the new territorial states. In Elizabethan England and during Phillip II's reign in Spain, nearly 75 percent of all government expenditures were used to wage war or repay debts incurred from past military adventures.[8] By the seventeenth and eighteenth centuries, even in peacetime, the upkeep of the armed services consumed 40 to 50 percent of a country's expenditures. In wartime it could rise to 80 or 90 percent.[9]

In *The Rise and Fall of the Great Powers*, historian Paul Kennedy examines the symbiotic relationship that developed over the centuries as the nation-state increasingly relied on the banking community to help finance its military adventures. The private financial houses in Europe, especially in Amsterdam, London, Lyons, and Frankfurt, were able to reap windfall profits in the form of interest on the loans they extended, which were used, in turn, to provide the finance capital for much of the Industrial Revolution.[10]

It should be emphasized that from the beginning of the modern territorial state, the cost of financing a professional military establishment always exceeded the revenue that could be collected in the form of taxes. The state continually had to rely on private financing to support its military and secure its territory. In this sense, the state was neither sovereign nor secure but, rather, carried on the shoulders of the financial community. The bankers often used their leverage to secure military access to foreign markets as well as special privileges in the form of state trading monopolies.[11]

Kennedy points out that European monarchs were often unable to pay back loans, especially in the wake of military defeats or downturns in the economy. Then, too, the cost of waging war increased dramatically in just a few short centuries. In the sixteenth century, wars were measured in millions of pounds, in the late seventeenth century in tens of millions, and by the eighteenth century waging a war might cost upward of 100 million pounds.[12] It is not surprising that states often defaulted on their debts and devalued their currency. By the late seventeenth and early eighteenth century, the spiraling cost of financing war and an increasingly unstable relationship between the banking community and the state forced what historians refer to as the "financial revolution" in Europe. Modern banking practices were implemented and sophisticated credit systems were introduced to regulate loans for the financing of wars.

The new partnership between the financiers and the state continually fed on itself; the financial community provided loans to the government, which, in turn, let out contracts to shipbuilders, armsmakers, and merchants, thus stimulating the growth of the capitalist economy. Says Kennedy, "In many respects, this two-way system of raising and simultaneously spending vast sums of money acted like a bellows, fanning the development of Western capitalism and that of the nation-state itself."[13]

14

ARMED TO THE TEETH

IN HIS 1961 farewell address to the nation, Dwight David Eisenhower warned of a new and potentially ominous threat to the peace and security of the United States:

> The conjunction of an immense military establishment and a large arms industry is new in the American experience. The total influence—economic, political, even spiritual—is felt in every city, every state house, every office of the federal government. In the councils of government, we must guard against the acquisition of unwarranted influence, whether sought or not by the military-industrial complex. The potential for the disastrous rise of misplaced power exists and will persist.[1]

Eisenhower thought of the military-industrial complex as a historical anomaly, a force that had developed out of the special circumstances dictated by post–World War II Soviet expansion and the Cold War. In point of fact, Eisenhower's warning might just as easily have been made a hundred times over by politicians and social critics throughout the five centuries spanning the political life of the nation-state. The military-industrial complex is endemic to the modern age. It is intimately bound up with the emergence of territorial states and the systematic conquest and enclosure of the global commons. The relationship between militarism, capitalism, and the state goes far beyond the financing of war to include the very birth and development of industrial production.

It was the increased demand for artillery, guns, and cannonballs in the fifteenth century that helped force a change from handicraft production to industrial production in the fifteenth century. By the end of the century France had thirteen foundries, all producing cannons.[2] Over the next two centuries, foundries were built throughout the continent. Stoking furnaces and firing guns became the Promethean symbol of the age. By the sixteenth century large tracts of European forests had been denuded to fuel the giant ovens and build the naval armadas of the new territorial states. Experiments were made substituting coal for charcoal, and in the eighteenth century an Englishman, Abraham Darby, perfected a coal-burning process.[3] The transition from a renewable to a fossil-fuel energy source marked a turning point in the manufacturing revolution and the final weaning of industrial production from the old smithing processes that had characterized earlier technology.

Over and over again, industrial innovations were devised to assist nation-states in their wars of conquest. Division of labor was used in the munitions factories well before Adam Smith's pithy observation of the benefits of manufacturing pins by the same process. Standardization of parts was introduced in the manufacture of muskets. In 1785, the Frenchman Le Blanc produced the first muskets containing interchangeable parts. Before that time even the minute details of production, including screws and threads, were each individually crafted and varied in weight, size, and contour, making them unsuitable as replacement parts.[4] In 1799 an American, Eli Whitney, introduced the idea of mass production. Under contract with the U.S. War Department to produce a large number of muskets, Whitney became frustrated over the long delays that resulted from teaching workers the necessary skills to make the various component parts of the finished product. Whitney developed the idea of mass-producing standard interchangeable parts that could be easily assembled by unskilled laborers.

In the nineteenth century, Napoleon II offered an award to anyone who could come up with a new cheap process of making steel strong enough to withstand the explosive force of powerful artillery shells. The Bessemer process won the contest. The new method gave France, and later other countries, the capacity to build more powerful weapons of destruction. The Bessemer process was subsequently used to forge the construction material of the later Industrial Revolution.[5]

Although the industrial process was first used to manufacture armaments, its modus operandi was soon extended to the military organization itself. Between the fifteenth and eighteenth centuries the feudal knight was transformed into the modern professional soldier. In medieval Europe, armies were recruited for short periods of time, the length of service generally not exceeding forty days. The transition from a highly ritualized form of personal combat to the more professional mechanized form of modern warfare was, to paraphrase Lewis Mumford, an "engineering feat."[6] In the new territorial states soldiers were identically trained, clothed in uniforms, drilled in unison on specially prepared parade grounds, and billeted in standardized barracks. Armies and navies were regimented to meet exacting standards of performance, and individual soldiers were trained to perform specialized tasks. There were now infantrymen, cavalrymen, artillerymen, men who handled ordnance, men who handled transportation, and men who handled corpses. There were field and support staff—in short, there developed a complex system of division of labor that bore all the earmarks of the industrial process. The professional army predated the professional business enterprise and provided a training ground in the art of reducing people to a machinelike status.

The new warfare states required standing armies, men ready to protect territorial and commercial interests at a moment's notice. The idea of huge numbers of identically clothed men drilling and dwelling together created a kind of walking image of the Cartesian vision. The sheer presence of this new mechanized man often overwhelmed local communities. In 1790, Berlin boasted a military population of twenty thousand in a city totaling less than ninety thousand inhabitants. Mumford writes:

The presence of this mass of mechanized and obedience-conditioned human beings necessarily touched every aspect of life. The army supplied the model in the discipline . . . [and] were copied by the new industrialists, who governed their factories like absolute despots.[7]

The French under Louis XIV were the first to make the complete transition into a fully modern, professional standing army and navy in the late seventeenth century. The French war ministry was established to oversee the full range of military operations, becoming the first formal military bureaucracy in modern times. France was also the first nation to implement a military draft. On September 5, 1798, the French government enacted a conscription law, calling up all men between the ages of twenty and twenty-five to an indefinite length of service. Two hundred thousand young Frenchmen were conscripted in the first draft. It was said that the only way a young Frenchman could end his military service was by death, contagious disease, or infliction of a wound so serious that he could not walk onto the battlefield.[8]

Speaking before the Council of State in 1804, Napoleon captured the military significance as well as the human pathos of the new practice of drafting civilians into service: "The law of conscription is the dread and desolation of families, but forms the security of the State."[9]

Outfitting one hundred thousand French soldiers with identical uniforms created "the first large-scale demand for standardized goods."[10] When the sewing machine was invented in 1829 by Thimonnet of Lyons, the French war department was the first to use it.[11]

The military-industrial complex has had a profound impact on virtually every aspect of modern life, even the design of city streets. Medieval streets were narrow and winding, more closely resembling paths or walkways. They were organic creations, the result of centuries of spontaneous development of living quarters and market areas. The French were the first to see the military value of building wide, straight avenues. The new thoroughfares were precisely drawn and, in their expanse and length, gave the impression of strength and order. When used as a parade ground for the fast movement of cavalry and artillery and the quick step of the well-drilled infantrymen, they radiated power. The new avenues also served a security function, providing a straight, unencumbered line of travel for the fast deployment of troops and cannons. Napoleon III was not unaware of the dangers that lurked in winding alleys and narrow streets. They gave an advantage to the lone sniper or the spontaneous mob. He ordered all of the cul-de-sacs and narrow passageways closed to make room for the grand boulevards.[12] In the United States, the founding fathers hired the French architect Pierre Charles L'Enfant to design the nation's new capital in Washington, D.C. He laid out the city in broad boulevards which came together like spokes of a giant wheel. L'Enfant believed that the enclosure of the capital city in circles offered the best military means of defending the city against attack. His rationale went up in smoke as the British burned the capital just a few decades later in the War of 1812. Still, the image of giant wheel-like avenues and broad linear-shaped boulevards could not help but conjure up the Cartesian vision of an orderly machinelike universe, where life itself was forced to operate within well-defined, mathematically precise borders.

While the great powers have changed over the past five hundred years, the military-industrial complex has remained a recurrent feature of virtually every developed nation-state on earth. Since World War II the nations of the world have spent over $17 trillion for military weapons and for maintenance of standing armies, navies, and air forces. In 1990, the more than hundred nations of the world spent over $1 trillion on preparation for war or actual combat.[13]

The armed forces of the world now total nearly 29 million men and women. Another 80 million people are employed in the arms industry.[14] According to Michael Renner of the Worldwatch Institute, military outlays exceeded world economic output in the first half of the 1980s.[15] In fact, the nations of the world now spend more money on military security than the poorer 50 percent of humanity earns each year.[16] The superpowers and key nations in Western Europe account for over 75 percent of all military spending.[17] At the same time, multinational companies produce and sell over $50 billion in arms to developing nations each year.[18] Since 1960, over $800 billion in weapons have been marketed to second and third world nations.[19] It is no wonder that military purchases now account for more than 25 percent of all second and third world debt.[20] Only two nations in the world have no military forces—Costa Rica and Iceland.[21]

In no other period of history have human institutions been so totally dedicated to military preparation and engagement. In the 1980s alone, twenty-two wars were fought around the world. In the last forty-five years nation-states have engaged in 120 armed conflicts.[22] Despite the many accolades that have been heaped on the modern age, a death culture lies on the dark side of the age of progress.

If we were to strip the military-industrial complex from the infrastructures of the great superpower states, we would be left with a pale shadow of their greatness. In the United States today the military share of total goods consumption is over 10 percent.[23] The Pentagon's investment in plants and equipment in the United States is nearly 38 percent. There are currently over twenty thousand major defense contracting corporations and an addition-al one hundred thousand subcontractors working on Pentagon projects.[24] Six multinational corporations alone account for 25 percent of all the defense contracts: Rockwell International, General Dynamics, General Electric, McDonnell Douglas, Boeing, and Lockheed.[25] In 1983 the U.S. military owned industrial equip-ment, land, and buildings valued at $475 billion, an amount equivalent to half the holdings of all U.S. manufacturing corporations.[26] Currently, over 70 percent of all research and development monies in the United States go to military-related activity.[22]

The military-industrial complex in the United States has swelled to such monstrous proportions that were it a separate nation, it would rank as the world's thirteenth largest power.[28] In the 1980s the United States spent more than $2.3 trillion on military security.[29] Equally impressive, $46 out of every $100 of new capital in the United States was expended on the military economy by the 1980s.[30]

The American taxpayers end up contributing a large amount of their yearly income to prop up the military-industrial complex. In 1986, the average family paid $5,800 in taxes: $3,103 went to the military, while only $115 went to housing, $138 to nutrition programs, and $126 to education.[31] Even this inordinate outlay of taxpayers' earnings is not enough to finance U.S. military ventures. Like every other nation-state in the modern age, the United States has had to borrow large sums of money to pay for military expenditures that continually exceed government revenues. In 1987, 53 cents of every dollar spent by the U.S. government went to pay back debt from past wars and military expenditures.[32]

Nations like the United States and the U.S.S.R. have increasingly relied on the military-industrial complex to help enclose and exploit vast regions of the global commons. Today, industrialized nations and developing nations alike find themselves riddled by debt, unable to pay back even the interest on past loans, as they desperately attempt to keep up with the cost of increases in military expenditures. The debt crisis now threatens to plunge civilization into the throes of a massive economic depression in the coming decade. This is part of the price humanity has been forced to pay to "secure" itself in the modern world.

15

EVERYONE'S A SOLDIER

WHILE THE FINANCIAL toll of waging modern warfare has been extraordinary, the human toll is almost beyond comprehension. In the struggle to secure global resources, the human species has suffered terrible losses. Over one hundred million people have been killed in the twentieth century by the military machines of nation-states in their relentless drive to subdue and enclose the earth's ecosystems.[1] Although it has gone largely unnoticed by historians and anthropologists, the nation-states of the industrial age, in their quest for complete dominance over nature and people, fundamentally altered the rules of conduct in military engagement. The result has been the inclusion of vast civilian populations as expendable military targets in wartime.

Many Americans in the late 1960s were shocked and repulsed viewing nightly television coverage of women, children, and old people being maimed and killed by American soldiers in Southeast Asia. The American experience in Vietnam is not unique. The devaluation of human life began at the very dawn of the industrial age as market forces conspired with Enlightenment ideas about nature and human nature, reducing all phenomena to the status of a mere resource or commodity. And, of course, resources are expendable; their prime purpose, after all, is to be used. Human resources, like natural resources, have been spent in various ways: in the industrial mills, on the assembly lines, in the financial

114

houses, and, increasingly in the past century, on an expanded military battlefield—which now envelops the global commons and the entire human complex.

The idea of the civilian as combatant is novel, and it is inextricably linked to the military-industrial complex that forms the power center of the nation-state. Military and political leaders are well aware that waging a modern war depends as much on the strength of the industrial complex that churns out the weapons of destruction as it does on the brains of generals and the courage of field troops. The Union armies, it is said, won the Civil War despite their generals, thanks to their superior resource base and industrial infrastructure. Because the modern nation-state is directed to war making, both on the front lines and behind the lines, the concept of soldiers has been increasingly extended to include welders and engineers, the assembly line workers and plant foremen, the scientists and mathematicians—in short, the entire phalanx of industrial soldiers, their families, and the civilian population that make up the military-industrial complex of a nation. A total of 135,000 men, women, and children were killed in the allied fire-bombings of the industrial city of Dresden during World War II.[2] The casualties exceeded those of Hiroshima. The allied powers viewed the entire city—its factories, rail links, phone lines, and work force—as combatants.

The radical change in the status of the civilian between the medieval and modern world is illustrative of the larger historical processes that denatured the planet and reduced humankind to an instrument of production.

The concept of civilian immunity during war developed slowly over the centuries of Western history. St. Augustine was the first of the Christian faith to articulate the principles of noncombatant immunity in his exegesis on the just war concept in the late fourth century. The Church viewed war as an act of retributive justice, a way of punishing evil and restoring spiritual order. The Church was adamant in its belief that war was never justifiable as a means of securing power over other people or lands. War was never to be fought for purposes of revenge or gain but only to uphold the moral order. Writing in the thirteenth century, St. Thomas Aquinas said, "True religion looks upon as peaceful those wars that are waged not for motives of agrandizement, or cruelty, but with the object of securing peace, of punishing evildoers, and of uplifting the good."[3]

Despite the lofty intentions of the Church and the carefully chosen words of theologians like St. Augustine and St. Thomas Aquinas, the reality of war in medieval Europe was often at odds with official doctrine. As Richard Shelly Hartigan points out in his authoritative history, *The Forgotten Victim,* churches were often looted, farms and villages ransacked and burned, and women and children tortured and killed.[4] Then, in the last decade of the tenth century, just before the first millennium of the Christian era, a rather unusual social phenomenon emerged in Europe. The first grassroots peace movement in Western history started in France and then spread across the continent. Mass protests against the unrestrained violence of feudal war resulted in two parallel movements: the Peace of God and the Truce of God. The first movement attempted to limit the destruction of war by outlawing military action against specific civilian targets. The second movement was aimed at limiting the incidence of war to specific times or seasons of the year.[5]

As popular protest increased in number and intensity, the Church joined in, giving the movement the authority it needed to prevail. A Pact of Peace, the first of its kind in Western history, was signed between noblemen and the Church in France in 998. The agreement mandated the protection of laborers, merchants, clerics, and other noncombatants during war and made violations punishable by individual excommunication or communal interdiction—the excommunication of an entire community if the military action of a feudal lord were condoned or supported by his subjects.[6]

At the Council of Elne in 1027, and in subsequent peace councils at Nabone in 1043, 1045, and again in 1054, the rules safeguarding noncombatants were extended and further clarified. Serfs and their property were afforded protection during war. Later, at a second council at Elne in 1065, domestic animals were brought under the umbrella of noncombatant immunity as well.[7] In 1059, Pope Nicholas II issued a decree protecting all pilgrims, clerics, and poor people from military attack. Europe's first peace movement peaked in 1095 at Clermont when Pope Urban II officially endorsed the principles of the Truce of God.[8]

The Church's decrees changed the temperament of war in medieval Europe, affording the civilian population a measure of security they had never known before. Church doctrine also changed the practice of war, transforming the feudal warrior into the Christian knight. The new soldier of the twelfth century owed his first loyalty to the faith. He was charged with defending the Church, which included both its property and its parishioners. The chivalric code bound the knight to the rules of peace that had been laid out by the various church councils. It also bound him to a code of professional honor, another new idea in warfare.

Over the next several centuries, the ecclesiastical doctrine governing noncombatants and the conduct of war extended into secular law. In 1625, Hugo Grotius, the father of modern international law, published a lengthy treatise on the rights of noncombatants, which amplified church doctrine to include non-Christians as well under the umbrella of civilian immunity during wartime.

The principle of noncombatant immunity continued to gain momentum both in law and in practice until the early eighteenth century and the emergence of the first modern territorial states. The meteoric rise of the professional army in that century changed the goal and the conduct of military action. Wars of territorial and military conquest replaced just wars and religious crusades. New weapons of depersonalized mass destruction put an end to ritualized combat. While codes of conduct continued to be defined and refined by jurists, they became far less important in the actual conduct of war. Still, their existence provided an overarching moral standard, even if increasingly violated, by which to judge the behavior of nations.

In 1862, Francis Lieber, a German immigrant to the United States, drafted the first professional code governing the conduct of modern war for the Union army. The resulting manual, which Lincoln signed into law in 1863, bore the inauspicious and rather bureaucratic title of *General Order Number 100, Instructions of the Government of Armies of the United States in the Field*.[9] The points of conduct Lieber outlined were subsequently modified and used by other nations and ultimately became the basis of the Hague Convention of 1899 and 1907. The Hague Convention established rules governing the treatment of prisoners and civilians in occupied territories, the status of neutral parties and hospital personnel. Property rights, freedom of transit, correspondence between civilians in occupied regions were also defined.[10] The juridical victory was to be short-lived.

The "guns of August" shattered a fifteen-hundred-year struggle to humanize war and secure the rights of nonbelligerents. World War I was the first global military conflict in history. It was also the first fully mechanized war, in which victory was measured as much by the industrial capacity of the combatants as by the military maneuvers in the field. Codes of conduct governing warfare and the humane treatment of civilians seemed a quaint reminder of an idyllic past in the path of tanks rumbling down the military boulevards of Europe and poison gas wafting its way over miles and miles of deep trenches filled with young men.

Although nation-states continued to pay lip service to the notion of protecting the noncombatant, the new "industrial wars" forced a broadening of the definition of enemy to include "women making munitions in a factory and children filling sandbags for defense against air attacks."[11] Approximately 6,000 people died every single day for 1,500 days in World War I. While nearly three million died by direct violence, another six to eight million died from long-term privation.[12] In World War II, more civilians were killed than soldiers.[13] In the 1950s, civilians accounted for 52 percent of the war-related deaths. By the 1980s, civilian deaths during war were 85 percent of the total casualties.[14] In southern Africa alone, over 750,000 children have died due to war in the 1980s. Bangladesh, Korea, Nigeria, Iran, Iraq, Vietnam, Kampuchea, and China have each experienced over one million deaths, mostly civilians, in wars since 1945.[15]

With the advent of nuclear weaponry, the concept of noncombatant has become moot. The entire globe has now been reduced to a single battlefield and every human being defined as a military target. Today, a thirty-minute war could obliterate most of the human population and all other life on the earth.

16

THE POLITICS OF
GEOGRAPHY

D U R I N G   T H E modern age, nation-states have relied on a combination of market forces and military force to help enclose and secure the global commons. The near total commodification of nature and militarization of society are awesome accomplishments and likely to be remembered as the crowning achievements of the nation-state era.

In pursuit of both commercial and military objectives, the nation-states have developed a unique code of conduct governing political activity in the international arena. Geopolitics has become the universally accepted political philosophy of the nation-state era. Its strategic assumptions are rooted in the Enlightenment catechism and have become the modus operandi by which nations extend their influence and secure their power in the world today.

Although the term "geopolitics" is widely used, its anthropological origins, philosophical underpinnings, and historical development have remained somewhat of a mystery, even among its many practitioners. Yet nation-states almost exclusively rely on the theory and practice of geopolitics in their efforts to secure commercial and military advantage. To a very real extent, today's global environmental and economic crises are the result of a geopolitical way of thinking about and acting on the world. For that reason the art of geopolitics needs to be thoroughly understood and critiqued if alternative theories of international security are to be envisioned that are more in keeping with the principles of ecological sustainability, peaceful coexistence, and elementary economic justice.

The word *geopolitics* was conceived by a Swede, Rudolph Kjellen. Geopolitics is "the science that conceives the state as a geographical organism or as a phenomenon in space."[1] The living state is characterized by its territory and people; its form of government and economy; its space, size, and shape; and its relationship to the sea, among other considerations.

Kjellen, like many other intellectuals of his day, was enamored of the evolutionary theories of Charles Darwin and Alfred Wallace, and used the new ideas in biology to redefine the notion of the state. The nation-state, which had long been regarded as an inanimate machine, was suddenly made animate and conscious. As with other organisms, Kjellen argued, the state is always attempting to grow and expand, to seek out new territories, to conquer and exploit.[2] Imperialist ventures, then, were not so much the product of greed or blind ambition, but, rather, the result of natural evolutionary forces at work.

> . . . Strong states with a limited area of sovereignty are dominated by the categorical imperative to enlarge their area by colonization. It is clearly a case, not of the lust for conquest, but of natural and necessary growth.[3]

The new science of geopolitics was systematically laid out by a German professor of geography, Frederick Ratzel. In 1882, he published his *Anthropogeographie*,[4] the first of many works in which the author wove together the science of geography and the art of politics into a set of theories which were to become as influential in the thinking of twentieth-century politics as the writings of Machiavelli, Bacon, Descartes, and Locke had been at the beginning of the nation-state era.

Ratzel, like Kjellen, argued that land and people join together to form an organic whole, an organism that grows, expands, and changes in accordance with the evolutionary laws of biology. The geographer interpreted evolutionary theory to mean that every living creature seeks to enlarge both itself and its territory. In

Politische Geographie, published in 1898,[5] Ratzel borrowed extensively from Darwin, arguing that states are "rooted organisms" that constantly compete with each other for scarce space. The law of natural selection, which favors the most biologically fit, applies as equally to nations as to species.[6]

The theory of geopolitics provided an ideal rationalization for the conquest and enclosure of the global commons and the increasing military struggle between nation-states, each eager to expand territorial boundaries and markets. Where past imperialist ventures were justified either by the need to Christianize the world or extend the principles of liberty, fraternity, and equality, new justification could be found in the laws of natural selection. By constantly seeking to enlarge its commercial domain and military rule, the nation-state was merely fulfilling its biological destiny.[7]

Frederick Ratzel's theories were expanded in subsequent years by other political geographers, and while they differed with regard to details, they all accepted the Darwinian notion of nature "red in tooth and claw." Throughout the twentieth century, the nation-state struggle has been viewed as a relentless battle of survival of the fittest, a contest in which each party attempts to secure its own autonomy in a hostile environment by enlarging and enclosing its territorial domain and increasing its power over others.

In *Sea as a Source of Greatness of a People,* published in 1900, Ratzel reiterated the underlying biological theme of the new science of geopolitics.[8] All states, he proclaimed, "stand under the law of progress from small to big spaces."[9] In the same work, he extends the biological imperative to include the oceanic commons, arguing that "Germany must be strong on the seas to fulfill her mission in the world."[10]

Ellen Churchill Semple, an American disciple of Ratzel, took up the banner of geopolitics on behalf of U.S. interests, stating that ". . . man is a product of the earth's surface. Big spacial ideas, born of ceaseless regular wandering, outgrow the land that bred them and bear their legitimate fruit in wide imperial conquest."[11] The new science of geopolitics provided an appropriate academic gloss for the expansionary spirit of the times and found a welcome audience among industrialists, politicians, and military strategists.

While geopolitics borrowed heavily from evolutionary biology

121

to justify the expansionary self-interest of the state, it retained the mechanistic utilitarianism of Descartes, Locke, and other Enlightenment thinkers when it came to exploiting the environment. Geography was presented on a flat one-dimensional plane. Nature was viewed as if it were made up of discrete phenomena, bits and pieces of material that could be treated in isolation and reduced to the status of economic resources. The idea of nature as a system of interacting relationships that are constantly affected and changed with the passage of time was absent from much of the geopolitical thinking. Although the term "ecology" had already been coined by the German scientist Ernst Haeckel in 1866, the scientific study of ecosystems was still in an embryonic stage and not yet developed enough to influence political thinking as either metaphor, model, or context.[12]

Geographers, for the most part, tend to busy themselves with spatial rather than temporal concerns, and their bias has been amply reflected in the science of geopolitics. To a great extent, geopolitics is a politics of spatial relationships and is far more concerned with strategic locations than dynamic processes. Still, even location has been narrowly conceived by the proponents of geopolitics to advance a strictly commercial and military agenda.

It is worth remembering that throughout human history, location has always been imbued with sacred meaning. People belonged to the land and the land was hallowed ground immersed in spiritual significance. The enclosure and commodification of the global commons changed humanity's long-standing relationship to the land. The land was disenchanted. It was fenced in, then stripped into sections and pieces. After centuries of people belonging to the land, the land now belonged to people. By the twentieth century, location was devoid of any remaining sacred value, reduced to an economic resource, and finally, with the ascendency of geopolitics, a strategic resource. Geopolitics made all of nature into a military map, so much strategic value was placed on navigable rivers, warm water ports, mountain barriers, rainfall seasons, and mineral deposits. In this sense, the science of geopolitics is the final acknowledgment of the dark side of modernity. Never before in history has all of nature been defined in purely strategic military terms.

122

Nicholas Spykman, a distinguished geopolitical thinker of the early twentieth century, defined several key geographic components that he said should affect the foreign policy considerations and formulations of every nation-state.

> Size affects [the nation's] relative strength ... natural resources influence population density and economic structure, which are themselves factors in the formulation of foreign policy. Location with reference to the equator and to oceans and landmasses determines nearness to centers of power, areas of conflict, and established roots of communication, and location with reference to immediate neighbors defines position in regard to potential enemies, thereby determining the basic problems of territorial security.[13]

Spykman was quick to point out the strategic importance of coal, oil, iron, and other minerals without which modern warfare could not be fought. Those countries that control the largest deposits of fossil fuels, metals, and minerals, and have a military-industrial complex of sufficient size to harness them for military and commercial use command the strategic advantage in the war of all against all.

The increasing mechanization and automation of weapons and warfare shifted the emphasis of geopolitics, making mineral resources as important as geographic barriers and food production in determining geopolitical advantage. In fact, the shift in military focus from the lay of the land to what lies under its seams reflects the profound transition from defensive to offensive military preparedness, and from power based traditionally on size of population to power based primarily on industrial capacity. Wars are increasingly fought with capital-intensive machinery and less with legions of men.

In the United States alone, the military consumes 40 percent of the thallium and titanium, 20 percent of the cobalt, copper, and garnet, 30 percent of the germanium and thorium, and, as was mentioned earlier, 6 percent of the petroleum.[14] Guaranteeing access to vital minerals, metals, and oil is a prime national security objective of the United States and every other industrialized nation. In 1985, Secretary of Defense Caspar Weinberger reiterated the long-standing commitment of the U.S. government to "protect U.S. economic interests worldwide by maintaining steady access to energy supplies, other critical resources, and foreign markets."[15]

Oil has figured prominently in strategic military thinking during most of the twentieth century, triggering regional conflicts and influencing world war. It's no wonder. The United States is dependent on foreign imports for one third of its oil needs.[16] France, Japan, England, and Germany are all dependent on foreign imports. In both World War I and World War II, Germany sought expansion into foreign territory, in part, to secure access to oil to run its industrial machines. France's eight-year colonial war to hold on to its Algerian colony was in large part motivated by a desire to secure the African nation's rich oil reserves. Nigeria successfully averted a secessionist movement by oil-rich Biafra in the late 1960s by waging a bloody civil war against the province. In 1974, Vietnam and China clashed on the Paracel Island in the South China Sea in anticipation of suspected offshore oil deposits. China prevailed.

In 1953, the United States and the United Kingdom helped support the overthrow of the Iranian government, which two years earlier had nationalized its oil industry, posing a potential threat to the Western powers. With the cooperation of the newly installed Shah of Iran, the United States established an oil consortium, ARAMCO, assuring U.S. oil companies a 40 percent share of Iranian oil production, with 40 percent going to the Anglo-Iranian Company, another 14 percent to Royal Dutch Shell, and 6 percent to Compagnie Française de Pétrole.

In 1960, five developing nations formed an oil cartel, the Organization of Petroleum Exporting Nations (OPEC). By 1983, OPEC boasted eight member states that accounted for one third of the world's oil production and two thirds of the known oil reserves.[17] During the 1973–74 oil crisis, Americans became aware of the tremendous strategic advantage that the OPEC cartel enjoyed, as gasoline prices quadrupled and long lines became commonplace at neighborhood gas stations.

The United States and the Soviet Union have both maintained a steady presence in the Middle East ever since World War II, each hoping to secure influence, access, and control over the region's rich oil reserves. In 1980, President Carter made clear the strategic importance of Middle Eastern oil, warning that "an attempt by any outside force to gain control of the Persian Gulf region will be regarded as an assault on the vital interests of the United States of America, and such an assault will be repelled by any means necessary, including military force."[18]

In the summer of 1990, Saddam Hussein of Iraq invaded the tiny oil-rich nation of Kuwait. Just a few days later, President Bush ordered air, land, and naval forces to the Middle East to "protect" U.S. oil interests. Within a few weeks the U.S. government had deployed over two hundred thousand troops to Saudi Arabia in the swiftest mobilization of military equipment and personnel in history. The President informed the American public that the domestic economy had become more dependent on Middle Eastern oil than at any other time in history, and that the billion-dollars-a-month military commitment to keep American soldiers stationed in the desert of Saudi Arabia was essential to protect the national security interest of the nation.

Minerals have also been a source of continuing friction and open conflict as every industrial nation has sought access to or control over the raw materials necessary to secure its military-industrial complex. In his anthology *Global Resources and Industrial Conflict,* Arthur H. Westing chronicles some of the wars that were fought in the present century over precious minerals. The Lorraine region near Luxembourg, one of the few rich iron ore ranges of Europe, has been fought over by France and Germany for the better part of the twentieth century. In 1944, the Soviet Union annexed the Petsamo territory in Finland, in part to secure possession of nickel deposits. The Congo civil war in the early 1960s was fought over copper deposits in Katanga province.[19]

Today, chromium has become a metal of vital national security interest, as it is an essential alloy in the making of stainless steel and there are no substitutes for it in the production process. Most of the chromium reserves are found in the Soviet Union, Zimbabwe, and South Africa, giving all these nations a geopolitical advantage. South Africa is of particular strategic importance in the global game of geopolitics because it contains "vast reserves of such strategic minerals as chromium, cobalt, cerancium, manganese, platinum, vanadian, gold, and diamonds."[20]

With the dawn of the nuclear age, uranium has suddenly become a strategic metal. Most of the world's uranium deposits are found in Canada, Australia, the United States, South Africa, the Soviet Union, and China, giving these nations a distinct geopolitical advantage in the nuclear arena.

The industrial nations, then, continue to maintain a strong military presence and exert their influence and power around the world, in part, to secure continued access to raw materials. Much of the geopolitical thinking of the past century has centered on the strategic implications of mineral and oil deposits. Helge Hveem of the University of Norway concludes that a shortage of 15 percent to 30 percent in the supply of a dozen basic minerals—including titanium, platinum, cobalt, tin, chromium, aluminum, copper, silver, nickel, and tungsten—could result in a serious downturn in the U.S. economy.[21] In 1979, the British business journal *The Economist* estimated that a 20 percent reduction in aluminum imports alone could result in a 3 percent reduction in the U.S. gross national product.[22]

By enclosing virtually every strategic resource of the planet, nation-states have created their own self-perpetuating form of economic and military warfare. To grow and expand in a global economy, nation-states must continue to secure access to raw materials and markets. In the modern era, virtually every ounce of coal, uranium, tin, cobalt, and the like has been staked out, fenced in, and made the commercial possession of a state power, to be used as a carrot on a stick to secure commercial advantage or military domination. The result is a world rife in political and economic intrigue, a world that has been torn and shattered by regional conflicts and world wars and left environmentally decimated by both commercial and military exploitation.

17

GEOPOLITICAL GAMES

GEOPOLITICAL THINKING HAS dominated the external affairs of states during the twentieth century, and much of the intellectual credit is attributable to the theories espoused by a single man. Sir Halford Mackinder was a British geographer. In 1919 he published *Democratic Ideals and Reality*, in which he outlined a theory of geopolitics that to this day has continued to influence the foreign policy of nations.[1]

Mackinder's theory is known as the heartland thesis. The geographer took a careful reading of world history and, applying it to the geography of the planet, concluded that the pivot area, which has long determined the fate of empires and people, is Central Asia. Because of their superior mobility, the nomadic horsemen of Central Asia once effectively dominated the Eurasian continent from the China Sea to the English Channel. Their hegemony was challenged and then eclipsed by the rise of the great maritime powers of northern and western Europe after 1500. For four hundred years the balance of power rested with the great coastal sea powers—first Portugal and Spain, later the Scandinavian countries and the Netherlands, and finally England.

Mackinder believed that with the advent of the railroad and the telegraph the era of unchallenged maritime power was no longer assured. The railroad, Mackinder argued, provided Central Asia with a new, superior form of mechanized "horsepower" that might well tilt the balance of power once again from maritime to land-based power.[2]

Realizing that the final enclosure of the global commons made the entire planet a single geopolitical field, Mackinder set about the task of redefining regions in terms of the new strategic reality. Mackinder identified the pivot area of Asia—extending along the great central continental plain—as the heartland, or center, of the world, an area occupied by the Soviet Union. A second geopolitical region surrounds the heartland. The "inner crescent" includes Germany, Austria, Turkey, India, and China. A third geopolitical region, the "outer crescent," forms a second ring of encirclement around the heartland and includes Britain, South Africa, the United States, Canada, Australia, and Japan.[3]

Mackinder surveyed the globe and noted that nine twelfths of the surface of the planet is covered by the great oceans. Of the remaining three twelfths, which makes up the landmass, two twelfths are composed of what he called the "world island," the contiguous areas of Europe, Asia, and Africa.[4] Mackinder argued that the pressure point of world history has always been located in the plains of Eastern Europe and Western and Central Asia, where landlocked people have continually pushed outward to the Atlantic Ocean on the western front and the Pacific Ocean to the east.

With the railroad, telegraph, and telephone forming a powerful land link across the heartland and the entire world island, the possibility now existed that a single powerful state, or alliance of states, might emerge in Eurasia, with access to both vast industrial and agricultural resources and to the oceans on each side, allowing it to build a great naval armada and ultimately dominate the entire globe.

Being a loyal Englishman, Mackinder was anxious to find the appropriate geopolitical strategy that would continue to assure British hegemony in this new twentieth-century world. The key, according to Mackinder, is the inner crescent of states that form a "vast buffer zone" in any future conflict between sea power and land power.[5] Eastern Europe, then, and especially Germany, became the critical geopolitical factors in shaping military strategy.

Mackinder's theory rests on the central assumption that whoever controls Eastern Europe ultimately controls the destiny of civilization. His famous dictum, which has served as gospel and guidepost for much of the political and military thinking of the century, states:

> Who rules East Europe commands the Heartland. Who rules the Heartland commands the World Island. Who rules the World Island commands the world.[6]

Mackinder believed that Germany was in the best strategic position to control Eastern Europe and dominate the heartland. He warned that German expansion into Eastern Europe or, worse still, a German-Russian alliance could effectively arrest control over all Eurasia, threatening and eventually undermining British hegemony, which had always been based on maritime encirclement of the world island. To prevent either German or Russian dominance or a joint alliance of the two powers, England and the United States forged alliances with Russia against Germany in both world wars.

Mackinder's heartland thesis is not without its shortcomings. To begin with, the geographer grossly exaggerated the value of the railroad as an effective means of tying together the great landmass of Eurasia. He also somewhat underestimated the inherent strategic advantage of maritime power in the geopolitics of world dominance. As William Thompson and George Modelski pointed out in their history *Sea Power in Global Politics,* "A power aspiring to or exercising world leadership requires capacity for global reach and sea power is tailor-made for that purpose." According to Thompson and Modelski, a careful analysis of the Columbian era suggests that for the past five centuries, "changes in the position of world leadership are associated with shifts in the distribution of sea power."[7] Naval theoreticians like Alfred Thayer Mahan argued as such during the early decades of the century and their thinking inspired Britain, at least, to support what it called a "two-power" standard: maintaining a naval fleet that was "at least equal to the sum of the two next-largest fleets in the world." In 1916, the United States passed a naval act authorizing the building of "a navy second to none," realizing that its long-term security interests rested squarely on the decks of its great warships.

The introduction of the submarine in World War I greatly expanded the naval domain to the deep reaches of the oceanic commons, opening up a new strategic front and making the oceans even more important in global geopolitical thinking.[8]

Most important of all, Mackinder overlooked the advent of air power, which brought the atmospheric commons into the geopolitical arena for the first time. Interestingly enough, when Mackinder delivered his lecture on "The Geographic Pivot of History" for the World Geographical Society in London in 1904, a certain Mr. Amery rose from the audience with an observation that, in hindsight, turned out to be a prophetic insight of incalculable import. He remarked that "both the sea and the railways are in the future going to be supplemented by the air as a means of locomotion, and when we come to that . . . a great deal of this geographical distribution must lose its importance, and the successful powers will be those who have the greatest industrial bases."[9] Forty years later, British and American bombers flew sorties over Germany and Eastern Europe, bombing and destroying the rail links transporting German soldiers and ordnance to both the Eastern and Western fronts.

Despite flaws and errors in judgment, the Mackinder theory has remained a point of reference for geopolitical thinking up until this day. Certainly, concern over the control of the Eurasian heartland greatly affected the thinking of the post–World War II era. Even during the war, Harry S Truman restated the long-held Anglo-American sentiment that neither Germany nor Russia should be allowed to control the "world island." When Germany invaded Russia the then Missouri politician remarked, "If we see Germany is winning we ought to help Russia and if Russia is winning we ought to help Germany and that way let them kill as many as possible. . . ."[10]

In the last months of the war, Russian troops cut a path through Eastern Europe directly to the doorsteps of Berlin. With the support of Communist partisans in each country, the Soviets began a process of establishing client regimes. Thus, on the eve of the Yalta Conference, which was to decide the postwar disposition of Europe, the Soviets were well on the way to creating a secure perimeter stretching the length and breadth of the "inner crescent."

The struggle for control of the inner crescent among Churchill, Roosevelt, and Stalin set the framework for the discussions at Yalta. The Russians were determined to annex Poland, Stalin arguing that a pro-Soviet regime was "not only a question of honor, but one of security . . . of the life and death of the Soviet state."[11] Stalin reminded the allies that twice in the twentieth century Germany had been able to invade Russia by way of the Polish corridor. While Roosevelt seemed sympathetic, Churchill drew the sword at the prospect of a Russian takeover.

When the Soviets failed to live up to their agreement at Yalta to allow free elections in Eastern Europe after the war, the allies went on the offensive. Churchill visited the United States and warned of an "iron curtain" descending over Europe. President Truman warned the American people that "the Soviet Union and its agents have destroyed the independence and democratic character of a whole series of nations in Eastern and Central Europe," which was affecting the long-range national security interests of the United States.[12] Truman urged and won congressional approval for the Marshall Plan to rebuild the shattered economies of Western Europe, in order to counter the Russian threat. At the same time, the allied powers began discussions on the formation of a North Atlantic Treaty Organization, a military alliance aimed at containing the Soviets well inside the inner crescent.

The final showdown between East and West came in 1948 in Germany, which had been jointly occupied by the allied powers since the end of the war, although in reality the Soviet Union controlled the eastern part of the country, and the other allies controlled the west. The city of Berlin remained jointly occupied and cordoned off into sectors controlled by each power. The Western allies agreed to allow the formation of a West German assembly to draw up a national constitution and introduce a postwar German currency. The plan was to establish a West German state that would include the powerful industrial region of the Ruhr and provide a base for the long-term billeting of American military forces.

On June 23, 1948, the Western powers announced the circulation of the new German deutsche mark in the western zones of occupation. The next day, the Soviet Union cut entry into Berlin.

The American forces countered the Soviet land blockade with a historic airlift, shuttling supplies into West Berlin around the clock. The Berlin airlift was successful, forcing the Soviets to accept the reality of a new West German state with American troops permanently positioned in it. The Berlin airlift also demonstrated the superiority of airpower over land power, changing the dynamics of geopolitical thinking for the rest of the century.

On August 24, 1949, the Western allies implemented the NATO Alliance, dividing Eurasia on the western side of the inner crescent. The Soviets countered six years later, on May 14, 1955, with the formation of the Warsaw Pact, securing the eastern side of the inner crescent. With the division of Europe, the West assumed that the Soviet Union would be unable to extend its control to the Atlantic and gain hegemony over the world island. The Soviet Union, in turn, assumed that the Western maritime powers would be unable to penetrate the inner crescent and the Polish corridor leading into the Soviet heartland of Central Asia.

The Communist victory in China in 1948, and later the North Korean invasion of South Korea, kindled concern that the Soviet Union might seek new alliances in the East, giving the Russians clear passage to the Pacific Ocean. Determined to contain the Soviets, and mindful that access to the great ocean on its eastern flank might give it a geopolitical advantage and perhaps even eventual control over the world island, the United States initiated a policy of complete "containment," designed to encircle the Soviets on all sides. NATO was followed by the Central Treaty Organization (CENTO) in West Asia and the South East Asia Treaty Organization (SEATO), effectively sealing up the Russians along a wide geographic front.

The post–World War II political configuration, which is only now unraveling as we approach the twenty-first century, is steeped in geopolitical thinking. It is rather remarkable that a theory which was suspect from the beginning and held in contempt by more than a few of the best minds of the day could nevertheless have held sway, influencing the politics of an entire century.

Even more curious is the theory's influence today in the wake of both the nuclear and space age and the revolutionary changes in warfare that make the very notion of strategic geographic advantage increasingly irrelevant. Still, geopolitics continues to dominate the thinking of the superpowers, a fact made more ominous by advances in military technology of such overwhelming destructive capability that they dwarf the playing field for which they were designed. The lethal combination of geopolitical thinking and space-age military technology remains the central threat to the continued existence of the planet and human civilization.

The nuclear age has fundamentally altered the context of political relations, casting a final doubt on the underlying assumptions upon which our modern notions of security are based. The very idea of global expansion and national autonomy become unrealizable goals in a nuclear world.

A brief survey of the geopolitics of the post–World War II era and the changes in military technology of the past half century demonstrate the intellectual bankruptcy of our current thinking about security and the urgent need to entertain new approaches to international politics in the coming century.

18

ENCLOSURE
IN A NUCLEAR AGE

IN AUGUST 1945, the United States dropped atomic bombs on the Japanese cities of Hiroshima and Nagasaki. When President Truman reported the bombings to the American public, he claimed a limited objective: to shorten the war in the Pacific and thus save the lives of American military personnel. Many historians now believe that behind the public utterances, administration officials had in mind a second, more far-reaching objective—to establish the geopolitical ground for the postwar world. According to historian Gar Alperovitz, Truman had hoped that the destructive force of the atomic blasts would frighten the Soviets and force Stalin into accepting a much reduced role in postwar Europe. The United States had not, however, anticipated how close the Soviets were to detonating their own nuclear device. In 1949 the Soviets successfully tested a nuclear bomb, dashing any lingering hopes the United States might have entertained about hegemony over the geopolitical arena.[1]

Even with the coming of the nuclear age, geopolitical thinking continued to reflect the assumptions of an earlier generation of geographers and military tacticians. With the Soviets enjoying a superior strategic advantage on the Eurasian landmass, U.S. foreign policy analysts concluded that the only effective way to counterbalance the threat of a complete takeover of the world island was through nuclear deterrence. From the early 1950s, the United

States has maintained a policy of encircling the Soviet Union with nuclear weapons.[2] Land bases along the inner crescent and naval bases along the outer crescent have provided staging areas for launching bomber and missile attacks against a potential movement of Russian tank units across the border into West Germany.

Tensions between the two new superpowers heightened during the early 1950s, with the Soviets feeling besieged by the nuclear encirclement policy of the West, and the United States and its allies feeling increasingly vulnerable because of what they regarded as Soviet-sponsored aggression in the third world, where Communist insurgents were battling to overthrow pro-Western governments. In January 1954 President Dwight D. Eisenhower and Secretary of State John Foster Dulles announced a new foreign policy whose twisted assumptions graphically illustrate both the pathological thinking upon which geopolitics is based and the potential cataclysmic consequences that flow from its continued use as an instrument of foreign policy.

The policy was called "massive retaliation." Concerned with the "nibbling away" of the "free world" by Communist-inspired "liberation" movements, Dulles warned that any form of Communist aggression anywhere in the world might risk the launching of a full-scale nuclear attack by the United States against the Soviet Union.[3] The Dulles doctrine underscored the great change that had taken place in the notion of security as a result of the enclosure of the global commons and the increased reliance on far-flung resources and markets. Where just five hundred years ago vulnerability lay just beyond the city gates and security just inside the city walls, today vulnerability extends to events in every corner of the globe, and security rests on the ability and willingness to destroy every living creature on the face of the earth. Security in the nuclear age has become a dance macabre to the very edge of existence.

According to Dulles, "the way to deter aggression is for the free community to be willing and able to respond vigorously at places and with means of its own choosing," including the possibility of massive retaliation. "The ability to get to the verge without getting into the war is the necessary art. If you cannot master it you will inevitably get into war. If you try to run away from it, if you are scared to go to the brink you are lost."[4] Nine years later the United States and the Soviet Union faced off in the Cuban missile crisis, bringing the world to the brink of nuclear annihilation. In that instance, the Soviets blinked, losing face and saving civilization.

In the 1960s, the doctrine of "massive retaliation" gave way to "flexible response." Under the new doctrine, any aggression by Warsaw Pact nations would be met first with NATO conventional forces. If conventional weapons proved insufficient, the allies would escalate to tactical nuclear weapons, and as the last resort, a long-range nuclear attack on the Soviet Union. In 1964, Secretary of Defense Robert McNamara announced a further refinement in strategic nuclear policy, which he euphemistically called "Mutual Assured Destruction" (MAD).

> The cornerstone of our strategic policy continues to be to deter deliberate nuclear attack upon the United States, or its allies, by maintaining a highly reliable ability to inflict an unacceptable degree of damage upon any single aggressor, or combination of aggressors, at any time during the course of a strategic nuclear exchange—even after absorbing a surprise nuclear strike.[5]

The MAD doctrine rests on the assumption that the enemy will not attack first because its own cities and population would be destroyed in retaliation.

As long as nuclear missile accuracy was still crude and unreliable, the superpowers felt they had no choice but to target large industrial and population areas to ensure victory. In the past decade, however, a new generation of highly accurate land-based ICBM missiles were developed which can travel thousands of miles, striking within hundreds of feet of a selected target. The new rocketry raises the possibility of a precision nuclear exchange designed exclusively to knock out enemy missile silos, airbases, and other military targets. A military doctrine—nuclear utilization targeting strategy (NUTS)—has been developed to accompany the new technological capabilities.[6] Today, the Pentagon relies on both MAD and NUTS. Submarine-based ICBMs are still highly inaccurate and are therefore targeted against cities. The more accurate land-based ICBMs are targeted against the enemy's strategic nuclear forces.

Over the years, the strategic nuclear doctrines have changed, reflecting the greater sophistication in weaponry and the changing temperament of the public and foreign policy communities. Still, today, as at the beginning of the nuclear age, the security of every man, woman, and child on the planet continues to lie in the "threat" of using a weapon that could destroy all of civilization and much of nature in less than half an hour.

The potential of a nuclear conflagration has expanded and deepened over the past several decades with the commercial enclosure and militarization of each sphere of the global commons. Bacon's dream of "shaking the earth to its foundation" has been given new meaning as nuclear strength has been extended from the land and ocean surface to the oceanic depths, the atmosphere, the electromagnetic spectrum, and outer space. Today, one thousand land-based missiles tipped with 2,450 nuclear bombs sit in underground silos waiting for their trip over the ocean. Thousands of additional nuclear warheads are tucked under the wings of bombers aloft in the atmospheric commons virtually around the clock. Along the ocean floor, thirty-two ballistic missile submarines lie in wait with five thousand additional nuclear bombs. Each Trident submarine is armed with enough warheads to destroy 192 of the largest cities in the Soviet Union in a matter of minutes.[7]

Even the electromagnetic spectrum has become a base of operation for nuclear warfare. The electronic communications revolution has radically transformed the art of warfare since World War II. Where power and speed used to be the primary variables in both offensive and defensive warfare, they have now been joined by two new considerations, transparency and stealth.[8] In an age where time is being continually compressed and space continually shrunk by new military technology, the ability to detect quickly enemy matériel and movement, as well as effectively hide from an adversary, becomes an increasingly important strategic consideration in war. The electromagnetic spectrum has become the new staging area for harnessing sophisticated computing technology, advanced sensors, and communication systems into an interactive network of electronic spies whose job is to monitor military movement in every sphere of the global commons.

The transparency and stealth revolutions introduce a new psychological dimension to warfare. While the art of "hide and seek" has always played a prominent role in warfare, the omnipresent eye of modern spy technologies creates a condition of permanent paranoia. The idea of a safe haven becomes absurd. There are no truly private places left anywhere on the planet when an infrared sensor can detect the heat of a single body from hundreds of miles away and a satellite can photograph a human face from outer space.

The rules of engagement have changed considerably from the days when adversaries met face-to-face in combat. Even in the waning years of the chivalric code, armies preferred to confront each other openly, believing that cloak-and-dagger tactics were a sign of cowardice.

Telescopic spyglasses were the first modern transparency technology, used by ship captains.[9] They tripled the range of vision, giving them a unique military advantage on the high seas. On land, the increasing power and accuracy of firearms forced the introduction of stealth technology in combat. The shift from musket to breech-loading rifle and machine gun increased the range and sweep of trajectory from a few hundred to a few thousand yards. The armies of the nineteenth century, with their brightly colored uniforms, became sitting ducks for the new weaponry. Camouflage, the first modern stealth technology, was introduced by the English, who switched to khaki uniforms after the Boer War.[10] The French were the first to introduce techniques for camouflaging both soldiers and equipment. A camouflage section was added to the French army and the high command began hiring well-known artists, including Forain and Segonzac to "dissimulate the big guns and other conspicuous objects."[11] By the end of World War I, the French camouflage section boasted three thousand artists. Their insignia was a chameleon.[12]

Today's advances in transparency and stealth technologies combine new knowledge in the earth sciences with new communication tools. In his essay "Whole Earth Security," Daniel Deudney points out that new discoveries in oceanography, geophysics, aeronomy, and astrophysics have provided scientists with a wealth of data on features of the planet that had previously remained unknown and unexplored, including "the floating continental plates, the Van Allen radiation belts, the jet streams, and the protective ozone layer."[13]

The Pentagon has financed most of the research into these previously hidden layers of the global commons, realizing that "detection and tracking requires intimate and continuous knowledge of the natural phenomena against which weapons must be distinguished."[14] The U.S. military also supported much of the pioneering research in computing that is so crucial in detection and monitoring activity. As Deudney points out, the switch from vacuum tube to transistor technology was partially financed by the Department of Defense in order to pack greater computing power into the nose cones of missiles. The National Security Agency, the federal agency charged with the task of monitoring Soviet communications and gathering intelligence data from around the world, "reportedly maintains a dozen acres of the largest computers linked together to make billions of calculations per second." The American public might be surprised to learn that this rather obscure agency "maintains electronic files of every electronic signal ever recorded of the Soviet Union." In addition, the Pentagon's "worldwide military command and control system" relies on a combination of satellites, computers, and ground receiving stations to monitor virtually everything of military significance on the earth.[15]

In the new era of nuclear warfare, invisible electronic walls replace the hard walled surfaces of medieval and early modern cities. The first such electronic walls, the Defense Early Warning System, or DEW line, was set up over Canada and the northern United States in the 1950s. The DEW line was the first of a series of radar barriers designed to detect incoming planes and missiles.[16] Today, the North American Aerospace Defense command (NORAD) can track an object the size of an astronaut's glove in outer space. A ground radar system made up of infrared sensors and giant forty-inch telescopes can see objects in outer space that are an inch and a half in size.[17]

In addition to its plethora of new transparency technologies, the Pentagon recently unveiled its new stealth bombers, billion-dollar attack planes specially designed to evade enemy radar. A stealth submarine is currently being built by General Dynamics for the Department of the Navy. All of the sophisticated new transparency and stealth technologies have made Earth's electromagnetic spectrum a critical military arena in the geopolitics of the nuclear age.

Increasing reliance on the electromagnetic spectrum has inevitably led to increased military interest in the space commons. In March 1983, President Ronald Reagan announced that the United States would initiate a new military program that administration officials called the Strategic Defense Initiative and that the popular media called the "Star Wars" program. While the question of the militarization of space has been raised as far back as 1956, with the Russian launch of the first space satellite, the space commons has remained an adjunct to geopolitical thinking, its usefulness still lying in the intelligence-gathering arena.

The President outlined an ambitious plan to establish a defense shield around the earth, which could intercept and destroy incoming Soviet missiles from staging areas in outer space. Using space battle stations, the Pentagon envisioned employing a new generation of energy-directed weapons—X-ray lasers, microwaves, electromagnetic and particle beam weapons—to destroy Soviet missiles shortly after launch or while traveling through outer space on their flight path to American and allied targets. Enemy missiles that successfully penetrated the outer space "peace shield" would be shot down as they reentered Earth's atmosphere.

The enclosure and militarization of the space commons has become the newest goal in the postwar "nuclearization" of the global commons. The SDI program is also seen as a way to breathe new life into a sagging military-industrial complex.

During the 1980s, billions of dollars were invested in the Star Wars program despite the fact that many prominent physicists and computer scientists viewed the concept as theoretically suspect and technologically unfeasible. Still, the idea attracted many supporters from the foreign policy community and military establishment who, no doubt, saw the Star Wars shield as a bold new complement to traditional geopolitical strategy. The idea of encircling the

140

Soviet Union and the world island from outer space added an important new element to geopolitical thinking. The militarization of the space commons would give the United States a new line of defense, a second tier on the "outer crescent" that could bolster the superiority it already enjoyed on the world's oceanic commons. By controlling both the oceanic and space commons, the United States's encirclement of the Soviet Union would be nearly complete.

Speaking before the Senate Armed Services Committee in February 1984, Secretary of State Caspar Weinberger voiced the administration's enthusiasm for the Star Wars program, asserting that it would give back to the United States the strategic geopolitical advantage it enjoyed for a brief moment of time after World War II—when it was the only nation with nuclear weapons and could claim clear military superiority over the global commons.[18]

Nuclear weapons and missiles have now given the United States and other nations power even greater than the forces of nature. Indeed, the ingenuity of modern man has far exceeded the expectations of Enlightenment thinkers, creating machines of such overwhelming force that the natural world itself can be eliminated with the push of a button.

Ironically, in our quest to become ever more autonomous from the environment, we have created weapons of mass destruction that are increasingly autonomous as well. Now their autonomy threatens ours. The Department of Defense is increasingly replacing human decision making with preprogrammed computer scenarios in its strategic decision making. Military planners point out that nuclear missile systems are becoming so complex, and the time between launch and delivery to the target is becoming so compressed, that human beings are simply too slow to respond effectively to the critical data in time to make the appropriate counterresponse. The Department of Defense's Advance Research Project Agency (DARPA) advocates automating our nuclear defenses against attacks and predicts that "where systems must react so rapidly . . . it is likely that almost complete reliance will have to be placed on automated decisions."[19]

Preprogramming World War III is a terrifying prospect. Nonetheless, our children's generation may well grow up in a world where computer programs will decide the fate of the earth. This prospect becomes all the more frightening given the history of false alarms that have triggered full-scale nuclear alerts in the past. The Department of Defense's computers have often erred, identifying flocks of birds and other objects as incoming missiles. Nuclear catastrophe has been averted by human intervention only at the last minute on several occasions. The abandonment of human decision making in the form of preprogrammed computer responses could well result in an accidental nuclear war in the future.

The military battlefield has now been extended far out into space and far down into the oceans. Virtually every sphere of the global commons has been enclosed and exploited for military advantage. The nation-states have used the tools of modern science and technology to secure the world and in the process have created a world that is less secure with each passing day. The nuclearization of the global commons—the land, oceans, electromagnetic spectrum, atmosphere, and space realms—now puts every living thing on the planet within striking distance.

Today, the United States and the Soviet Union claim a combined arsenal of fifty thousand nuclear warheads, the equivalent of fifteen billion tons of TNT, or three tons of TNT for every man, woman, and child on earth.[20] Some of our hydrogen bombs are so powerful that in sheer megatonnage they exceed the total firepower expended during all of World War II by all parties to the conflict. The U.S. stockpile is now sufficient to destroy every Soviet city fifty times over.[21] Analysts estimate that within twenty minutes of the commencement of an all-out nuclear war, 160 million Americans would die.[22] In a global nuclear exchange, over 60 percent of the human race would perish immediately and another 25 percent over time.[23] Those who did survive would likely have to face the prospect of a nuclear winter.

The impact of a nuclear exchange would force vast amounts of dust into the atmosphere, perhaps as much as 200 million tons. The heavy dust particles in the atmosphere could block up to 90 percent of the sunlight from reaching the earth's surface and cause a plunge in worldwide temperatures by 10 to 15 percent centigrade.[24] Agricultural production would cease over much, if not all, of the globe. Radical fluctuations in the weather could mean additional calamities, including super hurricanes, tornados, earthquakes, and floods on an unimaginable scale. The ozone layer would be seriously, if not irreversibly damaged, leaving human beings, animals, and plants vulnerable to massive doses of deadly ultraviolet radiation once the dust eventually settled.[25]

This, then, is the ultimate price we may have to pay for the military enclosure of the globe. For five hundred years nation-states have fought each other for control over each of the earth's commons. To secure their objective they have developed more powerful and sophisticated incendiary weapons. Now with the nuclear bomb, they have enough incendiary power at their disposal to extinguish most of life and much of the material scaffolding of civilization. The nuclearization of the global commons has made the present generation the least secure in human history.

The late social critic Arthur Koestler observed that "from the dawn of consciousness until August 6, 1945, man had to live with the prospects of his death as an individual; since that day when the first bomb outshone the sun over Hiroshima, mankind as a whole has had to live with the prospect of its extinction as a species."[26]

In ancient China, the philosopher Mencius was once asked how best to defend the state and secure the lives of its subjects. He said, "Dig deeper your moats; build higher your walls; guard them along with your people."[27] Today, in the expedient world of geopolitics and nuclear armaments, there is simply no place left to hide and no corner left to secure. Everyone becomes vulnerable and no one is safe.

At present, at least six nations have nuclear stockpiles. Several others are suspected of either having nuclear explosives or the capability of making them. Upon learning that India had detonated a "peaceful nuclear device," then Prime Minister Zulfikar Ali Bhutto of Pakistan warned the world that his people would "eat grass" if necessary to finance their way into the nuclear club.[28] As long as superpowers and developing nations alike continue to look to nuclear weaponry as their salvation, the prospect of real security will continue to elude the human race.

An analogy often used by peace activists best illustrates the reductio ad absurdum of geopolitical thinking in a nuclear age.

They ask us to imagine two people in a room full of gasoline, one holding up eight matches, the other only three. Can the one with eight matches dare claim a geopolitical advantage by dint of his superior firepower? In a world populated by nation-states each wielding a nuclear club, everyone becomes a potential victim of what the Russian nuclear physicist Andrei Sakharov called "collective suicide."[29]

19

GENE WARS

THE SUPERPOWERS AND other industrialized nations have spent untold billions of dollars in their attempts to secure and exploit the land, ocean, atmosphere, electromagnetic spectrum, and now the space commons for military purposes. In recent years, military attention has also turned to the microscopic commons, the earth's biological gene pool. Breakthroughs in genetic engineering technology have renewed military interest in biological weapons and generated grave concern over the prospect of a new biological arms race that could well prove as destabilizing and deadly in the future as the nuclear arms race.

Biological warfare (BW) involves the use of living organisms for military purposes. Biological weapons can be viral, bacterial, fungal, rickettsial, and protozoan. They can be used to destroy animals, crops, and people. Biological agents can mutate, reproduce, multiply, and spread over a large geographic terrain by wind, animal, and insect transmission. Once released, many biological pathogens are capable of developing viable niches and maintaining themselves in the environment indefinitely. Traditional biological agents include yersinia pestis (the plague), tularemia, rift valley fever, coxiella burnetii (Q fever), eastern equine encephalitis, and smallpox.

Biological warfare has never been widely used because of the expense and danger involved in processing and stockpiling large volumes of toxic materials and the difficulty in targeting the dissemination of biological agents. Advances in genetic engineering technologies over the past decade, however, have made biological warfare a viable possibility for the first time in history.

In a May 1986 report to the Committee on Appropriations of the U.S. House of Representatives, the Department of Defense (DOD) pointed out that recombinant DNA and other genetic engineering technologies are finally making biological warfare an effective military option. Genetic engineers are cloning previously unattainable quantities of "traditional" pathogens. The technology can also be used to create "novel" pathogens never before seen. The report concluded:

> . . . [Advances in biotechnology] permit the elaboration of a wide variety of "novel" warfare materials. . . . The novel agents represent the newly found ability to modify, improve, or produce large amounts of natural materials or organisms previously considered to be militarily insignificant due to problems such as availability, stability, infectivity, and producibility.[1]

The report goes on to say:

> Potent toxins which until now were available only in minute quantities, and only upon isolation from immense amounts of biological materials, can now be prepared in industrial quantities after a relatively short developmental period. This process consists of identifying genes, encoding for the desired molecule, and transferring the sequence to a receptive microorganism which then becomes capable of producing the substance. The recombinant organisms may then be cultured and grown at any desired scale. . . . Large quantities of compounds, previously available only in minute amounts, thus become available at relatively low costs.[2]

With recombinant DNA technology, it is now possible to develop "a nearly infinite variety of what might be termed 'designer agents.' "[3] The DOD report concludes that the new developments in genetic engineering technology enable "the rapid exploitation of

146

nature's resources for warfare purposes in ways not even imagined ten to fifteen years ago."[4] In August 1986, Douglas J. Feith, then deputy secretary of defense, noted the near impossibility of defending against this newfound ability to genetically engineer biowarfare agents:

> It is now possible to synthesize BW agents tailored to military specifications. The technology that makes possible so-called "designer drugs" also makes possible designer BW. . . . It is [becoming] a simple matter to produce new agents but a problem to develop antidotes. New agents can be produced in hours; antidotes may take years. To gauge the magnitude of the antidote problem, consider the many years and millions of dollars that have been invested as yet without success in developing a means of countering a single biological agent outside the BW field—the AIDS virus. Such an investment far surpasses the resources available for BW defense work.[5]

In many ways, current research in gene splicing parallels earlier research in the nuclear field in the 1940s and 1950s. The data base developed from nuclear technology was convertible to both military and industrial purposes. Similarly, the data base being developed for commercial genetic engineering in the fields of agriculture, animal husbandry, and human medicine is potentially convertible to the development of a wide range of novel viruses that can attack human, plant, and animal populations.

Recombinant DNA "designer" weapons can be created in many ways. The new technologies can be used to program genes into infectious microorganisms to increase their antibiotic resistance, virulence, and environmental stability. It is possible to insert lethal genes into harmless microorganisms, resulting in biological agents that the body recognizes as friendly and does not resist. It is even possible to insert genes into organisms that affect regulatory functions that control mood and behavior, mental status, body temperature, and other functions. Scientists say they may be able to clone selective toxins to eliminate specific racial or ethnic groups whose genotypical makeup predisposes them to certain disease patterns. Genetic engineering can also be used to destroy specific strains or species of agricultural plants or domestic animals, if the intent is to cripple the economy of a country. In addition, advances have been made in the creation of genetically engineered microbes that are designed to self-destruct after a given period of time. The implications of this development, and other advances in genetic engineering, are extraordinary.

The new genetic engineering technologies provide a versatile form of weaponry that can be used for a wide variety of military purposes, ranging from terrorism and counterinsurgency operations to large-scale warfare aimed at entire populations. Unlike nuclear technologies, genetic engineering can be cheaply developed and produced, requires far less scientific expertise, and can be effectively employed in many diverse settings.

Under the rubric of defense research, the U.S. Department of Defense launched a significant research and development effort in the 1980s. In 1981, the Pentagon budget for "defensive" biological warfare research was only $15.1 million. By 1986, the DOD budget had grown to $90 million.[6] The various branches of the armed services now work with virtually every major pathogen in the world, from exotic viral diseases such as hemorrhagic fevers, chikungunya, and dengue fever to newly discovered viruses such as AIDS. The Department of Defense claims that most of the work is unclassified and intended to provide the military with defensive protection in the form of vaccines and antidotes. Despite DOD assurances that its biological warfare program is defensive in nature and not in violation of the Biological Weapons Convention, signed by the United States and many other nations in 1972, observers are alarmed over the increased commitment of funds for genetic engineering research.

The Reagan Administration was particularly concerned over what it perceived as a "gene gap." In the fall of 1984, Secretary of Defense Caspar Weinberger told members of Congress that he had obtained "new evidence that the Soviet Union has maintained its offensive biological warfare programs and that it is exploring genetic engineering to expand its program's scope." Weinberger went on to warn Congress that "it is essential and urgent that we develop and field adequate biological and toxin protection."[7]

Convinced that the Soviets were violating the Convention and

148

broadening the gene gap by launching a rigorous research and development program in genetic weaponry, the DOD announced intentions to respond, in turn, with its own ambitious "defensive" program. Whether or not the Soviet Union or the United States has been violating the Biological Weapons Convention, as each has accused the other, is still a matter of conjecture and speculation, despite the rhetoric of both sides. Nonetheless, other nations are likely to react to the new U.S. intention to accelerate defensive research by increasing their own research and development efforts.[8] The missile gap paranoia of the past several decades is likely to be followed by the gene gap paranoia of the 1990s as each nation's accusations and counteraccusations tear away at the fabric of the Biological Weapons Convention, preparing the groundwork for a deadly arms race with genetic engineering weaponry.

The militarization of the genetic commons poses a new security threat quite unlike anything we have experienced in the past. By extending the art and technology of warfare into the microscopic world of chromosomes and genes, the war states of the modern age threaten to wreak havoc on the most intimate commons that exists on Earth, the building blocks of the biological process. Targeting and destroying the blueprints of life undermines the last bastion of security in an increasingly destabilized world.

PART THREE

THE CULTURE OF PRIVACY

20

PERSONAL SECURITY AND THE PRIVATIZATION OF LIFE

POLITICAL SECURITY CONCERNS have, in the past, focused almost exclusively on institutional arrangements and power relationships. A new approach to political security is called for—one that can probe below the politics of society to address the politics of individual consciousness.

It is important to emphasize that our worldviews are not merely social abstractions, but, rather, the embodiment of our sense of self in the world. Transforming the politics of civilization will require a transformation in the personal politics of each human being. Healing the planet and healing ourselves are indispensable parts of the same restorative process.

The struggle for personal security, like the struggle of nations for economic, political, and military security, has been fought along the same Enlightenment plane during the whole of the modern age. The modern worldview, with its emphasis on the flight from nature and the drive for autonomy, has increasingly isolated Western man and woman from the environment, each other, and our own physical nature. More and more walls have been erected around our species and its individual members, creating an invisible prison that becomes increasingly cramped and insufferable with each passing day.

In medieval Europe, the individual was not yet separated from the natural world or the human community. Security was still found in close proximity rather than in isolation. The enclosure of the village commons undermined the human bond with nature that had been painstakingly erected over the centuries. As the landlords, merchants, and, later, industrialists enclosed sphere after sphere, severing traditional relationships between people, land, and nature, a radical new concept of human life emerged in the form of the bourgeois man and woman of the modern age. The rise of the bourgeoisie represents the beginning of a human enclosure movement.

Unlike other groups of the premodern era, the bourgeoisie is distinguished by its systematic withdrawal from the external world of group participation and its enthusiastic retreat into a new psychic world of self-reflection and self-absorption. The passage from the medieval world of sacred, communal arrangements to the industrial world of secular, market forces brought with it the fall of public man and the meteoric rise of the private individual.

The idea of self was not well developed in the Middle Ages. Up until the time of the enclosure movements, the well-being of the community and the expression of the common will took precedence over the needs of the individual. For that reason, personal achievement was barely recognized as an end in itself. Rather, a person's status was measured in terms of his or her contribution to the commonweal.

The notion of intimacy was also virtually nonexistent in medieval life. On the village commons and in the palace courtyards, people were always in each other's presence. Rarely, if ever, did individuals stray from the pack or venture out on their own. Historian Georges Duby says that "in the medieval era, solitary wandering was a symptom of insanity. No one would run such a risk who was not deviant or possessed or mad."[1] Withdrawal from group activity was frowned upon and openly chastised. In men, such behavior was ridiculed as effeminate and was often associated with greed or miserliness.

The architecture of the medieval period reflected the sense of undifferentiated group participation. In the early medieval era, the homes of the nobility were little more than barnlike structures. In the late medieval period a few rooms were added on, but most of the daily activities took place in public, in what was called the

154

"great hall." Over the years, the great hall has been steadily reduced in size and now exists only as a small ceremonial passage where people are announced and where coats and hats are checked.[2]

The medieval manor house was more like a "public house" than a home as we think of it today. Aside from the slew of servants and apprentices that lived there, the extended family might include dozens of relatives, in-laws, and close family friends on extended visits. The few large rooms that existed in the medieval manor house were general-purpose areas. People often ate, slept, worked, and played together in the same room. The household functioned more like an internal commune. While there existed a clearly delineated hierarchy, everyone, from the head of the household to the lowliest servant, lived together under a common roof, sharing daily routines in direct contact with one another. In the cottages of the poor there was even more crowding; the average peasant could live a lifetime without ever being truly alone. In pre-Napoleonic Europe, over 75 percent of the population lived in "squalid hovels," generally one-room cottages where twenty or more family members and friends shared a space that rarely exceeded twenty square yards. Three generations might share the same bed. It was also not uncommon to share whatever remaining space that existed with farm animals, who provided a minimum of warmth for the inhabitants.[3]

Gradually, the public character of medieval life began to metamorphose. By the eighteenth century, a noticeable change had taken place in the social life of Western Europe, reflecting the vast changes occurring in economic relationships. It was noted earlier that the old economic security based on communal ties and a subsistence-based economy was giving way to a new form of economic security based on the individual accumulation of money and the exercise of power over others in the open marketplace. As the communal notion of economic security gave way to the idea of the financially autonomous individual, it was accompanied by a parallel movement in the social life of Europe. The communal orientation of the medieval household was increasingly challenged by a new trend toward individual withdrawal and privacy. The emergence of the bourgeois individual and the increasing privatization and walling in of human experience represent the psychic counterpart of the worldwide enclosure movement and commodification of nature. The enclosure of the external commons and the privatization of the internal household served as cause and effect for one another. Together, they helped mold the economic, social, and psychic dimensions of the modern age.

A popular French expression of the nineteenth century proclaimed that "private life should be lived behind walls."[4] It is no wonder, then, that the great hall was the first room abandoned by the new bourgeoisie. After 1500 the hall was converted in many English palaces and homes to a dining area for servants, while the heads of the household retreated upstairs to dine in their chambers. The separation of the landlord's family from the servants and others in their employ continued over the coming century. By the late sixteenth century the French and English began introducing backstairs and basement rooms in their households. Henceforth, the servants were expected to work out of public sight as much as possible. At the end of the day they climbed up the backstairs to their small garrets in the attic so as not to disturb the rest of the household.[5] In the eighteenth century, landlords introduced bellpulls to summon servants. These innovations served to further separate landlord from servant in both time and space.[6] Yi-Fu Tuan chronicles the withdrawal process:

> Whereas in the seventeenth century servants might banter with their master or mistress and Louis XIV gallantly took off his hat to any charwoman he encountered in the corridors of Versailles, in the nineteenth century servants who entered the family wing to clean up must try to be invisible to their employers, a trick made possible by an intricate system of backstairs and corridors.[7]

The withdrawal of landlord from servants was accompanied by a further withdrawal of family members from visitors, friends, and other family members. Rooms were added to the domiciles of the rich and poor alike, providing enclosures within enclosures where individuals could find refuge from "the crowd." Between the mid-sixteenth and mid-seventeenth centuries the number of laborers' houses having three or more rooms rose from 56 to 79 percent.[8] The general-purpose rooms of an earlier era were replaced with parlors, dining rooms, bedroom chambers, and butteries, or storage rooms. Private rooms signified the division of functions in the home and predated the division of labor in the workplace by a century. The privatization of space in the household provided the opportunity for self-reflection and intimacy, aspects of sociability that played a lesser role in the public life of the Middle Ages.

The transformation from public to private life was dramatically expressed in the bedroom. Most moderns would be surprised to learn of the communal nature of medieval sleeping arrangements. Yet, until very recently, night, like the day, was a shared experience. The notion of privacy in the bedroom would have seemed quite strange and out of place to medieval sensibilities. In Saxon times, the bed was little more than a sack filled with straw. By the late medieval age, portable beds had become fashionable. Several beds were often set up each night in the same room, where the landlord and his mistresses slept alongside visitors, valets, and chambermaids.[9] Members of the same sex often shared a common bed. Michelangelo slept with his workmen, four to a bed. Even as late as the American Colonial era the Reverend John Cotton of Massachusetts wrote to his cousin, Cotton Mather, "to thank you for your late courteous entertainment in your bed." Louis XIV shared his bedchamber with his nurse until he married.[10]

The permanent bed was first introduced in the sixteenth century. By the seventeenth century, the four-poster bed with canopy was commonplace in the homes of the burghers and nobility. Even then the bedroom was considered a public place where visitors and friends often intermingled and socialized well into the night. Curtains were added to the beds, affording the first touch of true privacy. According to accounts, it was not unusual for a couple to make love or sleep behind the closed curtains while relatives and friends just a few feet away ate, drank, and carried on.[11] In fact, on wedding nights, custom required that relatives and guests accompany the couple to their wedding bed. "The bridal bed had to be mounted in the presence of witnesses if the marriage was to be valid." The next day the bridal couple exhibited the stained sheets to family and friends as proof of their union. The consummation of marriage was as much a public event as a private act.[12]

The idea of sleeping together in the same bed and room with relatives, friends, and occasionally strangers gradually gave way to sleeping alone in a single bed behind the closed doors of a solitary bedroom. Bodily contact, which was an ever-present feature of communal life, became a source of increasing embarrassment and finally a taboo as people separated from each other, journeying further and further into a new world of privacy and individualism.

The privatization of life gave new impetus to the idea of shame. Bodily functions became more and more concealed from public view and scrutiny. Sexual relations were fundamentally transformed. In the medieval era, sex was a far more open activity. While extramarital affairs were condemned by the Church, they were often tolerated by society, and the bastard children of various liaisons were often raised side-by-side with other siblings. Eventually, sexual relations became a completely private act between adults, and public demonstrations of lust or eroticism were increasingly frowned upon and finally condemned by law as well as custom.[13]

The breakup of the communal commons and the dismemberment of public life continued apace between the fifteenth and nineteenth centuries. The rise of the private sphere and the emergence of the autonomous individual is reflected in the most commonplace aspects of daily life. The bath, which today we regard purely as a function of hygiene, served a somewhat different role in parts of medieval Europe. Bathing was done to eliminate body odor and was largely a communal activity in northern Europe, especially in Scandinavia and Germany. Every village of any size boasted one or more public baths. Communal bathing was a richly orchestrated social activity that bound the members of the community in a common experience of ablution and regeneration. The fifteenth-century Florentine writer Poggio, whose own Renaissance culture was leaving communal life behind, told of his surprise upon visiting the public baths in Baden, Germany:

> Above the pools are galleries where the men sit watching and conversing. For everyone is allowed to go to other people's

baths, to contemplate, chat, gambol and unburden the mind, and they stay while the women enter, and leave the water, their full nakedness exposed to everyone's view. No guard observes who enters, no gate prevents one from entering and there is no hint of lewdness. . . . The men encounter half-naked women while the women encounter naked men. . . . People often take meals in the water. . . . Husbands watched as their wives were touched by strangers and did not take offense, did not even pay attention, interpreting everything in the best light. . . . Everyday they go to bathe three or four times, spending the greater part of the day singing, drinking, and dancing.[14]

In many towns the custom was to undress at home and then parade through the streets to the baths. "How often the father wearing but his breeches, with his naked wife and children, runs through the streets from his house to the baths. . . . "[15] The body had not yet been closed off and hidden away from the outside world.

The Protestant reformers effectively put an end to public baths, equating social bathing with licentious behavior and sin. By the eighteenth century, even private bathing was held suspect by church elders, who preferred to limit bodily pursuits as much as humanly possible so that the Christian believer could be free to concentrate on the sublime. So zealous was the Reformation Church on this score, that throughout Western and Northern Europe, where the Reformation had taken hold, a near paranoia set in regarding bathing of any kind, with public fear of contact with water reaching near hysterical proportions.

The public's fear of the bath subsided in the eighteenth century. By the nineteenth century, interest in bathing was renewed under a new banner—personal hygiene. As the medieval community and later the public became aware of the relationship between hygiene and the spread of disease, the function of the bath was transferred from a shared experience to a private act to ward off disease. Over a period of three centuries, the bath was stripped of its communal significance, and reduced to a strictly personal utilitarian function. The notion of bodily pleasure was subsumed by the notion of hygiene.

The changing relationship to the bedroom and bath reflect the emergence of a man and woman who coveted autonomy and privacy. The new sensibility was also evident in the changing style in furniture. The chair made its debut around 1490 at the Palazzo Strozzi in Florence.[16] Before that time people sat on wood benches, which lined the walls of the great halls, or on simple portable benches and three-legged stools. The closest antecedent to a chair was the ceremonial throne, a simple seat reserved for princes and kings who, by dint of their sovereign status, most closely approximated the autonomy of divine authority. In France, during the height of the Renaissance, uniform series of chairs came into vogue for the first time, reflecting the new elevated status of the individual. "Now everyone has his chair," observed historian Siegfried Giedion. "The chair has ceased to be an honorary symbol of unusual distinction and is placed in a series around the table."[17] Still, it would be another two centuries before the chair become a standard item in the palaces and wealthy bourgeois homes of Europe.

Medieval interiors reflected the austere influence of the monasteries, with their hard flat surfaces and spare surroundings. People often sat on cushions or stretched out on the floor. Many preferred to squat, without any material supports at all. Pictures of medieval life depict people packed together on benches, floors, and stairs, their bodies cramped together in random fashion. This was often the case, even among the rich and powerful. Today, we feel as if our space is being violated if someone brushes up against us or shares an armrest in a theater or plane.

The idea of constructing a piece of furniture to accommodate the individual human anatomy was revolutionary. If, in the new scheme of things, each man was to be truly an island onto himself, then the chair offered a visible expression of the new sensibility.

In the late sixteenth century padded chairs with comfortable back support began to appear, reflecting the new bourgeois man and woman's passion for material comforts. Historian John Lukacs once remarked that "The interior furniture of houses appeared together with the interior furniture of the mind."[18] What better symbol for the new age than the chair? Here was a constant reminder of the new separation between people. The chair reinforced the idea of the autonomous individual, secure in his private space, isolated from the responsibilities and obligations of the larger community.

By the twentieth century, engineers had taken over the design of chairs from the craftsmen and upholsterers, creating mechanized recliners that moved and pivoted in synchronization with the movement of the occupant. The La-Z-Boy recliner became a symbol of the post–World War II era, a visible sign of the autonomous, secure middle-class male.

21

KIDS, MIRRORS,
AND LAWNS

FOR COUNTLESS CENTURIES, human security had been lodged in the local community. In the modern era, security was suddenly usurped, on the one hand by the birth of the nation-state, on the other by the emergence of a unique institution, the nuclear family. In the process, the immediate community was left an empty vessel, a status it still retains today.

The nuclear family, like the nation-state, is a relatively recent phenomenon. According to historian Georges Duby, the idea of "family," as we know it, was nonexistent in the Middle Ages. The concept first originated in the fifteenth and sixteenth centuries and became an integral part of modern social life only in the eighteenth century; even then, it was a phenomenon largely restricted to the bourgeois middle class and aristocracy.[1] Before that time the family was viewed more as a small subdivision of the larger communal order and was loosely held together by the conjugal bond. Children identified far more with their age group than with their siblings, and while they felt a certain kinship with their birth parents, they mixed freely with the entire adult community. In fact, even the notion of childhood was undeveloped. Rather, children were perceived as younger members of the community. Medieval historian Philippe Ariès points out that parents loved their children as parents have throughout history, "but they cared about them less for themselves, for the affection they felt for them, than for the contribution those children could make to the common task."[2]

From the age of seven, most children left their birth homes altogether, the remainder of their childhood to be spent in other homes, where they served as apprentices. From the beginning of their apprenticeship, they were considered small adults and were expected to contribute to the commonweal, to the extent that their training and experience allowed. Children participated in adult life, then, from a very early age. In the workshops, in the fields, even in the taverns, children were integrated into the work and play of the larger community. Childhood was still an undifferentiated age, in which affiliation was first, and foremost, with the commune.[3]

The enclosure movement, the emergence of a market economy, and the rise of a new class of wealthy merchants, bankers, and factory owners all helped facilitate the development of the modern family and the idea of an extended childhood. Greater economic sophistication required more abstract learning as well as more specialized training, which could only be effectively mastered in a prolonged school education. Schools, which for a good part of the medieval age were used almost exclusively to train clerics, expanded to include a general education. School isolated youngsters from the adult world, giving them a separate new status as children. It also brought children and parents closer together. A child's schooling became the responsibility of his parents. Their responsibility for his welfare increased as the community's role in his life diminished. While the children of the well-to-do were often shipped off to boarding school, they were still under their parents' charge. Children were no longer left to be apprenticed to another household but, rather, raised to adulthood by their own parents. For the first time, says Ariès, "the family centered itself on the child."[4] By the nineteenth century, the family had superceded the community as the fundamental social unit in the lives of most Europeans and new world inhabitants.

The segregation of children and their families from the larger community buttressed other forces that were transforming Western civilization from a communal to a private way of life. The increasing interiorization of social life drew more attention away from the community and onto the individual. The word *I* began to show up with greater regularity in literature by the early eighteenth century.[5] *Self* became a new all-embracing prefix, with words like *self-love, self-knowledge,* and *self-pity* entering the popular lexicon. In literature, the autobiographical form made its debut. Self-portraits and family portraits came into fashion, and everywhere there was a new fascination, near obsession, with the individual. Self-reflection and introspection became pastimes, and the incipient field of psychology made its first tentative stirrings in the mid-nineteenth century.

The interest in self was reflected, literally, in the sharp rise in mirror production. Mirrors were first manufactured in large numbers around the mid-1500s. Small mirrors often accompanied the new printed books of Gutenberg and other craftsmen. Hand and pocket mirrors were also used as adornment in dress. By the late seventeenth century, European craftsmen were producing large plate glass. Giant wall mirrors became commonplace in bourgeois homes and in the estates of the wealthy. Mirrored rooms, like the famed Hall of Mirrors at Versailles, became fashionable. Social historian Morris Berman reminds us of the unique nature of this innovation. In medieval days, says Berman, excessive preoccupation with personal appearance was unusual. People "were not terribly concerned with how they appeared in the view of others."[6] The individual had not yet been separated from the community. People lacked a sense of personal definition. The increasing isolation of the individual from the collective went hand in hand with self-reflection and self-interest, both of which found adequate expression in countless hours before the reflection mirror.

Proclamations of liberty, fraternity, and equality may well have inflamed the passions of republican mobs on the continent and yeoman farmers in the new world of North America. But it was the quiet trinity of privacy, individual self-interest, and personal autonomy that captured the spirit of the new bourgeoisie. As the modern family became the breeding ground as well as the refuge for the new sensibilities, it began to hold society at a distance, to push it back beyond a steadily extending zone of private life.

This new sense of personal detachment and isolation spawned a novel architectural phenomenon in the late nineteenth century—the suburb. The new suburban living arrangement systematically removed the home, in both time and space, from the work life of the community. The suburb has come to epitomize the notion of privacy: families secluded behind fences and separated from the outside world by a surrounding expanse of lawn, the contemporary counterpart of the medieval moat.

The suburban house proved to be the ideal architectural match for the moderns. Like its occupants, it was detached, autonomous, and isolated from the external environment. Sociologist Kenneth Jackson reports that after 1870 "the new idea was no longer to be part of a close community, but to have a self-contained unit, a private wonderland walled off from the rest of the world."[7]

In the medieval era crowding provided a sense of security. As late as the eighteenth century, the Dutch were still building row houses, which had been the custom in cities since the days of ancient Rome. In the United States, over 71 percent of the resident population of the nation's capital, Washington, D.C., still lived in attached row houses in the 1920s. In many cities, row house construction was the rule until the end of the Second World War.[8]

The suburbs offered a far different kind of security, one ensconced in isolation, in varying degrees of separation from strangers and neighbors. The sense of isolation became ever more pronounced with the elimination of the front porch and the invention of air conditioning and television, which drew everyone further indoors and away from the community. Jackson rightfully observes that "there are few places as desolate and lonely as a suburban street on a hot afternoon."[9]

Today, 60 percent of all U.S. metropolitan residents live in suburbs. Two thirds of the nation's 86.4 million homes are single-family domiciles.[10] Still, even this pale facsimile of grounding is transitory. In any given five-year period, between 25 and 35 percent of all households change residences.[11] Meanwhile, the security most Americans thought they could purchase with a mobile life-style and suburban mortgage has become problematic, as drugs, crime, and teenage suicide have become a regular feature of the suburban landscape.

The drive for privacy and autonomy that so characterizes the suburban life-style is often expressed in very peculiar ways. None surpasses the compulsion for "keeping up the lawn." *Lawn* is an English word and dates to the year 1548. It means land.[12] Some historians trace its origin to the first enclosure acts and the early attempts at privatizing the village green.[13] In its modern guise it projects much of the anxiety that continues to dog the contemporary quest for an autonomous, secure existence.

In 1870, Englishman Frank J. Scott wrote a treatise on "The Art of Beautifying Suburban Home Grounds." He urged his new suburban disciples to "let your lawn be your home's velvet robe."[14] The well-manicured lawn has come to be identified with material opulence and middle-class virtue. It is a sign of passage and conveys a clear message to the world. The occupants have arrived. The secure autonomous existence they have sought is reflected in every blade of grass. At the same time, their lawn is their physical grounding, their last slim connection to the land, to nature.

Lawn tending in 1989 was a $25 billion industry. In the United States 31 million acres are currently planted in lawns, or about fifty thousand square miles, an expanse equal to the entire state of Illinois. Fifty million people spend $4 billion annually for lawn accessories alone and devote hours on end to stewarding their piece of the world.[15]

The enclosure and privatization of open space, which had begun on the village commons a half millennium earlier, had all but completed its journey. The well-to-do middle class found themselves isolated from their neighbors by a "crabgrass frontier" and further isolated in their own homes from other family members, each of whom had staked claims on their own living space.

22

STORE-BOUGHT AND
MACHINE-MADE

I T I S O N E of the anomalies of the modern age that in
the attempt to become more autonomous and secure, the bulk of
the population in the industrialized nations have become more
dependent on forces over which they have little or no control. At
one time a household would engage in a range of productive
activities, including raising livestock, growing vegetables, baking
bread, canning food, and making clothes. One by one, these productive tasks have been snatched away from the home by the
expanding industrial process and the forces of the marketplace.
The near total commercialization of family functions has coin-
cided with the near total commodification of nature.

The expropriation of family functions by the industrial and
commercial sectors is a relatively new phenomenon. Labor historian Harry Braverman says that as late as 1890 families living in
highly industrial regions like the coal and steel communities of
Pennsylvania were still producing virtually all of their food at
home—over half the families raised their own poultry, livestock,
and vegetables, purchasing only potatoes at the market.[1] Just one
hundred years ago in New York City, the borough of Queens and
much of the borough of Brooklyn were still semirural and men and
women in many families worked in the textile factories and commercial markets, while the children and elderly tended to

the animals and gardens. According to the U.S. Census Bureau, between 1889 and 1892 over half the families surveyed in the United States were still baking their own bread. While men's clothes were generally store-bought, women and children's clothes were still stitched and tailored at home—first by hand, then with the help of the Singer sewing machine, which enjoyed a ubiquitous presence in homes across the country.[2]

The increasing mechanization and automation of manufacturing lowered the cost of store-bought items after the turn of the century. A new industry, mass advertising, began to preach the advantages of factory-made over homemade, convincing Americans that producing their own goods at home was old-fashioned, out of step with the times, and, worse yet, an embarrassment to be overcome. Between 1899 and 1939, the amount of flour consumed by commercial bakeries rose from one-seventh to two-fifths of the total produced. The production of canned vegetables increased fivefold, canned fruits twelvefold.[3] Braverman astutely observes that "the source of status is no longer the ability to make things but simply the ability to purchase them."[4] For the first time in history, self-sufficiency was discouraged.

In less than two generations, the modern urban and suburban family was largely stripped of the last vestige of control over its own sustenance, forced to rely on its purchasing power alone to secure its economic well-being. Here was a strange form of security; the wage earner of the twentieth century had been made virtually dependent on the goodwill of private capital to secure his existence. If a corporate employer lays off workers, shuts down plants, or moves its operation to the next community or overseas, individual employees often have little recourse but to uproot their families and follow the capital trail, retrain for other jobs, if available, or—increasingly—go on the public dole.

The expropriation of household functions by the commercial market not only undermined the economic security of the family but its emotional security as well. Just as the communal bonds of the medieval commons gave way to the enclosure and commodification of the land, family bonds have given way to the increasing commodification of family functions. Braverman summarizes both the process and its dehumanizing consequences:

168

Thus the population no longer relies upon social organization in the form of family, friends, neighbors, community, elders, children, but with few exceptions must go to the market, not only for food, clothing, and shelter, but also for recreation, amusement, and security for the care of the young, the old, the sick, and the handicapped. In time, not only the material and service needs but even the emotional patterns of life are channeled through the market.[5]

The expropriation and commercialization of family functions has weakened traditional family ties, leaving family members further isolated from one another. According to one recent survey, the average working couple now spends a total of four minutes each day in "meaningful conversation." Parents spend less than thirty seconds each day in "meaningful conversation" with their children.[6]

Nowhere is the sense of alienation and isolation more apparent than at dinnertime, the traditional time for families to come together in shared tasks and camaraderie. To begin with, many American families do not eat at home anymore. It is estimated that one out of ten lunches and dinners are eaten at fast food establishments.[7] On those days when families eat at home, a great number rely almost exclusively on prepackaged frozen dinners, eliminating the shared experience of preparing a meal. Seventeen percent of all meals are now cooked in microwaves in a matter of minutes.[8] Even at home, families often do not eat together at the same time. Only a little over half of all U.S. families say they eat dinner together each day.[9] Sitting at the same table still does not guarantee a shared experience. Forty percent of all households now eat dinner with the television or videocassette recorder on, consuming packaged commercial entertainment.[10]

While the production functions of the home have been eliminated altogether, many traditional housekeeping chores have also been taken out of human hands and given over to machines, further weakening the remaining social bonds and obligations between family members. In the past one hundred years the interior of the home has been filled with more and more mechanical contrivances, transforming the long-standing organic ambiance of the human habitat into a mechanized vision of reality.

For example, the open flame of the hearth, which had warmed the home and cooked the food of human beings since time immemorial, was replaced by the coal-burning furnace and cast-iron range between 1830 and 1880.[11] Between 1880 and 1930 the gas range and centralized oil and gas heat replaced coal, and later electric ranges and electric furnaces competed with oil and gas.[12] Cleaner, more efficient, and far more convenient, gas, electric energy, and central heating radically changed the sociology of the household. Family members were no longer responsible for "keeping the home fires burning."

The hearth had always been the soul of the home, the gathering place for family members, the secure center of family life. The Southern agrarian, Andrew Lytle, tells us that when the Tennessee Valley Authority began to build dams in the 1930s, it once had to purchase a house whose chimney fire had "not gone out in one hundred years." According to Lytle, "The TVA had to move the chimney intact, its coals covered and hot, to its new location."[13] Even today, in many rural communities the hearth and chimney of old homes are allowed to remain standing long after their frames have become so much dust in the wind, as they are regarded as the spirit of the household.

With central heating, the center of the home, its grounding both symbolically and practically, was irretrievably lost. The crackling warmth of the hearth provided a far different experience of security than the invisible, evenly distributed heat blown into a room from concealed ducts along ceilings, or the more visible warmth of steam pipes hissing and rattling along the wallboards. Of course, few among us would prefer a drafty wood-burning fireplace to the comfort of central heating. Still, the point that needs to be emphasized is that the hearth provided a kind of security, or centering experience, for which there is no counterpart in the modern home.

The crusade to mechanize the home dates back to 1912 and a series of articles authored by Christine Frederick on "The New Housekeeping" published in the *Ladies' Home Journal*. Frederick urged housewives across the country to apply scientific principles and engineering standards in the home. In a later book, *Household Engineering, Scientific Management in the Home,* the author explained to her erstwhile converts how they might take the principles of modern scientific management used in giant industrial factories and engineer them to the needs of the home, so that it, too, might function like a small, efficient factory.

> For years I never realized that I really made eighty wrong motions in the washing alone, not counting others in the sorting, wiping, and laying away. Do we not waste time by walking in poorly arranged kitchens? Could not the housework train be dispatched from station to station, from task to task?[14]

Frederick, and others who followed, set about the task of streamlining the functions of the home. Just as Eli Whitney had restructured his factory along new mechanized lines two centuries earlier, the new home engineers and home economists introduced the ideas of division of labor and compartmentalization into the kitchen first, then, in order of importance, the wash and bathrooms, the living and cleaning rooms, and finally the bedroom. Historian Siegfried Giedion recounts the great enthusiasm of the times as housewives, eager to be thoroughly modern and scientific, took command like so many entrepreneurs casting around for the ideal mix of time, labor, energy, and capital.

> Instantly the tremendous resources of industry were made available. The work process in the kitchen was scientifically investigated down to the last detail of food preparation. Expert staffs of engineers, chemists, architects, nutritionists, and practicing cooks studied everything connected with the kitchen. The principles of scientific housekeeping could at last be put into practice. In little time the streamlined kitchen was complete.[15]

With the coming of electricity after the turn of the century, the new "home engineers" were soon surrounded by an array of automatic and semiautomatic machines using electrical current.

The washing machine, the electric iron, the refrigerator, the vacuum cleaner, the electric garbage disposal, and the electric fan followed in close succession. Air conditioning made its public debut after World War II. These and countless other mechanical devices have transformed the middle-class household into a kind of mechanized utopia, a clean, efficient, effortless world, isolated from the indignities and troubles that exist just beyond the "crab-grass frontier."

23

HOMO CONSUMPTOR

CONSUMPTION FOR CONSUMPTION'S sake has now become a primary task and overriding preoccupation of the middle-class household in every industrialized nation. Indeed, consumption has now become the single thread that binds the shared interest and future vision of the individual and the state. Consumption is the passion of modern man just as eternal salvation was the passion of medieval man.

The term "consumption" dates to the early fourteenth century and has both French and English roots. In its original form, to "consume" meant to destroy, to pillage, to subdue, to exhaust.[1] It is a word steeped in violence, and up until the present century it had only a negative connotation. Today, however, Americans identify more as consumers than as citizens. Consumption has become the primary well from which the body politic draws its security in the modern world. Never before in history has security rested on such a narrow base.

Our species now consumes over 40 percent of all the energy produced by photosynthesis on the planet, leaving only 60 percent for all the other creatures. With the human population expected to double early in the next century, our species will be consuming over 80 percent of the planet's photosynthetic energy, leaving little or nothing for millions of other species.[2]

Most of the earth's nonrenewable energy is being consumed by a tiny fraction of the human population in the wealthy industrial countries. As mentioned earlier, the United States is currently consuming over one third of the world's fossil fuel energy even though we only make up 5 percent of the world's population.[3] In 1987, the United States consumed over 76 quadrillion BTUs of fossil fuel energy, 50 percent more than the total consumption of all of Western Europe combined, even though its population exceeds ours by 40 percent.[4]

The average family in the United States now affects the environment forty times more than an average family in India, and one hundred times more than an average family in Kenya.[5] The per capita energy consumption in the United States is 350 times greater than that in Haiti.[6] The sheer volume of terrestrial energy that flows through the average American home is astounding. The engineer and futurist Buckminster Fuller once calculated that a middle-class American uses up enough energy to support two hundred human slaves.[7]

The American home, like the American office, factory, and farm, has been transformed into a guzzler of resources. From every corner of the planet, nature's storehouse is being systematically raided to meet expanding consumption demands, primarily in the United States, Western Europe, and Japan. We have depleted the earth's endowment, consuming the body of the planet into our economy, our homes, and ourselves. The legacy of our consumption is now everywhere around us and circling ever closer. Barren stretches of desert in the sub-Sahel of Africa, miles of smoldering ashes in the rain forests of the Amazon, scarred mountain ranges in the strip-mining regions of Minnesota's Mesabi range, accumulating carbon in the upper atmosphere, acidic waters in the Alpine lakes, and toxic chemicals leaching out from underground landfills are all a dark reminder of the consequences of the modern journey to secure human existence.

The early modern philosophers and their heirs promised future generations that greater consumption—material progress—would mean greater personal security. Instead we find ourselves more isolated and less secure—at war with the environment, at odds with our fellow human beings, and without an alternative approach to securing ourselves in the world.

Man is, by nature, an acquisitive animal. We have always been collectors, but it is only in the modern era that our objects have come to possess us. Many Americans shop as a form of personal recreation. Buying things makes people feel good about themselves. To acquire is to belong, to take part, to be a member of good standing in the larger community. Shopping has, for many, become a self-validating experience. It makes modern man and woman feel secure, if only temporarily. Isolated from others, we surround ourselves with things. They become a surrogate, engaging our time and attention, love and affection, as if they were sentient and capable of responding in some meaningful way to our innermost needs to communicate and share ourselves.

Our lives have become increasingly cluttered with material things in direct proportion to our loss of communion with nature and each other. Our machines and things take up far too much time and space, leaving little else to fill what remains of each dimension. Of course, our aloneness allows us to turn inward, but instead of using the opportunity to reflect on our condition, to seek answers for our worsening predicament, we often opt for self-indulgence and fleeting amusements. Sociologist Christopher Lasch has characterized the new preoccupation with self and momentary pleasures as "the culture of narcissism," living for self-aggrandizement today, with little thought for past obligations or future commitments.[8]

The narcissist's worst enemy is the past. He resents having his time spoken for and his immediate interests curtailed. The past reaches into the present, controlling and tempering behavior in the form of promises that need to be kept or fulfilled. Customs, traditions, covenants, contracts, and constitutions are the time-honored chain that links the great divide of past and present into a meaningful continuum. The narcissist feels yoked and seeks liberation from such constraints. He reasons that since he cannot possibly affect what already preceded him, he should not be unfairly imprisoned by demands from the grave.

At the same time, the narcissist has little interest in the future beyond his own immediate time line. Since he will not be here to taste its fruits, to enjoy its pleasures, he feels no need to steward its coming or moderate his own pursuits in anticipation of the needs of others to follow, even his own children.

This is the world of rational self-interest that John Locke, Adam Smith, and other thinkers envisioned several hundred years ago. Our science, technology, economics, and political philosophy provide a convenient backdrop for the narcissism of the modern age. The consumption ethic preaches the value of the moment. Advertising, installment buying, credit card purchases—all promote and validate immediate self-gratification at the expense of the past, the future, and others. As long as expanding consumption and notions of security remain inextricably intertwined, modern man will continue to devour more and more of nature in less and less time, driving him further afield from the secure world he desperately seeks.

24

DESCARTES ON WHEELS

OUR MODERN IDEAS about security have no parallel in history. Traditionally, security has been a grounding experience. To be secure was to be tied to the land, bonded to the community, and anchored in time—both the cyclical time of the changing seasons and the sacred linear time that connects the creation with the final judgment. Today mobility, not grounding, becomes the new image of security. Modern man and woman want to be free to roam, to explore new frontiers, to break new ground.

Our obsession with mobility is best expressed in the American love affair with the automobile. More than any other technology of contemporary life, the automobile personifies autonomy and mobility. Even the name embodies these two essential features of Enlightenment thinking: *auto,* connoting automatic and autonomous, and *mobile.*[1] Today, 36 percent of all households have one automobile, 35 percent have two, and 18 percent have three or more. Every twenty-four hours, thirty thousand new drivers and twenty-eight thousand new cars are added to the road.[2] The automobile allows every person to experience the joy and exhilaration of overcoming temporal and spatial limits. Accelerating three thousand pounds of mechanical force, one experiences firsthand the temporal "will to power" of which Nietzsche and others spoke.

The automobile has come to symbolize the rite of passage in modern civilization. Car ownership provides the individual with a sense of his own uniqueness and individuality. In our highly mobile culture, people come to think of the automobile as a guarantor of personal freedom and security. It is a badge of membership in the modern world of mechanism.

For some, the automobile is an extension of being, for others a surrogate. Advertisers are quick to exploit all of the bodily substitutions built into the modern automobile. Automobiles are said to be quick, agile, powerful, masculine, lean, elegant, graceful, smooth, streamlined, and dependable. The automobile exemplifies the qualities and features we would like to incorporate in our own bodies, and when we are behind the wheel, we experience the physicality of our automobile as our own. This is especially true among young adults, experiencing the pride of drivership and ownership for the first time. It is no wonder that the image most associated with the automobile is sexuality. Teenage men and women are drawn to the sexual power and lure of the automobile. It becomes both an extension of and a substitution for their own sexuality. Henry Ford is said to have been so concerned about the seductive power of the automobile that he designed the seats in such a way as to prevent any meaningful sexual encounter. His efforts proved ineffective. As one auto commentator observed, "The Model-T had so much headroom that all but the tallest could achieve their pleasures standing up."[3]

The automobile allows one to master and dominate one's environment from behind closed windows and locked doors. The automobile exudes control and detachment at the same time. The driver can be in the world without having to be of it. He can control events around him while retaining a sense of anonymity. Many drivers will vent their aggressions and hostilities from behind the wheel while never daring to do so face to face.

Like the suburban home that it is so closely associated with, the automobile is a private space where an individual can feel safe, secure, and above all, autonomous in the world. Automobile manufacturers have long projected the image of the private home onto the car. The Ford Motor Company used to advertise their automobile as "a living room on wheels."[4] What better symbol of modern security than the automobile, which combines both mobility and individual privacy in a single machine.

The automobile has been an omnipresent force in twentieth-century life. It has not only dramatically affected the consciousness of contemporary culture but the global environment and economy as well. In fact, the automobile has proved to be the single most environmentally destructive work of technology in history.

Each gallon of gas burned releases 22 pounds of carbon dioxide into the atmosphere. In a year, the average car emits five tons of carbon dioxide into the air.[5] With over 120 million automobiles in the United States, automobile emissions account for 33 percent of all carbon dioxide and 45 percent of all nitrous oxide released into the sky, making the car the single largest contributor to global warming.[6]

The automobile is also responsible for 60 percent of the total air pollution in most U.S. cities.[7] Cars emit 69 percent of all the lead, 70 percent of the carbon monoxide, and are responsible for 60 percent of the ground ozone.[8] Every day, "250,000 tons of carbon monoxide, 25,000 tons of hydrocarbons, and 8,000 tons of oxides of nitrogen" are spewed out from auto exhausts.[9]

The car consumes vast amounts of the earth's resources. Autos consume "20 percent of all the steel, 12 percent of the aluminum, 10 percent of the copper, 5 percent of the lead, 95 percent of the nickel, 35 percent of the zinc, and 6 percent of the rubber used in the United States."[10] One enthusiastic supporter in the 1930s exclaimed:

> Think of the results to the industrial world of putting on the market a product that doubles the malleable iron consumption, triples the plate-glass consumption, and quadruples the use of rubber. . . . As a consumer of raw material, the automobile has no equal in the history of the world."[11]

Here is a machine costing thousands of dollars, intentionally designed to be replaced every thirty-six to forty-eight months. Between 1900 and 1984, 647,507,000 automobiles, trucks, and buses were junked in the United States alone.[12]

The automobile consumes the environment in still another way.

From 1936 to 1985, U.S. drivers burned 3 trillion gallons of fuel, making the automobile the largest single consumer of nonrenewable energy in the twentieth century.[13] The automobile also consumes the land. The first cement road was laid out in 1909 and extended from Detroit to the Wayne County state fairgrounds in Michigan.[14] Today, over 2 percent of the total land surface and 10 percent of the arable land have been paved over in the United States.[15] In Florida, over 1.6 million acres of agricultural land were converted to highways in one ten-year period between 1974 and 1984.[16] According to a study conducted by the Institute of Transportation and Traffic Engineering of the University of California, over 100,000 people each year are uprooted and displaced by new highway construction.[17]

Building and maintaining highways consumes vast amounts of the earth's resources. In 1961, it was estimated that every million dollars of highway construction used up "16,800 barrels of cement, 694 tons of bituminous materials, 485 tons of mineral materials, 24,000 pounds of explosives, 121,000 gallons of petroleum products, 99,000 feet of lumber and 600 tons of steel."[18]

Interestingly, the impetus for the construction of thousands of miles of highway in the United States was national security. The Interstate Defense Highway Act, the largest public works project in the history of civilization, was enacted in the 1950s, in large part to meet the perceived security needs of the country. Now, over three decades later, the U.S. government has paid out over $379.6 billion to build an integrated network of highways across the country. The cost of maintaining these highways is equally staggering. Between 1980 and 1987, repair costs exceeded $409 billion.[19]

Besides consuming vast amounts of the earth's resources, the automobile has also killed millions of animals and human beings. In the United States alone, thousands of animals are killed by automobiles every single day of the year.[20] An average of 48,000 people are killed in auto accidents every twelve months. In the past thirty years, over one million Americans have lost their lives in traffic accidents.[21] The National Safety Council estimates that more Americans have been killed by automobiles than were killed in all the wars this country fought in the past two hundred years.[22]

Despite all the advances in automotive engineering and highway construction and expansion, motorists in Los Angeles today often average less than 10 miles per hour in rush-hour traffic.[23] In Tokyo suburbs, drivers normally allow ninety minutes for a twenty-mile trip.[24] In São Paulo, commuters spend four hours each day going to and from work.[25] According to a study conducted by the Federal Highway Administration, urban freeway congestion results in 6.9 billion hours of delay each year and 1.3 billion gallons of wasted fuel. The total cost of the delays to American drivers exceeds $9 billion annually.[26] This is a high price to pay for mobility when one stops to consider that half of all automobile trips in the United States are under three miles, a distance that could be walked in less than one hour at no appreciable cost to the environment or the pocketbook.[27]

In the modern war against nature, the automobile ranks as the single most destructive tool in the nonmilitary arsenal. Still, in all the debates on global warming, resource management, and other environmental ills, the automobile has been treated more as a sacred cow than a destructive force. Politicians have shown little enthusiasm for confronting the automobile or the auto culture head-on, perhaps sensing its deep psychological significance in the life of every American. Then, too, politicians are not unmindful of the influence the automobile exerts on the American economy.

Today we seek to be as autonomous and mobile as possible. The secure man and woman are often thought of as those with the least encumbrances and ties and the most options from which to choose. Autonomy, mobility, and security have become virtually interchangeable. To be modern is to be an itinerant voyager, tasting bits and pieces of experience in life's various ports of call but never setting up residence long enough to experience a sense of spatial rootedness and the profound ritual of eternal return: nature's recurring birth process that has assured human beings from the beginning of time of their rightful place in the grand temporal scheme of things.

We have become much too nimble and quick to fully appreciate and take part in the slow rhythms of the natural world—spring floods melting away the cold silence of another winter, new life springing forth from a thousand coves and eddies, a hot summer sun baking the earth, turning greens to browns, the ripening scents of fall, the long-awaited harvest, the winter solstice, the quiet sleep that descends over the long hours of darkness before a new spring dawns. For the ancients and for those moderns who have had the good fortune to be grounded in such natural events and rhythms, the sense of security in being caught up and carried along the slow cycle of eternal return is like no other.

Primordial security, the security that comes from a deep, instinctual, bodily relationship to nature, was lost when Western man and woman were forced from the land and denied their ancestral and biological right to belong to the soil from which they descended. Today, only a faint biological reminder of that former union exists. Like all other species, human beings are born with myriad biological clocks entrained to the rhythms of the circadian day, and the lunar and circannual cycles. Our bodies' rhythms reach out to the rhythms of the land and nature. The temporal bonds forged over evolutionary history are tenacious, but increasingly stymied by the artificial temporality we have imposed on ourselves in the fast-paced, highly mobile culture of the modern world.[28]

How strange this modern world has become. Being on the move, constantly on the go, directing our energies to new frontiers, new vistas, hoping all along that our increasing restlessness will stir us to a secure haven.

If mobility is linked to security in the modern mind, then the notion of soaring is associated with progress. Soaring to new heights and new speeds assures greater progress. Art deco, streamlining, the Chrysler Building, the British Concorde are the soaring images of modern prowess. When soaring is mixed with mobility, the two forces create a powerful potion. When the mix explodes, as it did in the spacecraft *Challenger* in 1986, an entire generation of youngsters experiences the humbling of a powerful myth.

The *Challenger* was the archetypical expression of the modern notion of mobility and progress. Mechanical, streamlined, efficient, and mathematically engineered to be precise and flawless, the *Challenger* personified the Baconian-Cartesian vision. The space shuttle is a powerful mechanical force of computing skill laid against material strong enough to defy both earth's gravity and the sun's heat. The *Challenger* could escape nature's grasp altogether, ascending into the heavens. Enclosed inside their capsule, a crew of seven astronauts lived, for a brief few seconds, in a totally artificial, autonomous environment.

The *Challenger* was, perhaps, the most sophisticated symbol of the modern age. Its sudden catastrophic failure and fiery plunge has etched a painful memory into the collective consciousness of the next generation. Even the best engineered plans of the brightest scientists of our day were unable to secure the ship and crew.

Modern man and woman, then, have let go of their hold on the land and many of the ties that previously bound them to their fellow human beings, preferring a world of soaring mobility and progress, serviced and protected by machines of all kinds and surrounded by every conceivable creature comfort. Where human security had traditionally been embedded in the time and space of nature, the security of the modern age is sought in overcoming time and space altogether.

PART FOUR

SECURING THE BODY POLITIC

25

THE FLIGHT FROM THE
ANIMAL SHADOW

THE LAND, THE changing seasons, the life and death in nature are all constant reminders of the finiteness of existence. On a personal level, the most intimate expression of our own mortality is our physicality, our bodies. It is our bodies that anchor us to the soil and to a fixed duration of existence. Human bodies are fragile and unpredictable. They wither and die. In contrast, the tools of analytical reasoning, the principles of mathematics and mechanics do not fall victim to earthly mortality. They are forever applicable. While machines wear out and need to be replaced, the principles of construction and operation remain impervious to the ravages of time.

It is no wonder that Enlightenment thinkers began to champion forms of human reasoning that were predictable, orderly, objective, and detached, and that seemed to operate independently of the limitations of mortal existence. Other human qualities like wildness, instinct, and sensuality, which were more closely associated with the body, were disparaged and actively repressed, as their presence constituted a powerful reminder of human mortality.

The early Church, interestingly enough, helped seed the eventual harvest of Enlightenment thought. St. Augustine warned the faithful to be aware of the temptations of the flesh. Church fathers viewed the human body as fallen and depraved. The Christian

187

believer was asked to fix his sights on the heavens and to unite with Christ. Sensuality, spontaneity, and lust were associated with base animal instincts and were condemned by Church doctrine. The Church was anxious to wean its new converts away from animal worship and fertility rites, which had been at the center of religious experience from the outset of the neolithic era.

By stripping people of their close bonds with nature, the Church left Western man and woman without any secure grounding in the physical world. Human beings were left to dangle in this world in expectation of ultimate security in the next world. By the time the new commercial interests had succeeded in luring the faithful away from their preoccupation with Judgment Day and toward more secular affairs like profit, rents, and compound interest, Western man had already detached himself from his own physical body. The new bourgeois man and woman of the modern age were already "living in their head," and their heads were filled with thoughts of double-entry bookkeeping, inventory accounts, statistics, mathematical equations, and market shares. Bodily thoughts and sensations were systematically repressed to make room for the cold, calculating, machinelike mind of the industrial age.

The new security was to be found in mechanical logic and in machines that could overcome the limitations of time and space, speed the flow of material resources, expand the production and consumption curve, and advance the course of unlimited material progress. In its more rarefied form, material progress provided a new earthly surrogate for eternal salvation.

The transition from body to mind, from flesh to detached utilitarian thought, paralleled the other forces sweeping Western and Northern Europe during the early modern period. As European man and woman began to separate from the land and from their long-standing communal bonds, they also began separating from their own bodies and bodily nature, leaving their physicality outside as their minds increasingly retreated behind closed doors and interior spaces. In the new private sphere of the individual, security was found in disembodied, rational thought.

At the same time, the machine began to serve as a surrogate for the body. Machines replaced animal power, human legs and feet, the throwing arm, the clasped hand, the skilled fingers, and the trained eyes of the craftsmen. Increasingly, sophisticated machines of communication and transportation allowed modern man and woman to compress time and space and secure greater control over the natural world from an increasing distance.

The separation of mind from body and the substitution of machines for human physicality began in earnest during the Renaissance and has continued without respite to the present day. The withdrawal from the human body and the withdrawal from all of nature are inseparably linked and need to be examined together as two dimensions of a single experience.

In today's world, we tend to classify people as modern or old-fashioned, depending on their willingness or reluctance to embrace new fashions, styles of behavior, and technology. At the beginning of the modern era, people were classified quite differently, as either civilized or brutish. Their status was wholly dependent on whether or not they had effectively emancipated themselves from an animal-like existence and embraced a new world of refined manners, rational thoughts, and orderly and predictable behavior.

The struggle of people to separate themselves from other animals and disavow their own animal nature dates back to the emergence of monotheism in Western culture. Well before the Renaissance and even the early teachings of the Church, the Hebrew prophets wrestled with their own flock over their continued attachment to fertility religions and animal worship. Moses admonished the chosen people at the foot of Mount Sinai for lying prostrate before the golden calf.

Still, as long as human beings were tied to the land and beholden to the changing seasons and nature's benevolence, the close association with animals and animal gods and goddesses continued to hold sway, often competing with Hebrew scripture and Christian doctrine. In fact, the history of the early Church is replete with examples of internecine religious warfare, as ecclesiastical authorities periodically attempted to eliminate from their ranks any remaining vestige of animal idolatry.

The rapid urbanization of Western culture after the seventeenth century went hand in hand with the severing of the remaining bonds between people and animals and the detachment of human

189

beings from their own animal nature. Enlightenment thinkers joined with church authorities in condemning human behavior that they considered bestial, brutelike, and unworthy of the new civilized man and woman of the Age of Reason. Man's animal nature became something to overcome, a dark force to suppress and defeat. Bacon and other modern thinkers were as concerned with subduing the wild forces of human nature as they were the wild forces of the rest of nature. Exercising rational, detached, objective power over animals in nature and the animal inside human nature became equally important.

The brutal suppression of the human body in the early modern era transformed the animal side of human existence into a "shadow self," a condition from which modern man has yet to recover. Psychologist Carl Jung refers to the shadow as those features of the human personality that lie repressed in the unconscious.[1] They are the parts of ourselves that we hide from and ignore.

The shadow is a recurring theme throughout human history. Primitive people are often afraid to let their shadow fall on certain objects. In some cultures it is said one's shadow should never fall on pregnant women, or on a mother-in-law. Shadows should never fall on the dead or on coffins and, for that reason, the dead are buried at night by some primitive tribes. The shadow is viewed in myth and ritual as a person's spiritual double and has been long regarded as the dark side of being. The shadow is the ever-present reminder of the individual's own mortality. It is, in the words of psychologist Otto Rank, "the announcer of death."[2] In some primitive cultures, a person's health is diagnosed by the size and tone of his shadow. A weak shadow means the owner will soon become ill. A strong shadow is a guarantee of continued good health. Rank tells us that among some tribes, "the sick are brought into the sunlight in order that their shadow may be recalled and with it the departing soul."[3]

By the late medieval era, the animal side of human nature was beginning to haunt the collective psyche of Western civilization. Animal urges were an embarrassing reflection of the instinctual drives and uncontrollable impulses in nature that needed to be subdued. Pre-Enlightenment and Enlightenment thinkers were anxious to elevate man from his animal origins. In the orderly

190

and predictable new world of mechanics and mathematics, of reason and calculation, there was simply no room for the wild, unpredictable, and chaotic forces of nature.

The final suppression of man's animal nature corresponded with the final taming of the European continent and the colonial subjugation of new lands overseas. At first, the domestication of the wild actually brought people and animals closer together. As late as the fifteenth century, humans and their domestic animals were still living under the same roof. The traditional "long house" combined house and stable. Farmers and cattle entered the home from the same entrance and were separated inside only by a lone wall.[4]

The relationship between farmers and their domestic animals was intimate. Humans and animals got up together, left the house together in the morning, toiled all day in the fields together, and returned home at day's end to bed down together for the night. So close was the relationship that the language used to describe human beings and human activity was often laced with animal images and symbols:

> Children were "kids," "cubs" or "urchins"; a boy apprentice was a "colt". . . . A woman expecting a baby was said to have "got upon the nest." Her husband would address her affectionately as "duck" or "hen"; less affectionately as "cow," "shrew," "bitch," or "vixen." When she got old she would become a "crone," that is, a ewe who has lost her teeth.[5]

The enclosure and commercialization of nature radically changed the relationship between humans and animals. Where animals were once regarded as part of the household, both literally and figuratively, they were later regarded as commodities, worth so much per pound. By the late Elizabethan era the English had banished animals from the home altogether, sequestering them in stables and barns. Any lingering memory of former living arrangements was a source of embarrassment and not much talked about. It is said that the English "despised" the Irish, Welsh, and Scots because they still slept under a common roof with their animals.

Such behavior was suddenly looked on as "very beastly and rudely in respect of civility."[6]

In early modern England, says historian Keith Thomas, the attitude toward animals came to reflect the attitudes people most despised and loathed in themselves and others. People projected their own worst fears about themselves onto animals and condemned any and all human behavior that reminded them of their animal origins.

> Men attributed to animals the natural impulses they feared most in themselves—ferocity, gluttony, sexuality—even though it was men, not beasts, who made war on their own species, ate more than was good for them, and were sexually active all the year round.[7]

Christian doctrine and lore reinforced the idea that animals and animal-like behavior were sinful and evil. The Antichrist was depicted as a beast and the devil was often depicted as a human animal chimera. Evil spirits were also said to take up residence in the bodies of cats, dogs, rats, and other animals.

The Protestant reformers, though at odds with the Church on the fundamentals of the faith, bolstered the Vatican in its crusade against the evils of a fallen animal world, including man's fallen animal nature. Human bodily functions were a source of particular discomfort, as they were a constant reminder of the animal shadow that lurked behind every man, ready to jump out and pounce if left unrestrained. The New England clergyman Cotton Mather made the following entry in his diary in 1700:

> I was once emptying the cistern of nature, and making water at the wall. At the same time, there came a dog, who did so before me. Thought I . . . how much do our natural necessities abase us, and place us . . . on the same level with the very dogs. . . . Accordingly, I resolved that it would be my ordinary practice, whenever I step to answer the one or other necessity of nature, to make it an opportunity of shaping in my mind some holy, noble, divine thought. . . . [8]

192

Nakedness, which had never caused much of a stir in the past, suddenly became a matter of deep public concern. Only animals roamed naked. Men wore clothes, distinguishing them from the beasts. Long hair also became suspect for the first time and for the same reason. Bacon wrote that "beasts are more hairy than man . . . and savage man more than civil."[9] Night work was also shunned because, in the words of English jurist Sir Edward Coke, it is "the time wherein man is to rest, and wherein beasts run about seeking their prey."[10] Even swimming was condemned. Man was born to walk upright on solid ground, proclaimed a Cambridge theologian in 1600. Only fish swim.[11]

It is during this period that it became rather commonplace to use animal epithets to denigrate others. Such references could be heard in stately public forums as well as in street brawls and household spats. John Milton ridiculed his adversaries, calling them "owls and cuckoos, asses, apes, and dogs."[12] Nehemiah Wallington attacked the Royalists as "tigers and bears for cruelty . . . boars for waste and destruction . . . swine for dumbness . . . wolves for greediness."[13] Karl Marx called Thomas Malthus a "baboon."[14] Anthropomorphic innovation in the use of language continues today.

Throughout the modern era, animals—both domestic and wild—served as a constant reference point in man's struggle to civilize himself and rid himself of his animal nature. Indeed, the flight from the animal shadow has influenced modern man's relationship to nature perhaps more than any other single force.

26

MORALS, MANNERS, AND MENUS

THE BATTLE TO tame, subdue, and ultimately suppress the animal inside each person was fought on many different battlefields. None proved more important than the dining table, where a revolution in eating habits occurred between the fifteenth and nineteenth centuries. The term "civilized" was actually first associated in the public mind with the preparation and consumption of food and drink. The revolution in manners is largely attributable to the work of Erasmus. His book on proper table manners and etiquette, *De Civilitate Morum Puerilium (On Civility in Children)*, first published in 1526, became the bible of the new bourgeois class.[1] Erasmus believed that the essence of proper table etiquette lay in a complete and thorough disassociation from any behavior or activity that was animal-like in nature.

> Don't smack your lips like a horse . . . don't gnaw the bones like a dog; don't lick the dish like a cat; don't shake your hair like a colt; don't neigh when you laugh, like a horse, or show your teeth like a dog; don't move your whole body like a wagtail; don't speak through your nose: it's the property of cows and elephants.[2]

Eating habits in medieval Europe reflected the communal spirit of the times.[3] The meals of the nobility were often lavish and sumptuous affairs. Feasts were common. Guests would dine amid the noise of singing troubadours, the antics of clowns and acrobats, and the yelping of dogs. Dining was a gregarious occasion, a time for bantering and posturing, laughter and loud noise. People would be seated on long flat benches, in no particular order. Ornate tapestries lined the dining hall. The floors, however, were another matter. They were littered with the garbage of present and past meals, and more closely resembled a compost heap. Erasmus described the scene as an "ancient collection of beer, grease, fragments, bones, spittle, excrement of dogs and cats, and everything that is nasty."[4] Guests were served a meal that was as undifferentiated as the setting. A variety of whole birds—sparrows, herons, egrets, and bitterns—were heaped one on top of another on huge dishes and served to the guests. Stews were also popular and might include rabbits and other small animals, mixed in with every kind of vegetable and flower grown within a ten-mile radius. Food was served en masse, and everything was smothered in thick gravies or indiscriminately flavored with every kind of herb and seasoning available.[5]

Dining was a communal event. There were few utensils, and they were shared by all the guests. People ate from a trencher, which was then a thick slice of stale bread (a wooden plate was later substituted for the bread). At meal's end, the diners would often pass along their soaked, stained bread to the dogs underfoot or to the poor waiting outside. Dogs and other animals constantly roamed the room, eagerly awaiting a tossed bone or other morsel.[6]

Erasmus's treatise on table manners signaled the beginning of a fundamental shift in European life. The bawdiness of medieval dining was challenged by the reformers, who were anxious to civilize even the most banal aspects of day-to-day activity. In the early modern era, every effort was made to separate the experience of dining from anything that hinted at animality. A host of new innovations were implemented to create distance between humans and the food they prepared and consumed. New boundaries were also established between diners, reinforcing the new elevated status of the individual vis-à-vis the collective.[7]

The new sense of detachment from nature was exemplified in the changes in the way meat was prepared and served. In the great halls of medieval castles, whole pigs and large sections of oxen were roasted on spits in the center of the room. On the Lord's day, an entire lamb might have been prepared with "a puddinge in the bellye."[8] In the medieval household it was common practice to place the whole animal or large parts of it on the dining table. Whole birds with their feathers stuck back in to make them look alive were served up, as were whole rabbits, quarters of veal, and the like.[9] Carving was honed to a fine art and was always left to the head of the family as a sign of deference to his sovereign authority over the household.[10]

Beginning in the early modern era, much of the food preparation was removed from public scrutiny and fussed over behind the scenes in the kitchens and sculleries. The newly urbanized societies, especially in France and Germany, became increasingly squeamish at the sight of whole animals served up at the table. Serving a whole dead animal was no longer regarded as a pleasurable experience. It was too forceful a reminder of killing and death and the thin line that separated humans from their prey; only beasts tear into a whole animal. The new culinary standards began to stress concealment. More and more of the carving was done by the cooks in the kitchen, leaving the host with little more than the ceremonial carving role. Heads were removed from fish, foul, and animals, and meat was increasingly divided into small portions, filleted out of sight of the diners and then served to eliminate any identification with the animal that was being eaten.[11]

By the mid-nineteenth century, English society had caught up with the new dining sensibilities on the continent. In *The Habits of Good Society*, published in 1859, the authors condemn the "unwieldy barbarism" of carving an entire joint in front of one's dining guests. "The truth is that unless our appetites are very keen, the sight of much meat reaking in its gravy is sufficient to destroy them entirely, and a huge joint especially is calculated to disgust the epicure."[12]

The flight from animality at the dining table manifested itself in other ways as well. In the medieval era, people most often ate with their hands, aided only by a sharp knife. Cutting into whole animals with sharp instruments and tearing off flesh with one's bare hands became a sign of savage, animal-like behavior in the sixteenth century. The knife was associated with the violence of the hunt. Wielding a small sword or lance at the dinner table seemed menacing and dangerous, providing still another reminder of the dark instinctual animal forces that lurked just beneath the surface of human civility.[13] When the Chinese first encountered the eating habits of Europe, they were aghast. "The Europeans are barbarians," they would say. "They eat with their swords."[14]

The knife's role in dining was greatly circumscribed in the early modern era. Its end was blunted in the late 1500s and an elaborate code was established on how it was to be used. Diners were instructed never to raise their knife to their mouth like a primitive. In 1560, Calviac told his readers that proper care should be taken in handling a knife at the table, lest one's gesture be regarded as an unfriendly act of aggression. "If you pass someone a knife, take the point in your hands and offer him the handle."[15] Parents still instruct their children to do the same today.

The fork was introduced in the late medieval era to eliminate eating food by hand.[16] As with the other innovations in eating habits, public concern continued to focus on emancipation from animal-like behavior and from direct bodily contact with animals. The fork served both functions, effecting greater distance between humans and the animals they consumed. The very idea of grabbing meat in one's bare hands from a common bowl, which seemed so normal in medieval households, was regarded with repugnance in the seventeenth century.

The fork was first used in Venice and later found its way to France, Germany, and England.[17] Until the seventeenth century, it was used almost exclusively by the aristocracy and was usually cast in gold or silver. After that time, it became a standard utensil in bourgeois homes throughout Europe. The fork became associated with civility and good manners.[18] It created still another boundary separating people from nature. Like other tools of the modern age that would follow, the fork allowed people to manipulate and consume the things of nature from a distance, furthering the illusion, if only in a small way, that human beings were, in fact, separate from nature and on a higher plane than the beasts they were eating.

The radical changes in eating habits in the early modern era had

197

an effect beyond the separation of human beings from nature and their own animal nature. Many of the innovations helped further separate people from each other and, by so doing, weakened the already strained communal bonds while strengthening the role of the individual. The change in soup eating habits is a case in point. During the medieval era, people supped from the communal bowl, oftentimes spitting back undesirable bits of gristle into the cauldron as it made the rounds. A common ladle was added in the late medieval era to prevent the guests' mouths from touching the bowl. By the early modern era, individual spoons were used to dip into the shared bowl, and finally each individual was provided with his own bowl and spoon, completing the process of individuation. In like manner, individual napkins were added to the fare, replacing the shared tablecloth, which had long been used for wiping the grease and gravy off hands and mouths.[19]

The changes in dining also extended to questions of style and presentation. The undifferentiated, chaotic, and often unpredictable form of serving that characterized the medieval dinner was replaced with an orderly, predictable sequence of serving more befitting the Age of Reason. By the late seventeenth century, it became customary to serve the soup first, followed by fish, meat, and dessert.[20] While this change might seem rather uneventful to moderns, it should be remembered that at the medieval supper any food could come at any time and in any order. Custards and fruit tarts might accompany, precede, or follow stews and game birds, depending on nothing more than the whim or circumstance of the moment. Being able to predict not only what one would eat but also the order in which it would be eaten was reflective of the new kind of security based in linear thinking and rational planning. The spontaneity of medieval life gave way to the orderly rational life of the bourgeois home, laying the appropriate psychological groundwork for the Enlightenment worldview and the industrial age.

The new habits in dining even introduced a rudimentary form of division of function about the same time that such ideas were being introduced into the factories and marketplace. In the nineteenth century, a well-laid dining table might look more like a machine shop bench or surgical table with the dizzying array of utensils and instruments at hand. Each setting might include a number of different wineglasses, tailored to specific wines and liquors. Dinner knives and forks might be accompanied by fruit knives and forks as well as fish knives and forks.[21]

Changes in eating habits and a myriad of other mundane activities of day-to-day life were far more effective in reorienting human beings to "the new way of thinking" about nature and human nature than all of the university lectures, scholarly treatises, and tutorials combined. The modern worldview owes its very success in no small measure to the countless ways in which its central operating assumptions were integrated into the personal habits of the new man and woman.

27

EXORCIZING THE BEAST

OF ALL THE bodily functions, lust was most identified with man's "fallen" animal nature. The easy, even unas-
suming sexual practices of the medieval era were denounced,
suppressed, and condemned by church leaders and Enlightenment
thinkers alike. While sexual practices were driven underground or
strictly limited to a procreation function, the brunt of the new
moral outrage was aimed at "bestiality"—sexual relations with
animals. Bestiality became an obsession of the age. More than any
other act, it confirmed the presence of the dark side and threatened
to erase, in an instant, the walls that had been painstakingly
erected between man and nature and between man and his own
animal nature. For this reason, bestiality was considered the most
sinful of all human acts. "It turns man into a very beast, makes a
man a member of a brute creature."[1]

The Church seized on bestiality after the thirteenth century and
used it to ferret out any remaining pagan religious practices in
Europe. Before that time, the Church had pursued a live-and-let-
live policy in regard to ancient nature-worshipping cults. During
the Inquisition, church leaders tortured and burned to death nearly three quarters of a million people for witchcraft. In many of the
cases, bestiality was alleged to have occurred. Witches were accused of engaging in orgiastic rituals in which they committed
unspeakable sexual acts with the devil disguised as a large

animal: a goat, sheep, or dog. Men and women, along with their cows, sows, and donkeys, were regularly tried and burned at the stake for bestiality. Often the only evidence of any wrongdoing, if it can be called that, was the display of affection toward animals, which a century earlier would have been regarded as normal behavior. Many times older women would be convicted of bestiality and burned as witches simply because they lived alone with only a pet animal to keep them company.[2]

Bestiality was made a capital offense in England in 1534, and remained so until 1861.[3] Keith Thomas observes that incest, by contrast, was not made a crime until the twentieth century.[4] Despite the hysteria, there is no evidence to suggest that the incidence of bestiality in the sixteenth century was any greater than in any other time in Western history. According to Alfred Kinsey's report in the 1950s, approximately 8 percent of American males and 3.6 percent of females had engaged in sexual acts with animals. The figures increased dramatically among the farm population: between 17 and 50 percent of all adolescent boys had committed sexual acts with domestic animals. The figures are probably comparable to other societies at different periods in their history.[5]

The fear of human beings' animal nature reached new heights during the early modern era. The privatization and individualization of human life was accompanied by an almost fanatical need to escape any sort of identification with the animal world. Thomas says that "wherever we look in early modern England we find anxiety, latent or explicit, about any form of behavior which threatened to transgress the fragile boundaries between man and the animal creation."[6] The angst of the age was expressed in tales of werewolves stalking their urban prey along dimly lit backstreets, and children being snatched away from their homes by wolves and reverting back to a wild state.

Werewolves were a subject of great concern throughout Europe between the fifteenth and nineteenth centuries. Their existence was hotly debated before the Royal Society of London in 1663. French society was particularly caught up in the werewolf mania and arrested and convicted many alleged werewolves in French courts. Werewolf stories were popular in literature, no doubt fueling the public hysteria. Robert Louis Stevenson's tale of Dr. Jekyll and Mr. Hyde is perhaps the best example of the unconscious fears that gripped the new bourgeois man and woman of the urban age. Dr. Jekyll, the urbane, kindly doctor, leading a quiet and orderly middle-class life, epitomized the new scientific vision of reason and measured judgment. At night he transformed himself into his animal shadow, a ferocious, wolflike beast and committed violent sexual acts against helpless women.[7]

Stories of feral children were also widespread throughout Europe. Each new claim or discovery was greeted with both interest and alarm as it threatened to undermine the fragile boundary that had been artificially erected between human beings and their animal nature. The most famous of the cases was Victor, the "wild boy of Aveyron," discovered on the outskirts of a French village in the winter of 1800. When captured by local villagers, the boy was unclad, unable to walk upright, could not speak, and seemed impervious to heat and cold. He was taken to Paris, where he was placed in the care of scientists at the Society of Observers of Man. They described Victor as

> a disgusting, slovenly boy, affected with spasmodic, and frequently convulsive motions, continually balancing himself like some of the animals in the menagerie, biting and scratching those who contradicted him, expressing no kind of affection for those who attended him; and in short, indifferent to anybody, and paying no regard to anything.[8]

The society spent considerable time and expense over the next five years studying and analyzing Victor's behavior to ascertain both the nature of his upbringing and the potential of reintegrating him into human society. Although many in the public were convinced that Victor was in fact a wolf-child, the scientists concluded that he was most likely an idiot child who had been abandoned by his parents and had been fortunate enough to survive in the wild, living on the outskirts of human settlements. The description of Victor's physical condition and state of mind was similar to other accounts of "captured" wolf-children.[9] By and large they seem to confirm later analyses by psychologists like Bruno Bettelheim, who argued that in most cases the children in question were likely victims of autism and other forms of brain damage.[10]

While the public came to fear any transgression of the human-animal boundary, it was also fascinated by behavior that seemed to reinforce the prejudices of the period. The mentally insane, for example, came to be viewed as beasts, little different from wild animals. They were also a source of continued public amusement and even entertainment. London's Bethlehem Hospital for the Insane opened its doors to the public, who paid admission to view the insane as they would animals in a zoo. The spectators, who included the rich as well as the rabble, would taunt and tease the caged patients, often coaxing them with cheap gin to enliven their performance. The hospital admitted over 96,000 visitors each year, and by the time it finally closed its doors to the public in 1700, it had reaped a handsome profit.[11] In the new world, the Pennsylvania Hospital, America's first general hospital, opened its doors to the public in 1756. The mentally ill were confined to the cellar. Local residents would often treat their out-of-town guests to visits to the institution to gaze at naked inmates, chained to iron rings on the floor, being whipped by their keeper.[12]

The moral and intellectual crusade to subdue the animal side of human existence was used repeatedly and effectively by the new territorial states and colonial trading companies as a rationale and justification for subduing native people around the world. The enclosure and colonization of the new world was pictured as a grand historical struggle, pitting the civilized influences of Western culture against the brutish character of primitive people. Taming the wilderness and civilizing other people became part and parcel of the same imperialist mission. Speaking of the American frontier experience, historian Roderick Nash observed:

> ... Frontiersmen acutely sensed that they battled wild country not only for personal survival, but in the name of nation, race, and God. Civilizing the new world meant enlightening darkness, ordering chaos, and changing evil into good. In the morality play of westward expansion, wilderness was the villain, and the pioneer, as hero, relished its destruction. The

transformation of wilderness into civilization was the reward for his sacrifices. . . .[13]

The notion that all human beings were animal-like spawned the idea that some races of human beings were inherently more so than others. Modern race ideology was born during the early modern era and was first espoused by an Englishman, Sir William Petty, in 1677. He argued that the human race was made up of different species, some of whom were closer in lineage to the higher animals than to their fellow human beings.[14]

Petty's race theory was taken up and expanded upon in the eighteenth century by David Hume and other Enlightenment thinkers. In his *History of Jamaica,* published in 1774, Edward Long shared his view that the Negro was closer to the orangutan than he was to the white man in nature's hierarchy. Much of the racial theory of the time concentrated on the black race, in no small part to justify the lucrative slave trade, which was providing a cheap captive labor force for the newly enclosed lands of the new world.[15]

The European aristocracy even integrated race theory directly into their households. It became fashionable to own little black boys as "house pets." It was said that a proper lady "hath always two necessary implements about her, a Blackamoor and a little dog."[16] Black boys became household ornaments in England and on the European continent and, like other pets, trailed their mistresses throughout the house and even accompanied them in the bedchamber. Often the boys were outfitted like dogs; in the *London Advertiser* of 1756, a goldsmith announced that he could forge "silver paddocks for blacks or dogs; collars, etc." It was not uncommon for black houseboys to wear gold-plated collars engraved with their owners' coat of arms, with inscriptions like "My Lady Bronfield's black, in Lincoln's Inn Fields."[17]

Blacks, Indians, and aborigines were not the only groups to suffer from the new race theories. Many Englishmen regarded the Irish as little better than beasts, who drank raw blood and ate raw flesh. An English regiment told of finding dead Irishmen with "tails near a quarter of a yard long" in a garrison after a long and bloody battle. Over forty British soldiers came forward and testified under oath that they had viewed the corpses.[18] By the nineteenth century, race theory became the accepted doctrine among European intellectuals. Charles Darwin concurred with the intellectual view of the period, arguing that natural selection would eventually prevail among Homo sapiens, ensuring that "endless numbers of the lower races will have been eliminated by the higher civilized races throughout the world."[19]

Darwin lent his enthusiastic support to the eugenics dogma espoused by his cousin, Sir Francis Galton. Galton was interested in developing a selective breeding program to propagate the best stock of the Caucasian race. He reasoned that just as breeding programs had proven successful in animal husbandry, a human breeding program might prove highly effective at weeding out the more brutish representatives of the human species, leaving civilization with a purebred stock of highly civilized human beings.

In this century, Adolf Hitler rose to power, in part, by effectively preying upon the racial anxieties of a society caught between the accelerating influences of modernity and the traditional folk values of medieval life. The Third Reich combined a pathological fear of the "animal-like bestiality" of the Jew with the bureaucratic logic of Cartesian mechanism in the death camps and crematoria. In the end, over six million Jews and other minorities had been systematically gassed in the name of "pure blood."

28

DISCONNECTING
THE SENSES

IN THE STRUGGLE to gain autonomy, modern man has given up far more than his animal nature. He has journeyed to the interior of his physical being and surrendered the very senses that connect him to the natural world. The bonding senses—touch, smell, and hearing—have been dulled in direct proportion to the flight from nature and the human body. At the same time, sight—the most detached, expropriating, and rational sense—has been sharpened and has now gained near hegemony in the sensual hierarchy. Seeing has replaced feeling in the modern world, fostering the illusion that a disembodied autonomous mind can exist in a natureless world.

By amputating the intimate senses and elevating the most abstract of the senses, modern man has been left with few resources to free himself from his own isolation. In a world where the institutional fabric of private and public life has been wholly made over to suit the prerequisites of sight at the expense of smell, touch, and hearing, detached expropriation will inevitably triumph over intimate communion at every juncture. Left unused or underutilized, the intimate and instinctual senses lose their potency and definition, further isolating the individual and lessening the chance of reclaiming a deep, meaningful relationship with the outside world.

Ernest Schachtel points out that the intimate senses—taste,

touch, smell and, to a lesser degree, hearing—are more closely attuned to feelings of pleasure and disgust. They incite the instinctual animal side of our being.

> The pleasure which a perfume, a taste, or a texture can give is much more a bodily, physical one, hence more akin to sexual pleasure, than is the more sublime pleasure aroused by sound, and the least bodily of all pleasures, the beautiful.[1]

The Church—and to an even greater extent, the early Protestant reformers—feared the more intimate senses and did everything within their power to suppress them in the hope that human beings would not give in to their animal appetites and fall back into a beastlike state of existence. The asceticism of the monastery and the new Protestant churches served as a model for a social order in which the exercise of smell and touch were increasingly marginalized in day-to-day human affairs.

Enlightenment thinkers reinforced the suppression of smell and touch, arguing that the "feeling" senses were far too instinctual, spontaneous, and unpredictable. Like their church brethren, the philosophers regarded smell and touch as the more primitive, less developed senses.

Entrepreneurs and industrialists joined the ranks as well. They were concerned that the more intimate senses would promote indolence and undermine their attempts to create and maintain a productive, disciplined work force. They preferred to redirect the instinctual senses away from communal bonding and intimate participation with nature and toward the more limited role of pure consumption. Today taste, touch, and smell have been made hostage to the marketplace, where they are toyed with and incited shamelessly to promote ever greater consumption of goods and services.

29

ODORIFEROUS TERRORS

SMELL WAS THE first of the senses to be suppressed during the early modern era. Smelling and sniffing became associated with animal behavior. Intellectuals of the period were quick to point out that only human beings walked totally upright on two legs—other creatures always had their noses to the ground.[1]

The fact that animals rely more on their snouts and have a more highly developed sense of smell than human beings reinforced assumptions about man's higher nature. Then, too, smell was associated with lust and sexuality and the unbridled passion of animality, forces that came under increasing scrutiny during the transition to the modern era. The repression of smell has continued unabated during the entire modern era. As late as the twentieth century, Sigmund Freud wrote that the root of man's alienation from nature and his own animal instincts is "man's adoption of erect posture and the lowering in value of the sense of smell."[2]

Smells are not easy to define or measure. They are difficult to control and do not respect boundaries. They diffuse into the environment, cross borders, and mix freely with their surroundings. The olfactory sense is incompatible with the Cartesian worldview, with its emphasis on order, precision, linearity, and well-defined surfaces and borders. Smells are ephemeral. They lack the kind of hardness that so characterizes the atomistic world of Newtonian mechanics. Smells unite and commingle and, for that reason, pose a threat to the notion of autonomy and security.

A deadly fear of earthly and organic smells spread across much of the European continent in the eighteenth and nineteenth centuries. Public paranoia over certain odors seeping out of the ground, from the roots of trees, and from the pores of other human beings reached near hysterical proportions, especially in France. Familiar smells that had long provided a sense of continuity with the past and bonding with the present suddenly became suspect. The near phobia over various smells marked a rather macabre turn in human affairs. As with other animal species, Homo sapiens has always relied on smell to establish patterns of security and safe havens. In the modern era, many familiar smells became a dangerous threat and something to be avoided.

It is, perhaps, no mere coincidence that the enclosure of the European commons and the new sense of detachment from the land was accompanied by a new fear of "deadly" smells emanating from the bowels of the earth.[3] In 1774, Boissier de Sauvages warned that a dangerous "vapor rises from the whole surface of the earth as a result of subterranean heat. . . . It is to a greater or lesser degree abundant, denser than air, and it spreads out when nothing prevents it, and falls again in the evening."[4]

Government-appointed commissions issued lengthy reports on the dangers of "subterranean" fumes in agricultural regions. In 1786, a report was presented to the Société Royale de Médicine in France, by Monsieur de Chamseru, warning of the danger to any peasant "who bent down and brought his face too close to the soil he was turning over."[5] Many scientists expressed concern over "morbific vapors" that escaped from the earth during cultivation. Some authorities suggested that agricultural workers be "prevented from sleeping with their noses to the soil."[6] The land, which had provided the bounty and sustained and secured the existence of countless generations, was transformed from a fecund, life-giving source to a devilish terrain populated by evil winds blowing up from the fiery depths of the underworld.

Writers and philosophers of the period used olfactory metaphors to describe hell. The putrid and the demonic became synonymous in the public mind and earthly stench became associated with hell and the grim reaper. For the first time since the outset of the neolithic revolution, the soil itself became something to fear. Among urban dwellers, the fear ripened into public clamor for paving over the land, to seal up the "morbific vapors" and create an impenetrable boundary between man and nature. While paving dates back to Roman times, and was used to ease and speed the flow of commercial and military traffic, the new obsession with the "mysterious art of paving" was motivated to a great extent by a pathological fear of the earth and a desire to be isolated from it as much as possible.[7]

It was during the early modern age that organic smells, especially human and animal emanations, became deeply associated with disease and death. In medicine, doctors and scientists developed a complex taxonomy of smells to diagnose illness.

> Qualified practitioners can very well tell the odor that emanates from ulcers complicated by gangrene, every odor peculiar to consumptives, people laid low by dysentery, malign putrid fevers; and that odor of mice which is part of hospital and jail fevers.[8]

It was common for doctors to smell a patient's breath, stool, urine, and pus in order to identify both the illness and its state of progression. By 1760, French scientists had succeeded in classifying the various stages of putrefaction based on olfactory analysis. In a thesis published in that year, Féou detailed the various stages of decomposition of matter after death based on a taxonomy of smells. Immediately after death, the body emanates a "sweetish odor," which scientists call "vinous fermentation." In the next stage an acidic odor, "quite often similar to that of decaying cheese," sets in. This came to be known as the "acid ocaseous" stage.

> Finally the odor of decay appears; at first, it is stale, without pungency, but this staleness is nauseating . . . imperceptibly the odor becomes penetrating, then it is bitter and abominable.

210

The putrid taste is followed by a herbaceous taste and the odor of amber.[9]

The new interest in smell among doctors and scientists proved short-lived. Its scientific contribution was dubious. However, it did succeed in further heightening public anxiety over organic odors, especially animal and human smells. More than anything else, says French historian Alain Corbin, it revealed "the precarious nature of organic life."[10] Pungent and fetid animal smells became linked in the public mind with an olfactory shadow of death. The smells were everywhere; of course, they always had been, but once were of little concern. They were simply the background smells of nature that enveloped the organic world and provided the recurring cues of life's passage. Now, suddenly, they were associated with the threat of death. The stench of nature, animals, and humans became a source of alarm.

The war against the olfactory sense was fought along two fronts: disinfection and deodorization. The emerging bourgeoisie of the cities and the country's gentry joined forces to rid their environments of all olfactory traces of animality. The spatial interiorization and privatization of life were accompanied by a campaign to isolate the family and the individual from the smells of nature, the smells of the masses, and one's own bodily smells as well. Corbin summarizes the mood of the period in his book *The Foul and the Fragrant:*

> Disinfection and therefore deodorization also formed part of the utopian plan to conceal the evidence of organic time, to repress all the irrefutable prophetic markers of death: excrement, the product of menstruation, the corruption of carcasses, and the stench of corpses. Absence of odor not only stripped miasma of its terrors; it denied the passing of life and the succession of generations; it was an aid to enduring the endlessly repeated agony of death.[11]

Human defecation and urination were among the first bodily functions to be privatized. During the medieval era, men would often relieve themselves in public places or wherever convenient.

Visitors to the Louvre during the reign of Louis XIV "relieved themselves not only in the courtyards, but also on the balconies, on staircases, and behind doors."[12] While such behavior often posed a nuisance, the smell of human waste and stale urine was so much a part of the olfactory background of life, it was barely noticed amid the other pungent odors that hung over city and village alike.

By the early modern era, human waste became a source of increasing embarrassment. Defecation and urination, like other human activities, were removed from public places, privatized and concealed so as not to offend others with animal-like behavior. In 1569, a court regulation stated, "Let no one, whoever he may be, before, at, or after meals, early or late, foul the staircases, corridors, or closets with urine or other filth, but go to suitable, prescribed places for such relief."[13] Privies were moved inside and vast urban sewer systems were constructed to replace cesspools.

The London sewer system was constructed in the 1860s. Other European cities began construction around the same time. The advent of the flush toilet completed the process of concealment. Henceforth, relieving oneself became the most secretive and private of all human functions—even more so than sexual activity. One's "embarrassment" could be flushed down under the ground and washed away in huge tubes to an outlying river, lake, or ocean, without one ever having to risk violating the nostrils of another human being. Today, the lone toilet and the locked bathroom have become the quintessential symbol of privacy, and for some, the last secure refuge of the individual in the home.

The privatization and concealment of human smells even affected the interiors of individual households. Family members began to fear close olfactory contact with their relatives. In the early 1800s, sanitary reformers like Dr. Michael Levy began warning of what they called "the family atmosphere" or the "gaseous detritus of the family." Levy and others believed that each family emitted its own "miasmic exhalation" by dint of its unique bloodline. These noxious gases built up inside the home, posing a deadly threat to all of the inhabitants. Too much "miasmic intercourse" among family members in closed spaces could result in the spread of "specific endemic diseases."

Odoriferous fears inside the household helped strengthen the movement toward increasing individuation and privacy. Experts were near unanimous in urging that the household be rearranged so that each person was provided enough personal space to avoid "reciprocal contamination" from the harmful effects of the "domestic atmosphere."[15] Medical authorities attempted to measure the exact amount of personal airspace each person required in the home to prevent the buildup of "miasmic exhalations." In the nineteenth century, LeBlanc and Peclet argued that to ensure "domestic hygiene" each family member required six to ten cubic meters of air an hour.[16]

The concern over odoriferous contamination stretched the idea of privacy and autonomy even to the grave. French sanitary reformer Jean Philibert Maret argued that "morbific" rays "radiated from corpses," and that shared family tombs spread the "family atmosphere" beyond the grave, imperiling the health of those still above. Another Frenchman, Vicq d'Azyr, campaigned for a radical new idea, individual gravesites, which he said should be separated from the nearest neighbor by at least four feet.[17]

Paranoia over "morbific vapors," especially among the new urban bourgeoisie, led to innovations in ventilation. Airing, lifting, fanning, and beating became standard practices in the household. Specific instructions were given for aerating beds "to rid them of putrescent animal substances."[18]

Personal hygiene also became an important consideration, motivated more by disgust over the animal smells of the human body than by health considerations. Germs had not yet been discovered. The new fears triggered renewed interest in bathing. Hufeland suggested a bath once a week, an idea which, at first, scandalized the public. Other reformers came forth with equally radical ideas. Some went so far as to suggest a weekly change in underwear. Previously, the same undergarments might be worn for weeks or months at a time.[19]

The deodorization of the human body even affected a change in the use of perfume. Animal perfumes had long been popular. By the mid-1760s, however, musk, civet, ambergris, and other scents extracted from animals fell out of favor. Animal scents had traditionally been used to accentuate human odors, especially sexual odors. The new emphasis in perfumes was on masking any hint of either human or animal odors. Flower scents gained in popularity. Rosewater, lavender, violet, and thyme were considered less threatening and far less sexually provocative. Perfumed handkerchiefs and sachets became stylish and tobacconists perfumed men's snuff with jasmine and orange blossoms.[20]

The fear of human body odors extended beyond the family and home into the marketplace, where it played a decisive role in defining the boundaries between economic classes in the new industrial order. The aristocracy and emerging bourgeoisie seized on their new disgust of animal smells to draw greater distance from the peasants and laboring classes. It was believed at the time that each class, profession, and vocation could be identified by its unique scent. Dr. Jean-Joseph de Brieude asked rhetorically:

> Who could not tell a cesspool cleaner, tanner, candlemaker, butcher, etc., solely by the sense of smell . . . ? A certain quantity of those volatile particles which penetrate the workers is expelled from their bodies almost intact, along with their humors, with which they partly combine. . . . The odor that results is the very sign of the health of these workers.[21]

The poor among the population were singled out for particular abuse by the physicians and reformers of the day. Both the rural poor and the new urban poor were said to exhale an animal stench. Scientists and public officials began to focus on what they called the "secretions of poverty." It was widely believed that the poor were closer in physiology to the higher animals and had not yet acquired a truly human smell. A new image, "the dung man," emerged throughout Europe, according to Corbin, followed in succession by the foul-smelling proletariat and the filthy communists and anarchists.[22] The new olfactory boundary erected around the poor and laboring classes proved far more potent than philosophical abstractions in separating the classes and justifying the further exploitation of the masses by the ruling elite. After all, if the rural and urban poor were, biologically speaking, little better than brutes, then they could be manipulated as commodities or utilities, with no more remorse than might be expected in the tethering of a bull or the harnessing of a carriage horse.

The deodorizing zeal of the aristocratic and bourgeois classes, then, served as a convenient means of distinguishing themselves "from the putrid masses, stinking like death, like sin." At the same time, by emphasizing the threat posed by the fetidity of the laboring classes, those in power could continue to justify ruthless measures to subdue the masses and harness their labor to the new industrial machine.[23]

By the nineteenth century those in power had become almost paralyzed with fear over the animality of the masses. Their "organic stench" struck terror in the minds of the bourgeoisie, who continued to retreat behind closed doors, preferring to exercise control over the hordes from a safe distance.

The early efforts at establishing public health policies were motivated, in large part, by such fears. Disinfecting the masses was seen as a means of exercising control. Deodorizing the poor, it was said, would imbue the "crowd with a liking for cleanliness . . . order and discipline."[24] "Disinfection and submission," says Corbin, became inseparably linked in the bourgeois psyche.[25]

Today's high-technology environments are sanitized and odorless. We have surrounded ourselves with machines that are scentless. The rich organic smells of nature that people relied upon throughout evolutionary history to identify safe environments, establish secure relationships, and ward off dangers to health and well-being have been systematically suppressed. The sons and daughters of the post–World War II era were the first generation in history to grow up in a partially sealed-off environment. Our children's generation has been further separated from the smells of nature, increasingly experiencing the world from inside sealed bubbles—enclosed shopping malls, domed sports arenas, deodorized supermarkets, and the like. Their generation's security rests more and more on the workings of a machine culture that regulates temperature, the flow of energy, and other vital inputs in a totally artificial setting.

With each passing day, our sense of smell continues to atrophy as we become further removed from the smells of nature. Human beings are equipped to identify over ten thousand odors. Unfortunately, most Americans now can recognize fewer than two thousand smells, meaning that we have lost nearly 80 percent of our olfactory capacity.[26] If the American population were to lose 80 percent of its visual capacity in the next two hundred years, the loss would, no doubt, be experienced as a major threat to both personal and national security. Yet, we have expressed little or no alarm about the loss of our olfactory sense.

Experimental research over the past decade has begun to cast new light on the overriding importance of organic smells in securing human life. It appears that the olfactory sense plays a key role in maintaining the human species at every level of existence, from the primal drives to abstract reasoning. Its suppression poses a fundamental threat to the physiological and mental well-being of every person.

It has long been known that the loss of smell affects the loss of taste. Smell has provided our species with a powerful tool to identify friendly foods and reject poisonous or contaminated substances. The loss of the olfactory function weakens the sense of taste, leaving the individual less able to discern between what is safe to consume and what is not.

Recently, researchers have been discovering more subtle dependency relationships between smell and other human functions. For example, in a novel set of experiments conducted in the early 1980s, George Preti and Winnifred Cutler collected underarm secretions from one group of women and rubbed the extract under the noses of a second group of women on a regular basis.[27] After three and one half months, the two groups achieved menstrual synchrony. In another study, Cutler collected underarm secretions from seven men and applied the extract to the upper lips of six women who had "abnormal" menstrual cycles. The cycles of all six women sped up or slowed down until they reached the norm of 29.5 days. A second control group, whose lips were dabbed with only alcohol, continued to experience abnormal menstrual cycles. Sadly, instead of using the new data to urge a new bodily participation with nature and our fellow human beings, Cutler expressed excitement over the commercial possibilities of reducing bodily smells to a commodity status, purchasable in the marketplace. "My dream," said Cutler, "is that manufactured male es-

216

sence, in creams, sprays, or perfumes, can dramatically alter the well-being of women."[28]

New studies on smell are also demonstrating its importance in memory and recall. Smell, it appears, is the most powerful of all the senses in remembering past experiences and events, even eclipsing the pictorial images of sight. In one recent study, researchers exposed a test group to both pictures and odors; immediately afterward, subjects scored nearly 100 percent in picking out the pictures, but were only 70 percent accurate in detecting the smells. After four months, however, the visual memories of the pictures had faded to nearly zero, while the olfactory memories of the odors remained 70 percent accurate.[29]

As the metallic world of machines and computers becomes more pervasive, pushing the organic smells of nature further into the background, what is likely to happen to the human ability to recall? Again, it bears repeating that the machine world is scentless, except when a mishap triggers an electrical short or fire and the release of a toxic or noxious chemical.

Human events are increasingly experienced in a "smell-less" context. Deodorants mask our body odor. Disinfectants of all kinds mask organic excretions and secretions, eliminating any telltale signs of the natural world. Even the preparation of prepackaged foods in a microwave oven all but eliminates the aroma of the foods we cook and consume. Children growing up in hermetically sealed environments, devoid of natural smells, will likely suffer significant memory deprivation, as they are forced to rely more and more on limited visual images to resurrect past experiences and events.

The new scentless environments deprive human beings of one of the most fundamental tools of security. Reexperiencing smells associated with pleasurable past events is among the most comforting of life's experiences. The suppression of smells and the loss of olfactory recall isolate the individual not only from his own immediate organic environment, but increasingly from his own personal history and the feelings of deep personal security that arise from intimate bodily identification with past experiences.

30

A TOUCHLESS SOCIETY

THE FLIGHT FROM nature to an artificial environment and the accompanying desensualization of the human body have left modern man and woman with an arid and illusory milieu devoid of many of the familiar benchmarks of security. The traditional notion of "reality," which is based on a felt participation with the organic world, has become increasingly elusive with the suppression of the intimate senses. If the "real" traditionally includes the bodily experience of what it is to be alive, then the elimination of organic smells and the imprisonment of the olfactory sense in the modern era has greatly reduced our sense of reality and real participation in the world.

The experience of organic reality has been further compromised in the industrial age with the suppression and elimination of still another intimate sense, that of touch. Modern man and woman are the first in history to spend more time touching machines and tools than organic things. Homo faber, man the toolmaker, has systematically substituted the inorganic for the organic, the energy of the machine for the energy of life. Modern man spends much of his life touching cold, lifeless surfaces. Electricity, oil, engines, circuits, valves, and tubes have replaced nerves, blood, hearts, arteries, and veins.

The Spanish philosopher José Ortega y Gasset once remarked that "the decisive form of our intercourse with things is in fact touch. And if this is so, touch and contact are necessarily the most conclusive factor in determining the structure of our world."[1]

Consider the revolutionary change in tactile experience that has taken place in just the past two centuries. Even as recently as the early 1800s, the primary tactile experience was with the organic and with living creatures. People reached out and touched the soil, plants, domesticated animals, and other human beings all day long. Their hands grasped, cajoled, and squeezed living things. Their feet sank into the earth. Their bodies brushed up against the ox, the goat, the pig, and other creatures. People bunched together in their homes and lent each other a hand in the fields.

Today, in our highly urbanized industrial environment, tactile experience is primarily with inert materials—glass, steel, cement, plastic, silicon. Our bodies—our arms, legs, face—brush up against and handle a world that has been denatured. Real physical contact with what is alive has been greatly narrowed to a few gestures. In the post-industrial world of computer work stations, faxes, and cellular communication, the handshake is often the only physical contact that human beings enjoy during much of their waking hours. In social situations, the handshake is occasionally augmented by a peck on the face or a slight embrace, or an accidental brushing against each other in cramped quarters. At home, the tactile experience is only slightly expanded to include the cuddling of infants and small children, occasional sexual intercourse, and the stroking of the family pet.

Where machines used to partially mediate our relationships with the world, they now act as a surrogate environment. The psychic damage that has occurred as a result of the increasing loss of touch with the living world is beyond calculation. Today, Descartes's vision of a mechanized nature is no longer simply metaphor or poetic license, but very near an achieved goal of modernity.

The fear of touching many things that are alive, like the fear of smelling odors that emanate from animals, is deeply bound up with the fear of death. By disassociating himself from nature and surrounding himself with inert materials and machines, modern man could entertain the fiction of an autonomous existence and spare himself the angst of intimate sensual experience with anything that reminded him of his own mortality.

We touch through the skin, which is the most alive, most sensitive, and most mortal of all the organs. The skin is the largest organ system, comprising about 2,500 square centimeters on the newborn and about 18,000 square centimeters on the average adult male. The skin also makes up nearly 18 percent of human body weight.[2] It performs a number of vital tasks, all designed to secure human survival; its versatility is truly remarkable. In his book *Sunlight and Health,* Dr. C. W. Saleeby speaks admiringly of the skin's many roles:

> This admirable organ, the natural clothing of the body, which grows continually throughout life, which has at least four distinct sets of sensory nerves distributed to it, which is essential in the regulation of temperature, which is waterproof from without inwards, but allows the excretory sweat to escape freely, which, when unbroken, is micro-proof, and which can readily absorb sunlight. This most beautiful, versatile and wonderful organ. . . .[3]

The skin, as the body's main organ of protection, offers some interesting lessons on the fundamentals of security. Because of its porous nature, it encloses the body while simultaneously keeping it open to exchanges with the outside world. The skin mediates between the individual and the environment, constantly readjusting the body to changes in the outside world to ensure proper balance between autonomy and mutual relationship.

We participate most directly and intimately with the world through the skin and more specifically by way of touch. The tactile sense is our primary window to the world and is often called the "mother of the senses."[4] Even when all the other senses fail us, the tactile sense is able to make up for the losses. Helen Keller, who became deaf and blind in infancy, was able to learn about the world around her and make substantial contributions to it by communicating through the stimulation of her skin.

The retreat from touch, like the suppression of the olfactory sense, can often undermine the physiological and mental well-being of an individual. In a landmark study, psychologists R. G. Patton and L. I. Gardner found that babies denied maternal touch are more likely than other infants to have both their physical and mental growth retarded. In many of the cases reported, three-year-olds' bone growth was only half that of normal children. Adult problems with intimacy, including feelings of alienation and estrangement, detachment, isolation, personal inadequacy, and lack of identity are often traceable to tactile deprivation in infancy and early childhood.[5]

The loss of tactile intimacy often begins immediately after birth in modern society. In this century, breast-feeding, the most intimate and comforting of all human tactile experiences, became associated, at least in part, with animal-like behavior. Formula and bottle-feeding were touted as more scientifically safe and progressive ways of feeding infants. In an official manual on infant care published by the Department of Health, Education and Welfare in the 1960s, the authors reinforced the negative attitude toward human breast-feeding:

> You may feel some resistance to the idea of such intimacy with an infant who, at first, seems like a stranger. To some mothers it seems better to keep the baby at arm's length, so to speak, by feeding plans that are not so close.[6]

With formula feeding, as with so many of the functions of modern society, an artificial surrogate is substituted for the organic original, changing the nature of the exchange in a fundamental way. The post–World War II generation in the United States and other industrialized nations was the first to be suckled on rubber nipples affixed to glass, and later plastic, bottles. Denied the loving warmth of their mother's own breast, these infants were primed for an artificial, machine-mediated environment from the outset.

Of all the tactile experiences, none exceeds human breast-feeding for establishing a sense of emotional security in infants. Its widespread abandonment has likely had as great an effect in shaping the insecurities of a generation as all of the geopolitical and military considerations combined.

Human breast-feeding is vital in securing the physiological health as well as emotional well-being of a newborn. Human babies are born with little immunological defense. Mother's milk contains colostrum, which is rich in antibodies and helps protect the baby for the first six months until the baby has developed his or her own immunological defenses. In research studies comparing children who were breast-fed with those who were bottle-fed, scientists have found that by the age of ten, the non-breast-fed youngsters "had four times as many respiratory infections, twenty times more diarrhea, twenty-two times more miscellaneous infections, eight times more eczema, twenty-one times more asthma, and twenty-seven times more hayfever."[7]

Apparently, even the act of breathing, the most basic of all human functions, is adversely affected by bottle-feeding. The tactile experience of sucking on a breast is critical in developing proper breathing habits in babies. In the first few weeks after birth, infant breathing is generally shallow and unstable. Vigorous breast sucking stimulates respiration. Evidence suggests that bottle-fed babies are less likely to suck with the same enthusiasm as breast-fed babies, which may account for the higher incidence of respiratory tract disorders later in life. Other studies have shown that children breast-fed for four to nine months advance more quickly mentally, learning to talk and walk at an earlier age.[8]

In recent years, multinational corporations have expanded the market for formula feeding into third world nations, convincing mothers that their own milk is inferior to the scientifically tested, laboratory-produced substitute. Some of the advertising contains subtle messages designed to disparage the "primitive" nature of being suckled on a human teat.

The way babies are treated in a culture is symptomatic of the values that govern the society as a whole. Separating babies from their own mother's milk reflects the many other forms of detachment from nature that have come to characterize the modern age. The commodification and takeover of this most intimate maternal function by the corporation and the marketplace is consistent with the broad trend toward commodification of every aspect of the natural world.

Infant care changed dramatically during the industrial age, in large part reflecting the new value placed on individual autonomy. Interestingly, the new infant care techniques often increased infant mortality. Although it is not widely known, more than half the babies born in the United States in the nineteenth century died within the first year of life of a strange, inexplicable disease called marasmus, which is the Greek term for "wasting away." The disease was also referred to, on occasion, as infantile atrophy or debility.[9] In foundling institutions, infant mortality often reached near 100 percent as late as the first decade of the twentieth century. The mystery of the fatal illness was solved just before World War I when a Boston doctor, Fritz Talbot, visited the children's clinic in Dusseldorf. The American physician noticed a large old woman carrying a sick baby and inquired about her presence in the wards. His host replied, "Oh, that's old Anna. When we have done everything we can medically for a baby, and it's still not doing well, we turn it over to old Anna, and she is always successful."[10]

This chance encounter helped change infant care practices in the United States and Europe. In the 1920s, pediatricians in the U.S. began introducing a regular daily regime of "mothering" in the wards. Some hospitals required that every baby be "picked up, carried around, and mothered several times a day." In New York's Bellevue Hospital, infant mortality dropped from 35 percent to under 10 percent in the first few years of "mothering" on the wards.[11]

Although some compromises have been introduced into infant care, for the most part the practice of handling babies is still wed to a scientific paradigm that emphasizes therapeutic detachment, often at the expense of nurture and intimate bodily contact. Perhaps the best example of the problem is the successful campaign to eliminate the cradle at the turn of the last century. The crusade was led by Dr. Luther Emmett Holt, whose many textbooks on pediatric care were accepted as gospel by doctors and mothers alike. Holt ranted against the use of the cradle for over a generation, calling the practice "vicious" and "injurious." Caught up in the euphoria of twentieth-century modernity, and committed to applying the principles of scientific reasoning to every aspect of infant care, Holt and his contemporaries argued that the cradle was "old-fashioned" and unscientific. Worst of all, rocking the baby prolonged dependency. They urged its replacement with a prisonlike crib, which they said would make the child more self-reliant and autonomous at an earlier age.[12]

The radical transition from cradle to crib mirrored the radical changes going on in the culture as it struggled to redefine the notion of security. The cradle had served as an extension of the mother who, from the beginning of time, had cradled and rocked her infant in her arms to soothe and quiet him, to make him feel secure. The stationary crib, surrounded by bars, is a very different environment. The infant is isolated, hemmed in, and very much on his own.

Ashley Montagu points out that rocking an infant "produces a gentle stimulation of almost every area of the skin, with consequential beneficial physiological effects of every kind." As the mother rocks her infant in the cradle, her bodily motion becomes synchronized with the baby's. The heartbeats of each come together in a common sway, giving the baby "the reassurance of a familiar environment." Montagu sums up the anthropological significance of the cradle to generations of babies: "[The rocking] maintains the feeling of relatedness. A baby that is rocked knows that it is not alone."[13]

Replacing the rocker with the crib undermined the infant's bond with the mother. By emphasizing autonomy over relationship, the "experts" may well have achieved results quite different than they had intended. Instead of turning out more secure, self-reliant adults, the evidence suggests, the introduction and widespread use of the crib may have contributed to a host of physiological and mental maladies and, in the final analysis, a weakening of adult security among several generations of Americans.

Innovations like bottle-feeding and the crib were part of a larger effort to mechanize infant care over the last hundred years. The "scientization" of childbirth and neonatal care began with successful efforts by the medical community to eliminate midwifery in the latter half of the nineteenth century. In this century, the medical community launched a vigorous effort to introduce the principles of scientific management into every aspect of infant care. The experts advised parents to remain somewhat detached and aloof from their babies and to put them on regimented feeding schedules. If the baby cried between clock feedings, parents were told not to trust their "animal impulse" and pick up the baby and soothe him, but rather to ignore his pleas, relying on the prearranged schedule.[14]

Scientific objectivity, detachment, efficiency, and mechanization have been applied in the delivery room and the nursery with the same crusading zeal as to other areas of life, giving added force to the Cartesian vision of the world. With each new mechanistic encroachment on traditional infant care, human touch receded further into the background.

While it might come as a surprise to some, Americans are far less tactile with their children and each other than most other cultures. In one study comparing the tactile experience of parents and children between the ages of two and five in the United States, the Soviet Union, and Greece, American parents had "significantly less contact" with their children.[15] Often, American parents will substitute toys at a very early age as surrogates for their own bodily participation. The shift in tactile attention onto things is far more pronounced in highly advanced technological cultures in which material values and consumption rule over the entire body politic and extend down even into the crib. American parents are also less likely to allow their young to sleep in the same bed with them, as is still the custom in some other cultures. Anna Freud has observed that "It is a primitive need of the child to have close and warm contact with another person's body while falling asleep, but this runs counter to all the rules of hygiene which demand that children sleep by themselves, and not share the parental bed."[16]

American children, after the age of two, spend long hours by themselves, often with only their toys, or television sets, to keep them company. Deprived of bodily contact, very young children often have a difficult time sleeping and are forever pleading with parents to allow them to slip under the covers with them at night. The tactile loss is often compensated for by a near obsessive attachment to cuddly stuffed animals or old blankets, and an excess of thumbsucking—activities that are absent in cultures that encourage close bodily contact between parents and infants.

Surveying the results of a century of scientific management, Montagu concludes:

> Unsound as this kind of thinking is, and damaging as it has been to millions of children, many of whom later grew up into disturbed persons, the . . . mechanistic approach to child rearing is still largely with us. Hospital deliveries, the mechanization of obstetrics, the removal of babies from their mothers at birth, the failure to feed them soon after they're born, the elimination of breast-feeding and the substitution and encouragement of bottle-feeding . . . and so on, constitute some of the melancholy evidences of the dehumanizing approach to the making of people, as opposed to human beings.[17]

Since Montagu made his observations, new developments in biotechnology have further advanced the dehumanization and mechanization process. New human reproductive technologies, including artificial insemination, in-vitro fertilization techniques, frozen egg and embryo transfers, and surrogate motherhood make it possible, for the first time in history, to conceive a baby without intimate tactile contact between male and female. The social and psychological implications of conception in a petri dish have yet to be adequately explored. Certainly, as the new reproductive technologies combine with the new gene-splicing technologies in the coming decades, allowing prospective parents to begin the simple programming of traits into their offspring, the traditional notion of the parent-child bond will be even further eroded.

The introduction of surrogate motherhood has already reduced gestation to a business arrangement. Wombs can be rented for nine months, reducing even the female to a commodity status, purchasable at going market rates, which, at this writing, are approximately $10,000 per gestation. With the introduction of gene surgery on developing human embryos, the engineering principles of quality control, advance design concepts, quantifiability, and efficiency will further reduce human life to the status of an engineered, preprogrammed product.

Our detachment and increasing isolation from nature, other members of our species, our own bodies, and now our own progeny, and the subsequent commodification of each, are part of the same process of modernization that has reduced all of nature to a scientific and commercial paradigm.

31

ORAL AND VISUAL
CULTURES

THE SUPPRESSION OF the human senses is one
of the least examined aspects of the modern age. Yet, the severing
of sensual ties with the outside world has been a decisive factor in
the construction of the modern frame of mind. Nowhere is this
more apparent than in the events of the early modern era that
transformed Europe from an oral to a print culture.

The Gutenberg revolution shifted attention from the ear to the
eye, and in so doing effected profound changes in human consciousness and institutions. The coming of print elevated sight to
the top of the sensual hierarchy, making all the other senses mere
handmaidens. The ascendance of sight and the suppression of
sound helped assure the final triumph of the Cartesian vision, the
Baconian paradigm, the capitalist market, and the modern nation-
state. Although script existed among the Sumerians and Meso-
potamians six thousand years before Gutenberg, day-to-day culture had relied primarily on oral communication up until the
printing press revolution.

Our modern society is so dependent on visual communication
that it is difficult to appreciate how radically different the social
dynamic is in an oral culture. Walter J. Ong, professor of humanities in psychiatry, has written extensively on the subject of oral
versus print societies and offers some interesting and compelling
observations on the differences between the two.[1]

In oral cultures, learning is by apprenticeship. Information is passed on through word of mouth. Storytelling and proverbs are the most common forms of transferring knowledge between people and generations. In an oral culture, Ong reminds us, most language is stored in the mind. Information is not retrieved but, rather, recalled. For that reason, village elders are respected and deferred to, as they serve as repositories of the stored knowledge of a society. In oral cultures, wisdom is cherished above all else. Facts, statistics, and data are little-used concepts in a nonvisual society. Because virtually all the communication is mouth to ear, people are forced to interact in close proximity to one another. Oral cultures, by their very nature, are intimate. While communication is primarily oral, exchanges between people are full-bodied and integrate the other senses into the process. Human utterances take on different shades, tones, and meanings, depending on the inflection, body language, and tactile cues that moderate or amplify each sound as it is delivered. Oral cultures, then, are necessarily communal, intimate, and highly interactive.[2]

In contrast, print culture reinforces isolation over group participation. Writing and reading are activities best pursued in privacy. It is interesting to note that before the printing press, written manuscripts were most often written in a sing-song style, reflecting the oratorical and poetic dimensions of an oral culture, and were generally read out loud to a group. On the rare occasions when manuscripts were read alone, the reader would always speak the words aloud, again reinforcing the primacy of sound over sight. The manuscript was seen as an adjunct to speech—and as a less reliable medium of communication to boot. Even account books were read aloud in the medieval era to assure everyone involved that what was written on the ledger could be trusted. The word *audit* has somehow survived the transition into a print culture, and exists as a kind of historical reminder of the great store placed in oral communication in bygone times. In his commentary on the Gospel of Luke, Ambrose of Milan remarked that "sight is often deceived, hearing serves as guarantee."[3] Today, the opposite mentality prevails. Oral agreements between people do not hold nearly the same weight as written contracts. "See-

229

ing is believing" has replaced "You have my word on it" in the popular culture.

In all of its particulars, print reinforces the underlying assumptions of the modern age. To begin with, print detaches people from each other. The bonds of intimate human relationship are severed and replaced by a technological intermediary. The printed page creates a temporal and spatial boundary. Both the sender and the receiver of communication relate to each other indirectly and circuitously by way of symbols inked on paper. Print also establishes "autonomous discourse, discourse which cannot be directly questioned or contested as oral speech can be, because written discourse has been detached from the author."[4]

Print suppresses and deadens sound, turning human utterances into lifeless symbols. Because the printed word exists in a kind of timeless vacuum, it gives the appearance of immortality, making it seem far more powerful, even if far less interactive. The spoken word, by contrast, comes into and out of existence in a moment. It lacks a sense of permanence.

The printed word is a thoroughly artificial construct, while the spoken word is always natural. Ong explains:

> Written words are isolated from the fuller context in which spoken words come into being. The word in its natural, oral habitat is part of a real, existential present. Spoken utterance is addressed by a real living person to another real living person, or real living persons, at a specific time and in a real setting that includes more than mere words.[5]

Print creates a second world which is immune to the immediacy of human interactions and impervious to the ravages of time. It is not uncommon in the modern world for people to retreat into the world of books to escape from the realities of the outside world. The printed word evokes the modern notion of security, with the emphasis on detachment, privacy, autonomy, predictability, and enclosed artificiality.

Printing press technology also combines some of the essential features of industrial production. Gutenberg's press was the first modern machine to use the principles of assembly. The printed word preexists as individual lettered units, which are then assembled in a linear format to produce words and sentences that can be used over and over again to stamp out identical signatures on page after page. Print also "made possible on a large scale the quantification of knowledge, both through the use of mathematical analysis and through the rise of diagrams and charts."[6]

Finally, and perhaps not surprisingly, the printing press allowed words to be privatized and commercialized for the first time in history. In an oral culture, words, stories, tales, poems, and aphorisms were all collectively shared. They existed in common, as did the land. The thought that someone could own a sentence, or worse, sell it and profit from it, would have seemed quite strange in medieval Europe or, for that matter, in any other culture in human history.

The printing press revolution brought with it new legal terms, like copyright and plagiarism. Human language, like every other aspect of nature, was reduced, at least partially, to a commodity status that could be bought and sold for the right price in the capitalist marketplace.[7]

While print helped establish sight as the premier sense in the modern world, other forces came to bear as well, adding to its new elevated status. The invention of perspective in art during the Italian Renaissance proved fateful in speeding the transition to a primarily visual worldview.

Medieval art, like medieval life, was largely undifferentiated. The viewer of medieval paintings often feels as if he is inside a giant fishbowl, surrounded by one-dimensional forms floating over and underneath him in different sizes and shapes that are, more often than not, out of scale and proportion. By contrast, in the new genre of perspective art, the world is "revealed from the viewpoint of a single individual."[8] With perspective, the medieval world of intimate bonds and relationships gave way to a new world of landscapes in which a subject (the viewer) looks at a series of objects along a receding plane. The objects exist as they would in the real world in their proper proportions and scale, always with the viewer as the point of departure. Perspective accentuates detachment, the viewer looking out at the world from a distance, as if the vista were his exclusive domain. Perspective reinforced the other trends of the period that were beginning to emphasize the importance of the individual and precise measurement.

Today, perspective is so much a part of our visual field that it is difficult to comprehend a world where it played little or no role. Yet in medieval Europe, visual consciousness was tightly integrated with the other senses—hearing, taste, touch, and smell. Life was sensually clustered. The land, people, and senses formed a "reassuring cocoon in which life could unconsciously proceed."[9] The visual field extended upward to heaven rather than outward to the receding horizon.

Perspective soon moved from canvas to architecture. Builders began to redesign living space with an eye to landscapes. Unobstructed views became far more important, as did the entire horizontal plane. The shift from heavenly gaze to earthly vista mirrored the shift in worldview from the sacred to the secular realms. Perspective helped fundamentally alter European consciousness. Sight gained ascendency over sound, smell, and tactile experience, leaving human beings isolated and detached from the comings and goings of the natural world. Modern man and woman began to look at the world from a distance. The land became the landscape. More important, it became a field to exploit rather than a place to belong.

Sight affects consciousness very differently than sound. As Ong points out, sight is "the dissecting sense" while sound is the "unifying sense."[10] The eye takes apart. It seeks clarity and distinctiveness. The ear puts things together. It seeks harmony.

In mythology, the eye has always been regarded as a male symbol while the ear has been a traditional female symbol. The eye is the sense of expropriation and is often symbolized by the arrow or dagger. The eye targets and isolates objects in a visual field. It can survey a landscape and zero in on an object, as sound cannot. The eye cuts. In fact, even today, television directors talk of cutting from one visual scene to another. In the animal world, the eye has always been the source of aggression. Animals avoid the gaze of other animals. The stare is perceived as a hostile gesture, the precursor to a violent confrontation.

The ear is often symbolized by the mussel or conch. Unlike the eye, which can be opened and closed by an act of individual will, the ear is always open, even when a person is asleep. The ear takes the world in while the eye projects the will of the person outward. The ear is vulnerable to whatever lies in its surrounding auditory range. The eye is far more selective and can more easily screen out what it chooses not to address. The ear, then, is inclusive while the eye is exclusive. The ear range is circular, while the eye range is linear; one hears all around but sees in only one direction at a time. The eye is a powerful but limited sensory organ. It can scan surfaces with precision, but cannot penetrate interiors. The ear, by contrast, is far less able to discriminate between things in the environment, but sound is far more able to descend into the depths and become part of the interior of things.[11] Joachim-Ernest Berendt tells us that in Chinese tradition:

> The eyes constituted a yang type of sense organ: male, aggressive, dominating, rational, surface-oriented, analyzing things. The ears, on the other hand, are a yin sense: female, receptive, careful, intuitive and spiritual, depth-oriented, perceiving the whole as one.[12]

The eye, Yi-Fu Tuan reminds us, is not able to merge with things in its field of sight. It is always removed and acting at a distance. Yet, because it is removed, it is able to discern relationships.[13] Aristotle once remarked that human beings "prefer seeing to everything else, because above all the other senses, sight makes us know and brings to light the many differences between things."[14] The ability to discriminate, define, analyze, and make connections between phenomena makes sight the pre-eminent intellectual sense.

Interestingly, studies on newborns by psychiatrists Robert May and Anneliese Korner have shown that male babies tend to react more to visual stimulants whereas female babies react more readily to sounds. For that reason, mothers will more often make sounds to attract the attention of female babies while relying on the waving of hands or objects to attract male babies.[15] The pattern seems to have extended into later life. Studies conducted by Camilla Perrson Benbow and Julian C. Stanley of Johns Hopkins University have found that "men usually perform better in the visual-spatial field, women in language."[16] It is still a widely held belief in the popular culture that women are more receptive and better listeners and men are more detached and rational.

The increasing reliance on sight, at the expense of sound and the other more intimate senses, set the stage for the Baconian revolution in science. Nearly a century before Bacon spelled out the details of the modern scientific method, people were becoming accustomed to objectifying their environment. With perspective came detachment and the idea of dividing the world into subjects and objects. People came to think of themselves as observers rather than participants. Today, five centuries later, the observer status continues to gain momentum as people spend much of their leisure hours with their eyes focused on television screens.

The suppression of the more intimate senses and the elevation of the eye went along with the enclosure of the commons, the severing of communal ties, the privatization of space, and the commodification of nature. The fragmentation, division, and expropriation of the global commons could not have been accomplished without the use of the sense most able to dissect, sever, and marshal. Then, too, organizing, coordinating, and arranging an increasingly complex number of commercial activities and events, stretched over time and space and between far-flung markets, could not have been achieved without greater reliance on the sense most able to discern patterns and relationships and make measurements.

The balanced relationship that had long existed among sight, sound, taste, smell, and touch was abandoned during the early modern era to make room for a worldview immersed in visual imagery. The eye helped modern man become an individual. It fostered analytical thinking and rational thought. The eye allowed man to influence people and events from a distance. It helped him exploit ever larger domains for profit and gain. The telescope and microscope extended his visual domain even further, allowing him to gain control over the open seas and the heretofore invisible world of the microbe. The eye turned everything in nature into an object or utility that could be expropriated and commercialized.

The war against nature has been fought with the eye. Its first victims were the other senses that helped maintain the bonds of relationship with the natural world. Literary critic M. H. Abrams captured the enormity of the loss, as modern man and woman emerged from a largely oral and sensate culture into the clear sterile world of light and sight:

> Man has lapsed into a fixed and "narrowed" mode of "single vision" by means of the physical eye alone, which sees reality as a multitude of isolated individuals in a dehumanized world."[17]

Sight is the least participatory and the most isolated of the senses. It is also the most willed of the senses and is always projected outward onto the world. Its stance is largely aggressive and expropriating. In a world increasingly mediated by sight, autonomy is inevitably pursued at the expense of relationship. The crisis of modern security is very much a crisis brought on by the tyranny of the eye.

32

THE AGE OF SIMULATION

THE SEPARATION OF human beings from nature and the parallel detachment of human consciousness from the human body has transformed Western man into an alien on his own planet. Much of the outside world has become a kind of "no man's land," a scarred and polluted terrain full of danger—a foreboding environment where wars are fought, animals are slaughtered, forests are razed and burned, and human refugees wander aimlessly from place to place in search of safe havens. In the new indoor world, modern man and woman attempt to escape their last connection with the outside world by suppressing their own animal senses and freeing themselves from their own physical nature. A marvelous array of machines, big and small, have been invented to replace nearly every part of our bodies, providing us with mechanical surrogates from head to toe.

Our deep yearning for a mechanical analogue to nature was first expressed in the construction of automata, elaborate mechanized toys that mimicked living creatures, even human beings, in bodily function, movement, and gesture. The most elaborate of the automata were the brainchildren of a brilliant and imaginative French engineer, Jacques de Vaucanson. In 1738, Vaucanson amazed his fellow countrymen with the introduction of a fully automated flutist. The mechanized miniature of a human being "possessed lips that moved, a moving tongue that served as the airflow valve, and movable fingers whose leather tips opened and closed the stops of the flute." Voltaire was so taken by the sight of the lifelike, remarkable little creature that he dubbed Vaucanson "Prometheus's rival." Vaucanson's greatest work was a mechanical duck, an automata of such great versatility that it has not been surpassed in design to this day. The duck could drink puddle water with its bill, eat bits of grain, and within a special chamber visible to admiring spectators, duplicate the process of digestion. "Each of its wings contained four hundred moving pieces and could open and close like that of a living duck."[1]

Automata were the rage of Europe during the early industrial era. Engineers built little mechanical boys who wrote out poems and prose, petite mechanical maidens who danced to music, and animals of every kind and description performing wondrous feats. The toys, which became a favorite of princes and kings, were toured and put on exhibition throughout Europe. The automata provided a kind of proof to many that nature, like the automata that mimicked it, must indeed be animated by principles of mechanism just as Descartes and his contemporaries had argued. The visible presence of these strange little automated creatures could not help but excite the scientific and popular imagination and add impetus to the drive to find mechanized surrogates for everything in nature, even the human body.

During the first stage of the Industrial Revolution, machines of all kinds were invented to substitute for the human body. With the invention of electricity at the turn of the nineteenth century, a new category of machines was created to amplify and even replace human consciousness. Marshall McLuhan summed up the "bodily" impact of the two stages of invention:

> During the mechanical age we had extended our bodies in space. Today, after more than a century of electronic technology, we have extended our central nervous system itself in a global embrace. . . .[2]

McLuhan's now famous aphorism that "electronic man has no physical body" is fast becoming a reality in a world in which electronic communication has increasingly substituted for face-to-face communication between people. Today, electronic media have even eclipsed print in importance. Less than 20 percent of all the words delivered in America today are printed. Over 80 percent of all communications now go through the airwaves and telephone wires.[3]

Electronic technology represents the final disembodiment of the senses. The more intimate senses, smell and touch, are eliminated altogether. Sight and sound are disembodied by machines, turned into invisible waves and pulses, transported over great distances with lightning speed, and then reembodied by other machines in the form of facsimiles, artificially reconstructed versions of the originals.

Television is today's electronic sequel to the mechanized automata of the early industrial period. The mechanical representations of life have been replaced by electronic representations. With television, cinema, radio, stereos, cassette-disc players, and the like, modern man and woman can surround themselves with a second creation, an artificially conceived electronic environment that is virtually sealed off from the world of living nature.

Over 99 percent of the homes in the United States now have at least one television set. On any given evening, over 80 million people are watching television. It is not uncommon for 100 million people to all watch the same show at the same time.[4] Never before in history have so many human beings collectively experienced the same event simultaneously. Ironically, it is anything but a shared experience, in that each viewer is witnessing the events in the privacy of his or her own home, far removed from neighbors.

The average American household watches over six hours of television each day. The average viewer watches over four hours of television daily. Most Americans are spending nearly half their nonworking, nonsleeping hours in front of a machine watching "the phosphorescent glow of three hundred thousand tiny dots" flicker on and off at thirty times per second, creating electronic images of people, places, and things.[5] While the images entertain, inform, and educate, we tend to forget that they are not "real" experiences. They are simulations. In his book *Four Arguments for the Elimination of Television,* Jerry Mander points to the

238

profound anthropological significance of this powerful and ubiquitous new presence in our life: "America has become the first culture to have substituted secondary, mediated versions of experience for direct experience of the world."[6]

Television is the ultimate technological surrogate for real life. It represents the final separation from nature, a retreat into a private domain where, cut off from the outside world, the individual can view artificial electronic re-creations of reality. Millions of people have become voyeurs, passive spectators of experience. They can watch in horror as wars unfold before their eyes, be entertained by swashbuckling adventures, be romanced and beguiled by torrid love stories, tickled and amused by comedic antics, and saddened by the tragic accounts of others' misfortunes. All of the human emotions and feelings are aroused daily by television—millions of people reacting not to other flesh-and-blood people, not to a living environment, but rather to a machine pulsing electronic images into a semidarkened room.

The electronic images cannot be touched, smelled, or tasted. They are visual and only secondarily aural, and even then both senses are narrowly circumscribed, diminished in size, range, and volume. Television cannot begin to capture the color, resolution, pitch, and tones of real images and sounds in the outside world. The flicker of illuminated dots conveys a one-dimensional silhouette, a distorted and disembodied representation of life.

Television distorts temporal and spatial reality in other, even more fundamental ways. The images of people, places, and events are cut into seven- or eight-second frames or sound bites. The viewer is asked to suspend reality and accept cutaway shots in which the past, present, and future intermix, follow each other out of sequence, dovetail and parallel each other in a confusing array of combinations that bear no resemblance to the temporal and spatial realities of the real world.

Then, too, the medium has become so pervasive in our lives that it has become much of our experience of life. We often talk about television characters and situations as if they were an intimate part of our lives. So much of our waking experience is consumed by television that many viewers are unable to distinguish clearly the artificial from the real. Indeed, the artificial becomes the most real part of our lives, since it takes up so much of our time.

Television blurs the distinction between artificial and real as no other medium in history, creating a fundamental distortion in human consciousness that for many borders on dysfunctional pathology. "Marcus Welby, M.D." received over 250,000 letters from viewers during the five-year run of the show asking the fictional doctor for medical advice.[7]

In a study prepared for the National Institute of Mental Health, Dr. George Grebner, dean of the Annenberg School of Communications at the University of Pennsylvania, and Dr. Larry Gross found that television watchers form much of their view of the world from what they see and experience on the screen. Among other things, the researchers found that:

> heavy viewers of television were more likely to overestimate the percentage of the world population that lives in America; they seriously overestimated the percentage of the population that have professional jobs; and they drastically overestimated the number of police in the U.S. and the amount of violence. In all these cases, the overestimate matched a distortion that exists in television programming. The more television people watched, the more their view of the world matched television reality.[8]

As both a medium and a technology, television incorporates many of the operative principles of Enlightenment thinking. It separates people from the natural world, isolates them from their neighbors, suppresses some bodily senses and narrows others, emphasizes the artificial over the real, and reinforces the illusion of an autonomous, secure existence. From the safe haven of the television room, one can experience the outside world vicariously, without having to risk intimate participation or bodily contact.

While television helped further enclose human consciousness from the world of nature by conditioning the mind to live within an artificial environment, computer technology is creating a second artificial enclosure, which "promises" to replace living nature altogether. With computer technology, human civilization enters what may best be characterized as the age of simulation. At the Massachusetts Institute of Technology, Carnegie-Mellon University, and other elite schools of engineering, scientists are working feverishly on a new generation of computers that they say will create totally artificial environments. They call these new environments "virtual reality" to distinguish them from the kind of reality we have experienced up to now in our evolutionary history.[9]

At the advanced media lab at MIT, scientists are creating prototypes of computing machines that can simulate aspects of reality. Their goal is to construct an artificial "vivarium," a totally enclosed environment in which they can create and sustain facsimiles of life in isolation from the outside world. In the new world of simulation, the computer is not only used to create the simulated world of virtual reality but also becomes a machine surrogate for human companionship. Nicholas Negroponte of MIT states unabashedly that he regards his relationship to the computer not as "one of master and slave but rather of two associates that have a potential and a desire for self-fulfillment."[10] Negroponte, like many of his engineering colleagues, envisions the computing machines of the future more as personalized companions than work tools or mechanized forms of entertainment. He writes in his book *The Architecture Machine:*

> Imagine a machine that can follow your design technology and at the same time discern and assimilate your conversational idiosyncrasies. The same machine, after observing your behavior, could build a predictive model of your conversational performance. . . . The dialogue would be so intimate—even exclusive—that only mutual persuasion and compromise would bring about ideas. Ideas unrealizable by either conversant alone.[11]

The goal of advanced computing design extends far beyond the obvious and banal considerations of commerce, military preparedness, or even more lofty goals like education and discovery. After spending several months interviewing scientists at MIT and other engineering schools, futurist Stewart Brand concluded in his book

241

Media Lab that what scientists really desire with their mechanical creation is "companionship" and the security of a predictable artificial environment to wrap around them. Daniel Hillis of the media lab at MIT fantasied: "I would like to build a machine that can be proud of me," to which he added, "Thinking machines will be grateful to their creators."[12] The notion of an intimate mechanized companion that, while not completely predictable, is at least somewhat controllable and, of course, replaceable—to wit, an artificial surrogate to living creatures—reinforces the vision of Descartes, Bacon, and other early Enlightenment thinkers.

In his second book, *Soft Architecture Machines,* Negroponte turns the final screw on the age of modernity, envisioning the ultimate vivarium, or enclosed environment:

> The last chapter is my view of the distant future of architecture machines: they won't help us design; instead, we will live in them. . . . While proposing that a room might giggle at a funny gesture or be reluctant to be transformed into something else seems so unserious today, it does expose some of the questions associated with possible cognitive environments of tomorrow.[13]

Negroponte's vivarium is almost alive. It is virtual reality and, like the natural world, it can be silly, even obstinate. Still, it is a creation of human beings and therefore seems more easily manipulated and exploitable.

The autonomous interactive vivarium is years, if not decades, away. Scientists, however, have already successfully created limited virtual reality environments. At the Japanese government's mechanical engineering laboratory, scientists are experimenting in a new field of simulation called "tele-operations." Japanese scientists have already created a successful visual model with tele-operations, a robotized camera that allows the viewer to scan an environment hundreds or thousands of miles away with the help of a mobile robot. The observer can send the robot to distant places and then scan the terrain with his own eyes, as if he were actually there experiencing it firsthand. The observer places his head in a black-velvet-lined box equipped with two television receivers, one for each eye:

> The receivers are gauged so that the image that is reflected against the retina of each eye is exactly the same as if you were looking at the world unaided. Further, every movement of your head is duplicated on the robot, where two precisely placed video cameras transmit a human range of what is seen.[14]

Researchers are working on other tele-operation devices, including one that allows an individual to manipulate an artificial environment on a computer screen in the control room and have his actions duplicated precisely and virtually simultaneously by a robot working miles away in the real environment.

Scientists working in the new field of virtual reality are experimenting with high-technology systems that can simulate all of the senses, enabling people to affect the outside world by way of an array of artificial experiences. The Data Glove was pioneered in the 1980s by Thomas G. Zimmerman and Lyoring Haivell. The glove, which contains fiber-optic cables tucked inside the fingers and thumbs, is connected to a computer terminal. The glove allows someone in a central control room to work with the mechanical hands of a robot in the outside world. As the human hand clenches, grasps, squeezes, and turns, the pressures are transmitted electronically to the robot's hands, which mimics each gesture. In the not-too-distant future, researchers say they will be able to reverse the tactile experience. As the robot takes hold of an object or even a living creature in the outside world, the tactile feeling will be transmitted inside, to the controller's hand, allowing him to experience touch by way of electronic stimulation.[15]

Computer synthesizing machines using advanced digital design techniques can already simulate the sound of an entire orchestra. One person sitting at a console can electronically reproduce the sound of virtually any musical instrument with the kind of precision that a musician cannot hope to duplicate.

Scientists are even working on techniques that will simulate smells, providing the vivariums of the future with preprogrammed odoriferous releases designed to incite, soothe, energize, and divert. Aroma therapists are experimenting with scent machines that can time a steady release of odors through ventilation systems into enclosed work environments or households. Researchers at Duke and Yale universities are studying the impact of various odors on blood pressure, brain waves, and other physiological processes. The new developments in olfactory science, says Yale psychologist William Cain, are likely to have extraordinary impacts on human civilization in the coming decades. "We'll gain tremendous understanding of the basic neurophysiological ways in which odors regulate the body and influence the mind. And after we've mapped the hidden pathways of olfactory nerves, we'll be able to influence behavior, modulate mood, and alleviate pain."[16] Some scientists hope to simulate smell electronically, over distances, just as they've begun to do with touch. One could smell flowers or a sea breeze hundreds or even thousands of miles away by way of artificially transmitted electronic pulses.

Proponents of virtual reality are eager to simulate every aspect of the human environment in hopes of creating a totally artificial living space. With each new technological marvel, reality becomes more ephemeral and further removed from anything that might be thought of as natural. With laser-generated holography, scientists hope to fashion new artificial environments that are mere illusions, transporting us into a world lacking any semblance of physicality. Holographically furnished homes might include paintings and other artifacts that are no more real than the electronic images on the television screen.

Virtual reality represents the final retreat from organic reality and the last chapter in the modern drive for security. The substitution of artificial experiences for natural ones masks an almost pathological fear of the living world.

Grant Fjermedal, in *The Tomorrow Makers*, recounts the dreams and goals of scientists he interviewed at Carnegie-Mellon. Their vision of the future captures much of the artificiality of the modern sojourn.

At Carnegie-Mellon University, Hans Moravec and Mike Blackwell had talked of the day when experiences could be simulated so well that you could sit in a chair wearing a headset to captivate your eyes, ears, and nose and have sensors attached to hands and legs, which would enable you to visit the world from the safety and comfort of your home.[17]

The relentless pursuit of a mechanized form of autonomous existence, seemingly free from the hold of nature and the death sentence it imposes on all living creatures, has led scientists like Hans Moravec to experiment with the idea of "downloading" human consciousness. Moravec, who is a senior research scientist at Carnegie-Mellon's Autonomous Mobile Robot Laboratory, explains the process in a theoretical paper entitled "Robots That Rove." Using ultrasonic radar, phased array radio encephalography, and high-resolution, three-dimensional nuclear magnetic resonance holography, researchers might be able to scan parts of the human brain in order to develop a three-dimensional picture of its chemical makeup. A computer program could be written to simulate the behavior of each section of the brain. After each section of the brain has been "downloaded" into a written program, the entire simulation could be transferred into a computerized brain, which would think and act as the living original, complete with an identical set of memories.[18]

Many researchers in the new field of artificial intelligence believe that downloading is indeed possible. MIT's Marvin Minsky says, "If a person is a machine and you get a wiring diagram of it, then you can make copies."[19] Like the alchemists who dreamed of discovering the elixir for everlasting life, and the mechanical engineers of the industrial age who dreamed of inventing a perpetual motion machine, the new computer scientists of the age of simulation dream of replacing the organic brain with a simulated computer model in an effort to defeat the inevitability of death.

MIT professor Gerald Jay Sussman expressed the hopes and expectations of many of his colleagues:

"If you can make a machine that contains the contents of your mind, then the machine is you. To hell with the rest of your physical body, it's not very interesting. Now, the machine can last forever. Even if it doesn't last forever, you can always dump it onto tape and make backups, then load it up on some other machine if the first one breaks. . . . Everyone would like to be immortal. . . . I'm afraid, unfortunately, that I am the last generation to die."[20]

The idea of downloading human consciousness should not really surprise us. It stands as the last unexplored terrain in a five-hundred-year odyssey to find a mechanical elixir. With thoughts of downloading dancing in their heads, scientists have crossed the final boundary separating the secular from the sacred, the artificial from the real world. The modern journey ends in the laboratories of MIT and Carnegie-Mellon, where some of the best minds of science are currently devoting their energies and their lives to creating a mechanical surrogate for eternal salvation.

In the age of simulation, security and immortality are no longer sought in Christ on Judgment Day, or in unlimited material progress, or even in the specter of a classless society at the end of history. The new immortality is information, which can be collected, stored, edited, and preserved in perpetuity. Unlike living creatures, information does not rot and decay. Because it is mathematically derived and immaterial in nature, information can be transferred from one program to another and from one computing machine to another forever, without risk of diminution. While the software and hardware will eventually run down, the information will not and needs merely to be downloaded periodically to preserve its contents. Yoneji Masuda, a principal figure in the Japanese plan to become the first fully simulated information society, expresses unbridled enthusiasm for the new immortality:

Unlike material goods, information does not disappear by being consumed, and even more important, the value of information can be amplified indefinitely by constant additions of new information to the existing information. People will

246

thus continue to utilize information which they and others have created, even after it has been used.[21]

For some, the notion of transferring human consciousness to electronic programs that can be tucked inside automated computing machines is a chilling prospect. For others, like Moravec and his colleagues, downloading represents the long-sought-after fulfillment of Descartes's grand vision, the final reaffirmation of the modern quest for total autonomy from nature and absolute security for humankind.

PART FIVE

THE COMING OF THE BIOSPHERIC AGE

33

MECHANISTIC VERSUS THERAPEUTIC CONSCIOUSNESS

OVER THE COURSE of Western history, our state of mind regarding security has changed, sometimes fundamentally. As we have already noted, in the medieval age the quest for security was directed to the heavens. Humanity placed its faith in divine intervention and salvation. In the modern age, security was redirected to an earthly cornucopia at the end of history. Humanity placed its faith in what Nietzsche called "the will to power," hoping to secure itself by triumphing over both the forces of nature and its own physical nature. Modern man and woman no longer regarded themselves as part of a carefully constructed organic unity but, rather, as the chance result of natural selection at work in a heartless, amoral world devoid of divine guidance. The struggle for survival took precedence, in both the personal and public realms.

Today, our ideas about security are once again being redefined, this time within the context of the global environmental crisis and the nuclear nightmare, both of which challenge the underlying assumptions of a mechanistic worldview based on increased detachment and autonomy from nature and the accumulation of material possessions.

A new way of thinking about security is emerging, which is likely to have a profound impact on human consciousness in the coming century. For the new man and woman, security is found in

251

breaking down walls, resacralizing relationships, reparticipating in community, and stewarding nature.

The pre–World War II generation was the last generation of unquestioning loyalists of the Enlightenment tradition. They believed in rational, objective thinking and were suspicious of emotions and bodily feelings. They championed material productivity and personal autonomy above all other human considerations. They eschewed intimacy and let feelings and motives go unexplored. They were cut from the Cartesian mold. Their orderly, predictable worldview was shattered by the carnage of World War II and the grim reality of the Holocaust and the dropping of nuclear bombs on Hiroshima and Nagasaki.

Those born after the detonation of the atomic bomb grew up in a far different reality. Where their parents' generation had believed that security lies in the exercise of technological power, they began to realize that in a nuclear age, the distinction between victor and vanquished becomes meaningless. Where their parents' generation had preached the virtues of privacy and autonomy, they felt increasingly alienated and alone, cut off from meaningful contact with the outside world. The post–World War II generation became the first in history to consciously explore its own feelings with regard to security. In the process, it began to challenge many of the assumptions upon which much of the modern worldview is built.

In the modern age, ideas about security flowed from the outside in. Military security, economic security, and political security were all external considerations that each person internalized. The ways in which modern man and woman came to define security in the public arena influenced their private attitudes about security.

Personal relationships during the modern age mimicked much of the thinking of Baconian science and Cartesian mechanism. Detachment, objectivity, utilitarianism, and expediency found their way into personal relationships among spouses, between parents and children, siblings and acquaintances, just as they did in the workplace, on the battlefield, and in the environment. People came to think of each other as objects.

Today, the new thinking about security flows from the inside out. The point of departure is personal feelings. Many among the younger generation are beginning to reshape their ideas about military, economic, and political security as a result of a change in the way they view security in their own personal relationships. The "therapeutic" generation has come to understand the inherent limitations of Enlightenment thinking on a personal level, and there is growing evidence that these private changes in attitude are beginning to find their way into the public arena, affecting attitudes about the environment, national security, and the economy.

The sixties generation challenged the mechanistic attitudes that had so thoroughly permeated personal relationships, especially the value placed on autonomy over intimacy. As the middle class became increasingly exposed to psychology, therapy, and counseling in the schools, workplace, community, and through the media, they began to make the first tentative connections between security on the personal and societal level.

In personal life, if one attempts to overpower and control a friend or mate, or relate to him or her purely in an objective, detached manner, the relationship will inevitably weaken and erode. Both parties, the victimizer and the victim, will exhaust their energies on each other, leaving each depleted and spent and the relationship scarred and maimed. Similarly, if one or both parties to a relationship place personal autonomy above shared intimacy, they will inevitably grow apart and the relationship will wither and die. Relationships based on power, control, subjugation, detached objectivity, and autonomy can never be secure. On the other hand, if one reaches out and is vulnerable and open with a spouse or child, sibling or friend, participating directly with him or her out of a sense of mutual respect, trust, and love, the relationship will almost surely deepen, strengthen, and become more secure.

The therapeutic generation is just beginning to apply the lessons of personal relationships to the society at large, challenging the concepts of security that have dominated the modern age. If brute power, detachment, expediency, strict utilitarianism, and autonomy undermine and deplete personal relationships and make them less secure, then we should not be surprised if the same values applied to nature or to geopolitical thinking or the marketplace lead to the same result.

Both the sixties generation and their sons and daughters, now coming of age in the high schools and universities of America, are beginning to glimpse the tremendous social impact of therapeutic consciousness. The new thinking about security has been called "transformational politics." Many in the post–World War II generation believe that changing one's personal values and attitudes in relationships is a necessary precursor to changing societal norms and effecting institutional change at the national and international level. The new therapeutic consciousness emphasizes intimacy and bodily contact, a reenchantment of the senses. It is a powerful, countervailing force and a direct challenge to the older mechanistic consciousness, which is now careening toward a world of simulation and virtual reality.

The clash between mechanistic consciousness and therapeutic consciousness is manifesting itself at every level of human decision making. President Reagan's commitment to the Strategic Defense Initiative is a prime example of the old way of thinking that characterized the Cartesian era. For Reagan, security was first and foremost, an external condition that could best be addressed by the application of more sophisticated technology. He argued that security always comes from a position of superior technological power and strength. Reagan believed that Star Wars technology would ensure American inpregnability and autonomy against any Soviet threat.

The older mechanistic consciousness finds security in isolation from the environment and the community of life. The body of nature and the human body, which is a microcosm of nature, are feared. Technological substitution becomes the goal to which human consciousness is directed. It is ironic that this old way of thinking is still regarded by many as visionary and progressive, when, in fact, it represents an earlier stage of consciousness, one whose contours were shaped and defined several centuries ago.

Perhaps the newer therapeutic stage of consciousness, which is still in a formative period of development, has not yet been given a proper historical reception because it has yet to effect fundamental changes in humanity's relationship to nature, science, technology, politics, and economics. Today, therapeutic consciousness is still preoccupied with the intangibles of reparticipation. Rehealing the mind-body split, resurrecting the human body, and resacralizing our relationship with nature are necessary first steps to remaking our economic and political institutions and redirecting science and technology. As the new therapeutic consciousness begins to effect tangible changes in the external world in the coming decades, the results of this new way of thinking will offer a sharp contrast and a strong alternative vision to the older mechanistic thinking, with its emphasis on genetic engineering, computer simulation, and virtual reality environments.

Already, a few visible demonstrations of therapeutic thinking are beginning to work their way into the public life of the society. Holistic health, organic agriculture, soft path energy technologies, green and cruelty-free life-styles, socially responsible investment, self-managed worker-run enterprises, and the like are attracting considerable attention. All of these innovations appeal to the deep yearning for reconnection with our own bodies, recommitment to our fellow human beings, and reparticipation with the natural world.

Mechanistic consciousness and therapeutic consciousness project very different images of the earth, each flowing from radically different concepts of security. The late Buckminster Fuller updated the mechanistic view of Earth as a machine with the image of "spaceship Earth." His choice of metaphor could not be more appropriate. The idea of Earth as a self-contained, hermetically sealed, automated, and autonomous piece of hardware encircling the sun fits neatly into the Cartesian vision. Today, the spaceship metaphor is being projected onto every level of reality. The postmodern home, the electronic workplace, the enclosed shopping mall, the bubble-domed sports arena—all take on the appearance and ambiance of a spaceship environment.

Practitioners of the new therapeutic consciousness, in contrast, are beginning to experience the earth as a living organism, an image that is more closely attuned to the new spirit of shared participation with the body of nature. The resurrection of the earth as an organism profoundly alters our notion of security, creating the basis for both a cultural and political reformation in the coming century.

Interestingly, new developments in the science of biochemistry, geophysics, meteorology, and other earth sciences are lending credence to the organismic theory. Many scientists are beginning to view the earth as an organism or, at least, as a set of living relationships that work in tandem, creating a single organic unity. The organismic view of the planet is not a new conception. Before the modern age, every civilization in history viewed the earth as alive. Even the Church, with its otherwordly emphasis, still regarded the planet as a living creation.

In a strange way, the worldwide enclosure of the global commons helped trigger this new understanding of the earth as a living sphere. Detachment from nature allowed humanity to discover relationships and patterns from a distance. As humanity seized control of the various spheres of the planet—land, ocean, atmosphere, electromagnetic spectrum, and gene pool—it slowly began to realize that each realm could not be neatly sealed off and isolated from the others. The political, economic, and military boundaries nation-states placed around their newly acquired earthly possessions were continually being breached by nature. The environment could not be easily constrained in artificial enclosures or be mined, exhumed, manipulated, or consumed piecemeal without affecting other spheres and realms. The growing environmental crises, which reached global proportions in the 1970s and 1980s, underscored the interactive nature of the planetary environment.

The new ecological awareness has been slow in coming. Today the younger generation is beginning to understand that everything in nature is interrelated, and every event in nature has an effect on everything else, be it obvious and direct or subtle and indirect. Still, this awareness of interrelatedness is a relatively new phenomenon. For most of the modern age, scientists and technicians, politicians, industrialists, and military tacticians perceived the environment as a one-dimensional horizontal plane made up of passive matter that could be expropriated and exploited in a spatial vacuum—without consequences or repercussions to the rest of the earth's environment. Mechanistic consciousness perceived nature in Newtonian terms, as bits and pieces or discrete resources rather than interactive processes.

From the very beginning, the worldwide enclosure movement

narrowed its frame of reference to the geosphere, the solid surface of the planet. Even after the other earthly realms were invaded, enclosed, and commercialized, the thinking of the age remained fixed on the horizontal plane. To this day, geopolitics, which is a derivative science of the geosphere, continues to dominate the thinking of nation-states, multinational corporations, and military thinkers, despite the new ecological awareness of the younger generation. By remaining steadfastly ensconced in a geospheric reality, the powers that be continue to entertain the mechanistic vision, ignoring the growing body of evidence that points to the organic interrelatedness of all earthly phenomena.

34

GEOSPHERE TO BIOSPHERE

THE FIRST MODERN acknowledgment of the earth as a living organism is found in the works of Russian scientist Vladimir Vernadsky. He defined the term biosphere, although the word itself had been coined in 1875 by Edward Suess in describing his work on the geological features of the Alps. The biosphere includes the geosphere (the solid earth) but subsumes it within a broader, more inclusive realm. Vernadsky described the biosphere in a paper published in 1911 as "the envelope of life, namely, the area of living matter. . . . The biosphere can be regarded as the area of the earth's crust occupied by transformers that convert cosmic radiation into effective terrestrial energy—electrical, chemical, mechanical, thermal, etc."[1]

In his book *Biosfera,* published in 1926, Vernadsky broke with the scientific orthodoxy of the day, arguing that the geochemical and biological processes on the planet evolved together, each aiding the other. His views were sharply at odds with Darwinian theory, which viewed geochemical processes evolving separately, creating the atmospheric environment in which living organisms emerged, adapted, and evolved. Vernadsky believed that the cycling of inert chemicals on earth is influenced by the quality and quantity of living matter, and the living matter, in turn, influences the quality and quantity of inert chemicals being cycled through the planet.[2] Today, scientists define the biosphere as an

> ... integrated living and life-supporting system comprising the peripheral envelope of Planet Earth together with its surrounding atmosphere, so far down, and up, as any form of life exists naturally.[3]

The biosphere, then, is the film of dry land, water, and air enveloping the globe within which all of life exists. While the geosphere is one-dimensional and horizontal, the biosphere is two-dimensional. It encompasses the horizontal, but it emphasizes the vertical. The biosphere is very thin, extending only from the ocean depths, where the most primitive forms of life exist, to the upper stratosphere. The entire reach of the biospheric envelope is less than thirty to forty miles from ocean floor to outer space, a distance that, were it horizontal, could be traversed in under an hour by automobile. It is within this narrow vertical band that living creatures and the earth's geochemical processes interact to sustain each other.

In the 1970s, an English chemist, James Lovelock, and an American biologist, Lynn Margulis, extended our understanding of the biosphere with their Gaia hypothesis. The two scientists argue that the earth functions like a self-regulating living organism. It is their contention that the biota and the geochemical composition of the atmosphere work in a symbiotic relationship to maintain the earth climate in a relatively steady state, favorable to the continuous flourishing of life. Lovelock and Margulis point out that the earth's mean surface temperature has never varied by more than a few degrees from its current levels. It has continued to stay within a narrow temperature range, despite vast changes in the sun's output over the eons of evolutionary history. The fact is, our sun has been warming up over time. Astronomers believe that the sun's output may have increased by as much as 30 to 50 percent since the beginning of life on earth. Troubled by this apparent paradox, Lovelock looked for the answer in his native field of chemistry, only to reach a dead end. It was when he considered the relationship between biology and chemistry that the explanation suggested itself:

> It was then that I began to wonder if it could be that the air is not just an environment for life, but also a part of life itself. To put it another way, it seemed that the interaction between life and the environment, of which the air is a part, is so intense that the air could be thought of as being like the fur of a cat or the paper of a hornet's nest: not living, but made by living things to sustain a chosen environment.[4]

Lovelock points to the regulation of oxygen and methane as prime examples of how the cybernetic process between life and the geochemical cycle works to maintain a homeostatic climatic regime on earth. He reminds us that oxygen levels on the planet must be confined within the narrowest of ranges. A 1 percent rise in oxygen level on the planet would increase the likelihood of fire by 60 percent. A 4 percent rise would likely ignite the entire planet in flames, resulting in a complete conflagration of living matter on the land surface.[5] Oxygen production is maintained by photosynthesis. The green chloroplasts inside plant cells convert the sun's energy into chemical energy for the plant's nurturance and, in the process, convert carbon dioxide and water into oxygen. Animals, in turn, take in the oxygen, sustaining their lives, and emit carbon dioxide into the environment. Much of the carbon dioxide is then cycled back through the plant chain again, and so on.

While scientists have known for quite a while how the oxygen and carbon dioxide cycle interact, they have been in the dark as to how the oxygen levels remain so fixed in the wake of major changes in the sun's output and in the kinds and numbers of living creatures inhabiting the planet. To understand how the oxygen level remains fixed at 21 percent, it is necessary to understand how it reacts with other atmospheric gases. Lovelock uses methane to partially explain the process.[6]

It was less than thirty years ago that scientists realized that methane was a biological by-product, produced by bacterial fermentation. Microorganisms living inside ruminant animals, in termites, and peat bogs produce over 1,000 million tons of methane a year.[7] Methane migrates to the atmosphere, where it acts as a regulator, both adding and taking away oxygen from the air. As it reaches the stratosphere, methane oxidizes into carbon dioxide and water vapor. The water, in turn, separates into oxygen and hydrogen. The oxygen descends to earth, while the hydrogen escapes into outer space. Methane, then, can add to the existing levels of oxygen in the upper atmosphere. In the lower atmosphere, methane uses up oxygen, some two thousand megatons each year. Lovelock points out that "in the absence of methane production, the oxygen concentration will rise by as much as 1 percent in as little as twelve thousand years: a very dangerous change, and on a geological timescale, a far too rapid one."[8]

Lovelock and Margulis believe that when the oxygen in the atmosphere rises above a tolerable level, a warning signal of some kind triggers an increase in methane production by microscopic bacteria. The increased methane migrates into the atmosphere, dampening the oxygen content until a steady state is reached again. The constant interaction and feedback between living creatures and the geochemical content and cycles act as an organic unity, maintaining the earth's climate and environment and preserving life:

> It is an intriguing thought that without the assistance of these anaerobic micro-flora living in the stinking muds of the seabeds, lakes, and ponds, there might be no writing or reading of books. Without the methane they produce, oxygen would rise inexorably in concentration to a level at which any fire would be a holocaust, and landlife, apart from micro-flora in damp places, would be impossible.[9]

Much of what makes up the biosphere, then, either comes from living creatures or is modified by them. Lovelock reminds us that the oxygen and nitrogen of the air come directly from plants and microorganisms. Chalk and limestone deposits are the shells or bones of once living marine animals. Coral reefs and many islands are merely the burial grounds of untold animalcules. Lovelock cites these and other examples to drive home the point that life is not simply added to a static, inert world of matter "determined by the dead hand of chemistry and physics." Rather, says Lovelock, "The evolution of the rocks and the air and the evolution of the biota are not to be separated."[10]

The planet, then, is more like a living creature, a self-regulating organic entity that maintains itself in a steady state conducive to the continuance of life. According to the Gaian way of thinking, the adaptation and evolution of individual creatures becomes part of a larger process, the adaptation and evolution of the planet itself. It is the continuous symbiotic relationship between every living creature and the geochemical processes that ensures the survival of both the planetary organism and the individual species that live within its biospheric envelope. The narrow Darwinist argument of survival of the fittest becomes trivial, if not irrelevant, in this larger organic context. The body of the planet and the body of each species within it is entwined in an elaborate, mutually reinforcing set of finely choreographed relationships.

Just as the earth lives within a narrow temperature regime and geochemical band that are self-regulating, so, too, does each organism. The human body, like the planet, is made up of microorganisms, living matter, and chemicals—all interacting to maintain the health of the organism. The idea that each microorganism in the human gut is fighting for its survival and expansion becomes far less important than the mutual relationship that exists between it and the other bodily processes that together maintain the health of the larger organism.

The Darwinist argument that each organism must either grow and expand or wither and die is as misguided and dangerous in biology as it is when applied to geopolitics. Unrestrained growth of cells inside the body of an animal leads to cancer and the consumption of the animal. Unrestrained growth of a species within an ecosystem can overwhelm a habitat and lead to the destruction of the environment.

Interestingly enough, recent evidence suggests that the American public is beginning to shift its frame of reference from the geosphere to the biosphere. In a survey on geographic literacy conducted by the Gallup organization in 1988, only 57 percent of the respondents could identify England on a map. Only 55 percent of those surveyed could locate New York State. One in seven could not even identify the United States on a world map. One in four could not identify the Soviet Union. The respondents demonstrated even less knowledge of geopolitics. One in three Americans could not name a single member country of NATO; 16 percent of those polled thought that the Soviet Union was in NATO. One in ten college graduates made the same error. The respondents fared less well identifying the Warsaw Pact nations; 50 percent could not name a single member nation. One in nine thought the United States belonged to the Soviet Alliance.[11]

Yet, when the survey shifted from geospheric to biospheric questions, the results were dramatically different: 84 percent of the respondents were aware that CFCs may be destroying the earth's ozone layer, and 94 percent realized that the impact of ozone loss would be felt all over the planet. Of those surveyed, 68 percent were aware of the problems associated with acid rain. One in three was even aware of the problem of deforestation in Brazil and its impact on the rest of the planet.[12] Although it is regrettable that adult Americans appear far less geographically literate than they were forty years ago, it is encouraging to observe both the awareness and the sophistication shown in relation to issues affecting the entire biosphere.

35

PLANETARY RHYTHMS

THE TRANSITION FROM a mechanistic to an organismic image of the earth and the accompanying shift in attention from the geosphere to the biosphere fundamentally alter the human perception of time upon which all definitions of human security are based.

Time in the mechanistic culture is artificially segmented, enclosed, and tied to commodification. The mechanical clock divides time into hours, minutes, seconds, and, with the advent of the computer, nanoseconds and picoseconds. The schedule and now the program are used to usurp and enclose future chunks of time, largely for commercial purposes. "Time is money" has become the temporal signature of the modern age. Market efficiency has become the overriding temporal imperative of society.

Time in organic culture is circadian, lunar, and seasonal, tied to the rotation of the planet and the rhythms of nature. Ecosystem sustainability is the temporal goal of society. Rethinking the time values of civilization will be a formidable task. The linear time frame of geosphere politics will have to be bent into the cyclical loop of biospheric processes. The notion of an ever-accelerating rate of production and consumption rushing into an open-ended cornucopic future has led us to the present environmental and economic crisis. In the name of progress, we have mortgaged our planet's future and made our children's world far less secure. Reorienting the time frame of human culture to make it compatible with the circadian, lunar, and circannual cycles of the biosphere will mean rethinking the most essential features of our temporal values.

Industrial civilization is entrained to the pace of the combustion engine and the electronic circuit. Every other culture in the past has lived, more or less, within the temporal constraints established by the sun and the changing seasons. To a great extent, then, the global environmental threat is a temporal as well as spatial crisis. In the modern age, humankind imposed temporal fences as well as spatial fences around nature. The introduction of the mechanical clock and the arbitrary segmentation of time into uniform, precise, mathematically calculable units that could be manipulated to serve the interests of mechanization and the increased manipulation of nature and man is, perhaps, the most important and least recognized aspects of modernity. It is no wonder that historians like Lewis Mumford argue that the clock, not the steam engine, is the principal machine and dominant metaphor of the Cartesian era.

In the nineteenth century, Western man enclosed the earth into artificial time zones and imposed a single system of world time on the planet to better coordinate transportation and communications and integrate market activity. Today, human beings are forced to live within two very different time worlds, one imposed by nature, the other by man. Our internal biological clocks, like those of all other creatures, are oriented to the steady rotation of the planet and the workings of the biosphere. Our personal and public lives, however, are entrained to the fast-paced rhythms of clocks, computers, assembly lines, electronic grids, combustion engines, and rush-hour traffic. The pace continues to accelerate with the introduction of ever more sophisticated labor-saving and time-saving technologies.

The "will to power" in the modern age is as much temporal as territorial. The modern enclosure movement dislodged people from the traditional sense of time as well as place. Temporal imperialism has accompanied spatial imperialism around the globe. Forcing human beings off the land has also meant forcing them off a seasonal temporal orientation. The hourly wage earners of the industrial city were coerced, sometimes brutally, into accepting the artificial tyranny of the clock. Making people "punctual" became a central preoccupation of the modern age.[1]

Deaccelerating back into the biospheric temporal loop will require a revolutionary change in thinking and a restructuring of the economic and cultural landscape. The task begins with a reconsideration of efficiency, the dominant temporal value of the mechanistic worldview. Many observers of modern history would be quite surprised to learn that efficiency has enjoyed a very short reign as the temporal standard of civilization—less than one hundred years. In its modern guise, efficiency is defined as maximizing output in minimum time, expending the minimum labor, energy, and capital in the process.

Before the introduction of the steam engine, durability was the most important measure of craftsmanship. While speed of production and performance could be improved on and was, toolmakers inevitably came up against the temporal limits imposed by the biosphere. Speed was conditioned and constrained by the energy that could be harnessed directly from nature. Horse and ox power, wind and water wheels operated within the temporal framework of the biosphere.

The steam engine, and later the combustion engine, allowed humankind to entertain the notion of virtually unlimited acceleration. Today, we are quick to equate speed with power. Indeed, efficiency has become the chief weapon in the war against nature. We have developed more and more efficient technological means to speed up the expropriation and consumption of nature. In science, technology, economics, and war making, efficiency has become the critical mark of our prowess and the standard by which we judge our relative security. The more efficient we become as individuals and nations, the more productive and secure we are likely to feel in the modern world. It is no accident that our sense of national security is more threatened today by the gains in Japanese efficiency than by the building of Russian missiles. With increased efficiency, we are able to consume the natural world at an ever faster pace, while allegedly saving more time for ourselves in the process.

Every engineer dreams of designing and building the perfectly efficient machine, one that runs by perpetual motion, without assistance from or dependence on an outside force. Our obsession with efficiency is born out of the modern drive for an autonomous existence. We have come to believe that the more efficient we make our science, technology, economics, war-making ability, and private lives, the more autonomous we are likely to feel. Our drive to become ever more efficient is bound up with our yearning to be like the gods—a prime force, autonomous, all-powerful, and in control. Lest there be any nagging doubt on this score, consider how pervasive and coveted this single value has become. The very idea of challenging the merits of efficiency, or rejecting it outright as a value, seems wildly heretical, if not completely blasphemous.

The more efficient our mechanized society has become, the more detached we have become from nature, each other, and our own bodily existence. In an efficient culture, both machines and people become instrumental to increasing output in less time. Anyone who has ever had to work for a long period of time within an overly efficient environment knows the feeling of being treated like a machine and feeling like a machine. Efficient environments and efficient tools reduce bodily contact and the full use of the senses, especially touch, taste, and smell. Because the emphasis is always on minimizing human labor, the process itself ensures greater detachment and isolation from others and less direct participation and felt experience in the world.

Efficiency also isolates society from its own past and future. Efficiency is a present-oriented temporal value. Its concerns are purely instrumental. What counts is increasing output now. The past and future are seen as impediments to the full use and exploitation of the present.

In every culture that preceded the modern era, the present was always constrained by the past. Sacred rituals, holy days, and other commemorative events were a way of binding together the past and present in a shared relationship. The past maintained a hold on the present. The present generation was always expected to honor traditions, fulfill obligations, and meet expectations placed on it by those who came before. In custom-bound cultures much of the present, then, has always been committed in advance.

In an efficient society, the past is an albatross. By placing limits on the free use of time and space, the past restrains the playing field in which efficiency can operate. Custom and tradition more often than not limit efficient technological innovation. By substituting progress for tradition, mechanized society has effectively eschewed the past. Modern man prefers to set his gaze exclusively on the immediate horizon and the short-term material gains that can be secured by overcoming the limitations of time and space.

Modern society is the first in history to attempt to "liberate" itself from its history. Free of the restraints imposed by tradition, the efficient society exercises pure power in a vacuum. By accelerating the pace of production and consumption, and narrowing the temporal span to the present moment, modern man has created the first thoroughly expedient culture.

By the same token, an increasingly expedient society pays little regard to the future. Efficiency works best in a market economy where the immediate self-interest of buyers and sellers dictates supply and demand. The idea of stewarding resources and protecting the environment on behalf of future generations is inimical to the process of resource optimization and market efficiency.

By detaching themselves from both the past and the future, human beings are left alone, adrift in the continuum of time and history, without meaningful connection to what has come before and what will come after. The efficient society severs the traditional bonds of security, the threads of obligation and commitment that traditionally join the generations together in a seamless temporal web. Human beings are left with only their technological prowess to ease their sense of historical isolation in an ever more expedient world.

While efficiency has enjoyed near hegemony as the temporal standard in the geospheric culture, it will need to be modified by the temporal requisites of sustainability in the biospheric culture. An ever more efficient culture is an ever less sustainable one. By continuing to accelerate the production and consumption of nature's resources in less time, mechanized society has strained the carrying capacity of the biosphere. Although greater efficiency will be necessary in the use of energy, it can no longer be the exclusive standard by which we judge all other market activity. No society can long sustain its relationship with the biosphere if it continues to develop technological means of accelerating the expropriation and use of nature's resources in less and less time. The advanced industrial nations have long since passed the critical juncture where technological transformation of nature's resources into economic utilities matched the ecosystem's ability to absorb, recycle, and replenish.

The "green revolution" in agriculture is a good case in point. Regarded by many as the most efficient form of agriculture in history, it is also becoming obvious that it is the least sustainable. While green revolution technology boosted production in a short time with the use of petrochemical fertilizers, pesticides, and high-yield monocultures, it did so at the expense of eroding and poisoning the soil base, undermining the genetic diversity of agricultural crops, and increasing the effect of global warming (as mentioned earlier, nitrous oxides emitted from petrochemical fertilizers are a potent greenhouse gas).

Modern architecture also underscores the inherent limitations in pursuing efficiency to the exclusion of other temporal values. High-tech prefabricated building materials and more efficient design standards allow architects to erect more structures in less time and with less human labor. Yet, for the most part, contemporary architecture is far less sustainable than the architecture of the early modern era.[2] American visitors to Europe are often impressed by the age, condition, and esthetic appearance of ancient European architecture. Office buildings, houses, streets, and infrastructure in cities like Amsterdam in the Netherlands and Siena in Italy are over five hundred years old and still remarkably well preserved. How many American cities and suburbs are likely to last as long? The earlier architecture required a greater initial commitment of time and human labor. In that sense, it was less efficient. But, perhaps for that very reason, it ultimately proved to be more sustainable.

An efficient environment can never be a truly joyful, playful, spontaneous, and empathetic environment. That is because everything becomes secondary to increasing material output in shorter time intervals. People, like machines, become instrumental to the task at hand. The younger generation, caught between mechanistic and therapeutic consciousness, geospheric and biospheric

269

thinking, is just beginning to grasp the shortcomings of efficiency as an exclusive means and end by which to organize social life. Author and environmental activist Andrew Kimbrell observes that we would never treat our loved ones in a purely efficient manner. Personal relationships require the expenditure of time, labor, energy, and capital. Love and understanding cannot be forced into schedules and programmed like so many inputs. Knowing another person in a deep way requires direct participation. Empathy grows out of shared experience. No one seriously interested in nurturing a relationship would consider maximizing the output in the minimum time, while expending the minimum labor, energy, and capital in the process. Efficient relationships are rarely sustainable ones.

What is true in personal relationships is equally valid in economic and environmental relationships. Sustaining our relationship with the biosphere will require a wholesale reorientation in temporal standards. Society will need to broaden its temporal horizon beyond the expediency of the moment and the marketplace and renew its commitment to both past and future generations and to the cycles of nature. Ultimately, we will need to understand that true security can never be experienced or realized when relationships are based exclusively on efficiency, be they personal relationships or economic and environmental relationships.

While time in the geospheric culture is measured by the clock and the computer, time in the biospheric culture needs to be experienced through close empathetic involvement with nature. A new biospheric temporal orientation is already beginning to challenge the conventional mechanistic time orientation in a wide range of human activities.

Consider agriculture once again, this time within the context of an emerging biospheric temporal framework. High-technology farmers are constantly engaged in the pursuit of new, more exotic forms of plant and soil manipulation in order to speed production and increase output beyond the natural carrying capacity of the ecosystem. In contrast, organic farmers are developing a sophisticated store of knowledge about the delicate balance of relationships that govern the environment and the seasonal cycles.

They are introducing organic fertilizers and natural pest controls and are paying close attention to restoring the natural rhythms of production and recycling. Organic farmers see their role as nurturing rather than marshaling. Their concern is to preserve the soil base and natural plant strains to ensure adequate reserves for future generations.

Architecture is another field that is beginning to experience the tug between the more traditional geospheric temporal values and the new biospheric temporal orientation. Although many architects still prefer to erect buildings that are autonomous in design and detached and isolated from the environment, a new generation of biosphere-oriented architects build with a different purpose in mind. They are combining traditional wisdom, a sophisticated understanding of the earth sciences, and the most advanced design concepts and building materials to erect passive solar buildings. The new biospheric structures are often so elegant and unobstrusive, so integrated with the sequences, durations, and tempos of the natural world that for all practical purposes they become part of the community of life that makes up the larger ecosystem.

Biospheric buildings, then, are designed to be compatible with the surrounding environmental rhythms. Ecological architects see their buildings not as fortresses, but as environments within the environment, extensions of their surroundings that fully participate with the beats and periodicities of the larger setting—the heat and light of the sun, the lunar and seasonal cycles, and the currents and tides of the winds and water.

Energy technology is still another case in point. In engineering departments of universities and some private corporations researchers are working with wind, solar, and water power in an effort to develop appropriate technologies that rely on and are congenial with the rhythms of nature.

Even more intimate fields, like medicine, are also experiencing a change in temporal attitudes. Conventional medicine puts a premium on speed and efficiency. Often, the goal is to supercede rather than complement the natural restorative rhythms of the body. The emerging holistic health movement, on the other hand, emphasizes the need to work with, instead of against, the body's own restorative timetable. The body is not treated in isolation but as an integral part of the larger environment with which it is in constant rhythmic participation. The emphasis is on letting the entire environment assist in helping to restore the proper temporal relationships of the body.

An ecological approach to medical treatment places greater attention on prevention than cure. For example, consider the two major diseases that confront industrial society today: cancer and heart disease. While these diseases have always existed, they have assumed epidemic proportions in the past several decades. A host of clinical studies point to a causal relationship between the high-stress, carcinogenic environment we have created and the triggering of cancer and heart disease. The ecological school of medicine focuses its research on finding ways to eliminate the source of the problem. Concern is directed toward reducing stress by slowing down the frenetic pace of life, changing nutritional habits, and cleaning up the polluted environment.

Nowhere is the contrast between the mechanistic approach and the biospheric approach to time orientation more vividly portrayed than in the workplace. The conventional time orientation emphasizes speed and expediency. Toward that end, personal involvement in the work cycle is reduced to a minimum. Individual workers are isolated from both the process and each other. Although they are caught up in the work cycle, they often do not participate in it. Instead, they are swept up into the temporality imposed on them by machines and management, forced to conform to a rigidly defined set of mechanical and electrical sequences, durations, and rhythms over which they have little or no control.

A new generation of worker-owned-and-operated companies is attempting to establish a radically different temporal orientation, one that integrates the time needs of the individual workers with the time imperatives of the production process. In democratically run enterprises, each worker has a voice and a vote in the decisions that affect his or her life on the job. Group participation in every aspect of the work process ensures that each individual will have some say in establishing the tempo of work-related activities. Worker-run companies place greater emphasis on face-to-face interaction and on trying to accommodate the unique temporal needs of each employee. Many worker-run companies use appropriate small-scale technologies, tools that are designed to work in tandem with the natural biological rhythms of the human body and the rhythms of nature.

These are but a few of the many examples of a new temporal standard that is beginning to inch its way into the public domain, influencing the thinking of a world in transition to a new biospheric consciousness. In the final analysis, synchronizing social time with ecological time will require patience and understanding and, above all, direct bodily experience within the biosphere. It is only by felt participation with nature that we can begin to integrate our rhythms with "hers." This is the price of membership in the biospheric loop.

Reorienting the temporal standards of society to be more compatible with the temporality of the planet does not mean going back to a premodern mode of existence, as some would suggest. It does mean developing a far more sophisticated and elegant temporal orientation—one that combines traditional wisdom and our newly found ecological awareness with a new generation of institutional arrangements and technologies that can sustain the planet and resacralize our relationship to it.

36

RECLAIMING THE
GROUND OF BEING

THE TRANSITION TO a biosphere culture will radically transform our thinking about space and spatial relations just as it will affect our temporal orientation.

Activity in the geosphere culture is measured in terms of isolated events. Dates and places take on inordinate importance. Strategic locations or territories are the critical spatial classifications. In the biosphere culture, activity is viewed in terms of interrelated processes. Ecological context becomes the primary spatial influence.

In the geosphere culture, expansion and centralization take command. As described earlier, modern man's race across the geosphere has been marked by the enclosure, privatization, and commercialization of nature. The modern age has been characterized by imperialist conquest and an all-out war against nature. Our science has been directed to the task of reducing, dividing, and vivisecting nature to manageable proportions that can be easily and quickly consumed and discarded. Our technology has been amplified to allow us to extend our reach over vast distances at great speeds.

In the biosphere culture, homeostasis and decentralization would govern. Because everything in the biosphere is understood to be interrelated and mutually interdependent, any arbitrary enclosure or privatization of nature would be considered potentially harmful. Science, then, in a biosphere culture would be directed to reinforcing relationships and processes in nature. Technology would be designed to a temporal and spatial scale that was compatible with the workings of local ecosystems.

In the geosphere culture, security comes from exercising control over events from a distance. Autonomy is the ultimate objective. In the biosphere culture, security comes from reintegrating oneself into the cyclical processes that make up the body of nature. Participation in the organic community becomes the goal.

The new biospheric consciousness begins, then, with a reassertion of spatial grounding. The modern enclosure movement destroyed the most basic element of security, a sense of belonging. Enlightenment thinkers, nation-state politicians, and now multinational corporate adventurers have all attempted to convince the public that possession can serve as a meaningful surrogate for belonging. Repeatedly in the preceding pages, the point has been made that the more we possess, the more we are possessed. Our possessions, especially those of a technological nature, isolate us from the world around us. They become pale substitutes for bodily contact, human warmth and affection, and meaningful participation with the natural world. They allow us to create an artificial reality, a "virtual environment" that is deadened to the smells of aliveness, the touch and sounds of animality, the texture of nature's wrap.

We ought make no mistake about the psychic toll of the drive to enclose the global commons. Millions of people have been wrenched away, often brutally, from the ground of their being. The very words *ground* and *being* have been so thoroughly purged from the lexicon of modern culture that today only our philosophers and playwrights toy with their meaning—and then rarely touch on their ontological importance to the body politic. Yet, these are the words of revolutionary change for tomorrow's generation.

Everywhere modernity has tread, it has severed people from their ancestral ground, stripping them of their sense of being in the world. The loss of geographical centeredness came swiftly in the twentieth century with the introduction of the automobile and the laying of the electronic grid. Reminiscing about his childhood, Siegfried Sassoon recalled that anyone living more than ten miles away was beyond calling distance: "Dumborough Park was twelve miles from where my aunt lived. . . . My aunt was fully two miles beyond the radius of Lady Dumborough's 'round of calls.' "[1]

Now it matters little whether someone is ten miles or two thousand miles away. The telephone, television, fax machine, and other technological wizardry have introduced a new kind of electronic nomadism into the culture. The physicality of place has become irrelevant to much of the social interaction in modern society. It is more than a little ironic that AT&T's slogan in recent years has been "Reach out and touch someone" when that is exactly what cannot be done over the telephone. Still, these commercials strike a responsive chord among a public eager to reestablish bodily contact with friends and loved ones.

Of all the technological innovations of the electronics revolution, none has had a bigger impact on our sense of ground and being than television. Simply by switching channels, one can be transported to any one of a number of different times and places in the world, without ever being in the world. Physical location loses all sense of traditional meaning. The electronic media introduces a new artificial sense of being, imposed on an electronic ground that is everywhere, simultaneously, and touches down anywhere the impulses are directed.

Media historian and critic Joshua Meyrowitz believes that the electronic media's major contribution to our changing consciousness has been its ability to disorient our sense of "situational geography." With electronic media—telephone, television, radio, and computers—physical place and social place become distended in time and space: "Where we are physically no longer determines who and where we are socially."[2] Meyrowitz concludes: "One of the reasons that many Americans may no longer seem to know their place is that they no longer have a place in the traditional sense of a set of behaviors matched to physical locations and the audiences found in them."[3]

The new electronic rootlessness fosters a deep sense of alienation that is unique in human experience. It is instructive that our generation spends so much time worrying over whether world leaders, associates, close friends, and family members are "losing touch with reality." How could it be otherwise in a world where "reality" is increasingly acted out on an electronic field? Electronically mediated experience is out-of-body experience—not of the kind that leads to revelation, but, rather, disorientation, writ large.

Historian Otto Spengler argued that every culture creates its own unique spatial imprint which, in turn, influences and shapes the unfolding of its social reality. In the modern world, space is being disembodied of substance, reduced from hard matter to energy waves. There is no longer any firm place for modern man to stand on. Dislodged from his ancestral land by the worldwide enclosure movement, he now finds himself dislodged from even his "social place" by the electronic revolution, making him easy prey for manipulation by the state and the multinational corporations.

A popular Woody Guthrie song of the American labor and civil rights struggles begins with the words "We shall not, we shall not be moved. . . ." Reclaiming the ground is the first step toward reclaiming our place in the organic scheme of things. In his "Letter on Humanism," Heidegger reminds us that *humanus* comes from the word *humus,* which is the Latin word for a nourishing and fertile ground.[4] In Hebraic mythology, God is said to have fashioned Adam from the clay of the earth. All living creatures owe their existence to the soil. In life and in death the earth claims every living creature. It is progenitor, nourisher, and final resting place. In the Bible, it is written: "From dust to dust."

The artificial pull of the state and the multinational corporation, though powerful, is still not sufficient to wrest our physicality away from the earth's own gravitational pull, which continues to draw every human being and creature back to its bosom. In *The Will to Power,* Nietzsche observes that in the modern world "we are losing our center of gravity by virtue of which we have lived; we are lost for a while. . . ."[5] Finding our way back requires a burrowing into the earth's seams.

In the modern age, the sense of "being" gave way, almost entirely, to a sense of "becoming." The "will to power" uprooted humanity's long-standing sense of community. Restoring community means replanting our feet squarely in the earth's soil.

Biospheric consciousness embraces the entirety of the earth

community. When man and woman stand erect on the earth's surface, they become both incarnate and transcendent, their bodies reaching down to reparticipate with the flesh of the planet, their spirits reaching up to embrace heavenly rapture. Leonardo da Vinci's line drawing of "man extended" captures the intentionality of biospheric grounding. The body extends both vertically and horizontally. The arms and legs reach out in every direction, forming an elongated circle that mirrors the dimensions of the biosphere.

Relocating our bodies back into the biosphere is both a metaphysical and physical act. In the age of geospheric consciousness, man and woman entertained the illusion of being "the center." Perspective ruled, making all of nature a separate object of expropriation. In the new age, the biosphere moves from margin to context and from object to ground. Human physicality and consciousness are rooted in the larger earth organism, reintegrated, if you will, into the extended community of life that forms a protective seal around the planet.

The new biospheric grounding flows from a deep understanding that our being is part of the earth's being. Our physical being, like the goods and services of our economy, is borrowed from the biosphere. Every breath we take contains a quadrillion—or 10^{15}—atoms that have been breathed in by other human beings in just the past few weeks and at least a million atoms that have been breathed by every human being on the planet. We are constantly exchanging atoms with other creatures and with the earth itself. Each year, over 98 percent of the atoms that make up our bodies are exchanged for new atoms that existed previously somewhere else in nature. In just five years, the entire physical body is replaced. Our very physicality—the organs, blood, tissue that make up our bodies—is continually being exchanged with the environment. In a physical sense, we are borrowed and are as indebted to the biosphere as the goods and products we fashion from nature. The idea that we are somehow independent and autonomous forces, separate from nature, is pure fiction. We are made of the stuff of the biosphere, and are part of the dynamic process that maintains the biosphere.

The great twentieth-century physicist Erwin Schrodinger recognized the true nature of our being:

> Thus you can throw yourself flat on the ground, stretched out upon Mother Earth, with the certain conviction that you are one with her and she with you. You are as firmly established, as invulnerable as she. . . . As surely as she will endow you tomorrow, so surely will she bring you forth anew to new striving and suffering. And not merely "someday"; now, today, every day, she is bringing you forth, not once, but thousands of times, just as every day she engulfs you a thousand times over. For eternally and always, there is only now, one and the same now; the present is the only thing that has no end.[6]

Schrodinger's account of human beings' relationship to the earth is a description of the workings of the living biosphere.

In West Africa and among older black women in the American South, the eating of clay, or geophagy, is still practiced. The geographer Guy Davenport tells of his great delight as a child being taken to his nurse's house to eat clay:

> The eating took place in a bedroom, for the galvanized bucket of clay was kept under the bed, for the cool. It was blue clay from a creek, the consistency of slightly gritty ice cream. It lay smooth and delicious looking in its pail of clear water. You scooped it out and ate it from your hand. The taste was wholesome, mineral and emphatic.[7]

This sense of belonging, of oneness with the earth, which is now preserved in fading rituals and anecdotal stories, reflects the centeredness of an earlier age, a ground that has been lost in the mad dash of an ever-accelerating modernity. Yet, the ancient practice of geophagy provides a powerful metaphor for the new metaphysics.

If geospheric consciousness is steeped in autonomy, then biospheric consciousness is, most certainly, steeped in indebtedness. We borrow from the biosphere and we return. When we despoil the biosphere—clog its arteries with poison, pollute its environs, choke its atmosphere with deadly gases, denude and parch its soil—we reap the consequences. They flow back into the very sinew of our physical being. We are made up of air, earth, water, and fire, the chemical and mineral elements and gases of the biosphere. We take into ourselves, into our organs and tissues, into our flesh and fluids, the stuff of the biosphere. As we degrade and pollute it, we become degraded and polluted in the process. When we expropriate and exploit the biosphere, reduce and diminish its grandeur, we become reduced and diminished as well. Our being and the earth's being are inseparably linked. Each exists inside the other. Each is beholden to the other.

Biospheric consciousness, then, begins with a healing of the body of nature. We realize that we individually become whole to the extent that the biospheric community is made whole. We resacralize our being by resacralizing the being of the planet. Ultimately, our personal peace and security can only be assured if the peace and security of the biosphere is guaranteed.

Securing the peace of the planet will require challenging the will to power of the state and, even more so, the multinational corporation. A firm rootedness in the biosphere is a powerful counterforce to the furtive nomadism of the transnational enterprise. A Desana Indian of the Colombian Amazon defined security as "a man standing upright, firmly planted on that ground as a cosmic axis, stepping firmly."[8] Reclaiming the ground of our being means reembodying our physicality and rehealing the mind-body split.

To become whole, we will need to reenchant the senses. We participate with the planet and the ground of our being to the extent that we fully experience it. Whether our experience and, ultimately, our participation is rich and meaningful or only meager and superficial will depend on how creative we are in fashioning new ways to use the intimate as well as the more abstract and detached of our senses.

Reintegrating our being into the spatial framework of the biosphere will require a radical change in our thinking about technology. In the modern age, power came from surrounding ourselves with technological appendages to inflate our own being while diminishing and miniaturizing nature. The great folly of modernity has been one of scale. The battle over nuclear power best exemplifies the question of scale and the gap in thinking that separates a mechanistic from an organismic approach to technology. Nuclear energy represents the quintessential thinking of the modern age. The immense concentration of energy generated by nuclear power plants is grossly out of proportion to the energy distribution in the surrounding environment. Amory Lovins captured the problem of pathology of scale when he remarked that using nuclear power as a source of energy is like using an electric chain saw to cut through butter.[9] Biospheric centeredness is the route by which humanity reestablishes a proper sense of scale in the world.

It should be emphasized that the new spatial thinking about centeredness differs fundamentally from premodern ways of thinking about space and is, therefore, not simply an attempt to journey back to the past. The new way of thinking about place is neither parochial nor xenophobic but, rather, inclusive and global and represents a new vision of spatial relationship. Centeredness in the local biome is perceived as part and parcel of a larger centeredness that expands to fill the whole of the biosphere. Belonging, in the new ecological context, means participating with and taking responsibility for one's own small neighborhood of the biosphere.

37

ACCOUNTING
FOR THE EARTH

THE NEW BIOSPHERIC temporal and spatial
sensibilities will require a rethinking of conventional economic
theory. The contrast between geospheric and biospheric economics is best exemplified in the radically different approaches to
national income accounting.

Every government in the world today still relies on gross national product (GNP) as a measure of economic performance. Economists define the GNP as the total value of goods and services
generated in a twelve-month period. Governments and multinational corporations continue to adhere to the assumptions of
Englightenment thinkers like John Locke, who argued that nature,
left unattended, remains in a wasteful and unproductive state. It
was Locke who argued for the enclosure and commodification of
as much of nature as humanly possible, so that it might be properly transformed by toil and tools into a storehouse of ever-
expanding wealth.

From a biospheric perspective, the contemporary conception of
GNP appears naïve. Nature, in the new organic scheme of things,
is viewed as an endowment. Living creatures have both intrinsic
value and utilitarian value. Inanimate materials have thermody-
namic value. Human ingenuity and technology merely transform
that value into goods, products, and services, which are used

generally for a brief moment in time, only to be returned to the environment as waste. Some of this waste is recyclable, while the rest is irretrievably lost as spent energy or dispersed matter. Additional energy is expended and emitted into the environment in the process of collecting, transforming, producing, and exchanging goods, products, and services. The GNP, then, is more appropriately an index of the temporary value of the goods and services produced at the expense of the natural endowment that is used up in the process of making them and the waste and pollution that is discarded into the atmosphere, land, and ocean at various stages of extraction, production, and consumption.

Most economists and virtually every government leader would shudder at the idea that the GNP is as much a measure of resources consumed and pollution generated as of wealth created. They would be nonplussed by the notion that every economic act degrades the environment in some way, and impoverishes others now and in the future.

First world economists have long argued that the more wealth generated by the industrial nations, the greater the largesse available to everyone else. This is sometimes euphemistically referred to as the "trickle-down theory." Needless to say, even before the new ecological awareness and understanding of the workings of the biosphere, many third world leaders rightfully countered that greater wealth for the rich nations ultimately meant that less of the earth's endowment would be available for everyone else. As mentioned in an earlier chapter, with 5 percent of the world's population, the United States consumes 30 percent of the earth's resources and emits over 25 percent of all the carbon dioxide, CFCs, and other pollutants into the environment.

Still, the powers that be cling to the worn-out cliché of economists like Adam Smith who argue that each person, pursuing his own self-interest, inevitably advances the public good by adding to the stock of wealth or capital available to society. We continue to think of economics in terms of growth when it is essentially increased borrowing. The ancients understood as much; until the modern age, every culture regarded economic activity as borrowing from nature. Economics was immersed in indebtedness. Gift giving and sacrifices, which were the first primitive form of economic exchange, were acknowledgments that living creatures borrowed from each other and from the environment.

The very fiber of our physiological being, the accoutrements of civilization, the artifacts and tools of culture, the monuments we erect to the gods and each other are all borrowed from nature, and to nature they eventually return. Economics is merely the borrowing and transforming of nature's riches for our temporary enjoyment and sustenance. Technology, far from being an autonomous force that frees us from nature, simply borrows, transforms, exchanges, consumes, and discards the things of nature. Technology is as dependent on nature and the biosphere as we are. Tools can only transform what is already in nature. They cannot create something from nothing.

In geospheric thinking, the environment is viewed as merely an input or factor of production, or, at worst, an externality. In biospheric thinking, the environment is the context in which economic activity takes place. Economics is that human activity which intervenes in the environment and which manipulates it toward the ends of human sustenance and survival. Economics, far from being separate and autonomous from nature, is deeply enmeshed in it and conditioned by it.

Acknowledging the true nature of economic activity is, perhaps, the most difficult of the challenges facing civilization. If economic activity is indeed merely borrowing from nature, then the whole notion of economic security in the modern age becomes suspect. Borrowing implies indebtedness, mutuality, and shared relationships with nature. The very idea of an autonomous economic existence becomes unsupportable if we are, in fact, dependent upon nature. The drive to enclose and privatize the global commons, to commercialize nature and put a price tag on each other's labor to gain greater autonomy and security appears more like a tragic folly than a well-reasoned historical sojourn.

For nearly half a millennium, modern man and woman have created every imaginable boundary and restriction to separate us from any association with nature, even to the point of denying our own animal nature. Yet, our new understanding of the biosphere dashes any hopes we might have had about creating an inside, tucked away and sealed off from the outside. Even our

284

high-tech vivaria, virtual environments, and simulated realities are merely temporary scaffolding inside the ebb and flow of the biosphere.

The belief that new technological innovations could continue to guarantee material growth has so thoroughly permeated the thinking of the modern age that any suggestion of inherent limits is generally dismissed as unduly pessimistic or antiprogressive. Consequently, our environmental deficit now threatens to dwarf our national deficit.

For years our politicians and business leaders have engaged in heated public discussions on the need to balance the federal budget and retire the national debt. Far less attention has been given to the debt between civilization and the biosphere, which has now reached crisis proportions. The United States and other nations are consuming the earth's endowment faster than the biosphere can absorb and recycle the polluted waste and replenish the stock of natural resources our children's generation will need to sustain their economic future. Global warming, ozone depletion, acid rain, deforestation, desertification, and species extinction represent the greatest environmental debt any civilization has ever accumulated. Balancing our budget with the biosphere will require a new approach to economic policy based on synchronizing society's production, consumption, and recycling schedules with those of nature.

38

BIOSPHERE POLITICS

RENÉ DUBOS CAPTURED the spirit of biosphere politics in the aphorism "Think globally, act locally." An effective biospheric politics will necessitate a redrafting of political borders to make them compatible with the new ecological way of thinking about space.

The spatial map of the nation-state is based on market extension and the effective reach of the military to secure expanding markets. The multinational corporations eliminate spatial boundaries altogether, treating the entire global commons as a single market. Biospheric politics will need to create a new, competing spatial map whose governing configuration more clearly follows the geographical lines of regional ecosystems on the local level, while encompassing the entire biosphere on an international level.

Because biospheric politics is based on sustainable economic development, rather than ever-accelerating production, the ecosystem rather than the market dictates the spatial limits of political rule. Equally important, as biospheric consciousness is global and rooted in an organismic worldview, new international political institutions will need to be created to oversee and protect the entire biosphere of the planet.

The task of the new organismic politics, then, is to ensure ecosystem sustainability on the local level and biospheric security on the global level. Just before his death, the British historian Arnold Toynbee turned his attention to the biosphere, believing that its destruction at the hands of modern industrial production signaled a potential irreversible cataclysm for both human civilization and the planet. Toynbee argued for new political arrangements at both the local and global level to address what he feared would be the greatest challenge to the continuance of human civilization:

> The present-day global set of local sovereign states is not capable of keeping the peace, and it is also not capable of saving the biosphere from manmade pollution or of conserving the biosphere's nonreplaceable natural resources.... What has been needed . . . is a global politic composed of cells on the scale of the Neolithic Age village-community. A scale on which the participants could be personally acquainted with each other, while each of them would also be a citizen of the world-state.[1]

While the geospheric politics of the nation-state and multinational was designed to enclose and commodify the global commons, the biospheric politics of the new age is designed to eliminate the arbitrary political and commercial barriers that have clogged the biospheric arteries and make whole the planetary organism. The political challenge of the new biospheric politics is to tear down the walls of enclosure and reopen the global commons, to treat the planet as a single unified organism.

On the local level, the new biospheric political vision is rooted in what ecologists and planners call the "bioregion." In his book *Dwellers in the Land,* Kirkpatrick Sale defined a bioregion as

> ... any part of the earth's surface whose rough boundaries are determined by natural characteristics rather than human dictates, distinguishable from other areas by particular attributes of flora, fauna, water, climate, soils, and landforms, and by the human settlements and cultures those attributes have given rise to.[2]

Geographers and ecologists divide bioregions into ecoregions, georegions, and morpharegions. An ecoregion encompasses the "broadest distribution of nature, vegetation, and soil types. . . ." In America, ecoregions like the Ozark Plateau and the Sonora Desert often extend over hundreds of thousands of square miles, covering several states. Ecoregions are generally distinguished by their "spread of trees and grasses." The Ozark Plateau, for example, reaches across several states and is naturally bounded by the Missouri, Mississippi, and Arkansas rivers. Its forests, Sale observes, are primarily oak and hickory, clearly delineating them from the pine forests of the South and the prairie grasses to the west. Its calcareous and chert soil, Sale notes, distinguishes it from the noncalcareous deposits to the east and sandstone and shale to the south and west. The North American continent contains forty distinct ecoregions, most of which cross every kind of political and commercial boundary.[3]

Ecoregions are further divided by ecologists into georegions, smaller ecosystems tucked inside the larger ecosystem and sharing common characteristics, as well as exhibiting unique features. River basins, watersheds, valleys, mountain ranges, and unique flora and fauna generally distinguish georegions. The central valley of California, says Sale, is a good example of a georegion inside a larger ecosystem, the northern California ecoregion. The central valley is a rich twenty-thousand-mile stretch of land bordering the Sacramento and San Joaquin rivers, whose topography and climate make it ideal for agriculture. While it is very much an integral part of the larger California ecoregion, its geography and biology are quite different than those of the Klamath mountain range and Sierra foothills, which are also part of the same ecoregion.

Georegions can be further divided into morpharegions, smaller, ecologically unique patterns that extend over several thousand square miles. Sale points to the Connecticut River basin, "running between the Green and White mountains all the way from Canada down to the Long Island Sound."[4]

Before European colonization, American Indian tribes lived within the temporal and spatial parameters of well-defined ecoregions; the Mahican along the Hudson River watershed, the

Seminole in the southeastern Everglades, the Pawnee on the prairie grasses of the Platte River. Even today, modern governance has retained a hint of ecoregionalism. Shared geographic resources, including fresh water supplies and minerals, weather patterns and climate, and, increasingly, regional pollution which settles into specific geographic pockets, bring together locales and states— sometimes cooperatively, often competitively—in various eco-regions.

Still, existing political boundaries are often arbitrary. Many state and local boundaries, for example, were drawn along the path blazed by the railroad and are more closely tied to market reach than ecosystem prerequisites. Redrawing political boundaries to match ecosystem boundaries is among the most formidable and pressing political issues facing every country in the world as humanity makes the transition from geospheric to biospheric consciousness. Only when political and ecosystem boundaries are made compatible with one another will it be possible to regulate properly economic activity so as to make it sustainable and congenial with the temporal and spatial limitations of the environment human communities dwell in.

Ecosystem dynamics provide a useful analogy to help shape the thinking of the new biospheric politics. Ecologists refer to the two phases of evolutionary succession in an ecosystem as the pioneer and climax stages. In the pioneer stage, a succession of flora and fauna proliferate and extend outward, consuming as much energy as is available to them. Pioneer communities produce more organic matter than they consume. The excess matter changes the physicality of the habitat and provides new sources of food which, in turn, change the kinds and number of species that develop at subsequent stages. Over a period of time, the succession of flora and fauna develop mutually dependent, symbiotic relationships and consumption of matter and energy come into equilibrium. The climax community is

> "self-perpetuating and in equilibrium with the physical habitat. . . . In a climax community, in contrast to a developmental or unstable [pioneer] community, there is no net annual accumulation of organic matter. That is, the annual produc-

tion and import is balanced by the annual community consumption and export.[5]

Climax communities are far more stable than pioneer communities. The biota and the environment exist in a homeostatic relationship. The excess production of the pioneer community has been replaced by the sustainable production that preserves both the habitat and the biota that dwells within it.

The climax ecosystem serves as a useful guide and overarching metaphor for political and economic decision making. Sustainable development, a much bandied about term in the international community today, is, after all, patterned after the workings of the mature climax ecosystems.

Bioregional awareness is beginning to grow and is already having an effect on traditional domestic politics as well as on geopolitics. Within countries like the United States, bioregionalism is becoming an issue and a force to be reckoned with, largely because of resource shortages and the problems of mounting pollution. For example, shortages in fresh water are forcing locales and states to think bioregionally, especially in the West, and to set up new bioregional authorities. Air pollution is forcing a similar bioregional response. In places like Southern California, the climate, weather patterns, prevailing winds, and mountain chains conspire to lock air pollution into a bioregional pocket. The Southern California Air Quality Control Board was established to address the problems of air pollution on a bioregional level. In 1989, the board announced a long-term regional plan for Southern California which includes the phasing out of all gasoline-powered automobiles by the early part of the next century. Increasingly, new regional planning agencies (quasi-political governing bodies) are being established to regulate economic activity and oversee ecosystem preservation and maintenance on a bioregional scale.

On an international level, new regional agencies are being established among nation-states to regulate and manage resource allocation and pollution abatement, often in contiguous bioregional areas. There are over two hundred distinct biogeographic zones in the world. Most cut across nation-state boundaries. For example, there are two hundred international river basins, most of which are shared by several nations. With water becoming an increasingly scarce resource, nations are forming regional water commissions and agencies such as the ones regulating the Rhine and Danube rivers, and the Baltic Sea. United Nations agencies, including the Food and Agricultural Organization (FAO) and the United Nations Environmental Program (UNEP) have also established similar subagencies and commissions to regulate economic and environmental activities that spill over national boundaries and are bioregional in impact.[6]

In Central America, six nations have come together to create and jointly administer "peace parks." The parks are tropical forests that border on two or more of the countries and are part of the larger bioregion. For years, these border areas have been hotly contested and have been used as staging areas for armed conflicts. The "peace parks" represent a change in thinking from geopolitics to biosphere politics. Increasingly, countries inhabiting a common bioregion are beginning to realize that their individual survival depends on joint cooperation in preserving the larger bioregion in which they dwell. There are now sixty-eight border parks straddling sixty-six nations.[7]

Nation-states are showing some willingness to relinquish their power, vesting extranational agencies with regulatory power over economic and environmental activity that cuts through national borders. A few nations have actively pursued multilateral bioregional alliances. More often than not, however, nations around the world continue to let conventional geopolitics rule over biospheric politics. It is interesting to observe that while every nation on earth boasts a foreign policy based on geopolitics, not one has developed an "environmental foreign policy" as the U.N. Brundtland Commission Report has recommended.

Increasingly, bioregional interests are clashing with nation-state and multinational corporate interests around the world. Currently, there are over 103 different separatist movements fighting for independence in forty-nine nations.[9] Most of these movements are made up of ethnic, religious, and racial groups that are at odds with the policies of their national governments and are seeking separate homelands. Kirkpatrick Sale points out that, upon closer examination, their struggles

> ... are rooted in geographical differences as well, and many of the groups in specifying their homeland demarcate what clearly can be regarded as a bioregion, most often something like a georegion. This is particularly easy to see in places like Wales, Corsica, Jura, or Catalonia, where the ethnic region is virtually identical with an obvious geographic feature, but it is no less true of Brittany, Alsace, or Croatia—or for that matter Baluchistan, Kashmir, Sarawak, Eritrea, Quebec, or Dine [Navajo land].[10]

The political evidence suggests that the most fiercely contested battles between bioregional interests and nation-state prerogatives are likely to be fought inside the Soviet Union, Eastern Europe, and India in the years ahead.

39

MULTINATIONAL MACHINATIONS

THE CHIEF IMPEDIMENT to a new biospheric temporal and spatial orientation is the multinational corporation. The giant global companies represent the final institutional stage of mechanistic consciousness and geospheric thinking. In both their operating procedures and objectives, the multinationals epitomize the values and assumptions upon which the modern worldview is based. Their role in the world and their impact upon the world need to be understood, critiqued, and ultimately contested if society is to have any hope of entertaining a new biospheric conciousness.

In the past century, the corporation has grown in stature and outreach in direct proportion to the proliferation of air travel and the extension of the electronic grid across oceans and continents. Now it threatens the long-standing hegemony of the nation-state. The enclosure and commercialization of the atmosphere and the electromagnetic spectrum ultimately worked to the advantage of the corporation and to the detriment of the nation-state. Air travel shortened distances and broke through traditional geographic barriers. Electricity sped up communication to near simultaneity. The obliteration of space in the last half of the twentieth century has made the nation-state appear more and more like a political dinosaur. Because it is tied to territory, the nation-state is limited in its ability to move at will. It is a spatially bound institution, forced to adjust to an increasingly temporally bound world. The multinational corporation is not tied to a particular territory. It is free to roam the world at will, to exist everywhere without permanent residence anywhere.

International economist Charles P. Kindleberger once remarked that "the international corporation has no country to which it owes more loyalty than any other, nor any country where it feels completely at home."[1] No other governing institution in history has ruled with such great spatial detachment and with so little human accountability. The multinational is free of allegiances, historical restraints, and traditions and owes no obligations to any one people or community. It is the first human institution in history to be so thoroughly steeped in temporality and so devoid in spatial grounding.

The multinational corporation is the embodiment of abstract power. Because it has no ties to a particular place, it can exercise power over the entire face of the globe. Because it has no home territory to defend, it does not require its own military apparatus to secure its worldwide interests. While it depends on the goodwill and military protection of whatever host country it is doing business in, if its employees, assets, or raw material markets are threatened, it can shift operations, often overnight, to other regions of the globe without suffering crippling losses.

Many of today's multinational corporations have amassed greater economic power than nation-states. By the early 1970s, General Motors' annual sales exceeded the gross national product of Switzerland, South Africa, and Pakistan. Royal Dutch Shell boasted assets in excess of the worth of Iran, Venezuela, and Turkey.[2] Goodyear Tires' commercial clout exceeded that of many nations.[3] A U.S. Chamber of Commerce study conducted in the 1970s predicted that by the turn of the century a few hundred multinational corporations would likely control over half of the productive assets of the planet.[4] These corporate behemoths control raw materials, labor pools, primary and secondary markets, and enjoy a near monopoly over global communications and transportation systems. Some companies, like Exxon and British Petroleum, have naval fleets that rival those of the superpowers. Others, like ITT, employ tens of thousands of people in dozens of

294

countries. Corporate CEOs exercise a degree of control over world events that only a few heads of state can match. Political scientist Richard Barnet sums up the significance of these new quasi-political institutions in the affairs of civilization.

> In the process of developing a new world, the managers of firms like GM, IBM, Pepsico, GE, Pfizer, Shell, Volkswagen, Exxon, and a few hundred others are making daily business decisions which have more impact than those of sovereign governments on where people live; what work, if any, they do; what they will eat, drink, and wear; what sorts of knowledge, schools, and universities they will encourage; and what kind of society their children will inherit.[5]

The power of the multinational is quite ephemeral compared with the spatially bound empires of the past. It rules not by force of arms but, rather, by force of communications. Its chief tool is efficiency, the ability to manage production by controlling vast areas of the earth's commons—the land, sea, atmosphere, electromagnetic spectrum, outer space, and gene pool. Its domain is the entire globe. The multinational corporation seeks to be everywhere, simultaneously—to assume unchallenged commercial control over the entirety of the global commons. The temporal imperialism exercised by the multinational corporation is far more ambitious and far-reaching than the spatial imperialism of its nation-state predecessor.

If the cannon and gunpowder revolution can be justifiably credited with the meteoric rise of the nation-state, then today the electronic computer and satellite communication technology certainly enjoy comparable credit for the success of the multinational corporation. As media critic Jerry Mander points out, "Computers not only aid today's multinational corporate enterprises, they make them possible."[6] Without sophisticated computer networks, the transnational companies would simply not be able to "keep track instantaneously with millions of pieces of information from all over the world."[7] Today's multinational corporations do business everywhere but are "not located anywhere except in the computer itself."[8] The multinationals take their power with them wherever they go; they reside deep inside the microworld of silicon chips and electronic circuits that guard the data and information used to program the temporal and spatial affairs of local communities and whole continents. IBM's Jacques Maisonrouge points to the advantages multinational corporations enjoy in coordinating activity on a worldwide basis:

> With the magic of today's communications technologies, we were able to set up a network between the United States and Europe. By use of facsimile equipment we could transmit not only messages, but drawings as well. An engineer in our laboratory in Poughkeepsie, New York, can talk with and jointly design circuits with an engineer in Hursely, England, transmitting designs back and forth as they work.[9]

With the lifting of the Iron Curtain and the entry of Eastern Europe and the Soviet Union into a global marketplace, the multinationals are now in a position to gain even greater control over every aspect of global commerce. Today's multinational corporations talk in terms of a single market, what economist Peter Drucker calls the "global shopping center."[10] The fundamental goal is to transform the loyalties, identifications, and affiliations of people all over the world. Already, white collar and management employees in various countries are beginning to identify first with their multinational corporate employer and only secondarily with their host country. This is especially true for companies that have a deliberate policy of moving personnel every few years to different regions of the world.

As the multinationals segment more and more of their operations among various locales, corporate identification can be expected to increase, posing a serious threat to traditional national loyalties. For example, Barnet points out that with satellite communications and containerized shipping, many multinationals have established global factories. Massey-Ferguson, a Canadian multinational firm, "assembles French-made transmissions, Mexican-made axles, and British-made engines in a Detroit plant for a Canadian market."[11] The global car is already an on-line reality.

Where personal security used to be bound up with the state and

296

expressed in patriotic metaphors, today it is found in shared corporate credit cards, corporate medical insurance, corporate-sponsored vacations, and corporate-subsidized housing. Increasingly, large numbers of people in different regions of the globe identify themselves as members of the ITT family or the McDonald's family. Their security rests in the hands of their multinational employers.

Global production represents one aspect of the final commercial enclosure of the planet into a single market. The other is the creation of a single consumer market for corporate goods and services. McDonald's, Kentucky Fried Chicken, Pepsico, and other multinational companies are spending billions of dollars in advertising to create the global consumer, a person whose first affiliation and loyalty is with a brand name—Levi's, Christian Dior, Fiat, Apple Computer. One international business group several years ago went so far as to suggest that its corporate members "hype" the idea that "consumer democracy is more important than political democracy."[12]

The battle between the multinationals and the nation-states for the loyalty of the masses is already heating up and is likely to become more fierce in the years ahead. William I. Spencer, former president of the First National City Corporation, which conducts business activity in ninety countries, echoed the sentiment of many of his colleagues when he remarked: "The political boundaries of nation-states are too narrow and constricted to define the scope and sweep of modern business."[13]

Perhaps even more to the point is Maisonrouge of IBM:

"The world's political structures are obsolete. They have not changed in at least a hundred years and are woefully out of tune with technological progress. The critical issue of our time is the conceptual conflict between the search for global optimization of resources and the independence of nation-states."[14]

What makes the multinational such a formidable force is, as Maisonrouge suggests, its ability to optimize resources on a global scale.

In its drive to "optimize" the use of global resources, the multinational has become the main obstacle in the development of a sustainable worldview. The unrestrained acceleration of production and the artificial stimulation of consumer demand are incompatible with the ecological carrying capacity of the biosphere. Because their very purpose is to optimize resource use, the multinationals invariably place profit above the environment. Unlike the nation-state, they can simply pillage an ecosystem and flee, making them potentially far more dangerous in the years ahead.

The corporate drive for unchallenged control over the global commons, however, is not inevitable. To create the conditions for biospheric consciousness it will be necessary to challenge the will to power of the multinational with a new temporal and spatial sense of grounding in local communities around the planet. Only by reestablishing an organic sense of time and space will it be possible to moderate the excesses of corporate power and develop alternative institutions that are compatible with the workings of the biosphere.

40

DISARMING THE EARTH

As our ideas about security undergo fundamental change, we will need to reassess the geopolitical thinking that has dominated so much of the politics of the modern age. Biospheric realities are already forcing such a reevaluation. In every region of the world, biospheric politics is beginning to challenge traditional geopolitics, raising the specter of wholesale change in the practice of international relations in the years ahead. The emerging controversy over the proper conduct of foreign affairs is raising the question of the future of the arms race and long-standing military alliances, as well as the role of the military-industrial complexes that prop up virtually every major terrestrial power on the planet.

Nowhere is the difference between traditional geopolitical thinking and the new biospheric thinking more apparent than in the confrontation between the United States and Iraq in the Middle East. While President Bush committed billions of dollars to defending American oil interests in the Middle East and jeopardized the lives of hundreds of thousands of U.S. soldiers in the process, a far more prudent biospheric strategy might have avoided the crisis altogether. The fact is, had the United States and other industrial nations embarked on an ambitious program to conserve energy and develop alternate energy technologies, they would not have found themselves so vulnerable to Saddam Hussein's reckless adventure. If the President and Congress had simply raised the automobile fuel-efficiency standards from 27.5 miles per gallon to 35 miles per gallon or raised the gasoline tax by fifty cents per gallon, or taxed the automakers for every large gas-guzzling automobile they produce, the American economy would not have needed a single gallon of oil from the Middle East and the United States would not have had to risk American lives and waste billions of dollars in military deployment halfway around the world.

It is likely that in the years ahead a new generation of political leaders will begin questioning much of the outmoded thinking of classical geopolitics and begin fashioning foreign and domestic policies that are more congenial to the new biospheric way of thinking about the world.

Making the transition to a biosphere culture will require a significant demilitarization of the planet and a restructuring of the economies of every developed nation away from a military-industrial complex and toward a sustainable bioregional infrastructure. The task is a formidable one. The professional military and the art of mechanized warfare have accompanied the nation-state into every region and sphere of the globe, securing eco-systems, resources, and markets for colonial expansion and imperialistic adventures.

Today, three interrelated factors have combined to make the practice of modern warfare increasingly irrelevant in the conduct of international relations. First, the technology of warfare has radically changed in this century, making the art of geopolitics virtually useless. Second, the costs of securing the global commons and a global market economy by way of military might is economically unfeasible. Third, the dual biospheric threats of resource scarcity and global pollution have now eclipsed traditional national security concerns, posing a new and far greater threat to the security of the planet.

Modern geopolitical thinking continues to emphasize the spatial bias of military thinking, despite the increasing evidence that speed of delivery has changed the fundamentals of warfare, making military security a virtual technological impossibility.

Even though superpower military strategists still plan for wars as if geography mattered, the introduction of high-speed bombers, intercontinental rocketry, and nuclear bombs have made geopolitics a rather futile exercise. Writing on the question in *Whole Earth Security*, Daniel Deudney captures the strategic significance of the shift in military technology toward a purely temporal context.

> Circumnavigation of the earth by ships is measured in months, by airplanes in days, by missiles in minutes. The colonization of space by directed energy weapons could culminate this trend, as a terrain awesomely vast by terrestrial standards will be traversed by destructive forces traveling at the speed of light.[1]

Fred Ikle, a Defense Department official, put it best when he said, "Speed is the tightening noose around our neck." As long as speed was not a significant enough factor to obliterate space, military defense of territory and people was still a possibility.[2] It was only a hundred years ago that standing armies faced off against each other in fixed positions on rolling plains. Today, any geographic area of the earth can be invaded at will and pulverized in a matter of minutes by missiles carrying nuclear warheads. In a few years, new directed energy weapons will be able to travel at the speed of light, as Deudney points out. Strategic locations and spatial advantages have been rendered virtually useless by the new fast-paced military technology.

Gene Sharp, director of the Program on Nonviolent Sanctions in Conflict and Defense at Harvard University, says that with modern warfare "the capacity to defend in order to deter [an attacker] has been replaced by the capability to destroy massively without the ability to defend."[3] When space can no longer be defended or secured, there is no longer a great deal of strategic value to waging war. Talk of securing the heartland, the rimland, and the world island seems comically misplaced in a world where spatial advantage is no longer a meaningful concept.

Even if it were technologically possible to defend territory against a nuclear attack, the cost of securing a military hold over the entire global commons far exceeds the financial capabilities of any of the superpower states. Even in the early years of the modern nation-state, when military occupation was limited to specific stretches of land and sea, the costs generally exceeded the revenue-raising abilities of the government, forcing countries into borrowing and long-term debt management. Today, as Deudney points out, "security is something no nation can have without controlling the earth's commons, and no one nation can control the commons without ruling the earth."[4] The United States, the wealthiest nation in the world, has accumulated a debt of well over $3 trillion, much of which is directly attributable to the enormous costs of military preparedness. The costs of developing new, more sophisticated military technologies continues to rise, as does the national debt, as the superpowers desperately attempt to secure military hegemony over the land, the sea, the atmosphere, the electromagnetic spectrum, and outer space. Military enclosure of the global commons by any one nation or pact of nations has proven financially impossible and is now forcing a reassessment of priorities in Moscow, Washington, and other capitals.

Finally, the rapid deterioration of the biosphere (and the human civilization that is dependent on it) has now reached crisis proportions, creating a new and perilous threat to individual and national security that exceeds in magnitude the traditional security threats that have engaged the nations of the world during the modern age. The greenhouse effect, ozone depletion, acid rain, species extinction, deforestation, and desertification now threaten the entire global commons and could well destroy the biospheric processes that maintain life on our planet. In a recent speech delivered before the U.N. General Assembly, former Soviet Foreign Minister Eduard Shevardnadze acknowledged that the issue of global environmental security is forcing the human race to think beyond the limited sphere of national security concerns for the first time. In an extraordinary departure from conventional geopolitical thinking, Shevardnadze warned the nations of the world that "the biosphere recognizes no divisions into blocs, alliances, or systems. All share the same climatic system and no one is in a position to build his own isolated and independent line of environmental defense." Anticipating the new era of biospheric politics, the Soviet foreign minister proposed that the U.N. Environmental Program be turned "into an environmental council capable of making effective decisions to ensure ecological security."[5]

Shevardnadze's concerns are shared by a growing number of human beings around the world. In a recent public opinion survey conducted in the United States, over 77 percent of those polled said they regarded global environmental problems as "a very serious threat" to national security.[6] Unfortunately, nation-states continue to carry on business as usual in the global market economy, even while professing to be concerned about biospheric security. The Brundtland Commission on Environment and Development chastised the nations of the world for their continued reluctance to integrate biospheric thinking into domestic and foreign policy initiatives. The authors of the commission's report juxtaposed the new biospheric reality against the old geopolitical thinking, placing the dilemma squarely in front of the world community.

> The earth is one but the world is not. We all depend on our biosphere for sustaining our lives. Yet each community, each country, strives for survival and prosperity with little regard for its impact on others.[7]

For most of the modern era, debates over national security generally revolved around the issue of guns versus butter. Striking the proper balance between war making and commercial development has pitted hawks against doves for the better part of the twentieth century. In reality, the two options have more often than not fed off each other, as war making has spurred the growth of military-industrial complexes in many nations, as noted earlier. Still, by devoting government revenues and private capital to war production, nations have had fewer resources available to spend on education, health care, and programs designed to help the poor. President Lyndon Johnson experienced the guns-versus-butter issue firsthand in the 1960s as he attempted to finance an unpopular war in Southeast Asia and a domestic war on poverty at the same time. He overreached and consequently failed on both fronts.

Today, the guns-versus-butter argument has been subsumed by the guns-versus-environment argument. The Worldwatch Institute estimates the initial cost of reversing the global environmental crisis at around $774 billion over the next ten years.[8] (It should be noted that this figure may prove far too conservative.) Financing global efforts to protect topsoil from desertification, reforest the continents, develop programs for energy conservation, and explore new renewable sources of energy will require a shift of 10 percent or more in the military budget of every nation into biospheric protection.

The cost benefit comparison between guns and environment is striking and clearly underscores the difference in thinking between geopolitical security and biospheric security. For the $100 billion cost of the Trident II submarine and the F-16 jet fighter programs, the U.S. government could clean up the three thousand worst hazardous waste sites in the United States. For the cost of the stealth bomber program, estimated at $68 billion, the government could pay for two thirds of the projected costs of the clean water program over the next ten years. If the $6 billion cost of developing the Midgetman Intercontinental Ballistic Missile (ICBM) were transferred to biospheric protection, it could pay for the annual cost of cutting U.S. sulfur dioxide emissions by eight to twelve million tons per year, significantly easing the acid rain problem. For the cost of three B-1B bombers, the federal government could finance its entire program on renewable energy research for two years. Three weeks of global military spending could pay for primary health care for all the children in the third world, preventing over five million deaths from diarrhea and other diseases. Four days of global military spending, which is estimated to run about $8 billion, could finance a five-year action plan to protect the world's remaining tropical forests. Two days of global military spending switched to biospheric security efforts could finance the annual costs of halting third world desertification. The cost of one nuclear weapon test alone could finance the installation of eighty thousand hand pumps, giving third world villages access to clean water.[9]

The dramatic developments in the Soviet Union and Eastern Europe in recent years have radically changed the political dynamic in the world and cast doubt on conventional geopolitical thinking. Equally important, *glasnost, perestroika,* and the lifting of the Iron Curtain around Eastern Europe has for the first time raised the very real possibility of a new biospheric politics. With the economy of the Soviet Union near shambles from years of Cold War military expenditures, and its environment depleted and polluted from years of neglect, it has partially abandoned traditional geopolitical considerations, choosing to concentrate on its own economic development and environmental restoration. In 1989, Mikhail Gorbachev announced that Russia's Eastern European satellites would be free to choose their own course of development, without fear of Soviet meddling. Within months, the Communist regimes in East Germany, Hungary, Czechoslovakia, and Rumania fell. Communist rule gave way to free elections and new political leaders emerged throughout Eastern Europe. East and West Germany, with the encouragement of the United States and the Soviet Union, have reunified into a single Germany. Several former Warsaw Pact nations have asked for the removal of Soviet troops from their soil. Meanwhile, the Soviet Union has announced an across-the-board cut of 20 percent in Soviet arms production and has begun converting Soviet arms factories to commercial production.[10]

Responding to Soviet military cuts and the changes in Eastern Europe, the United States and its Western European allies are proposing serious cuts in NATO defenses. Some Western European nations are calling for the dismantling of NATO, signaling the end of the Cold War. Barring unforeseen circumstances, NATO and the Warsaw Pact Alliance will likely be disbanded entirely by the end of the current decade. The military savings to the United States will be significant. Currently, over 60 percent of the Pentagon budget goes to NATO and the defense of Europe. In 1986, American taxpayers each contributed an average of $1,155 in taxes to finance NATO operations.[11] If the $170 billion in NATO savings were applied to global environmental security, it would mark a significant change in U.S. foreign policy, away from conventional geopolitics and toward a new biosphere politics.

Shifting military spending to biospheric spending will necessitate a wholesale conversion of the military-industrial complex to a sustainable environmental economy. Labor unions and think tanks have already begun to initiate studies and make detailed proposals for converting plants from war production to peace production, emphasizing sustainable economic development and environmental stewardship. Workers at the General Dynamics shipyard in Massachusetts proposed converting their plant from building warships to the construction of "floating plants to convert ocean thermal energy into electricity." Similar "plantships" are already being built in Japan. Workers at the McDonnell Douglas aerospace plant in Southern California have proposed retooling their operations to build mass transit vehicles, wheelchairs, and other medical equipment and energy conservation equipment.[12]

A recent study by the Council on Economic Priorities estimates that for every billion dollars spent on military procurement, roughly 28,000 jobs are created.[13] The same expenditure on public transit would create 32,000 jobs and on education would create 71,000 jobs.[14] Another study, conducted by Employment Research Associates, found that overall Pentagon spending in 1981 resulted in the loss of 1.5 million jobs in the U.S. economy. The same study concluded that each $1 billion spent by the Defense Department resulted in the loss of 18,000 jobs in the U.S.[15]

Converting the military-industrial complex to a sustainable economic development complex will require a combination of public assistance in the form of state and federal tax dollars and the infusion of large sums of private capital. The economic and environmental advantages of conversion are obvious. Still, convincing federal and state legislators and the financial community to invest in a new green economy is quite another matter. Some state legislatures and city councils are beginning to pass new legislation and to rewrite existing statutes to encourage conversion. Tax incentives, changes in zoning laws, allocation of research and development funds, and new state-financed public works projects are among the various devices being used to leverage a transition into a more sustainable green economy. Effective across-the-board conversion, however, will require massive amounts of capital from the private sector. That capital, surprisingly enough, is available and from an unexpected source. Pension funds are a new form of wealth that has emerged only in the past forty years. They are now worth over $700 billion dollars and are the largest single pool of capital in the world.[16] Pension funds at present own at least 20 to 25 percent of the equity in U.S. corporations and hold over 40 percent of the bonds. Pension funds are now the largest source of investment capital for the U.S. capitalist system.[17]

Pension fund capital comes from the combined deferred savings of 19 million union members and the public employee funds of the various state governments. Over the years, the unions and the states have relinquished control over this powerful capital tool to the financial establishment. The banks, in turn, have used these capital assets to shift jobs and production around the world, oftentimes undermining both the job security of the workers, whose funds they are using, and the local economies from which these funds were generated.[18]

With pension fund capital, millions of American workers have become a major new ownership class. In recent years, labor leaders and state officials have begun pressing for greater participation by union members and taxpayers in deciding how pension funds are invested. Of the ninety-nine largest pension funds in the United States, forty-one have begun committing billions of dollars in pension funds to social investments that promote peace, sustainable economic development, job security for their members, and a healthy economy. Some are just beginning to invest in economic activities aimed at creating a green economy.[19]

Without access to workers' deferred savings, the international banking community and the multinational corporations they serve would be reduced to shells, having little effective control over global resources and the global marketplace. Biospheric grounding begins with the assertion of control over funds that belong to working people in each community and bioregion. Because pension funds are locally generated and are a unique form of collective capital, they are ideally suited for creating a bioregional economic infrastructure and promoting sustainable development on a regional scale.

Thinking globally, and acting locally, means taking responsibility for how one's funds are invested in the world. Millions of Americans have the potential power to direct hundreds of billions of dollars of their own deferred savings to investments locally and abroad that reflect the new green worldview. Translating that potential into a force for fundamental economic change will depend on the popular resolve to create a new biospheric politics in the years ahead.

41

OPENING UP THE GLOBAL COMMONS

MOVING BEYOND GEOPOLITICS to a new biospheric politics will require more than good intentions and expressions of goodwill. It has become acceptable, even fashionable, in first-world countries to think of the planet as Gaia, to acknowledge the importance of the biosphere and begin using terms like sustainability and stewardship. While a shift in language and the use of metaphor can serve as a powerful conditioner to reorient life-styles and worldviews, if the fledgling biospheric consciousness does not lead to a green movement for fundamental institutional change, it may well end up as little more than superficial gloss, incorporated into the advertising strategies of the multinationals and the political slogans of world leaders.

The late social philosopher Herbert Marcuse observed that in market-oriented cultures even revolutionary ideas become saleable commodities, their contents watered down and sanitized by the corporate powers to be made presentable and palatable to the widest possible buying public. Already, multinationals are reorienting their corporate image to incorporate the green theme, and politicians are jumping on the environmental bandwagon, professing their concern over the fate of the earth.

Biospheric consciousness and politics mean far more than a sensitivity to cleaning up the environment. In a biosphere culture, life-style itself becomes a political issue, as citizens in each community begin to draw the connections between personal consumption choices and the effects those choices have on the environmental health of the planet and the economic well-being of people in other lands. Although political pressure must continue to be exerted on the national level and in the international arena, patterns of living in every community will also have a direct and immediate impact on the biosphere.

Being grounded in a community means relying more on the bioregion and less on the global market to supply basic needs. Virtually every bioregion in the world has the resource potential to provide the basics of life. Of course, the advantage of the global market over the bioregional market is one of variety. An integrated world economy brings the vast resources of the global commons to the front door. One can purchase kiwi fruit from Australia and grapes from Mexico year-round, as well as mahogany and teak veneer from the Asian rain forests—and thousands of other items. The cost of having the resources of the planet available at our beck and call extends far beyond the price of purchase. A global market affords the rich and well-to-do middle classes of the first world with an opulent consumer life-style. But it does so at the expense of destroying the carrying capacity of the planet's ecosystems, undermining the health of the biosphere, and impoverishing the lives of millions of human beings in second and third world nations.

The bioregional market emphasizes necessities over luxuries and biospheric sustainability over geospheric expediency. Attention is placed on utilizing readily available resources in imaginative ways to provide food, clothing, shelter, transportation, and energy. Bioregional politics places the interests of humanity and the biosphere above personal whims and caprices. By establishing a sense of grounding in a local bioregion, people are making a political commitment to use only their fair share of the earth's resources.

Environmental stewardship and economic equity begins by reducing our consumption in the global marketplace and transferring our economic interests and activities, as much as possible, to our own local bioregions. Nowhere is this more important than in energy use. The wealthy nations of Western Europe, the United States, and Japan have been sucking up the nonrenewable energy of the planet in a frenzied attempt to maintain a profligate energy life-style. Meanwhile, villagers in the sub-Sahel of Africa are forced to walk for days at a time to gather up enough firewood to cook a single meal. Implementing radical energy conservation programs and alternative energy strategies—solar, wind, geothermal—are among the highest priorities of the new bioregional politics. Living within the energy limits set by the local bioregion and dictated by the standards of equity and conscience will go a long way toward addressing both the resource deficit and the global pollution crisis.

Of all the issues that connect human beings to each other and the biosphere, none is more important in establishing a sense of economic equity and environmental stewardship than the sharing of food. Eating high up on the planetary food chain is a luxury, not a necessity. That luxury is now threatening the land, the biosphere, and the lives of human beings around the globe.

Today, millions of people on the planet face malnourishment and starvation so that Americans and Western Europeans can enjoy a rich meat diet. In an earlier chapter, the environmental and economic consequences of worldwide cattle production for export was discussed. Cattle ranching is causing massive deforestation and desertification, dislodging people from their ancestral lands, creating a new class of environmental refugees, fanning political unrest and revolutionary movements, causing mass starvation, and destroying the biosphere. The elimination of beef and other meat from the human diet is now required if we are to have any hope of saving the planet and ensuring our children's future. The anthropological significance of giving up meat is profound and far-reaching in impact. From an environmental and economic perspective, it represents a watershed event in the history of the human species—a recognition that the health and well-being of the planet and the human race depend on eating lower on the food chain. From an ethical perspective, it marks an acknowledgment of our kindred spirit with the rest of the animal kingdom and our empathetic regard for the intrinsic value of all of earth's

311

creatures. Eliminating meat consumption and resacralizing our relationship to the living creatures of the planet are integral parts of the new biospheric consciousness and the new politics of extended community.

Reestablishing a sense of "ground" in the biosphere means reparticipating with the earth at every level of human existence. Breaking out of the arbitrary enclosures that have separated the ecosystems of the earth into exploitable domains and commercial corridors is the single most pressing task on the biospheric political agenda. A new green politics will need to reopen the global commons.

An Earth-oriented politics will be as diverse as the ecosystems that make up the planet and as unified as the biospheric process that unites it into a single organism. "Thinking globally and acting locally" means participating deeply in the local community and bioregion and sharing responsibility internationally for the ecological well-being of the planet.

Reopening the global commons will mean challenging the longstanding prerogatives of both the nation-states and the multinationals. The power and reach of both of these two governing institutions will need to be tempered to assure a modicum of biospheric security in the coming centuries. Human communities will need to join together across national borders and commercial trading markets to demand a more equitable sharing of Earth's resources among all of its inhabitants, humans and animals alike.

To begin with, whole areas of the planet's landmass need to be placed into public trust, to preserve what remains of the earth's genetic diversity. A limited number of "nature-for-debt" swaps have already been successfully negotiated. Lending institutions have agreed to retire a portion of the debt of developing nations in return for an agreement by the host countries to preserve rain forests and other ecosystems as land preserves or national parks. Nature-for-debt swaps need to be expanded and made more flexible. In some instances, debt retirement ought to be made conditional on an agreed-upon plan for sustainable development of a particular region, to ensure its long-term preservation while allowing for short-term economic use by the indigenous population.

Developed nations like the United States need to match international initiatives with ambitious domestic programs to buy up large tracts of land from the private sector and place them in public trusts. The commercial leasing of all public lands to the private sector should be conditional on meeting rigorous sustainable-production standards established by the government. Local communities and regional planning authorities ought to be able to place appropriate zoning restrictions on any private commercial use of publicly leased land.

Only by placing ecosystems in public trusts will it be possible to reverse the process of rampant short-term exploitation of the environment, which is endemic to private commercial ownership. Of course, there is no automatic guarantee that public ownership will ensure preservation and sustainable development. That will depend on the public's willingness and commitment in every country to protect the ecosystems under their charge.

Unfortunately, for the better part of two centuries, the U.S. business community has been able to exert tremendous influence on the leasing of public lands, often securing their commercial use for a pittance of their fair market value. Western ranchers lease millions of acres of public rangeland for a fraction of the land's worth on the open market. Lumber companies lease public forestlands in Alaska and the Northwest for nominal fees while reaping huge profits. The same story is repeated over and over again with offshore oil rights and coal leases, mineral and mining rights, and the like. U.S. corporations have been raiding the public lands of our country, plundering and depleting the rich natural endowment of the continent for short-term profit for as long as anyone cares to remember. Reversing that process will require a new sense of public vigilance. The American people will have to see themselves as guardians of the nation's ecological endowment and be willing to exercise stringent control over the commercial use of public lands.

While the land and the terrestrial ecosystems need to be better utilized to sustain human life, they are not simply regarded as "things" and "places" people privately own. The very idea of private ownership of part or all of an ecosystem is inimical to biospheric political thinking. In the new biospheric age, human

313

beings belong to the earth rather than the earth belonging to human beings. By maintaining the land and the ecosystems in public trusts, the human community acknowledges its membership inside the larger biospheric community of the planet. If effectively administered, private commercial leasing of the public commons should be able to strike a proper balance between economic entrepreneurship and market-driven forces on the one hand and ecosystem preservation and public stewardship on the other.

Certainly, if the commercial enclosure and privatization of the commons is not reversed and placed in public trust to be administered and leased out for development purposes, then no effective counterweight will exist to curtail the appetites of the corporate sector for resource optimization. There is not a single multinational corporation in the world today that voluntarily tempers or modifies short-term profit maximization and market advantage to accommodate the long-term sustainability of the biosphere.

Reopening the land commons of the planet will need to be accompanied by a reopening of the genetic commons. As noted in an earlier chapter, the rich genetic diversity of the Southern Hemisphere is being systematically transferred to Northern Hemisphere industrial nations and multinational corporations that reap untold profit from its use. As the world economy shifts from nonrenewable to renewable sources of energy, and from industrial technologies to biotechnologies, control over precious genetic resources will increasingly determine the configuration of the new economic order. We need only remember that a prime objective of nation-state geopolitics has been to secure increasing control over nonrenewable resources to fuel the industrial machine and modern commerce. Genetic resource wars may well succeed oil and mineral resource wars in the decades ahead unless a new international understanding is reached to share equitably the biological diversity of the planet. As long as the microbes, plants, and animals are regarded solely as resources, they will inevitably be reduced to a dollar value and be fought over by states and corporations anxious to maintain both political clout and market advantage.

Biosphere politics differs fundamentally from geopolitics in its approach to the genetic commons. All living creatures are perceived as having sacred as well as utilitarian value. Spiritual ecolo-

314

gy, in contrast to utilitarian ecology, pays homage to the awe of nature and the wonder of creation. The lives of individual creatures and species are treated with deep reverence. Human beings view other creatures as fellow travelers in the biosphere deserving of respect and equal consideration. At the same time, it is recognized that the well-being of living creatures cannot be separated from the well-being of the planet, as all of the earth's creatures play a critical role in maintaining the health and vitality of the biosphere. Preserving genetic diversity, then, is viewed as a sacred responsibility and an ecological imperative. This being the case, the economic use of genetic resources is viewed as a sacred trust, as is the use of the land.

In the years ahead, the gene pool of the planet will be increasingly relied upon to provide food, fiber, energy, and pharmaceuticals. Equitably sharing the genetic "resources" of the planet among all human beings, in a sustainable fashion, is a prime goal of biospheric politics and distinguishes the new way of thinking from traditional geopolitical considerations. Security, in the the new scheme of things, is bound up in shared responsibility for preserving the biosphere on behalf of present and future generations of human beings and all other creatures.

Over one hundred nations have joined together in the past decade under the leadership of Mexico to demand an equitable and sustainable policy on the use of germ plasm or genetic resources. At a succession of U.N. Food and Agriculture Organization (FAO) conferences in the 1980s, third world nations proposed that an international system of gene banks be funded and established in the host countries where the genetic resources are found. Suggestions have also been made for the establishment of a commission on plant genetic resources to ensure free and open access to all genetic resources stored in gene banks around the world. Many Southern Hemisphere nations have also argued for a free exchange of patented varieties of plants, owned by the multinational corporations, since most of the commercial strains were derived from domestic or wild stocks taken originally from third world countries. Genetic-rights activists Pat Mooney and Carey Fowler sum up the third world arguments expressed at the FAO meetings:

315

Third world delegates argued that if plant breeders had "rights" of ownership, control, and compensation by virtue of laboring for a decade (often with "donated" third world genetic resources) to develop a new variety, then third world farmers, as a group, also deserved some rights and recognition. Was it not third world farmers who domesticated our important agricultural crops, observed, developed, and safeguarded the tremendous genetic diversity used by the modern plant breeder?[1]

In 1987, Peru suggested that a tax be levied on the export of patented seeds by the multinationals, to be used to finance seed banks in third world countries. The United States, Canada, the United Kingdom, Australia, and other high-tech nations have bitterly fought such proposals, hoping to maintain free and open access to the world's gene pool while exercising exclusive market control over the patented varieties and other products made from the gene pool.[2]

The developed nations and multinationals seem determined to further enclose and privatize the gene pool of the planet by extending patent protection over plants, microbes, and animals, while most third world nations seem equally determined to open up the genetic commons for equitable and sustainable sharing of the world's germ plasm. In the coming years, the battle between those advocating an open gene pool commons and those advocating enclosure will likely be played out against a larger backdrop, pitting the new biospheric consciousness against conventional geopolitics.

The opening up of the global commons will need to be extended from the land, its ecosystems, and the gene pool to the oceans, atmosphere, electromagnetic spectrum, and outer space. Because biospheric politics is based on an organic view of the earth, it requires a relatively open playing field where all of creation can commingle and interact for the mutual health and well-being of the planet.

The Convention on the Law of the Seas, which was signed by 119 nations in 1982 and heralded as a significant breakthrough in the management of the global oceanic commons, actually ended

316

up enclosing nearly 40 percent of the world's oceans in a single legislative stroke. As was noted in an earlier chapter, the convention granted nation-states exclusive economic control over coastal waters extending two hundred miles out to sea. This single treaty effectively enclosed a greater portion of the global commons than any war or imperialist adventure in modern history. Although the convention calls on national governments to pass laws to reduce ocean dumping, compliance is purely voluntary, thus making the document virtually worthless as a regulatory instrument. Even so, twenty-two nations, including the United States and Soviet Union, refused to sign the accord.[3]

Opening up the oceanic commons will require a complete revision of the Law of the Seas Convention, including narrowing the 200-mile coastal waters limit to the conventional 3-to-20-mile limit, which had previously been accepted as the world standard. The convention also needs statutes to regulate the commercial use of the oceans, including the imposition of penalties and fines for overfishing and dumping. An international governing body and regional commissions should be established to monitor, regulate, and enforce the provisions of a revised Law of the Seas Convention. The governments of the world should consider global and regional leasing arrangements, charging fees to nation-states and multinational corporations for commercial use of the oceanic commons. Governments and private corporations might also be taxed on the basis of the quantity and market value of their fish catch, or, in the case of seabed minerals and oil, the market value of their extraction. Leasing fees and taxes should be placed in an international fund to be used by the oceanic governing body and regional commissions to clean up the world's oceans and implement the provisions of the treaty.

Like the oceanic commons, the atmosphere will also need to be regulated as a global trust if the human community is to entertain any possibility of addressing the problems of global warming, ozone depletion, acid rain and air pollution. In June 1988, the prime ministers of Norway and Canada proposed a "Law of the Air" treaty to protect the atmosphere from global warming and ozone depletion. The two countries suggested that a world atmosphere fund be established, financed by a tax on fossil fuel consumption in the industrial countries. The money accrued would, in turn, be used to help finance energy efficiency programs, the transition to renewable energy sources, and the research and development of alternatives to CFCs.[4]

Taxing the polluting countries and corporations establishes an equity standard for cleaning up the atmospheric commons. Second and third world nations are justified in arguing that the United States and the Soviet Union should shoulder the brunt of the financial burden in addressing the global warming crisis, as they are jointly responsible for over 40 percent of the carbon emissions into the atmosphere.

Every nation in the world will need to finance changes in their infrastructure and institutions to adjust effectively to the destabilizing effects of global warming in the coming century. By taxing fossil fuel consumption and establishing a world atmosphere fund, money will be available to help second and third world countries finance the necessary changes they will need to make to counter the effects of global warming on their national economies.

The commitment to reopen the global commons, to live within the carrying capacity of the biosphere and bioregions, to share the earth's resources equitably among present and future generations, and to resacralize our relationships to the rest of the living kingdom are all considerations firmly grounded in the new organismic view of the planet. The notion of living inside an extended community of relationships and obligations, stretching from the bioregion to the biosphere, represents a new vision of personal and global security that is in sharp contrast to the detached, mechanistic view of the past, with its emphasis on dominance, control, subjugation, self-interest, and autonomy.

42

THE THIRD STAGE OF HUMAN CONSCIOUSNESS

REOPENING THE GLOBAL commons and de-militarizing the planet will necessitate an unprecedented mobilization of the human species. To be effective, the new biospheric politics will need to transcend national boundaries, political ideologies, and market forces, and become earth-oriented. Reintegrating ourselves back into the temporal and spatial contours of the local biome and the earth's biosphere will require a leap of human consciousness, a fundamental transformation of our sense of self and our relationship to the world around us.

The evolution of consciousness is, to a great extent, a history of our changing conceptions of security. Today, the new therapeutic consciousness and ecological way of thinking is being accompanied by a profound shift away from geopolitical notions of security and toward a new biospheric vision. To understand both the nature and magnitude of the changes taking place in the collective consciousness of much of the human family, it is useful to examine some of the underlying assumptions of twentieth-century psychology.

Sigmund Freud speculated that the unconscious of each individual contained the "memory traces of the experiences of former generations," or what he called the "archaic heritage."[1] (Jung and other psychiatrists of the twentieth century preferred to use the term "collective unconscious.") Many of the seminal thinkers in modern psychology agreed with the German biologist Ernst Haeckel that "ontogeny recapitulates phylogeny"—that each individual relives the history of the race.

Freud believed that in the early years of childhood "we have to cover the enormous distance of development from primitive man of the Stone Age to civilized man of today."[2] Certainly, in the realm of security, the patterns in child development and the patterns in the collective history of human civilization share many common features, suggesting a close relationship between the two.

Freud reminds us that in the earliest stage of development, an infant experiences an undifferentiated union with the mother. The concept of self has not yet been formed. The baby experiences his mother and the world around him as a whole. There are no subjects and objects, no sense of "I" and "other," only what Freud called the "oceanic" feeling of oneness. The unity is broken early on as the infant comes to realize that his every urge and desire cannot be met immediately. The baby begins to distinguish between his desires and the objects of desire being denied him. His mother's breast is not always available to him. The feeling of omnipotence, that "he is the world," becomes tempered by the reality of limits imposed on him from the outside. The "pleasure principle," as Freud referred to it, is challenged by the "reality principle."

As the baby discovers both his separateness from the mother and the outside world, as well as his dependence on forces over which he has little or no control, the experience becomes a source of deep anxiety from which he never fully recovers. He experiences this original separation as death and begins fashioning an array of mental defenses to deny the pain of what he is experiencing. The individual spends the rest of his life attempting to recapture the feeling of "oceanic" oneness while, at the same time, denying his original loss because the pain of separation, dependence, and death is more than he can bear.

The original feeling of oneness is the "life instinct," or Eros. Bodily touch, sexuality, the feeling of love and belonging are all interlaced in the "life instinct." Partially separated from the objects of his affection, by toilet training, schedules, and other outside interferences, the baby begins to repress his sense of loss by sublimating his bodily feelings which were once a source of so much pleasure. He substitutes the "death instinct" for the "life instinct" to compensate for his sense of anxiety and powerlessness.

320

Unable to control the events that are denying him his bodily pleasure, he begins to deny his separation by becoming detached. He represses his dependency on others by seeking autonomy. The baby increasingly attempts to control events, to dominate his surroundings, to assert his individuality. Most parents are well aware of the "terrible twos," the age in a child's development when he begins to assert himself, to claim a sense of autonomy in the world.

The "death instinct" casts an ever more menacing shadow over the child as he grows up. Longing for the "oceanic" oneness he originally experienced, yet denying his separation and dependency, the developing child becomes immersed in sublimation. He represses what he truly wants and desires, the exaltation of bodily union, by attempting to deaden his own yearnings. The war against nature, which we have spoken of at length in this book, begins in infancy as the child wages war on his own bodily feelings. The child compensates for his own loss of bodily participation and pleasure by surrounding himself with substitutes or surrogates. Freud would argue that the body of Christ and eternal salvation served as surrogates in the medieval era. In the modern age, machines and material possessions serve as substitutes for the body. The individual "projects the repressed body into things." Psychologist Norman O. Brown observes: "The more the life of the body passes into things, the less life there is in the body, and at the same time the increasing accumulation of things represents an ever fuller articulation of the lost life of the body." Brown goes on to say that "technological progress makes increased sublimation possible . . . the hidden aim of technological progress is the discovery and recovery of the human body."[3]

We noted throughout this book the increasing human compulsion in Western civilization to substitute machines of one sort or another for the human body. The "death instinct" hangs over the culture as it does each individual life, conditioning much of our thinking about security in the modern age. Today virtual environments, simulated realities, genetic engineering, and the downloading of consciousness represent the triumph of the "death instinct" over the "life instinct." Brown says:

What we call human progress, or higher civilization, means an increase in the domain of the death instinct at the expense of the life instinct. Sublimation is a mortification of the body and a sequestration of the life of the body into dead things.[4]

The repression of the life instinct, of bodily experience and participation, runs deep in the human psyche and wide over the cultural landscape. Fear of life, as Freud reminds us in *Civilization and Its Discontents,* is fear of death, a fear first felt at the moment the baby experiences the original separation from the "oceanic" oneness of being.[5] The flight from death and from the "life instinct" is the tortured path of human civilization.

We have spent the better part of recorded history and virtually all of modern history projecting the death instinct onto the building of great civilizations. In the medieval era, Western man set his hopes on eternal salvation to ward off the fear of his own mortality. In the modern age, the ideology of unlimited progress, material cornucopias, and classless societies helped ease the pain of man's own finite nature. Western theologies and ideologies have been buttressed with an array of physical tokens expressing the flight from death. From ancient pyramids to modern skyscrapers, man has erected countless monuments to his own immortality and surrounded himself with all sorts of artifacts, tools, and institutions to maintain the illusion of his independence from nature and the finiteness of his own existence.

In the modern age, the "death instinct" has run rampant, in the guise of Baconian science and Cartesian rationalism. Norman O. Brown says that "modern science serves both the reality-principle and the 'death instinct' " by "getting rid of our old loves"—bodily participation and physical communion with nature—and replacing those experiences with scientific and technological substitutes.

Thus science and civilization combine to articulate the core of the human neurosis, man's incapacity to live in the body, which is also his incapacity to die.[6]

For the past two thousand years, and especially in the modern age, Western man and woman have been increasingly absorbed by the "death instinct." Witness the increasing human detachment from nature and the human body and the increasing withdrawal into an enclosed cocoon of technological and economic autonomy. While the "death instinct" has turned people away from their own bodies and the body of nature, it has also spurred an increasing aggression against both. Freud suggests:

> Aggression in human nature—the drive to master nature as well as the drive to master man—is the result of an extroversion of the "death instinct," the desire to die being transformed into the desire to kill, destroy or dominate.[7]

The modern age has been characterized by this dual process of detachment from and domination over nature. Our notions of modern-day security, then, seem tragically imbedded in the death instinct. It is no wonder we now find ourselves surrounded by the signs of death wherever we look. The global environmental crisis, the specter of nuclear holocaust, the impoverishment of millions of human beings, and mass social alienation on a scale never before experienced are all visible manifestations of a civilization locked into a death chant. How else could we possibly explain how the planet and our species have arrived at the brink of annihilation? In *Civilization and Its Discontents,* Freud concludes his life's work with an observation on the history of human culture:

> And now, I think, the meaning of the evolution of civilization is no longer obscure to us. It must represent the struggle between Eros and Death, between the "instinct of life" and the "instinct of destruction," as it works itself out in the human species. This struggle is what all of life essentially consists of, and the evolution of civilization may therefore be simply described as the struggle for life of the human species.[8]

Changing our ideas about security will require a change in the collective consciousness of the human race and in the psyche of each individual on the planet. Healing the breach between the pleasure principle and the reality principle, resurrecting Eros, the "life instinct," and coming to grips with the "death instinct" and the hold it has enjoyed on our individual beings and the whole of culture will be decisive in structuring a new approach to the security of the planet in which we dwell.

Human history, like individual history, seems to be conditioned by the dialectical pull of two great competing forces, one seeking "unification and interdependence," or the "life instinct," the other seeking "separation and independence," or the "death instinct." Reconciling these conflicting drives appears to be the great unfinished task of human evolution at both the individual and cultural level.

Owen Barfield, the British solicitor and philosopher, has outlined three stages in the history of human consciousness that provide a useful starting point for integrating the two conflicting human drives into a new unified synthesis—one that is compatible with the new biospheric consciousness and an organismic view of the planet.[9] Barfield says that for the greater part of human history, including the vast stretches of Paleolithic history, human beings enjoyed intimate bodily participation with nature and their own bodily nature. There was little sense of differentiation between the individual and the group and between human beings and their surroundings. The human species was firmly imbedded in the temporal and spatial realms of the natural world and experienced, at least partially, the kind of "oceanic" oneness that the newborn infant feels. Mothers and Mother Earth were experienced in a similar fashion. Indeed, for most of human history human beings experienced the earth as a loving but often arbitrary and capricious mother and themselves as helpless children who depended on her benevolence. Human beings experienced intimacy and the pleasures of direct bodily participation with Mother Nature, and had not yet developed more than a fragmentary sense of their own individual identity and independence.

Beginning with the neolithic revolution and the domestication of nature, human beings slowly began to assert their will over nature, first in the form of agricultural practices and animal husbandry, later in smithing technologies, and finally in industrial production. With mastery over nature came increasing detachment and the embryonic development of individuality and self-awareness. In the modern age, the trend sped up exponentially

324

with the enclosure of the global commons, the commercialization of nature, the increasing privatization and individuation of human social life, and developments in science and technology. Today, human beings are increasingly self-aware but have gained their sense of individual identity at the expense of losing intimate communion with the natural world.

The evolutionary history of the species has recapitulated the evolutionary history of each individual's own development. The human race has evolved from a state of undifferentiated oneness with Mother Nature to a detached self-aware isolation from her. We have won, at least, the illusion of independence from nature, but we have lost a sense of relationship and kindred spirit with the earth. Humanity, then, has passed from the life instinct to the death instinct, from oceanic oneness with the earth to separation, control, and domination over the planet from a distance.

Today, the third great stage of human consciousness opens up before us: to make a conscious self-aware choice to reparticipate with the body of nature. The implications of such a leap in consciousness are obvious and far-reaching. Nowhere will the impact of the new consciousness be more heartfelt than in our individual and collective notions of security.

Geopolitical security was based on the death instinct and took us to the brink of Armageddon. Biospheric security is based on a reconciliation of the death instinct with the life instinct and helps establish a balance between separation and oneness, independence and dependence, detachment and participation. The great anxiety that has fueled so much of the personal and collective history of our species, especially in the modern age, is, as Norman O. Brown observes, "the anxiety of separation from the protecting mother."[10] That anxiety has increased in direct proportion to our increasing sense of individuality. With greater awareness of self and our own uniqueness comes the painful awareness of our own mortality. It is for this reason that the marked individualism of the modern age has been accompanied by such denial and repression of the life instinct and such open aggression against the living world. Unable to bear our own mortality, modern man and woman have lashed out against all of life, as if the death of living nature might somehow rid us of the constant reminder of our own frail existence.

The poet Rainer Maria Rilke provided the understanding we need to reconcile and integrate the life instinct and death instinct into a new unity. He said, "Whoever rightly understands and celebrates death, at the same time magnifies life."[11] Accepting death means accepting what Hegel called "the nature of finite things." Hegel reminded us that all living creatures "have the seed of passing away as their essential being: the hour of their birth is the hour of their death."[12] Only by accepting death, then, do we affirm life. Or we might well say that only by affirming life and our bodily participation in the life of our planet do we come to accept our own death and the death process.

The decision to reparticipate with the body of nature is quite different from the kind of original participation that characterizes the life of every infant and the early history of our species. The key difference is the ability to choose. It is the act of self-aware volition that distinguishes the mature consciousness of the biospheric era. To reparticipate with nature out of an act of love and free will, rather than out of fear and dependency, is what makes the third stage of human consciousness so fundamentally unique. By making a choice to reparticipate with the body of nature, the individual and the species is affirming life, accepting the inevitability of death, and celebrating the organismic unity that binds the parts to the whole. By freely choosing, each person retains his or her own unique identity while reveling in the oceanic oneness of the biosphere. From mother to Mother Earth, from undifferentiated oneness to self-aware reparticipation, from utter dependency to mutually accepted responsibility, the consciousness of the individual and the species reach out from a self-imposed exile to reembrace the earth, secure in the fullness of their grounding inside the biosphere.

Today, it is ours to choose. To make a self-aware choice to reparticipate with the biosphere. To heal the wounds we have inflicted on our planet and our souls. To make the world secure. To secure ourselves and our being. To take the leap.

NOTES

CHAPTER 1

1. National Alliance to End Homelessness, *Housing and Homelessness* (Washington, D.C.: National Alliance to End Homelessness, 1988), pp. 11–33.

2. National Alliance, *Housing and Homelessness,* p. 37.

3. There are more than 2.2 million hard-core cocaine addicts in the United States. One in every five persons arrested in this country—regardless of his or her crime—is a cocaine addict. U.S., Congress, Senate, Committee On the Judiciary, *Hard-Core Cocaine Addicts: Measuring—And Fighting—The Epidemic.* S. Prt., pp. 101–6, 101st Cong., 2d sess., 1990, p. iv.

4. National Institute on Drug Abuse, *National Household Survey on Drug Abuse: Population Estimates 1988* (Washington D.C.: U.S. Government Printing Office, 1989), p. 17.

5. Federal Bureau of Investigation, *Crime in the United States—1988* (Washington, D.C.: U.S. Government Printing Office, 1989).

6. Figures from National Rifle Association, *NRA Firearms Fact Sheet 1990* (Washington, D.C.: NRA-Institute for Legislative Action, 1990), p. 1. For the number of murders and injuries caused by these same firearms, see Lois A. Fingerhut and Joel Kleinman, *Firearm Mortality Among Children and Youth* (Washington, D.C.: National Center For Health Statistics, 1989); American Medical Association, Council On Scientific Affairs. *Firearm Injuries and Deaths: A Critical Public Health Issue* (Washington, D.C.: Public Health Reports, 1989), pp. 111–20.

7. U.S. Treasury Department, *Federal Reserve Bulletin, 1st Quarter, 1990,* p. 830; U.S., Congress, Congressional Budget Office, *The Economic and Budget Outlook: An Update,* June 1990; U.S., Department of

Commerce, U.S. Bureau of the Census, *Statistical Abstract of the United States—1990* (Washington, D.C.: U.S. Government Printing Office, 1990).

8. Professor Gerald Vaughn of the University of Tennessee Zoology Department estimates the current global extinction rate at 1,000 species per year, 14,500 times the rate during the Ice Age of the Pleistocene era. Paul and Anne Ehrlich corroborate these figures in *Extinction: The Causes and Consequences of the Disappearance of Species* (New York: Ballantine, 1981). The Ehrlich volume is important because it warns of the broader social consequences of the elimination of the world's plant and animal species.

9. The Worldwatch Institute estimates the number of "environmental refugees"—those people who have had to leave their homes because of environmental hazards or urban development—at over 10 million. Lester R. Brown et al., *State of the World 1989* (Washington, D.C.: Worldwatch Institute, 1989). See also Jodi Jacobson, "Environmental Refugees: A Yardstick of Habitability."

10. Two very unsentimental portrayals of rural life in pre-twentieth-century Europe are found in Jerome Blum, ed., *Our Forgotten Past: Seven Centuries of Life on the Land* (London: Thames and Hudson, 1982) and Peter Laslett, *The World We Have Lost: England Before the Industrial Age*, 3d ed. (New York: Scribner's, 1984).

11. The most authoritative study of Aquinas and his nature cosmology is found in Arthur O. Lovejoy, *The Great Chain of Being* (Cambridge, Mass.: Harvard University Press, 1936).

CHAPTER 2

1. G. Elliot Smith, *Human History* (New York: Norton, 1929), quoted in S. A. Coblentz, *Avarice: A History* (Washington, D.C.: Public Affairs Press, 1965), p. 24.

2. Arthur Hocart, *The Life-Giving Myth*, ed. Lord Raglan (London: Methuen, 1952), p. 99.

3. Hocart, *The Life-Giving Myth*, p. 101.

4. Ernest Becker, *Escape From Evil*, p. 79.

5. James Knight, *For the Love of Money: Human Behavior and Money*, p. 29.

6. Ibid.

7. Becker, *Escape From Evil*, p. 81.

8. John Ruskin, "Unto This Last" in *Works of John Ruskin*, vol. 17, ed. E. T. Cook and A. Wedderburn (London: Allen & Unwin, 1903–1912), pp. 44–45, 46.

9. Jacques Le Goff, *Your Money or Your Life*, pp. 24–25.

10. St. Thomas Aquinas, quoted in Le Goff, *Your Money or Your Life*, p. 29.

11. The relationship between money, time, and the modern notion of profits is addressed in a number of important studies. See, for example, Jacques Le Goff, *Time, Work, and Culture in the Middle Ages,* pp. 51–61. Ricardo J. Quinones, *The Renaissance Discovery of Time* (Cambridge, Mass.: Harvard University Press, 1972), pp. 5–8; Sebastian De Grazia, *Of Time, Work, and Leisure* (New York: Anchor/Doubleday, 1964).

12. Thomas Chobham, *Summa Confessorum,* ed. F. Broomfield (Paris: Louvain, 1968), p. 505, question XI, chapter 1.

13. Le Goff, *Time, Work, and Culture,* p. 30.

14. See Bronislaw Malinowski, "The Primitive Economics of the Trobriand Islanders," *Economic Journal* 17 (1921): 1–16. See also Norman O. Brown, *Life Against Death: The Psychoanalytic Meaning of History,* p. 26.

15. Elias Canetti, *Crowds and Power,* p. 448.

16. The transition from a "moral economy to market economy" is discussed in greater detail in Murray Bookchin, *The Modern Crisis,* pp. 77–97.

17. See Richard Rubenstein's commentary on the rationalization of the marketplace in *The Age of Triage: Fear and Hope in an Overcrowded World,* pp. 6–8.

18. Lewis Mumford, *The Culture of Cities,* p. 27.

19. Le Goff, *Your Money or Your Life,* pp. 12–15.

20. Ibid., pp. 75–80.

21. Ibid., p. 80 (parentheses and emphases Le Goff's).

22. Ibid., pp. 92, 93.

23. Social historian Fernand Braudel observes that "Any society based on an ancient structure which opens its doors to money sooner or later loses its acquired equilibria and liberates forces that can never afterwards be adequately controlled. The new form of interchange disturbs the old order, benefits only a few privileged individuals, and hurts everyone else." Braudel, *The Wheels of Commerce: The Structures of Everyday Life,* vol. 1, p. 437.

24. Thomas Hobbes, *Leviathan,* pt. 2, ed. C. B. Macpherson (Harmondsworth, England: Penguin Books, 1979), p. 295.

25. Max Weber, *Economy and Society,* vol. 2, ed. Guenther Roth and Claus Witich (New York: Bedminster Press, 1968), p. 636.

CHAPTER 3

1. Francis Bacon, "Novum Organum," *The Works of Sir Francis Bacon,* Book 1, Aphorism 71. The following treatment of Bacon is indebted to three studies, all of which see a direct relationship between the rise of Baconian science and the modern subjugation of the natural world: Carolyn Merchant, *The Death of Nature: Women, Ecology, and*

the Scientific Revolution, chapter 7; William Leiss, The Domination of Nature, chapter 3; Morris Berman, The Reenchantment of the World, pp. 14–18, 94, 96.

2. Quoted in John Herman Randall, The Making of the Modern Mind, p. 223.

3. Ibid., p. 224.

4. Bacon, "Novum Organum," The Works of Francis Bacon, vol. 4, p. 246. See also Francis Bacon, "The Masculine Birth of Time," in Benjamin Farrington, ed., The Philosophy of Francis Bacon (Liverpool, England: Liverpool University Press, 1964), p. 62.

5. Francis Bacon, "Description of the Intellectual Globe," in Works, vol. 5., p. 506; Leiss, Domination of Nature, p. 58; Merchant, Death of Nature, p. 172.

6. Francis Bacon, "Novum Organum," p. 114; Farrington, Thoughts and Conclusions, pp. 92–93; Merchant, Death of Nature, p. 172.

7. Francis Bacon, "De Augmentis," Works, vol. 4, pp. 320, 325; Merchant, Death of Nature, p. 171.

8. Bacon, "De Augmentis," pp. 320, 325.

9. The role of Cartesian mechanism in framing our modern worldview and cosmology is explored in several recent studies that examine the evolution of human/environmental relations. See, for example, Fritjof Capra, The Turning Point: Science, Society, and the Rising Culture, pp. 56–63; Berman, Reenchantment of the World, pp. 14–24, 102; Merchant, Death of Nature, pp. 235–253, 259–60; Stephen Walker, Animal Thought, pp. 2–20, 108; Lawrence LeShan and Henry Margenau, Einstein's Space and Van Gogh's Sky (New York: Macmillan, 1983), chapter 2.

10. Quoted in Samuel L. Macy, Clocks and the Cosmos: Time and Western Life and Thought, p. 76.

11. Quoted in John Herman Randall, The Making of the Modern Mind, p. 241. An account of Descartes's dream is found in Karl Stern, The Flight from Women, pp. 80–84. See also Susan Bordo, "The Cartesian Masculinization of Thought," pp. 439–56.

12. Randall, Making of the Modern Mind, pp. 241–42.

13. René Descartes, Discourse on Method and Meditation, 2d ed. Laurence J. Lafleur, tr. (New York: Macmillan, 1960).

14. Alfred North Whitehead, Science and the Modern World, p. 54, as quoted in Bordo, "Cartesian Masculinization of Thought," p. 450.

15. Descartes's mechanical vision of nature was modified in the current century with the introduction of the electronic and computer revolutions. As the industrial machine gave way to the electronic computer after World War II, Descartes's mechanistic view of nature gave way to the idea of nature as information. Mechanistic assumptions were projected onto nature and the cosmos for nearly four hundred years, until a new generation of systems theorists and cyberneticians began to project

the assumptions of information theory onto all earthly and extraterrestrial phenomena.

The computer, like the industrial machine that preceded it, has become an all-embracing metaphor to redefine the workings of the world. A powerful new form of reductionism is spreading through the intellectual community, capturing the attention of a whole generation of thought makers. Scientists talk excitedly about the "computerlike" way all physical and biological phenomena seem to behave. This new view of nature adds a veneer of legitimacy to the newest technology, as all of reality is seen as operating by a set of governing principles remarkably similar to those that govern the computer.

16. John Locke, "Second Treatise," in Locke, *Two Treatises of Government*, ed. Peter Laslett (Cambridge, England: Cambridge University Press, 1967), p. 315.

17. Locke, quoted in Leo Strauss, *Natural Rights and History*, p. 258.

18. Locke, "Second Treatise," p. 315.

19. John Locke, quoted in Strauss, *Natural Rights*, p. 315.

CHAPTER 4

1. Gilbert Slater, *The English Peasantry and the Enclosure of Common Fields*, p. 1. The literature on the enclosure movement is voluminous; however, the history of enclosure is generally not well known in American academic circles. The best sources on the enclosure movement in England are: R. H. Tawney, *The Agrarian Problem in the Sixteenth Century* (London: Longmans Green, 1912); William Tate, *The Enclosure Movement*; John L. and Barbara Hammond, *The Village Labourer, 1760–1832: A Study in the Government of England Before the Reform Bill*, abridged ed. (London: Longmans Green, 1920); Joan Thirsk, ed., *The Agrarian History of England and Wales, 1500–1640*, vol. 4.

2. Karl Polanyi, *The Great Transformation: The Political and Economic Origins of Our Time*, p. 35; Richard Rubenstein, *The Age of Triage: Fear and Hope in an Overcrowded World*, p. 10.

3. Rubenstein, *Age of Triage*, p. 43; Slater, *English Peasantry*, pp. 6, 110.

4. Thomas More, *The Utopia of Sir Thomas More*, Thirsk, *Agrarian History*, p. 239.

5. Slater, *English Peasantry*, p. 264.

6. Carl J. Dahlman, *The Open Field System and Beyond: A Property Rights Analysis of an Economy Institution* (Cambridge, England: Cambridge University Press, 1980), pp. 164–68, 183–86.

7. Rubenstein, *Age of Triage*, p. 46.

8. Quoted in F. Pollack and F. W. Maitland, *The History of English Law Before the Time of Edward I* (Cambridge, England: Cambridge University Press, 1968), pp. 262–63; Dahlman, *Open Field System,* p. 183.

9. Slater, *English Peasantry,* p. 4.

10. Thomas Hobbes, quoted in Dahlman, *Open Field System,* p. 183.

CHAPTER 5

1. Frances Moore Lappé, *Diet for a Small Planet,* 10th ed., p. 89.

2. Frances Moore Lappé and Joseph Collins, *World Hunger: Twelve Myths* (New York: Grove Press, 1986), p. 40.

3. Steven Sanderson, "The Emergence of the 'World Steer:' Internationalization and Foreign Domination in Latin American Cattle Production," in F. Lamond Tullis and W. Ladd Hallister, eds. *Food, the State and International Political Economy: Dilemmas of Developing Countries,* p. 130.

4. Frances Moore Lappé and Joseph Collins, *Food First: Beyond the Myth of Scarcity,* p. 289; Norman Myers, *The Primary Source: Tropical Forests and Our Future,* p. 130.

5. Lappé and Collins, *Food First,* p. 289.

6. Ibid., p. 290.

7. Ibid., pp. 290–91, 292.

8. Myers, *Primary Source,* p. 128.

9. Ibid., p. 135

10. Lappé, *Food First,* p. 48.

11. Myers, *Primary Source,* p. 133.

12. Ibid., p. 134.

13. Ibid., p. 133.

14. Lappé, *Food First,* p. 49.

15. Ibid., p. 50.

16. Myers, *Primary Source,* p. 131.

17. Ibid.

CHAPTER 6

1. Thucydides is quoted in George Modelski and William Thompson, *Seapower in Global Politics, 1494–1994,* p. 6. Contemporary ideas about the role of "seapower" have been greatly influenced by the writing of Alfred Mahan, particularly *The Influence of Sea Power Upon History, 1660–1783.*

2. Marvin S. Soroos, "The International Commons: A Historical Perspective," p. 13.

3. Ibid.

4. Ibid.

5. Sir Walter Raleigh is quoted in Modelski and Thompson, *Seapower in Global Politics,* p. 7.

6. Soroos, "International Commons," p. 13.

7. Sayre A. Swarztrauber, *The Three-Mile Limit of Territorial Seas,* p. 10.

8. Ibid., pp. 23–35.

9. Soroos, "International Commons," p. 14.

10. R. R. Churchill and A. V. Lowe, *The Law of the Sea,* vol. 1 (Oxford, England: Oxford University Press, 1983), p. 126.

11. Ibid.

12. Arthur H. Westing, *Global Resources and International Conflict: Environmental Factors in Strategic Policy and Action,* p. 117.

13. Ibid., pp. 15, 133.

14. Huxley quoted in James Nicholson, *Food From the Sea* (London: Cassell, 1979), p. 159; Soroos, "International Commons," p. 4.

15. Westing, *Global Resources,* p. 134.

16. Ibid., pp. 133, 116, 134.

17. Ibid., p. 133.

18. Soroos, "International Commons," p. 5.

19. Westing, *Global Resources,* p. 189.

CHAPTER 7

1. Benjamin Franklin, *The Writings of Benjamin Franklin,* vol 9, ed. Albert Henry Smyth (New York: Macmillan, 1906), p. 85; John C. Cooper, *The Right to Fly,* p. 10.

2. Franklin, *Writings of Benjamin Franklin,* p. 157.

3. Cooper, *Right to Fly,* p. 17.

4. Ibid., p. 20.

5. Civil Aerial Transport Committee (British Air Board) Command Paper No. 9218. Placed before British Parliament in 1918; Cooper, *Right to Fly,* p. 23.

6. Cooper, *Right to Fly,* p. 32.

CHAPTER 8

1. Anthony Smith, *The Geopolitics of Information: How Western Culture Dominates the World,* p. 121. For further policy implications concerning the global electromagnetic environment see Lynton Caldwell, *International Environmental Policy: Emergence and Dimensions,* pp. 234–40. The historical emergence of the twentieth-century global communication network is also addressed in Harold Innis, *Empire and Communication.*

2. Smith, *Geopolitics of Information,* p. 121.
3. Ibid., p. 122.
4. Ibid.
5. Ibid., p. 123.
6. Caldwell, *International Environmental Policy,* p. 235.
7. Ibid., p. 237.
8. United Nations Resolution 626 (VII) rightly states that no nation "impede the exercise of sovereignty of any state over its natural resources; but remote sensing satellites . . . lead to precisely this result. There is no way to stop them, although it might be possible to argue that all information collected be transmitted immediately to the country concerned before being published. But without the facilities for receiving the data, processing it and analyzing it expertly, what would such a provision be?" See also Smith, *Geopolitics of Information,* p. 129; Caldwell, *International Environmental Diplomacy,* p. 238.
9. Smith, *Geopolitics of Information,* p. 131.

CHAPTER 9

1. For an insightful and critical survey of biotechnology's role in modern agricultural practices, see Jack Doyle, *Altered Harvest: Agriculture, Genetics, and the Fate of the World's Food Supply.*
2. World Commission on Environment and Development, *Our Common Future* [The Brundtland Commission Report] (Oxford, England: Oxford University Press, 1987), p. 155.
3. Gary Nabhan has conducted an extensive study on the loss of seed varieties (germ plasm) in North America. His voluminous work *Enduring Seeds: Native American Agriculture and Wild Plant Conservation* documents the evolution of seed propagation in the United States and warns of the potential dangers in losing this important natural resource. According to most estimates, roughly half of all our farm animal species face extinction in the coming years. See, for example, Lisa Drew, "The Barnyard Restoration," *Newsweek,* 29 May 1989, pp. 50–51. For literature on the availability of extremely rare or "minor" animal breeds, contact The American Minor Breeds Conservancy, Box 477, Pittsboro, N.C. 27312.
4. Pat Mooney and Cary Fowler, "Vanilla and Biotechnology," Rural Advancement Fund International *Communiqué,* January 1987, p. 1.
5. Ibid.
6. Ibid., p. 2.
7. Andrew Pollack, "It May Taste Like Vanilla, But Is It Vanilla?," *New York Times,* 6 June 1987, p. A1; *Food Engineering,* November 1987, p. 50; Boyce Rensberger, "Tricking Cotton to Think Lab is Home Sweet Home," *Washington Post,* 29 May 1988, p. A3.

8. Mooney and Fowler, "Vanilla and Biotechnology," p. 2; *Food Technology,* April 1986, p. 122.

9. For a summary of the differing political opinions on the subject of animal patenting as well as the variety of species involved, see William H. Lesser, ed., *Animal Patents: The Legal, Economic, and Social Issues.*

CHAPTER 10

1. See Catherine Caufield, *In the Rainforest: Report From a Strange, Beautiful, Imperiled World,* pp. 1–10. See also Nigel Smith, *Rainforest Corridors: The Transamazon Colonization Scheme.* For a more recent survey of the Amazon region, see Susanna Hecht and Alexander Cockburn, *The Fate of the Forest: Destroyers, Developers, and Defenders of the Amazon* (London: Verso Books, 1989).

2. The Nature Conservancy's estimate (74,000 acres per day) is the equivalent of 40,000 square miles annually. Botanist Peter Raven, in his keynote address to the 1987 meeting of the American Association for the Advancement of Science, estimated the loss of tropical forests at 80,000 square miles each year.

3. Caufield, *In the Rainforest,* pp. 12–15.

4. William Booth, "Tropical Forest Loss May Be Killing Off Songbirds, Study Says," *Washington Post,* 26 July 1989, p. A1; Jack Connor, "Empty Skies," *Harrowsmith,* August 1988, pp. 35–45. John Terborgh laments that the rare Bachman's warbler is probably extinct due to the rapid deforestation of Cuba, the warbler's exclusive winter habitat, in *Where Have All the Birds Gone?: Essays on the Biology and Conservation of Birds That Migrate to the American Tropics* (Princeton: Princeton University Press, 1989).

5. Jessica Tuchman Mathews, "Redefining Security," p. 165.

6. National Academy of Science estimate, cited in Wilson Clark, *Energy For Survival* (Garden City, N.Y.: Anchor/Doubleday, 1976), p. 174.

7. Presently, 3.5 billion hectares of land—an area the size of North and South America combined—are affected by desertification. UNEP estimates that "80 percent of the dry range lands, 60 percent of the rain-fed crop lands, and a third of all the irrigated lands on earth are already affected by the march of the deserts." Quoted in Julian Cribb, "How to Stop the Desert's March," *World Press Review* 36 (April 1989):32; see also Michael Renner, "National Security: The Economic and Environmental Dimension," p. 30.

8. Jack Mabbutt, "A New Global Assessment of the Status and Trends of Desertification," *Environmental Conservation* 11 (Summer 1984):103–13.

9. Lester R. Brown et al, *State of the World 1988* (Washington, D.C.: Worldwatch Institute, 1988), p. 10.

10. Robert Mann, "Development and the Sahel Disaster: The Case at Gambia," *The Ecologist* (March–June 1987). See also Brown et al, *State of the World, 1988*, p. 10.

11. United Nations Environmental Program (UNEP), *Sands of Change*, Brief no. 2, 1988.

12. Jodi Jacobson, "Environmental Refugees: A Yardstick of Habitability," p. 12.

13. United Nations, *Living Conditions in Developing Countries in the Mid-1980s*, pp. 5, 8.

14. Ibid., p. 10.

15. Ibid., p. 49.

16. Ibid., p. 26.

17. Ibid., pp. 28, 11.

18. Ibid., p. 46.

19. Figures from Herman Daly, "The Ecological and Moral Necessity for Limiting Economic Growth" (paper delivered at the Conference on Faith, Science and the Future of the World Council of Churches, Boston, Mass., July 12–14, 1979).

20. Statistics for solid waste compiled by Institute for Local Self-Reliance Data, Washington, D.C., 1988. However, this figure excludes the more than 500,000 tons of infectious waste disposed of each year. See, for example, "The Sudden Rise of the Red-Bag Business," *New York Times*, 27 March 1988.

21. Jackson W. Davis, *The Seventh Year* (New York: W. W. Norton, 1979), p. 126.

22. Martin V. Melosi, *Garbage in the Cities: Refuse, Reform, and the Environment, 1880–1980*.

23. National Research Council, *Causes and Effects of Changes in Stratospheric Ozone: Update 1983* (Washington, D.C.: National Academy Press, 1984).

24. Thousands of tons of U.S. and European waste have already been shipped to Africa and the Middle East. According to the Worldwatch Institute, some 5,000 tons of toxic waste (including 150 tons of PCBs) were dumped on a small Nigerian port between 1987 and 1988, which forced the evacuation of more than 5,000 residents. See Lester R. Brown et al., *State of the World 1989* (Washington, D.C.: Worldwatch Institute, 1989), p. 70; Debora MacKenzie, "If You Can't Treat It, Ship It," *New Scientist*, 1 April 1989, p. 24.

25. Brown et al., *State of the World 1989*, p. 69.

CHAPTER 11

1. Irving M. Mintzer, "A Matter of Degrees: The Potential for Controlling the Greenhouse Effect," *World Resources Institute Research Report No. 5*, April 1987, p. i.

2. A. M. Soloman, "The Global Cycle of Carbon," R. M. Rotty and C. D. Masters, "Carbon Dioxide from Fossil Fuel Combustion: Trends, Resources, and Technological Implications," and R. A. Houghton, "Carbon Dioxide Exchange Between the Atmosphere and Terrestrial Ecosystems," cited in John R. Trabalka, *Atmospheric Carbon Dioxide and the Global Carbon Cycle.*

3. V. R. Ramanathan, "Trace Gas Trends and Their Potential Role in Climate Change," *Journal of Geophysical Research* 90 (1985), pp. 5547–66.

4. Ibid.

5. Kirk B. Smith, "Home Economics," cited in Jeremy Rifkin, ed., *The Green Lifestyle Handbook,* pp. 1–2. See also Andrew C. Kimbrell, "Steering Toward Ecological Disaster," in Rifkin, *The Green Lifestyle Handbook,* pp. 33–37; Dennis Hayes, *Rays of Hope,* p. 91.

6. Wilson Clark, *Energy for Survival,* p. 170.

7. Peter Farb, *Humankind* (Boston: Houghton Mifflin, 1978), pp. 181–82.

8. Hayes, *Rays of Hope,* p. 91.

9. Between 1984 and 1988, the production of packaging containers increased by more than 19 percent, while the production of plastic containers increased by nearly 50 percent. U.S., Department of Commerce, *The 1988 Industrial Outlook,* International Trade Administration, 1988, pp. 7-2, 7-4, 7-5.

10. John K. Cooley, "Oil Crunch Worries U.S. Military," *Christian Science Monitor,* 17 May 1979, p. 17.

11. Ibid.

12. Figures from U.S., Department of Agriculture, *Commercial Fertilizer Consumption Report* (Washington, D.C.: U.S. Government Printing Office, 1988); Lester R. Brown, "The Changing World Food Prospect: The 90s and Beyond," *Worldwatch Paper No. 85* (Washington, D.C.: Worldwatch Institute, 1985), p. 31.

13. National Research Council, *Global Change in the Geosphere-Biosphere.*

14. Gordon J. MacDonald, "Climate Change and Acid Rain," The MITRE Corporation, McLean, Va. (December 1985).

15. Robert Cowan, "Rapid Rise in Methane Gas May Speed Worldwide Climatic Changes," *Christian Science Monitor,* 15 March 1988, p. 17.

16. Ibid., p. 12.

17. Termite population figures are from Judith Stone, "Bovine Madness," *Discover,* February 1989, pp. 40–41.

18. Jerry E. Bishop, "Global Threat: New Culprit Is Indicated in Greenhouse Effect: Rising Methane Level," *Wall Street Journal,* 24 October 1988, p. A1.

19. Judith Stone, "Bovine Madness," p. 38.

20. Bishop, "Global Threat," p. A1.

21. Denzel and Nancy Ferguson, *Sacred Cows at the Public Trough*, p. 56.

22. World Conference on Global Warming, "The Changing Atmosphere: Implications for Global Security" (paper delivered, Toronto, Canada, June 1988), pp. 1–10.

23. Andrew C. Revkin, "Endless Summer: Living with the Greenhouse Effect," *Discover*, 27 September 1988, p. 50.

24. Ibid.

25. Ibid.

26. James Hansen, NASA Goddard Institute for Space Studies, quoted in Revkin, "Endless Summer," p. 20.

27. Revkin, "Endless Summer," pp. 18–19.

28. W. R. Rangeley, "Irrigation and Drainage in the World" (paper delivered at the International Conference on Food and Water, Texas A & M University, College Station, Tex., May 26–30, 1985).

29. Ibid.

30. Richard Akerr, "Report Urges Greenhouse Action Now," *Science*, 1 July 1988, p. 23.

31. Ibid.

32. Quoted in Jill Jaeger, *Developing Policies for Responding to Climate Change* [The Bellagio Report], pp. 1–2.

33. Jesse Ansubel, quoted in Anthony Ramirez, "A Warming World," *Fortune*, 4 July 1988, p. 104.

34. Ramirez, "A Warming World," p. 104.

35. Cited in Sharon Begley, "A Gaping Hole in the Sky," *Newsweek*, 11 July 1988, p. 22.

36. National Aeronautics and Space Administration, "Knowledge of the Upper Atmosphere," January 1986; Environmental Protection Agency, "Analysis of Strategies for Protecting the Ozone Layer" (paper delivered at Working Group Meeting, Geneva, Switzerland, January 1985).

37. Donald Douglas, quoted in Begley, "A Gaping Hole," p. 21.

38. Alan Teramura, quoted in Begley, "A Gaping Hole," p. 22.

39. Richard Adams, quoted in Begley, "A Gaping Hole," p. 23.

40. Begley, "A Gaping Hole," p. 23.

CHAPTER 12

1. Lewis Mumford, *The Culture of Cities*, p. 79.

2. See Fernand Braudel, *The Wheels of Commerce: Civilization and Capitalism, 15th–18th Century*, pp. 25–137.

3. Frank Barnaby, *The Gaia Peace Atlas: Survival into the Third Millennium*, p. 48.

4. Braudel, *Wheels of Commerce*, pp. 433–36.

5. Ibid., p. 448.

6. Cited in Braudel, *Wheels of Commerce*, p. 439. A broader discus-

sion of the rise and development of corporate capitalism is found in Immanuel Wallerstein, *The Modern World-System II: Mercantilism and the Consolidation of the European World-Economy, 1600–1750,* especially chapter 6.

7. Braudel, *Wheels of Commerce,* p. 439.
8. Brian Gardner, *The East India Company: A History,* pp. 58, 18.
9. Ibid., p. 59.
10. Ibid., pp. 68, 69.
11. Ibid., p. 75.
12. Richard Barnet and Robert Muller, *Global Reach: The Power of the Multinational Corporations,* pp. 72–73.

CHAPTER 13

1. Lewis Mumford, *The Culture of Cities,* p. 83.
2. Machiavelli, quoted in Mumford, ibid.
3. Mumford, *Culture of Cities,* p. 83. Machiavelli, in Book 7 of *The Art of War,* details the military strategy of besieging and defending fortified cities. See Machiavelli, *The Chief Works and Others,* vol. 2, trans. Allan Gilbert (Durham, N.C.: Duke University Press, 1965).
4. John H. Herz, *The Nation State and the Rise of World Politics: Essays on International Politics in the 20th Century,* p. 476.
5. Paul Kennedy, *The Rise and Fall of the Great Powers: Economic Change and Military Conflict from 1500 to 2000,* p. 26.
6. Ibid., p. 27.
7. Mumford, *Culture of Cities,* p. 349.
8. Kennedy, *Rise and Fall of the Great Powers,* p. 72.
9. Ibid., p. 147.
10. Ibid., p. 77.
11. See Fernand Braudel, *The Wheels of Commerce,* vol. 1, pp. 430–40; Wallerstein, *The Modern World System,* 2, chapter 3.
12. Kennedy, *Rise and Fall of the Great Powers,* p. 77.
13. Ibid., p. 149.

CHAPTER 14

1. Dwight David Eisenhower, quoted in Frank Barnaby, *The Gaia Peace Atlas,* p. 50.
2. Lewis Mumford, *Culture of Cities,* p. 88.
3. Ibid., p. 87.
4. Ibid., p. 90.
5. Lewis Mumford, *Technics and Civilization,* p. 91.
6. Ibid., p. 93. Mumford went so far as to say that the army is "the

ideal form toward which a purely mechanical system of industry must tend," p. 89.

7. Mumford, *Culture of Cities*, p. 89.

8. Lawrence L. Gordon, *Military Origins* (New York: A. S. Barnes, 1971), p. 196.

9. Quoted in Gordon, *Military Origins*, p. 197.

10. Mumford, *Technics and Civilization*, p. 92.

11. Ibid., pp. 92–93.

12. Mumford, *Culture of Cities*, p. 96.

13. Michael Renner, "National Security: The Economic and Environmental Dimension," p. 8.

14. Ibid.

15. Ibid.

16. Frank Barnaby, *Gaia Peace Atlas*, p. 14.

17. Renner, "National Security," p. 7.

18. Barnaby, *Gaia Peace Atlas*, p. 52.

19. Renner, "National Security," p. 7.

20. Barnaby, *Gaia Peace Atlas*, p. 52.

21. Ibid., p. 46.

22. Renner, "National Security," p. 12.

23. Ibid., p. 19.

24. Ibid, p. 22.

25. U.S., Department of Defense, *Program Acquisition Costs by Weapon System*, 4 February 1986, pp. 1–4.

26. Renner, "National Security," p. 22.

27. Center for Defense Information, "Militarism in America," *Defense Monitor*, no. 3 (1986): 3; Elliot Currie and Jerome Skolnick, *America's Problems: Social Issues and Public Policy*, 2d ed., p. 401; see also Renner, "National Security," p. 18.

28. Center for Defense Information, "No Business Like War Business," *Defense Monitor*, no. 3 (1987): p. 1.

29. U.S., Office of Management and Budget, *Budget of the United States Government, Fiscal Year 1988*, Table 3-2.

30. Seymour Melman, "Looting the Means of Production," *Ploughshares*, November–December 1982.

31. Jobs with Peace, *A National Budget for Jobs with Peace* (Boston: Jobs with Peace Campaign, 1986); see also Currie and Skolnick, *America's Problems*, pp. 391–92.

32. Figures from Committee for a Sane Nuclear Policy, Washington, D.C., 1988.

CHAPTER 15

1. Frank Barnaby, *Gaia Peace Atlas*, p. 97.

2. Richard Shelly Hartigan, *The Forgotten Victim: A History of the*

Civilian, p. 119. The Dresden fire-bombing is the central theme of Kurt Vonnegut's celebrated *Slaughterhouse-Five*. Though a fictional account of the tragedy, the novel reveals many of the horrors of the Dresden fire-bombing. Kurt Vonnegut, *Slaughterhouse-Five* (New York: Dell Books, 1968).

3. St. Thomas Aquinas, *Summa Theologica,* p. 502.

4. Hartigan, *Forgotten Victim,* p. 65.

5. Ibid., p. 66.

6. Ibid., p. 68. According to Hartigan, this peace campaign spread northward to include all of France and eventually parts of Germany. Later the movement spread south into Catalonia.

7. Ibid., pp. 68–69. Loren C. MacKinney writes that this peace movement "fostered the development of public opinion in eleventh-century France, and actually brought forth a distinctly new public conscience on matters concerned with law and order." MacKinney, "People and Public Opinion in the 11th-Century Peace Movement," *Speculum* 5 (1930):204.

8. Hartigan, *Forgotten Victim,* p. 69.

9. Ibid., p. 113.

10. Ibid., p. 115.

11. Ibid., pp. 118–19.

12. Richard Rubenstein, *The Cunning of History,* pp. 7, 11.

13. Barnaby, *Gaia Peace Atlas,* p. 100.

14. Michael Renner, "National Security: The Economic and Environmental Dimension," p. 13.

15. Barnaby, *Gaia Peace Atlas,* p. 99.

CHAPTER 16

1. Quoted in Robert Strausz-Hupe, *Geopolitics: The Struggle for Space and Power,* p. 42.

2. Michael Pacione, *Progress in Political Geography,* p. 48.

3. Quoted in Pacione, *Progress in Political Geography,* p. 42.

4. Frederick Ratzel, *Anthropogeographie.*

5. Frederick Ratzel, *Politische Geographie.*

6. See also Stephen Kern, *The Culture of Time and Space, 1880–1918,* p. 224.

7. Interpreting Ratzel, Strausz-Hupe writes that "[the] urge to territorial expansion is seen as the manifestation of a natural law, and the population pressure of a growing nation as culminating in a struggle for existence as bruteless and lawless as is, according to the theory of evolution, the struggle for survival in nature." Strausz-Hupe, *Geopolitics,* p. 25.

8. Frederick Ratzel, *Das Meer als Quelle der Volergrosse* (Munich: 1900); Kern, *The Culture of Time and Space* (Cambridge, Mass.: Harvard University Press, 1983), p. 225.

9. Ratzel, ibid., pp. 1, 5; Kern, ibid., p. 224.

10. Ratzel, ibid., pp. 1, 5; Kern, ibid., p. 226.

11. Ellen Churchill Semple, *Influences of Geographic Environment on the Basis of Ratzel's System of Anthropo-Geography*, pp. 1–2, 175.

12. Haeckel referred to ecology as "the science of the relations of living organisms to the external world, their habitat, customs, energies . . . etc." in *The Wonders of Life*, p. 80.

13. Nicholas J. Spykman, *The Geography of Peace*, p. 5.

14. Frank Barnaby, *Gaia Peace Atlas*, p. 102.

15. C. W. Weinberger, *1985 Annual Report to the Congress: Fiscal Year 1986*, p. 25.

16. Arthur H. Westing, "Global Resources and International Conflict: An Overview," in Arthur H. Westing, ed., *Global Resources and International Conflict: Environmental Factors in Strategic Policy and Action*, p. 11.

17. Alexander A. Arbatov, "Oil as a Factor in Strategic Policy and Action: Past and Present," in Westing, ed., *Global Resources and International Conflict*, p. 26.

18. Quoted in Arbatov, "Oil as a Factor," ibid., p. 26.

19. Westing, *Global Resources and International Conflict*, pp. 9, 10.

20. Ibid., pp. 10–11.

21. Helge Hveem, "Minerals as a Factor in Strategic Policy and Action," in Westing, ed., *Global Resources and International Conflict*, p. 68.

22. *The Economist* 271 (1979), p. 92.

CHAPTER 17

1. Sir Halford Mackinder, *Democratic Ideas and Reality*. The influence of Mackinder's ideas on modern geopolitics is discussed in a number of studies, including Nicholas J. Spykman, *The Geography of Peace*, pp. 35–43; Ciro E. Zoppo, *On Geopolitics: Classical and Nuclear*, pp. 4–6, 55–59; Peter J. Taylor, *Political Geography: World-Economy, Nation-State, and Locality*, pp. 38–41. An earlier account of Mackinder's heartland thesis in world politics is found in Robert Strausz-Hupe, *Geopolitics: The Struggle for Space and Power*, pp. 51–53.

2. See Taylor, *Political Geography*, p. 38.

3. Stephen Kern, *The Culture of Time and Space*, p. 257.

4. Strausz-Hupe, *Geopolitics*, p. 53.

5. Spykman, *Geography of Peace*, p. 41.

6. Mackinder's famous dictum is commented on in a number of different sources. See particularly, Taylor's discussion in *Political Geography*, p. 39.

7. Modelski and Thompson, *Seapower in Global Politics 1494–1994*, p. 17.

8. Ibid., p. 10.

9. Quoted in Strausz-Hupe, *Geopolitics*, pp. 166–67.

10. Quoted in James Chace and Caleb Carr, *America Invulnerable: The Quest for Absolute Security from 1812 to Star Wars*, p. 230.

11. Chace and Carr, *America Invulnerable*, p. 229.

12. Quoted in Chace and Carr, *America Invulnerable*, p. 244.

CHAPTER 18

1. James Chace and Caleb Carr, *America Invulnerable: The Quest for Absolute Security from 1812 to Star Wars*, p. 304.

2. Peter J. Taylor, *Political Geography: World-Economy, Nation-State, and Locality*, p. 43.

3. Chace and Carr, *America Invulnerable*, pp. 254, 305; Frank Barnaby, *Gaia Peace Atlas*, p. 72.

4. Quoted in Chace and Carr, *America Invulnerable*, p. 305.

5. Robert McNamara, "The Dynamics of Nuclear Strategy," pp. 443–51.

6. Barnaby, *Gaia Peace Atlas*, p. 132; Daniel Deudney, *Whole Earth Security: A Geopolitics of Peace*. Washington, D.C.: Worldwatch Institute, 1983, p. 36–37.

7. Center for Defense Information, Washington, D.C.: 1990.

8. See Daniel Deudney, *Whole Earth Security: A Geopolitics of Peace*, p. 20.

9. Ibid., p. 21. The role of navigation technology in ocean exploration is discussed at length in J. H. Parry, *The Discovery of the Sea*.

10. Stephen Kern, *Culture of Time and Space, 1880–1918*, p. 303.

11. Ibid.

12. Ibid.

13. Deudney, *Whole Earth Security*, p. 21.

14. Ibid., p. 22.

15. Ibid., p. 21.

16. Ibid., p. 22.

17. Ibid., p. 24.

18. Chace and Carr, *America Invulnerable*, p. 315.

19. Grant Fjermedal, *The Tommorrow Makers*, p. 123.

20. Barnaby, *Gaia Peace Atlas*, p. 136.

21. The Bulletin of Atomic Scientists, cited in Jeremy Rifkin, *Entropy: Into the Greenhouse World*, p. 176.

22. Rifkin, *Entropy*, p. 177.

23. Barnaby, *Gaia Peace Atlas*, p. 138; see also Daniel Deudney, *Whole Earth Security: A Geopolitics of Peace*, p. 14.

24. Barnaby, *Gaia Peace Atlas*, p. 138.

25. Ibid.

26. Arthur Koestler, quoted in Barnaby, *Gaia Peace Atlas*, p. 73.

27. Mencius, quoted in John H. Herz, *The Nation State and the Rise of World Politics: Essays on International Politics in the 20th Century,* p. 13.

28. Quoted in Michael Renner, "National Security: The Economic and Environmental Dimension," p. 12.

29. Andrei Sakharov, "The Danger of Thermonuclear War," p. 1006; Deudney, *Whole Earth Security,* p. 15.

CHAPTER 19

1. U.S., Department of Defense, Biological Defense Program, *Report to the Committee on Appropriations, House of Representatives,* May 1986, p. 4. A brief but informative survey of the development and use of biological and chemical weapons is found in Frank Barnaby, *Gaia Peace Atlas,* pp. 134–38.

2. Department of Defense, *Report to the Committee on Appropriations,* p. 8.

3. Ibid., p. 8.

4. Ibid., p. 4.

5. Testimony of Douglas J. Feith before the Subcommittee on Oversight and Evaluation of the House Permanent Select Committee on Intelligence, 8 August 1986.

6. Jonathan B. Tucker, "Gene Wars," *Foreign Policy* (Winter 1984–85), p. 60–69. See also Department of Defense Annual Report on Chemical Warfare, Biological Defense Research Program Obligations, October 1, 1984, through September 30, 1985, RCs: DDUSDRE (A) 1065.

7. Correspondence from Secretary of Defense Casper Weinberger to Senator Jim Sasser, November 20, 1984.

8. See also Jonathan B. Tucker, "Gene Wars," p. 68.

CHAPTER 20

1. Georges Duby, "Solitude: Eleventh to Thirteenth Century," in Georges Duby, ed., *A History of Private Life: Revelations in the Medieval World,* p. 510; Yi-Fu Tuan, *Segmented Worlds and Self: Group Life and Individual Consciousness,* p. 58.

2. W. H. Lewis, *The Splendid Century: Life in the France of Louis XIV,* p. 197; Philippe Ariès, *Centuries of Childhood: A Social History of Private Life,* pp. 392–94; Tuan, *Segmented Worlds and Self,* p. 70.

3. M. W. Barley, *The House and Home: A Review of 900 Years of House Planning and Furnishing in Britain* (Greenwich, Conn.: New York Graphic Society, 1971), pp. 40–41; Philippe Ariès, "The Family and the City," in Alice Rossi, ed., *The Family* (New York: Norton 1965), pp. 227–35; U. T. Holmes, Jr., *Daily Living in the Twelfth Century:*

Based on the Observations of Alexander Neckham in London and Paris (Madison, Wis.: University of Wisconsin Press, 1952), p. 231.

4. Georges Duby, "Private Power, Public Power," in Duby, ed., *A History of Private Life*, p. 3.

5. Tuan, *Segmented Worlds and Self*, pp. 68, 69.

6. Mark Girouard, *Life in the English Country House: A Social and Architectural History*, p. 219.

7. Tuan, *Segmented Worlds and Self*, p. 80.

8. Alan Everett, "Farm Labourers," in Joan Thirsk, ed., *The Agrarian History of England and Wales: 1500–1640*, pp. 442–43; Tuan, *Segmented Worlds and Self*, pp. 59–60.

9. Ariès, *Centuries of Childhood*, p. 394; Tuan, *Segmented Worlds and Self*, pp. 59, 75–77; Duby, "Solitude," p. 589.

10. Quoted in David H. Flaherty, *Privacy in Colonial New England* (Charlotte: University of Virginia Press, 1972), p. 77. See also Stephanie Coontz, *The Social Origins of Private Life: A History of American Families, 1600–1900*, pp. 73–106.

11. Ariès, *Centuries of Childhood*, p. 395; Tuan, *Segmented Worlds and Self*, p. 74; Norbert Elias, *The Civilizing Process: The History of Manners*, pp. 177–78.

12. Elias, *The Civilizing Process*, p. 177; Duby, "Solitude," pp. 589–90.

13. Elias, *The Civilizing Process*, pp. 178–80; see also Ariès, *Centuries of Childhood*, pp. 100–27.

14. Duby, "Solitude," p. 605.

15. Quoted in Elias, *The Civilizing Process*, p. 164.

16. Siegfried Giedion, *Mechanization Takes Command: A Contribution to Anonymous History*, pp. 268–69.

17. Ibid., p. 269.

18. John Lukacs, "The Bourgeois Interior," *American Scholar* 39 (Fall 1970):623; Tuan, *Segmented Worlds and Self*, p. 83.

CHAPTER 21

1. Georges Duby, "Solitude: Eleventh to Thirteenth Century," in Georges Duby, ed., *A History of Private Life: Revelations in the Medieval World*, p. 353.

2. Philippe Ariès, *Centuries of Childhood: A Social History of Private Life*, pp. 392–94; Yi-Fu Tuan, *Segmented Worlds and Self: Group Life and Individual Consciousness*, p. 368.

3. Ariès, *Centuries of Childhood*, p. 368.

4. Ibid., p. 369.

5. Tuan, *Segmented Worlds and Self*, pp. 9, 163.

6. Morris Berman, *Coming to Our Senses: Body and Spirit in the Hidden History of the West*, p. 48; Norbert Elias, *The Civilizing Process:*

The History of Manners, p. 79; Tuan, *Segmented Worlds and Self,* p. 82.

7. Kenneth Jackson, *Crabgrass Frontier: The Suburbanization of the United States,* p. 58.

8. Ibid., p. 57.

9. Ibid., p. 280.

10. Curt Suplee, "Slaves of the Lawn," *Washington Post Magazine,* 30 April 1989, p. 20.

11. Jackson, *Crabgrass Frontier,* p. 50.

12. *Oxford English Dictionary,* 2d ed., p. 719; Suplee, "Slaves of the Lawn," p. 16.

13. See, for example, Keith Thomas, *Man and the Natural World: A History of the Modern Sensibility,* p. 239.

14. Quoted in Suplee, "Slaves of the Lawn," p. 60; Jackson, *Crabgrass Frontier,* p. 60.

15. Suplee, "Slaves of the Lawn," p. 16.

CHAPTER 22

1. Harry Braverman, *Labor and Monopoly Capital* (New York: Monthly Review Press, 1971), pp. 273–74.

2. Robert Smuts, *Women and Work in America,* pp. 11–13; Braverman, *Labor and Monopoly Capital,* pp. 273–74.

3. George Stigler, *Trends in Output and Employment* (New York: National Bureau of Economic Research, 1947), pp. 14, 24.

4. Braverman, *Labor and Monopoly Capital,* p. 276.

5. Ibid., p. 248.

6. Independent agency survey conducted by Michael Fortino, Priority Management, Inc., Pittsburgh, Pa., June 1988.

7. Estimates from U.S., Department of Commerce, Bureau of the Census, *Statistical Abstract of the United States 1990* (Washington, D.C.: U.S. Government Printing Office, 1990).

8. Statistics from Food Marketing Institute survey cited in Laura Shapiro, "Eating Habits," p. 79.

9. Food Marketing Institute and *Better Homes and Gardens,* "A Study of Food Patterns and Meal Consumption." Washington, D.C., 1988.

10. Dena Kleinman, "Fast Food," *New York Times,* 6 December 1989, p. A6. For more academic treatment of the evolution of food habits in the United States, see Harvey Levenstein, *Revolution at the Table: The Transformation of the American Diet* (Oxford, England: Oxford University Press, 1988).

11. Siegfried Giedion, *Mechanization Takes Command: A Contribution to Anonymous History,* p. 527.

12. Ibid.

13. Andrew Nelson Lytle, *From Eden to Babylon: The Social and Political Essays of Andrew Nelson Lytle,* p. 227.

14. Christine Frederick, "The New Housekeeping," *Ladies' Home Journal*, September 1912; Giedion, *Mechanization Takes Command*, p. 521.

15. Giedion, *Mechanization Takes Command*, p. 616.

CHAPTER 23

1. Raymond Williams, *Keywords: A Vocabulary of Culture and Society*, pp. 78–79.

2. Jessica Tuchman Mathews, "Redefining Security," p. 172.

3. Fred C. Alvine and Fred A. Tarpley, Jr., "The New State of the Economy: The Challenging Prospect," in *U.S. Economic Growth From 1976 to 1986: Prospects, Problems and Patterns, Studies for the Joint Economic Committee of the U.S. Congress* (Washington, D.C.: U.S. Government Printing Office, 1976), p. 58; see also Jeremy Rifkin, *Entropy: Into the Greenhouse World*, pp. 117–18.

4. World Resources Institute, *World Resources 1990–91* (Oxford, England: Oxford University Press, 1990), p. 117.

5. Nathan Gardels, "A New Ecological Ethos," *New Perspectives Quarterly* 6 (Spring 1989):2.

6. Wilson Clark, *Energy for Survival*, p. 70.

7. Lester R. Brown et al., *State of the World, 1988* (Washington, D.C.: Worldwatch Institute, 1988), p. 33. See also Rifkin, *Entropy*, pp. 151–52.

8. Christopher Lasch, *The Culture of Narcissism: American Life in an Age of Diminishing Expectations*.

CHAPTER 24

1. *Oxford English Dictionary*, 2d ed., p. 806. Note that the earliest usage of the term required a hyphenated spelling: auto-mobile.

2. Statistics compiled by R. L. Polk & Company, Taylor, Mich. According to Polk, there were 27,732 new registrations every day in 1987, and there were 28,158 cars sold daily that same year. See also Jeremy Rifkin, *Entropy: Into the Greenhouse World*, pp. 159–60.

3. Peter Marsh and Peter Collett, "Driving Passions," *Psychology Today*, June 1987, p. 22. The article is excerpted from the authors' more recent *Driving Passions: The Psychology of the Car* (London: Faber & Faber, 1989).

4. Marsh and Collett, "Driving Passions," p. 18.

5. The Greenhouse Crisis Foundation, *The Greenhouse Crisis* (Washington, D.C.: The Greenhouse Crisis Foundation, 1989), p. 8. Copies available from The Greenhouse Crisis Foundation, 1130 17th Street, N.W., Suite 630, Washington, D.C. 20036.

6. Ibid.

7. Robert Goodman, *After the Planners* (New York: Simon & Schuster, 1971), p. 79.

8. D. Paul Sondel, "Everybody Needs a 'G.D.C.'," monograph, May 1989, p. 8. The author is grateful to Dr. Sondel for the use of this working monograph.

9. A. Q. Mowbray, *Road to Ruin,* p. 71; Wilson Clark, *Energy for Survival,* p. 171.

10. Mowbray, *Road to Ruin,* p. 15.

11. Quoted in K. R. Schneider, *Autokind Vs. Mankind,* p. 123.

12. Sondel, "Everybody Needs," p. 3.

13. Ibid., p. 5.

14. Ibid., p. 20.

15. Michael Renner, "Car Crash," *Worldwatch Magazine,* January–February 1988, p. 46.

16. Sondel, "Everybody Needs," p. 28.

17. Mowbray, *Road to Ruin,* p. 33.

18. Helen Leavitt, *Superhighway: Superhoax* (New York: Ballantine, 1971), p. 11.

19. Sondel, "Everybody Needs," p. 2.

20. Sandi Stadler, "Roadkills," *The Animals' Agenda,* October 1987, p. 32; Donald Dale Jackson, "Nobody Counts 'Squashed' Skunks," *Audubon,* March 1986, p. 78.

21. Leavitt, *Superhighway: Superhoax,* p. 251.

22. *National Safety Council Facts 1987* (Washington, D.C.: U.S. Government Printing Office, 1987). In addition, motor vehicles yearly emit 85 million tons of pollutants contributing to the incidence of lung cancer, emphysema, and other respiratory diseases—and thus hasten more than 100,000 deaths per year. Robert Erwin, "Dead End: America on Wheels," *The Progressive,* December 1974, p. 16.

23. *The Economist,* 8 February 1989, p. 20.

24. Sondel, "Everybody Needs," p. 13.

25. Ibid., pp. 13–14.

26. Ibid., p. 14; Jeffrey A. Lindley, *Journal of the Institute of Transportation* (January 1987).

27. Erwin, "Dead End: America on Wheels," pp. 16–17.

28. For a broader review of the relationship between social and natural rhythms, see the selected bibliography in Jeremy Rifkin, *Time Wars: The Primary Conflict in Human History.*

CHAPTER 25

1. Carl Jung, "After the Catastrophe," in *Collected Works,* Vol 10 (Princeton, N.J.: Princeton University Press, (Bollinger, 1970), p. 203;

see also Erich Neumann, *Depth Psychology and a New Ethic* (London: Hodder & Staughton, 1969), p. 40.

2. Otto Rank, *Beyond Psychology*, p. 76.

3. Ibid., p. 72.

4. Keith Thomas, *Man and the Natural World: A History of the Modern Sensibility*, p. 95.

5. Ibid., pp. 98–99.

6. Maurice Beresford and John G. Hurst, eds., *Deserted Medieval Villages* (New York: St. Martin's Press, 1972), p. 236; David Beers Quinn, *The Elizabethans and the Irish*, pp. 70–71.

7. Thomas, *Man and the Natural World*, pp. 40–41.

8. Cotton Mather, *Diary of Cotton Mather, 1681–1708*, p. 357.

9. Philip P. Weiner, "Man-Machine from the Greeks to the Computer," in Weiner, ed., *Dictionary of the History of Ideas* (New York: 1973–74), p. iii.

10. Quoted in Thomas, *Man and the Natural World*, p. 39.

11. Thomas, *Man and The Natural World*, p. 39.

12. Milton quoted in William Lamont and Sybil Oldfield, eds., *Politics, Religion and Literature in the 17th Century* (London: Dent Rowman and Littlefield, 1975), pp. 61–62.

13. Nehemiah Wallington, quoted in R. Webb, ed., *Historical Notices of Events* (1869), p. 243.

14. Karl Marx, *Grundrisse*, trans. Martin Nichalous (London: Harmondsworth, 1973), p. 606.

CHAPTER 26

1. Desiderius Erasmus, *De Cicilidate Morum Puerilium (On the Civility of Children)*, trans. Robert Whittinton, 1540; Yi-Fu Tuan, *Segmented Worlds and Self: Group Life and Individual Consciousness*, pp. 48–50; Norbert Elias, *The Civilizing Process: The History of Manners*, pp. 73–74.

2. Quoted in Keith Thomas, *Man and the Natural World: A History of the Modern Sensibility*, p. 37.

3. Tuan, *Segmented Worlds and Self*, p. 46, 58.

4. Quoted in Frederick J. Furnivall, *English Meals and Manners* (Detroit: Singing Tree Press, 1969), p. xvi; Tuan, *Segmented Worlds and Self*, p. 42.

5. Tuan, *Segmented Worlds and Self*, p. 42.

6. Ibid.

7. Ibid., p. 45.

8. Mildred Campbell, *The English Yeoman*, pp. 246–47.

9. Ibid., p. 247.

10. Tuan, *Segmented Worlds and Self*, p. 44.

11. Elias, *The Civilizing Process*, p. 118; Tuan, *Segmented Worlds and Self*, p. 44.

12. Quoted in Elias, *The Civilizing Process*, p. 121.

13. Tuan, *Segmented Worlds and Self*, pp. 45–46; Elias, *The Civilizing Process*, p. 68.

14. Elias, *The Civilizing Process*, p. 126.

15. Quoted in ibid., p. 123.

16. Tuan, *Segmented Worlds and Self*, p. 45; Elias, *The Civilizing Process*, p. 68.

17. Charles Cooper, *The English Table in History and Literature* (London: Sampson Low, Marston 7 Company, n.d.), pp. 17, 19; Elias, *The Civilizing Process*, p. 69; Tuan, *Segmented Worlds and Self*, p. 45.

18. Elias, *The Civilizing Process*, p. 69.

19. Tuan, *Segmented Worlds and Self*, p. 46; Elias, *The Civilizing Process*, p. 107.

20. Tuan, *Segmented Worlds and Self*, p. 43.

21. Gerard Brett, *Dinner Is Served: A History of Dining in England, 1400–1900*, p. 116.

CHAPTER 27

1. James Serpell, *In the Company of Animals: A Study of Human-Animal Relationships*, p. 126; Keith Thomas, *Man and the Natural World: A History of the Modern Sensibility*, p. 39.

2. Serpell, *In the Company of Animals*, pp. 125–26.

3. Ibid., p. 27.

4. Thomas, *Man and the Natural World*, p. 39.

5. Alfred C. Kinsey et al., *Sexual Behavior in the Human Male* (Philadelphia: W. B. Saunders, 1948), pp. 669–78; Alfred C. Kinsey et al, *Sexual Behavior in the Human Female* (Philadelphia: W. B. Saunders, 1953), pp. 505–9.

6. Thomas, *Man and the Natural World*, p. 38.

7. See Morris Berman, *Coming to Our Senses: Body and Spirit in the Hidden History of the West*.

8. Stephen Horizon, *Nature and Culture in Western Discourses*, p. 78.

9. Ibid., pp. 78–83.

10. See Bruno Bettelheim, *The Empty Fortress: Infantile Autism and the Birth of the Self*, pp. 351–72.

11. Yi-Fu Tuan, *Dominance and Affection: The Making of Pets*, p. 83.

12. Ibid., p. 83.

13. Roderick Nash, *Wilderness and the American Mind*, p. 24.

14. Thomas, *Man and the Natural World*, p. 136.

15. Ibid.

16. Quoted in Yi-Fu Tuan, *Dominance and Affection*, p. 141.

17. Tuan, *Dominance and Affection*, p. 142.

18. Thomas, *Man and the Natural World,* pp. 42–43.
19. Charles Darwin, *Life and Letters,* vol 1, p. 316. A fuller discussion of the eugenics movement and its relationship to both Darwinian science and modern conceptions of nature is found in Jeremy Rifkin, *Algeny: A New Word—A New World,* especially pp. 229–33.

CHAPTER 28

1. Quoted in Ashley Montagu, *Touching: The Human Significance of Skin,* p. 238.

CHAPTER 29

1. For an evocative discussion on the social and political suppression of odors in modern Europe, see Alain Corbin, *The Foul and the Fragrant: Odor and the French Social Imagination,* especially pp. 6–22. This chapter owes much to Corbin and the thesis that odors have historically been an important influence on social and political life. See also Yi-Fu Tuan, *Segmented Worlds and Self: Group Life and Individual Consciousness,* pp. 116–26.
2. Sigmund Freud, *Collected Papers,* ed. J. Reviere and J. Strachey (New York: International Psycho-Analytical Press), vol. 4, p. 215. (1924–1950), reprinted in *Collected Papers,* ed. Ernest Jones (NY: Basic Books, 1959); Norman O. Brown, *Life Against Death: The Psychoanalytic Meaning of History,* p. 188.
3. Quoted in Corbin, *Foul and the Fragrant,* p. 22.
4. Corbin, *Foul and the Fragrant,* p. 22.
5. Messieur de Chamseru, "Recherches sur la nyctalopia," *Histoire et Memoires de la Société Royale de Médecine* 8 (1786), p. 167ff.
6. J.-B. Theodore Baumes, "Mémoire . . . sur la question: Peut-on Déterminer par l'observation quelles sont les maladies qui résultent des émanations des eaux stagnantes. . . ." (1789), p. 234. Quoted in Corbin, p. 23.
7. Corbin, *Foul and the Fragrant,* p. 90.
8. Ibid., p. 41.
9. Quoted in Jacques-Joseph de Gardane, *Essais sur la putréfaction des humeurs animales* (1769), p. 121.
10. Corbin, *Foul and the Fragrant,* p. 20.
11. Ibid., p. 90.
12. Tuan, *Segmented Worlds and Self,* pp. 125–26.
13. Quoted in Tuan, *Segmented Worlds and Self,* p. 125.
14. Dr. Michael Levy, quoted in Corbin, *Foul and the Fragrant,* p. 163.
15. Corbin, *Foul and the Fragrant,* p. 163.

16. Ibid., p. 171.

17. Ibid., p. 102.

18. Charles Londe, *Nouveaux Elements* (1827), pp. 406, 407; Corbin, *Foul and the Fragrant*, p. 170.

19. Corbin, *Foul and the Fragrant*, p. 178. In medieval Europe, as Tuan notes in his *Segmented Worlds and Self*, p. 125, body odors were strong even among the upper classes. "King John (1167–1216)," writes Tuan, "took a bath once every three weeks, and his subjects presumably less often."

20. Corbin, *Foul and the Fragrant*, pp. 73, 74.

21. Dr. Jean-Joseph de Brieude, "Mémoire sur les odeurs que nous exhalons, considerérées comme signes de la santé et des maladies," *Histoire et Mémoires de la Société Royale de Médecine* 10 (1789): li–lii.

22. Corbin, *Foul and the Fragrant*, pp. 143–44.

23. Ibid., p. 143.

24. V. Moleon, *Rapports généraux sur les travaux du Conseil de Salubrité*, 2 vols. (Paris, 1828), I: 199.

25. Corbin, *Foul and the Fragrant*, pp. 90, 143, 144, 162.

26. Beryl Lieff Benderly and Joseph Alper, "Sorting Through Smells," *Health* (December 1988), p. 65.

27. George Preti and Winnifred Cutler study cited in ibid., pp. 65–66.

28. Quoted in John Leo, "Sexes: The Hidden Power of Body Odors," *Time*, vol. 128, 1 December, 1986, p. 67.

29. Benderly and Alper, "Sorting Through Smells," p. 65.

CHAPTER 30

1. José Ortega y Gassett, *Man and People*, p. 72.

2. Ashley Montagu, *Touching: The Human Significance of Skin*, p. 324.

3. C. W. Saleeby, *Sunlight and Health*, p. 67.

4. Montagu, *Touching*, p. 1.

5. R. G. Patton and L. I. Gardner, *Growth Failure in Maternal Deprivation*. See also Montagu, *Touching*, pp. 191–207. An interesting psychological discussion of the importance of breast-feeding is also found in Morris Berman, *The Reenchantment of the World*, pp. 158–65.

6. U.S., Department of Health, Education and Welfare, *Infant Care* (Washington, D.C.: U.S. Government Printing Office, 1963), p. 16.

7. Montagu, *Touching*, pp. 70, 72.

8. See, for example, C. Hoefer and M. C. Hardy, "Later Development of Breast Fed and Artificially Fed Infants," *Journal of the American Medical Association* 96 (1929):615–19.

9. Montagu, *Touching*, p. 82; see also Berman, *The Reenchantment of the World*, pp. 162–63.

10. Quoted in Montagu, *Touching*, p. 83.

11. Montagu, *Touching*, p. 84.

12. Ibid., pp. 122–25.

13. Ibid., pp. 134–35.

14. Ibid., pp. 126, 127–32.

15. Stephen Thayer, "Close Encounters," *Psychology Today,* March 1988, p. 31.

16. Anna Freud, *Normality and Pathology in Childhood* (New York: International Universities Press, 1965), p. 155.

17. Montagu, *Touching*, p. 128.

CHAPTER 31

1. Ong's books, which detail the differences between oral and print societies, include: Walter J. Ong, *The Presence of the Word: Some Prolegomena for Cultural and Religious History; The Interfaces of the Word; Studies in the Evolution of Consciousness and Culture;* and *Orality and Literacy: The Technologizing of the Word.* Ivan Illich and Barry Sanders also examine visual, technological language and its effect upon society in *ABC: The Alphabetization of the Popular Mind.*

2. Ong, *Interfaces of the Word,* pp. 230–71; Ong, *Orality and Literacy,* pp. 41–46.

3. Quoted in Ong, *Orality and Literacy,* p. 119.

4. Ong, *Orality and Literacy,* p. 78.

5. Ibid., p. 101.

6. Ibid., p. 130.

7. Ibid., p. 131.

8. Neil Evernden, *The Natural Alien: Humankind and Environment,* p. 85.

9. Yi-Fu Tuan, *Segmented Worlds and Self,* p. 129.

10. Ong, *Orality and Literacy,* p. 72. Other critical commentaries on the limiting aspects of the visual sense include Evernden, *The Natural Alien,* pp. 83–97; Hans Jonas, "The Nobility of Sight," in his *The Phenomenon of Life: Toward a Philosophical Biology,* pp. 135–56.

11. Joachim-Ernest Berendt, *Nada Brahma: The World Is Sound: Music and the Landscape of Consciousness,* p. 5.

12. Ibid.

13. Tuan, *Segmented Worlds and Self,* p. 118.

14. Aristotle, *Metaphysics,* 980a.

15. Berendt, *Nada Brahma: The World is Sound,* p. 142.

16. Ibid.

17. M. H. Abrams, *Natural Supernaturalism: Tradition and Revolution in Romantic Literature,* p. 341.

NOTES

CHAPTER 32

1. Vaucanson's automata were first described in the *Encyclopédie* of 1751. See also Siegfried Giedion, *Mechanization Takes Command: A Contribution to Anonymous History,* p. 35; Michael Uhl, "Living Dolls," *Geo,* July 1984, p. 86.
2. Herbert Marshall McLuhan, *Understanding Media: The Extensions of Man,* p. 53.
3. Stewart Brand, *The Media Lab, Inventing the Future at MIT,* pp. 18, 58.
4. Jerry Mander, *Four Arguments for the Elimination of Television,* p. 24.
5. Ibid., p. 192.
6. Ibid., p. 24.
7. Ibid., p. 255.
8. Ibid.
9. See Brand, *The Media Lab,* pp. 97–99, 112–13.
10. Nicholas Negroponte, quoted in Brand, *The Media Lab,* p. 149.
11. Nicholas Negroponte, *The Architecture Machine,* pp. 11–13.
12. Daniel Hillis, quoted in Grant Fjermedal, *The Tomorrow Makers,* p. 94.
13. Quoted in Brand, *The Media Lab,* p. 152.
14. Fjermedal, *Tomorrow Makers,* p. 233; see also Jeremy Rifkin, *Time Wars: The Primary Conflict in Human History,* pp. 173–74.
15. James D. Foley, "Interfaces for Advanced Computing," p. 130.
16. Quoted in Pamela Weintraub, "Sentimental Journeys," *Omni,* April 1986, p. 48.
17. Fjermedal, *Tomorrow Makers,* p. 229.
18. Ibid., p. 4.
19. Marvin Minsky, quoted in ibid., p. 7.
20. Gerald Jay Sussman, quoted in ibid., p. 8.
21. Yoneji Masuda, *The Information Society,* p. 150.

CHAPTER 34

1. Vladimir Vernadsky, quoted in James Lovelock, *The Ages of Gaia,* p. 312. Scientific papers about the Gaia hypothesis include: J. E. Lovelock, "Gaia as Seen Through the Atmosphere," *Atmospheric Environment* 6, (1972) (579); J. E. Lovelock and Lynn Margulis, "Atmospheric Homeostasis by and for the Atmosphere: The Gaia Hypothesis," *Tellus* 26, (1973) (2); Lynn Margulis and J. E. Lovelock, "Biological Modulation of the Earth's Atmosphere," *Icarus* 21, (1974) (471); J. E. Lovelock and S. R. Epton, "The Quest for Gaia," *New Scientist* 6 (February 1975).

2. Rafal Serafin, "Noosphere, Gaia, and the Science of the Biosphere," p. 124.

3. N. Polunin, "Our Use of 'Biosphere,' 'Ecosystem,' and Now 'Ecobiome,' " *Environmental Conservation* 11 (1984):198; Serafin, "Noosphere, Gaia, and the Science of the Biosphere," p. 125. A historical summary of the evolution and usage of the word *biosphere* is found in Lynton K. Caldwell, *International Environmental Policy: Emergence and Dimensions*, pp. 21–25.

4. James Lovelock, in William Irvin Thompson, ed., *Gaia: A New Way of Knowing*, pp. 87–88.

5. Ibid., p. 91.

6. Lovelock, *Gaia: A New Look at Life on Earth*, p. 72.

7. Ibid.

8. Ibid., p. 73.

9. Ibid., p. 74.

10. Lovelock, *Ages of Gaia*, pp. 33, 34.

11. Gallup Organization, "Geography: An International Gallup Survey—Summary of Findings," July 1988, pp. 4, 14, 29.

12. Ibid., p. 14.

CHAPTER 35

1. Studies that focus on the increasingly punctual nature of modern life include: Sebastian De Grazia, *Of Time, Work, and Leisure* (New York: Twentieth Century Fund, 1962); Stephen Kern, *The Culture of Time and Space, 1880–1918;* Sidney Pollard, *The Genesis of Modern Management* (Cambridge, Mass.: Harvard University Press, 1965); Lawrence Wright, *Clockwork Man* (New York: Horizon Press, 1969); Eviatar Zerubavel, *Hidden Rhythms: Schedules and Calendars in Social Life* (Chicago: University of Chicago Press, 1981) and *The Seven Day Circle* (New York: Free Press, 1985).

2. For additional critiques of modern architecture, see Tom Wolfe, *From Bauhaus to Our House*, and O. B. Hardison, *Disappearing Through the Skylight: Culture and Technology in the Twentieth Century*, pp. 94–142. As noted, there is a growing literature that looks at architecture from an integrated environmental perspective. See, for example, Michael Corbett, *A Better Place to Live: New Designs For Tomorrow's Communities;* Nancy and John Todd, *Bioshelters, Ocean Arks, City Farming: Ecology as the Basis of Design*. Anne Whiston Spirn also shows us ways in which urban planners could benefit from adopting ecological approaches to urban design and planning. She uses nature as the basis for her study and uncovers the history of the modern city and its fairly recent emergence from unspoiled wilderness in *The Granite Garden: Urban Nature and Human Design*.

NOTES

CHAPTER 36

1. Quoted in Stephen Kern, *The Culture of Time and Space, 1880–1918*, p. 217.
2. Joshua Meyrowitz, *No Sense of Place: The Impact of Electronic Media on Social Behavior* (New York: Oxford University Press, 1985), p. 115.
3. Ibid., p. 7.
4. Quoted in David Michael Levin, *The Body's Recollection of Being: Phenomenological Psychology and the Deconstruction of Nihilism*, pp. 267–68.
5. Friedrich Nietzsche, *The Will to Power*, Note 30, p. 20; Levin, *Body's Recollection of Being*, p. 271.
6. Erwin Schrodinger, "The Vedantic Vision," in *My View of the World* (Cambridge, England: Cambridge University Press, 1964), p. 22.
7. Guy Davenport, "The Anthropology of Table Manners from Geophagy Onward," in *The Geography of the Imagination: Forty Essays by Guy Davenport*, p. 347.
8. Quoted in Gerardo Reichel-Dolmatoff, *Amazonian Cosmos: The Sexual and Religious Symbolism of the Tukano Indians* (Chicago: University of Chicago Press, 1971), p. 94.
9. Amory Lovins, "A Light on the Soft Energy Path," in Stephen Lyons, ed., *Sun: A Handbook for the Solar Decade* (San Francisco: Friends of the Earth, 1978), p. 41.

CHAPTER 38

1. Arnold Toynbee, *Mankind and Mother Earth: A Narrative History of the World*, p. 593.
2. Kirkpatrick Sale, *Dwellers in the Land: The Bioregional Vision*, p. 55; see also Brian Tokar's excellent discussion of bioregions in his *The Green Alternative: Creating an Ecological Future*, pp. 27–32.
3. Sale, *Dwellers in the Land*, pp. 56–57.
4. Ibid., p. 58
5. Eugene P. Odum, *Fundamentals of Ecology* (Philadelphia: Saunders, 1971), p. 266.
6. World Commission on Environment and Development, *Our Common Future* (The Brundtland Commission Report) (New York: Oxford University Press, 1987), p. 316.
7. Michael Renner, "National Security: The Economic and Environmental Dimension," p. 43.
8. World Commission, *Our Common Future*, pp. 314–15.
9. Louis L. Snyder, *Global Mini-Nationalisms: Autonomy or Independence;* Sale, *Dwellers in the Land*, pp. 154–55.
10. Sale, *Dwellers in the Land*, pp. 155–56.

CHAPTER 39

1. Charles P. Kindleberger, quoted in Richard Barnet and Ronald Muller, *Global Reach: The Power of the Multinational Corporations,* p. 16.

2. Barnet and Muller, *Global Reach,* p. 15.

3. Ibid., p. 19.

4. Ibid., p. 1. Economist Judd Polk, the author of the U.S. Chamber of Commerce study, calculated that by the year 2000 multinationals would own production assets in excess of $4 trillion or "54 percent of everything worth owning for the creation of wealth."

5. Barnet and Muller, *Global Reach,* p. 15.

6. Jerry Mander, "Six Grave Doubts About Computers," *Whole Earth Review* 44 (1985):20. See also David Burnham, *The Rise of the Computer State;* David Burnham, "Data Protection," in Tom Forester, ed., *The Information Technology Revolution,* pp. 546–47.

7. Mander, "Six Grave Doubts About Computers," p. 20.

8. Ibid.

9. Jacques Maisonrouge, quoted in Barnet and Muller, *Global Reach,* pp. 35–36.

10. Peter F. Drucker, *The Age of Discontinuity,* chapter 5.

11. Barnet and Muller, *Global Reach,* p. 28

12. Ibid., p. 89.

13. Quoted in ibid., p. 19.

14. Quoted in ibid.

CHAPTER 40

1. Daniel Deudney, *Whole Earth Security: A Geopolitics of Peace,* p. 18.

2. Quoted in ibid., p. 37.

3. Quoted in Michael Renner, "National Security: The Economic and Environmental Dimension," p. 1.

4. Deudney, *Whole Earth Security,* p. 20.

5. Quoted in Renner, "National Security," pp. 44–45.

6. *Harper's,* July 1989, line 8, p. 17.

7. Quoted in Renner, "National Security," p. 39.

8. Renner, "National Security," p. 37.

9. Figures for military expenditures are from Renner, "National Security," pp. 48–49. Figures for biospheric protection and environmental cleanup costs are from Frank Barnaby, *The Gaia Peace Atlas,* pp. 106, 107, 109, 113, 218.

10. Renner, "National Security," p. 61.

11. Jack Beatty, "The Exorbitant Anachronism," *Atlantic Monthly,* June 1989, p. 41.

12. Barnaby, *Gaia Peace Atlas,* p. 411–12.

13. Robert DeGrasse, *Military Expansion, Economic Decline,* p. 2; Barnaby, *Gaia Peace Atlas,* p. 394. See also Marion Anderson, Michael Frisch, and Michael Oden, *The Empty Porkbarrel: The Employment Cost of the Military Buildup of 1981 to 1985* (Lansing, Mich.: Employment Research Associates, 1986), pp. 1–16.

14. DeGrasse, *Military Expansion,* p. 2.

15. Employment Research Associates, *The Price of the Pentagon* (Lansing, Mich.: Employment Research Associates, 1982); Elliott Currie and Jerome Skolnick, *America's Problems: Social Issues and Public Policy,* p. 396.

16. Michael deCourcy Hinds, "Public Pension Funds: The $700 Billion Lure," p. A1. The idea of using private and public pension funds for social investments was first popularized in Jeremy Rifkin and Randy Barber, *The North Will Rise Again: Pensions, Politics and Power in the 1980s* (Boston: Beacon Press, 1978). In 1988 the Reverend Jesse Jackson promoted the social investment idea in his presidential campaign and made the proposal that the federal government insure these investments.

17. Jeremy Rifkin, "Turning Arms Into a 'Green Dividend,' " *Washington Post,* Outlook Section, 15 April 1990.

18. Rifkin and Barber, *The North Will Rise Again,* pp. 83–194.

19. Hinds, "Public Pension Funds," p. A1.

CHAPTER 41

1. Pat Mooney and Carey Fowler, *Development Dialogue* 1–2 (1988), p. 259.

2. Ibid., p. 266.

3. Lester R. Brown et al., *State of the World 1988,* p. 18; see also Arthur H. Westing, *Global Resources and International Conflict,* Appendix 6, "Law of the Sea Convention of 1982," pp. 233–60.

4. Michael Renner, "National Security: The Economic and Environmental Dimension," p. 44.

CHAPTER 42

1. See P. Rieff, "The Meaning of History and Religion in Freud's Thought," *Journal of Religion* 31 (1951):115. As Norman O. Brown has pointed out, Freud abstained from adopting Jung's term but did state that "The content of the unconscious is collective anyhow." See Sigmund Freud, *Moses and Monotheism,* trans. K. Jones (London: Hogarth Press and the Institute for Psycho-Analysis, 1939), p. 208.

2. Sigmund Freud, *The Question of Lay Analysis,* p. 167; P. Rieff, "The Meaning of History," p. 430.

3. Norman O. Brown, *Life Against Death*, p. 297.

4. Ibid., pp. 297–98.

5. Sigmund Freud, *Civilization and Its Discontents*.

6. Brown, *Life Against Death*, p. 303.

7. Sigmund Freud, quoted in Brown, *Life Against Death*, p. 102.

8. Freud, *Civilization and Its Discontents*, p. 69.

9. Owen Barfield, *Saving the Appearances: A Study in Idolatry*.

10. Brown, *Life Against Death*, p. 109.

11. Rilke, quoted in Brown, *Life Against Death*, p. 108.

12. G. W. Hegel, *The Science of Logic* (London: G. Allen & Unwin, 1929), p. 142.

BIBLIOGRAPHY

Abrams, M. H. *Natural Supernaturalism: Tradition and Revolution in Romantic Literature.* New York: W. W. Norton, 1971.

Aquinas, St. Thomas. *Summa Theologica.* Translated by Fathers of the English Dominican. London: R. N. T. Washbourne, 1917.

Ariès, Philippe. *Centuries of Childhood: A Social History of Family Life.* New York: Random House, 1962.

_____. "The Family and the City." In *The Family,* edited by Alice Rossi, pp. 227–35. New York: W. W. Norton, 1965.

Aristotle, *Metaphysics.* Translated by W. D. Ross. Oxford, England: Clarendon Press, 1908.

Badcock, C. R. *Madness and Modernity: A Study in Social Psychoanalysis.* London: Basil Blackwell, 1983.

Barfield, Owen. *Saving the Appearances: A Study in Idolatry.* London: Faber and Faber, 1957.

Barnaby, Frank. *The Gaia Peace Atlas: Survival into the Third Millennium.* New York: Doubleday, 1988.

Barnet, Richard, and Muller, Robert. *Global Reach: The Power of the Multinational Corporations.* New York: Simon & Schuster, 1974.

_____. *Real Security.* New York: Simon & Schuster, 1981.

Beatty, Jack. "The Exorbitant Anachronism." *Atlantic Monthly,* June 1989, pp. 40–53.

Becker, Ernest. *Escape From Evil.* New York: Free Press, 1975.

BIBLIOGRAPHY

Berkes, F., et al. "The Benefits of the Commons." *Nature* 340 (13 July 1989):91–93.

Berman, Morris. *The Reenchantment of the World.* Ithaca, N.Y.: Cornell University Press, 1981.

_____. *Coming to Our Senses: Body and Spirit in the Hidden History of the West.* New York: Simon & Schuster, 1989.

Bettelheim, Bruno. *The Empty Fortress: Infantile Autism and the Birth of the Self.* New York: Free Press, 1967.

Birch, Charles, and Cobb, John B. *The Liberation of Life: From Cell to the Community.* Cambridge, England: Cambridge University Press, 1983.

Blum, Jerome, ed. *Our Forgotten Past: Seven Centuries of Life on the Land.* London: Thames and Hudson, 1982.

Bly, Robert. *News of the Universe: Poems of Twofold Consciousness.* San Francisco: Sierra Club, 1980.

Bookchin, Murray. *The Ecology of Freedom: The Emergence and Dissolution of Hierarchy.* Palo Alto, Calif.: Cheshire Books, 1982.

_____. *The Modern Crisis.* Philadelphia: New Society Publishers, 1986.

_____. *Remaking Society: Pathways to a Green Future.* Black Rose Books-Distr. University of Toronto Press 1989.

Boorstin, Daniel J., *The Discoverers.* New York: Random House, 1983.

Bordo, Susan. "The Cartesian Masculinization of Thought." *Signs: Journal of Women and Culture in Society* 2 (Spring 1986):439–56.

Botkin, Daniel B., et al. *Changing the Global Environment: Perspectives on Human Involvement.* New York: Harcourt Brace Jovanovich, 1989.

Botkin, Daniel B. *Discordant Harmonies: Ecology in the 21st Century.* Oxford, England: Oxford University Press, 1990.

Berendt, Joachim-Ernest. *Nada Brahma: The World Is Sound: Music and the Landscape of Consciousness.* Rochester, Vt.: Destiny Books, 1987.

Bramwell, Anna. *Ecology in the Twentieth Century: A History.* New Haven: Yale University Press, 1989.

Brand, Stewart. *The Media Lab: Inventing the Future at MIT.* New York: Viking, 1987.

Braudel, Fernand. *The Wheels of Commerce: The Structures of Everyday Life.* Vol. 1. New York: Harper & Row, 1979.

362

Bibliography

————. *The Wheels of Commerce: Civilization and Capitalism, 15th–18th Century.* Vol. 2. New York: Harper & Row, 1979.

Brett, Gerard. *Dinner Is Served: A History of Dining in England, 1400–1900.* London: Rupert Hart-Davis, 1968.

Brown, Norman O. *Life Against Death: The Psychoanalytical Meaning of History.* 2nd ed. Middletown, Conn.: Wesleyan University Press, 1985.

Brundtland, Gro Harlem. "The Test of Our Civilization," *New Perspectives Quarterly* 6 (Spring 1989):4–7.

Burnham, David. *The Rise of the Computer State.* New York: Random House, 1980.

Caldwell, Lynton K. *International Environmental Policy: Emergence and Dimensions.* Durham, N.C.: Duke University Press, 1984.

Callicott, J. Baird. *In Defense of the Land Ethic: Essays on Environmental Philosophy.* Albany: State University of New York, 1989.

Campbell, Mildred. *The English Yeoman.* New York: Barnes & Noble, 1960.

Canetti, Elias. *Crowds and Power.* Translated by Carol Stewart. London: Gollancz, 1962.

Cantor, Norman F. *Medieval History: The Life and Death of a Civilization.* 2nd ed. New York: Macmillan, 1969.

Capra, Fritjof. *The Turning Point: Science, Society, and the Rising Culture.* New York: Simon & Schuster, 1982.

Carroll, John E., ed. *International Environmental Diplomacy: The Management of Transfrontier Environmental Problems.* Cambridge, England: Cambridge University Press, 1988.

Caufield, Catherine. *In the Rainforest: Report From a Strange, Beautiful, Imperiled World.* Chicago: University of Chicago Press, 1986.

Chace, James, and Carr, Caleb. *America Invulnerable: The Quest for Absolute Security from 1812 to Star Wars.* New York: Summit Books, 1988.

Cohen, Mark Nathan. *The Food Crisis in Prehistory: Overpopulation and the Origins of Agriculture.* New Haven: Yale University Press, 1977.

Collingwood, R. G. *The Idea of Nature.* Oxford, England: Oxford University Press, 1945.

Coontz, Stephanie. *The Social Origins of Private Life: A History of American Families, 1600–1900.* New York: Verso Books, 1988.

BIBLIOGRAPHY

Cooper, John C. *The Right to Fly.* New York: Henry Holt, 1947.

Corbett, Michael N. *A Better Place to Live: New Designs for Tomorrow's Communities.* Emmaus, Pa.: Rodale Press, 1982.

Corbin, Alain. *The Foul and the Fragrant: Odor and the French Social Imagination.* Cambridge, Mass.: Harvard University Press, 1986.

Court, Thijs da la. *Beyond Brundtland: Green Development in the 1990s.* London: Zed Books, 1990.

Cowen, Robert. "Rapid Rise in Methane Gas May Speed Worldwide Climatic Changes." *Christian Science Monitor,* 15 March 1988, p. 17.

Currie, Elliott, and Skolnick, Jerome. *America's Problems: Social Issues and Public Policy,* 2d ed. Glenview, Ill.: Scott, Foresman, 1988.

Churchill, R. R., and Lowe, A. V. *The Law of the Sea.* Vol 1. Oxford, England: Oxford University Press, 1983.

Clark, Wilson. *Energy for Survival.* Garden City, N.Y.: Doubleday/Anchor Books, 1975.

Dahlman, Carl J. *The Open Field System and Beyond: A Property Rights Analysis of an Economy Institution.* Cambridge, England: Cambridge University Press, 1988.

Daly, Herman, and Cobb, John B. *For the Common Good: Redirecting the Economy Toward Community, the Environment and a Sustainable Future.* Boston: Beacon Press, 1989.

Darwin, Charles. *The Descent of Man and Selection in Relation to Sex.* New York: Appleton, 1896.

———. *The Life and Letters of Charles Darwin.* Edited by Francis Darwin. 2 vols. New York: Appleton, 1887.

Davenport, Guy. *The Geography of the Imagination: Forty Essays by Guy Davenport.* San Francisco: North Point Press, 1981.

Davis, Donald E. *Ecophilosophy: A Field Guide to the Literature.* San Pedro, Calif.: R & E Miles, 1989.

———. "Ecosophy: The Seduction of Sophia?" *Environmental Ethics* (Summer 1986):151–62.

DeGrasse, Robert. *Military Expansion, Economic Decline.* New York: Council on Economic Priorities, 1983.

Deudney, Daniel. *Whole Earth Security: A Geopolitics of Peace.* Washington, D.C.: Worldwatch Institute, 1983.

Devall, Bill. *Simple in Means, Rich in Ends.* Layton, Utah: Gibbs M. Smith, 1988.

Bibliography

Doyle, Jack. *Altered Harvest: Agriculture, Genetics, and the Fate of the World.* New York: Viking, 1985.

Drexler, Eric. "Interview: Eric Drexler." *Omni,* January 1989, pp. 67–68; 104–8.

Drucker, Peter F. *The Age of Discontinuity.* New York: Harper & Row, 1969.

Duby, Georges, ed. *A History of Private Life: Revelations in the Medieval World.* Vol. 2. Cambridge, Mass.: Harvard University Press, 1988.

Ehrlich, Paul, and Ornstein, Robert. "New World, New Mind," *New Perspectives Quarterly* 6 (Spring 1989):26–32.

Elias, Norbert. *The Civilizing Process: The History of Manners.* New York: Urizen Books, 1978.

Ellul, Jacques. *The Technological Society.* Translated by John Wilkinson. New York: Alfred A. Knopf, 1964.

Employment Research Associates. *The Price of the Pentagon.* Lansing, Mich.: Employment Research Associates, 1982.

Erwin, Robert. "America on Wheels." *The Progressive,* December 1974, pp. 15–19.

Evernden, Neil. *The Natural Alien: Humankind and Environment.* Toronto: University of Toronto Press, 1985.

Fallows, James M. *National Defense.* New York: Random House, 1982.

Farrington, Benjamin, ed. *The Philosophy of Francis Bacon.* Liverpool, England: Liverpool University Press, 1964.

Ferguson, Denzel, and Ferguson, Nancy. *Sacred Cows at the Public Trough.* Bend, Ore.: Maverick Publications, 1983.

Fjermedal, Grant. *The Tomorrow Makers.* New York: MacMillan, 1986.

Foley, James D. "Interfaces for Advanced Computing." *Scientific American,* October 1987, pp. 127–35.

Forester, Tom, ed. *The Information Technology Revolution.* Cambridge, Mass.: MIT Press, 1985.

Foster, Stephen William. *The Past Is Another Country: Representation, Historical Consciousness and Resistance in the Blue Ridge.* Berkeley, Calif.: University of California Press, 1988.

French, Marilyn. *Beyond Power: On Women, Men, and Morals.* New York: Summit Books, 1985.

Freud, Sigmund. *The Question of Lay Analysis.* London: Imago Publishing, 1948.

————. *Beyond the Pleasure Principle*. Translated by J. Strachey. New York: W. W. Norton, 1961.

————. *Civilization and Its Discontents*. Translated by James Strachey. New York: W. W. Norton, 1962.

Fry, Anthony. *Safe Space: How to Survive in a Threatening World*. London: Dent, 1987.

Gardner, Brian. *The East India Company: A History*. New York: McCall Publishing, 1972.

Giedion, Siegfried. *Mechanization Takes Command: A Contribution to Anonymous History*. New York: W. W. Norton, 1969.

Girouard, Mark. *Life in the English Country House: A Social and Architectural History*. New Haven: Yale University Press, 1978.

Glaeser, Bernhard, ed. *Ecodevelopment: Concepts, Projects, Strategies*. Oxford, England: Pergamon Press, 1984.

Grotius, Hugo. *Law of War and Peace in Three Books*. Translated by Francis W. Kelsey. Oxford, England: Clarendon Press, 1925.

Guha, Ramachandra. "Radical American Environmentalism and Wilderness Preservation: A Third World Critique." *Environmental Ethics* 11 (Spring 1989):71–83.

Haeckel, Ernest. *The Wonders of Life*. New York: Harper & Brothers, 1905.

Hall, Bob. *Environmental Politics: Lessons from the Grassroots*. Durham, N.C.: Institute for Southern Studies, 1989.

Hapgood, Fred. "Tiny Tech." *Omni*, November 1986, pp. 58–62; 102.

Hardison, O. B. *Disappearing through the Skylight: Culture and Technology in the Twentieth Century*. New York: Viking Press, 1989.

Harris, Marvin. *Cannibals and Kings: The Origins of Culture*. New York: Julian Press, 1963.

Hartigan, Richard Shelley. *The Forgotten Victim: A History of the Civilian*. Chicago: Precedent Publishing, 1982.

————. *The Future Remembered: An Essay in Biopolitics*. Notre Dame, Ind.: Notre Dame University Press, 1988.

Hayes, Dennis. *Rays of Hope*. New York: W. W. Norton, 1977.

Heard, Gerald. *The Five Ages of Man: The Psychology of Human History*. New York: Julian Press, 1963.

Heer, Friedrich. *The Medieval World*. Translated by Janet Sondheimer. New York: New American Library, 1963.

Heidegger, Martin. *The Question Concerning Technology and Other Essays*. Translated by William Lovitt. New York: Harper & Row, 1977.

Herz, John H. *The Nation State and the Rise of World Politics: Essays on International Politics in the 20th Century*. New York: McKay, 1976.

Hinds, Michael deCourcy. "Public Pension Funds: The $700 Billion Lure." *New York Times,* 2 December 1989, p. A1.

Holloway, David. *The Soviet Union and the Arms Race*. New Haven: Yale University Press, 1983.

Horizon, Stephen. *Nature and Culture in Western Discourses*. London: Routledge and Kegan Paul, 1988.

Illich, Ivan. "The Shadow Our Future Throws." *New Perspectives Quarterly* 6 (Spring 1989):20–25.

Illich, Ivan, and Sanders, Barry. *ABC: The Alphabetization of the Popular Mind*. San Francisco: North Point Press, 1988.

Innis, Harold. *Empire and Communication*. Toronto: University of Toronto Press, 1972.

Jackson, John Brinckerhoff. *Discovering the Vernacular Landscape*. New Haven: Yale University Press, 1984.

Jackson, Kenneth. *Crabgrass Frontier: The Suburbanization of the United States*. New York: Oxford University Press, 1985.

Jacobson, Jodi. "Environmental Refugees: A Yardstick of Habitability." *Worldwatch Paper No. 86*. Washington, D. C.: Worldwatch Institute, 1988.

Jaeger, Jill. *Developing Policies for Responding to Climate Change* (The Bellagio Report). Stockholm, Sweden: Beijer Institute's World Climate Programme—Impact Studies, April 1988.

Jonas, Hans. *The Phenomenon of Life: Toward a Philosophical Biology*. Chicago: Univeristy of Chicago Press, 1966.

Jones, Alwyn K. "Social Symbiosis: A Gaian Critique of Contemporary Social Theory." *Ecologist* 20 (May/June 1990):108–13.

Jung, C. G. *Man and His Symbols*. Garden City, N.Y.: Doubleday, 1964.

Kaldor, Mary. *The Baroque Arsenal*. New York: Hill and Wang, 1981.

Kaplan, Bernard. *Robots, Men and Minds*. New York: George Braziller, 1967.

Kennedy, Paul. *The Rise and Fall of the Great Powers: Economic Change and Military Conflict from 1500 to 2000*. New York: Random House, 1987.

Kern, Stephen. *The Culture of Time and Space, 1880–1918.* Cambridge, Mass.: Harvard University Press, 1983.

Knight, James. *For the Love of Money: Human Behavior and Money.* Philadelphia: Lippincott, 1968.

Lappé, Frances Moore. *Diet for a Small Planet.* 10th ed. New York: Ballantine Books, 1984.

Lappé, Frances Moore, and Collins, Joseph. *Food First: Beyond the Myth of Scarcity.* Boston: Houghton Mifflin, 1977.

Lasch, Christopher. *The Culture of Narcissism: American Life in an Age of Diminishing Expectations.* New York: W. W. Norton, 1979.

Le Goff, Jacques. *Your Money or Your Life: Economy and Religion in the Middle Ages.* New York: Zone Books, 1988.

———. *Time, Work, and Culture in the Middle Ages.* Chicago: University of Chicago Press, 1980.

Leiss, William. *The Domination of Nature.* Boston: Beacon Press, 1972.

LeShan, Lawrence, and Margenau, Henry. *Einstein's Space and Van Gogh's Sky: Physical Reality and Beyond.* New York: Macmillan, 1983.

Lesser, William H., ed. *Animal Patents: The Legal, Economic, and Social Issues.* London: Macmillan, 1989.

Levenstein, Harvey. *Revolution at the Table: The Transformation of the American Diet.* Oxford, England: Oxford University Press, 1988.

Levin, David Michael. *The Body's Recollection of Being: Phenomenological Psychology and the Deconstruction of Nihilism.* London: Routledge and Kegan Paul, 1985.

Lewis, W. H. *The Splendid Century: Life in the France of Louis XIV.* New York: Morrow Quill, 1978.

Lovejoy, Arthur O. *The Great Chain of Being.* Cambridge, Mass.: Harvard University Press, 1936.

Lovelock, James. *Gaia: A New Look at Life on Earth.* Oxford, England: Oxford University Press, 1979.

———. *The Ages of Gaia.* New York: W. W. Norton, 1988.

Lukacs, John. "The Bourgeois Interior." *American Scholar* 39 (Fall 1970).

Lytle, Andrew Nelson. *From Eden to Babylon: The Social and Political Essays of Andrew Nelson Lytle.* Washington, D. C.: Regnery Gateway, 1990.

Mabbutt, Jack. "A New Global Assessment of the Status and Trends of Desertification." *Environmental Conservation* 11 (Summer 1984): 103–13.

Mackinder, Sir Halford. *Democratic Ideas and Reality.* New York: W. W. Norton, 1962.

Macy, Samuel L. *Clocks and the Cosmos: Time and Western Life and Thought.* Hamden, Conn.: Archon Books, 1980.

Mahan, Alfred T. *The Influence of Sea Power Upon History, 1660–1783.* New York: Hill & Wang, 1957.

Malinowski, Bronislaw. "The Primitive Economics of the Trobriand Islanders." *Economic Journal* 17 (1921): 1–16.

Mander, Jerry. *Four Arguments for the Elimination of Television.* New York: Morrow, 1978.

Manes, Christopher. *Green Rage: Radical Environmentalism and the Unmaking of Civilization.* New York: Little, Brown, 1990.

Marsh, Peter, and Collett, Peter. *Driving Passions: The Psychology of the Car.* London: Faber & Faber, 1989.

Masuda, Yoneji. *The Information Society.* Washington, D.C.: World Future Society, 1980.

Mather, Cotton. *Diary of Cotton Mather, 1681–1708.* Boston: Massachusetts Historical Society, 1911.

Mathews, Jessica Tuchman. "Redefining Security." *Foreign Affairs* 68 (Spring 1989):172.

McCormick, John. *Reclaiming Paradise: The Global Environmental Movement.* Bloomington, Ind.: Indiana University Press, 1989.

McKibben, Bill. *The End of Nature.* New York: Random House, 1989.

McLuhan, Marshall. *Understanding Media: The Extensions of Man.* New York: McGraw-Hill, 1964.

McNamara, Robert. "The Dynamics of Nuclear Strategy." *Department of State Bulletin* (9 October 1967), pp. 443–51.

McNeil, William. *The Rise of the West: A History of the Human Community.* Chicago: University of Chicago Press, 1963.

Meining, Donald William. *The Shaping of America: A Geographical Perspective on 500 Years of History, 1492–1800.* New Haven: Yale University Press, 1986.

Melosi, Martin V. *Garbage in the Cities: Refuse, Reform, and the Environment, 1880–1980.* College Station, Tex.: Texas A & M University Press, 1981.

————. *Coping with Abundance: Energy and Environment in Industrial America*. Philadelphia: Temple University Press, 1985.

Merchant, Carolyn. *The Death of Nature: Women, Ecology, and the Scientific Revolution*. San Francisco: Harper & Row, 1980.

————. *Ecological Revolutions: Nature, Gender, and Science in New England*. Chapel Hill, N.C.: University of North Carolina Press, 1989.

Miller, Susanna. *The Psychology of Play*. New York: Penguin Books, 1968.

Modelski, George, and Thompson, William. *Seapower in Global Politics, 1494–1994*. New York: Macmillan, 1988.

Montagu, Ashley. *Touching: The Human Significance of the Skin*. New York: Columbia University Press, 1972.

More, Thomas. *The Utopia of Sir Thomas More*. Edited by H. B. Cotterill. London: 1937. (Classic series) *Utopia*, Paul Turner, tr. London: Penguin, 1965.

Mowbray, A. Q. *Road to Ruin*. Philadelphia: Lippincott, 1969.

Mumford, Lewis. *Technics and Civilization*. New York: Harcourt, Brace & World, 1963.

————. *Technics and Human Development: The Myth of the Machine*. Vol. 1. New York: Harcourt, Brace & World, 1966.

————. *The Culture of Cities*. New York: Harcourt, Brace, Jovanovich, 1970.

Myers, Norman. *The Primary Source: Tropical Forests and Our Future*. New York: W. W. Norton, 1984.

————. *Gaia: An Atlas of Planet Management*. New York: Anchor Press/Doubleday, 1984.

Nabhan, Gary. *Enduring Seeds: Native American Agriculture and Wild Plant Conservation*. San Francisco: North Point Press, 1989.

Naess, Arne. *Ecology, Community, and Life Style: Outline For an Ecosophy*. Cambridge, England: Cambridge University Press, 1989.

Nash, Roderick. *Wilderness and the American Mind*. 3d ed. New Haven: Yale University Press, 1982.

————. *The Rights of Nature: A History of Environmental Ethics*. Madison: University of Wisconsin Press, 1989.

National Research Council. *Global Change in the Geosphere—Biosphere*. Washington, D. C.: National Academy Press, 1986.

Negroponte, Nicholas. *The Architecture Machine*. Cambridge, Mass.: MIT Press, 1970.

_____. *Soft Architecture Machines*. Cambridge, Mass.: MIT Press, 1975.

Neumann, Erich. *The Origins and History of Consciousness*. New York: Pantheon, 1954.

Nietzsche, Friedrich. *The Will to Power*. New York: Random House, 1968.

Oakley, Francis. *The Medieval Experience: Foundations of Western Cultural Singularity*. New York: Scribner's, 1974.

Ong, Walter J. *The Presence of the Word; Some Prolegomena for Cultural and Religious History*. New Haven: Yale University Press, 1967.

_____. *The Interfaces of the Word: Studies in the Evolution of Consciousness and Culture*. Ithaca, N.Y.: Cornell University Press, 1977.

_____. *Orality and Literacy: The Technologizing of the Word*. London: Methuen, 1982.

Ortega y Gassett, José. *Man and People*. New York: W. W. Norton, 1957.

Pacione, Michael. *Progress in Political Geography*. London: Croom Helm, 1985.

Paehlke, Robert C. *Environmentalism and the Future of Progressive Politics*. New Haven: Yale University Press, 1989.

Parry, J. H. *The Discovery of the Sea*. Berkeley, Calif.: University of California Press, 1982.

Patton, R. G., and Gardner, L. I. *Growth Failure in Maternal Deprivation*. Springfield, Ill.: Charles C. Thomas, 1963.

Piddington, Kenneth. "Who Bears the Burden of Responsibility?" *New Perspectives Quarterly* 6 (Spring 1989):8–11.

Polanyi, Karl. *The Great Transformation: The Political and Economic Origins of Our Time*. Boston: Beacon Press, 1957.

Postel, Sandra, and Heise, Lori. "Reforesting the Earth." *Worldwatch Paper No. 83*. Washington, D.C.: Worldwatch Institute, 1988.

Quinn, David Beers. *The Elizabethans and the Irish*. Ithaca, N.Y.: Cornell University Press, 1966.

Raikes, Philip. *Modernising Hunger: Famine, Food and Surplus, Family Policy in the EEC & Africa*. London: Catholic Institute For International Relations, 1988.

Randall, John Herman. *The Making of the Modern Mind*. Boston: Houghton Mifflin, 1940.

Rank, Otto. *Beyond Psychology*. New York: Dover Publications, 1941.

BIBLIOGRAPHY

Ratzel, Frederick. *Anthropogeographie*. J. Elkhorn, 1882.

_____. *Politische Geographie*. Osnabruck, W. Germany: Otto Zeller Verlag, 1974.

Reichel-Dolmatoff, Gerardo. *Amazonian Cosmos: The Sexual and Religious Symbolism of the Tukano Indians*. Chicago: University of Chicago Press, 1971.

Renner, Michael. "National Security: The Economic and Environmental Dimension." *Worldwatch Paper No. 89*. Washington, D.C.: Worldwatch Institute, 1989.

Rheingold, Howard. *Tools for Thought: The History and Future of Mind-Expanding Technology*. New York: Simon & Schuster, 1985.

Rifkin, Jeremy. *Algeny: A New Word—A New World*. New York: Viking, 1983.

_____. *Time Wars: The Primary Conflict in Human History*. New York: Simon & Schuster, 1989.

_____. *Entropy: Into the Greenhouse World*. New York: Bantam Books, 1990.

_____, ed. *The Green Lifestyle Handbook*. New York: Henry Holt, 1990.

Roszak, Theodore. *Where the Wasteland Ends: Politics and Transcendence in Postindustrial Society*. Garden City, N.Y.: Doubleday, 1972.

_____. *Person/Planet: The Creative Disintegration of Industrial Society*. Garden City, N.Y.: Doubleday, 1978.

Rubenstein, Richard. *The Age of Triage: Fear and Hope in an Overcrowded World*. Boston: Beacon Press, 1983.

_____. *The Cunning of History*. New York: Harper & Row, 1975.

Sachs, Wolfgang. "The Virtue of Enoughness." *New Perspectives Quarterly* 6 (Spring 1989):16–19.

Sakharov, Andrei. "The Danger of Thermonuclear War." *Foreign Affairs*, Summer 1983, pp. 1001–16.

Sale, Kirkpatrick. *Dwellers in the Land: The Bioregional Vision*. San Francisco: Sierra Club, 1985.

Saleeby, C. W. *Sunlight and Health*. London: Nisbet, 1928.

Schnaiberg, Allan. *The Environment, From Surplus to Scarcity*. New York: Oxford University Press, 1979.

Schneider, K. R. *Autokind v. Mankind*. New York: Schocken Books, 1972.

372

Bibliography

Schrodinger, Erwin. *My View of the World*. Cambridge, England: Cambridge University Press, 1964.

Semple, Ellen Churchill. *Influences of Geographic Environment on the Basis of Ratzel's System of Anthropo-Geography*. New York: Henry Holt, 1911.

Serafin, Rafal. "Noosphere, Gaia, and the Science of the Biosphere." *Environmental Ethics* 10 (Summer 1988):121–37.

Serpell, James. *In the Company of Animals: A Study of Human-Animal Relationships*. London: Basil Blackwell, 1988.

Silver, Timothy. *A New Face on the Countryside: Indians, Colonists, and Slaves in South Atlantic Forests, 1500–1800*. Cambridge, England: Cambridge University Press, 1990.

Slater, Gilbert. *The English Peasantry and the Enclosure of Common Fields*. New York: A. M. Kelley, 1968.

Smith Anthony. *The Geopolitics of Information: How Western Culture Dominates the World*. New York: Oxford University Press, 1980.

Smith, Nigel. *Rainforest Corridors: The Transamazon Colonization Scheme*. Berkeley, Calif.: University of California Press, 1982.

Smuts, Robert. *Women and Work in America*. New York: Columbia University Press, 1971.

Snyder, Louis L. *Global Mini-Nationalisms: Autonomy or Independence*. Westport, Conn.: Greenwood Press, 1982.

Soroos, Marvin S. "The International Commons: A Historical Perspective." *Environmental Review* 12 (Spring 1988):1–30.

Spirn, Anne Whiston. *The Granite Garden: Urban Nature and Human Design*. New York: Basic Books, 1984.

Spykman, Nicholas J. *The Geography of Peace*. New York: Harcourt, Brace, 1944.

Stern, Karl. *The Flight from Women*. New York: Noonday Press, 1965.

Strauss, Leo. *Natural Rights and History*. Chicago: University of Chicago Press, 1953.

Strausz-Hupe, Robert. *Geopolitics: The Struggle for Space and Power*. New York: G. P. Putnam's Sons, 1942.

Swarztrauber, Sayre A. *The Three-Mile Limit of Territorial Seas*. Annapolis, Md.: Naval Institute Press, 1972.

Tate, William. *The Enclosure Movement*. New York: Walker, 1967.

Taylor, Peter J. *Political Geography: World-Economy, Nation-State, and Locality*. 2nd ed. New York: John Wiley & Sons, 1989.

BIBLIOGRAPHY

Taylor, William, et al. *Defense Manpower Planning: Issues for the 1980s*. New York: Pergamon Press, 1981.

Thirsk, Joan, ed. *The Agrarian History of England and Wales, 1500–1640*. Vol 4. Cambridge, England: Cambridge University Press, 1967.

Thomas, Caroline. *In Search of Security: The Third World in International Relations*. Boulder, Colo.: Reinner, 1987.

Thomas, Keith. *Man and the Natural World: A History of the Modern Sensibility*. New York: Pantheon, 1983.

Thompson, William Irvin, ed. *Gaia: A New Way of Knowing*. New York: Lindisfarne Press, 1988.

Todd, Nancy, and Todd, John. *Bioshelters, Ocean Arks, City Farming: Ecology as Basis of Design*. San Francisco: Sierra Club, 1984.

Tokar, Brian. *The Green Alternative: Creating an Ecological Future*. San Pedro, Calif.: R & E Miles, 1987.

Toynbee, Arnold. *Mankind and Mother Earth: A Narrative History of the World*. New York: Oxford University Press, 1976.

Trabalka, John R. *Atmospheric Carbon Dioxide and the Global Carbon Cycle*. Washington, D.C.: U.S. Government Printing Office, 1985.

Tuan, Yi-Fu. *Segmented Worlds and Self: Group Life and Individual Consciousness*. Minneapolis: University of Minnesota Press, 1982.

––––––. *Dominance and Affection: The Making of Pets*. New Haven: Yale University Press, 1984.

Tucker, Jonathan B. "Gene Wars." *Foreign Policy,* Winter 1984–85, pp. 60–69.

Tullis, Lamond, and Hallister, Ladd., eds. *Food, the State and International Political Economy: Dilemmas of Developing Countries*. Lincoln: University of Nebraska Press, 1986.

United Nations, Department of International and Social Affairs. *Living Conditions in Developing Countries in the Mid-1980s*. Supplement to the 1985 UN report on the world social situation. New York: United Nations, 1986.

U.S., Office of Management and Budget. *Budget of the United States Government, Fiscal Year 1988*. Supplement. Washington, D.C.: Government Printing Office, 1987.

Walker, Stephen. *Animal Thought*. Boston: Routledge & Kegan Paul, 1983.

Wallerstein, Immanuel. *The Modern World System II: Mercantilism and the Consolidation of the European World Economy, 1600–1750*. London: Academic Press, 1980.

Bibliography

Walter, Eugene V. *Placeways: A Theory of the Human Environment.* Chapel Hill, N.C.: University of North Carolina Press, 1988.

Weinberger, C. W. *1985 Annual Report to the Congress: Fiscal Year 1986.* Washington, D.C.: U.S. Department of Defense, 1986.

Wenz, Peters. *Environmental Justice.* Albany: State University of New York, 1988.

Westing, Arthur H., ed. *Global Resources and International Conflict: Environmental Factors in Strategic Policy and Action.* Oxford, England: Oxford University Press, 1986.

Whitehead, Alfred North. *Science and the Modern World.* Toronto: Collier Macmillan, 1967.

_____. *The Concept of Nature.* Cambridge, England: Cambridge University Press, 1930.

Wiener, Martin J. *English Culture and the Decline of the Industrial Spirit: 1880–1980.* Cambridge, England: Cambridge University Press, 1981.

Williams, Raymond. *Keywords: A Vocabulary of Culture and Society.* Oxford, England: Oxford University Press, 1985.

Wolch, Jennifer, and Dear, Michael. *The Power of Geography: How Territory Shapes Social Life.* Boston: Unwin Hyman, 1989.

Wolfe, Tom. *From Bauhaus to Our House.* New York: Farrar Straus Giroux, 1981.

Yates, Frances A. *The Rosicrucian Enlightenment.* Boston: Routledge and Kegan Paul, 1972.

Zoppo, Ciro E. *On Geopolitics: Classical and Nuclear.* NATO Advanced Research Workshop on Geopolitics Revisited in the Nuclear Age (Brussels, Belgium, 1983). The Netherlands: Nijhoff, 1985.

INDEX

Index

INDEX

Index

INDEX

Enlightenment thinkers, thinking, 2,
    34–37, 95, 119, 141, 177, 198,
    242, 252, 274, 282
  and body-mind split, 187–88, 190–
    91
  and devaluation of human life, 114–
    15
  incorporated in television, 240
  inherent limitations in, 253
  mechanistic utilitarianism of, 122
  personal security in, 153
  race theory among, 204
  and suppression of senses, 207
Environment(s), 4, 35, 253
  artificial, 218, 238, 240–42, 244–
    45, 285
  economics and degradation of, 283,
    284
  effect of automobile on, 179–80
  effects of enclosure movement on,
    71–80
  efficient, 269–70
Environmental problems/crises, 1–2, 6,
    13, 37, 76, 78–80, 90, 91, 95,
    251, 256, 264–65, 322
  geopolitics and, 119
  public concern regarding, 303–304
  as temporal crisis, 265
Environmental Protection Agency (EPA),
    88, 90
Environmental relationships, 37, 78, 87,
    270
Erasmus, 194, 195
Erosion, 44, 73, 80
Eugenics, 205
Eurasia, 128, 129, 130, 132, 134
Europe, 76, 103, 128
  see also Eastern Europe; Medieval
    Europe; Western Europe
Evolution, 258–59, 262, 324, 325
  and geopolitics, 120–22
Exchange, 21–22
Expediency, 252, 253
Exploitation of resources, 5, 71, 95,
    126, 269, 285, 313
  coercion and force in, 104–105
  electromagnetic spectrum, 62
  environmental effects of, 75–80
  genetic commons, 65, 66
  seabed, 57
Exxon (co.), 294
  oil spill, 76–77

Family(ies), 162–63, 164
  commercialization of functions of,
    167–72
Far East, 76
Farmworkers Union, 78
Feith, Douglas J., 147
Feudal principalities, 96, 97
Fiduciary relations, 16, 24–25
Financial autonomy, 22–23
Financial revolution, 105

Fish(ing), 56–57
Fjermedel, Grant, 244–45
Florence, 98
Food chain
  eating high on, 41, 50, 86, 311
Food supply, 44, 87, 123, 311–12
Food Technology magazine, 69
Forces of nature, 5, 16, 29, 36, 141
Ford, Henry, 178
Ford Motor Company, 178
Foreign policy, 123, 135–36, 291
Forest(s), 72–73, 88–89, 108
  see also Tropical rain forests
Forgotten Victim, The (Hartigan), 116
Fossil fuels, 67, 82–83, 84, 108, 123,
    174
Foul and the Fragrant, The (Corbin),
    211
Four Arguments for the Elimination of
    Television (Mander), 238–39
Fowler, Cary, 68, 315–16
France, 124
Franklin, Benjamin, 58–59
Frederick, Christine, 170–71
Freedom of Information Act, 64
Freud, Anna, 225
Freud, Sigmund, 208, 319–20, 321,
    322, 323
Fuller, Buckminster, 174, 255
Furniture, 159–60
Future (the), 13, 268, 270

Gaia hypothesis, 259–60, 262, 309
Galton, Sir Francis, 205
Gama, Vasco da, 99
Gardner, L. I., 221
Gene banks, 67, 315
Gene pool, 66, 145, 256, 295, 315,
    316
  enclosure of, 5, 71
Gene splicing, 65–66, 226
Gene wars, 145–49
General Dynamics (co.), 112, 140, 306
General Electric Company, 69, 112
General Motors, 294
Genetic commons
  enclosure of, 65–70
  militarization of, 149
  reopening of, 314–16
Genetic diversity, 312, 314, 315–16
Genetic engineering, 255, 321
  and biological warfare, 145, 146–48,
    149
  patents in, 69–70, 316
Genoa, 54, 98
Geochemical processes, 258–59, 262
Geographic literacy, 262–63
"Geographic Pivot of History, The"
    (Mackinder), 130
Geography
  and politics, 119–26
Geophagy, 279
Geophysics, 138–39, 256

Index

INDEX

INDEX

386

INDEX